Empires, Soldiers, and Citizens

Empires, Soldiers, and Citizens

A World War I Sourcebook

Edited by

Marilyn Shevin-Coetzee and Frans Coetzee

WILEY-BLACKWELL

A John Wiley & Sons, Ltd., Publication

This second edition first published 2013
Editorial material and organization © 2013 John Wiley & Sons Ltd.

Edition history: D.C. Heath and Company (1e, 1995)

Wiley-Blackwell is an imprint of John Wiley & Sons, formed by the merger of Wiley's global Scientific, Technical and Medical business with Blackwell Publishing.

Registered Office
John Wiley & Sons Ltd, The Atrium, Southern Gate, Chichester, West Sussex, PO19 8SQ, UK

Editorial Offices
350 Main Street, Malden, MA 02148-5020, USA
9600 Garsington Road, Oxford, OX4 2DQ, UK
The Atrium, Southern Gate, Chichester, West Sussex, PO19 8SQ, UK

For details of our global editorial offices, for customer services, and for information about how to apply for permission to reuse the copyright material in this book please see our website at www.wiley.com/wiley-blackwell.

The right of Marilyn Shevin-Coetzee and Frans Coetzee to be identified as the authors of the editorial material in this work has been asserted in accordance with the UK Copyright, Designs and Patents Act 1988.

Library of Congress Cataloging-in-Publication Data

Empires, soldiers, and citizens : a World War I sourcebook / edited by Marilyn Shevin-Coetzee and Frans Coetzee. – 2nd ed.

p. cm.

Includes bibliographical references and index.

   ISBN 978-0-470-65582-5 (cloth) – ISBN 978-0-470-65583-2 (paper)

 1. World War, 1914-1918–Sources. 2. World War, 1914-1918–Social aspects–Sources. 3. World War, 1914-1918–Campaigns–Sources. I. Shevin-Coetzee, Marilyn, 1955- II. Coetzee, Frans, 1955-

   D505.E47 2013

   940.3–dc23

                                                       2011043337

A catalogue record for this book is available from the British Library.

Cover image: Indian auxiliary troops in battle with German infantry during capture of Neuve Chapelle, Artois, March 1915. Colour print from drawing by Fabius Lorenzi, Paris, 1915. Photo © akg-images/ Jean-Pierre Verney.

Cover design by www.simonlevyassociates.co.uk
Ornament © Anja Kaiser / Fotolia.com

Set in 10.5/13pt Minion Regular by Thomson Digital, Noida, India.

Printed in Malaysia by Ho Printing (M) Sdn Bhd

1   2013

This book is dedicated to our daughter, Michelle Hanna Shevin-Coetzee, in the hope that her generation will never experience the horrors chronicled in the following pages.

Contents

List of Maps

Chronology

1914

June 28	Assassination of Archduke Franz Ferdinand of Austria-Hungary.
July 23	Austro-Hungarian ultimatum to Serbia.
July 24	Partial mobilization of Austro-Hungarian army.
July 30	Mobilization of Russian army.
August 1	Mobilization of French and German armies; Germany declares war on Russia.
August 2	German trade unions agree to support war.
August 3	Germany declares war on France.
August 4	German invasion of neutral Belgium; Britain enters the war against Germany.
Early August	Passage of Defence of the Realm Act (DORA) in Britain.
August	Sporadic anti-German riots in Britain.
August 23	Japan declares war on Germany.
August 26–30	Battle of Tannenberg (East Prussia).
September 6–9	Battle of the Marne.
Mid-September	Trench warfare begins.
September 20	France implements policy of industrial mobilization.
October 12	First Battle of Ypres.
October 18–19	Anti-German riots in Deptford, England.
November 1	Russia declares war on Turkey.
December 21	First German air raids on Britain.

1915

January	Introduction of food rationing in Germany.
February–March	Allied attempts to take the Dardanelles.
February–September	Intensive German submarine warfare begins.
March	Conclusion of Treasury Agreement with trade unions in Britain.

March 21	First German air raid on Paris.
April 8	Turkey initiates deportation and massacre of Armenians.
April 22–May 27	Second Battle of Ypres; introduction of gas warfare.
April 25	Allied land campaign against Turks in Gallipoli begins.
May 2–4	Russian retreat at Battle of Gorlice-Tarnow.
May 7	Sinking of the *Lusitania* by German U-boat.
May 8	Anti-German riots break out in England following news about the *Lusitania*.
May 23	Italy enters war on Allied side.
May 26	Formation of coalition government in Britain in which Asquith retains the office of Prime Minister.
July	Coalminers strike in South Wales; Munitions of War Act passed in Britain.
September	First Zimmerwald Movement Conference held in Switzerland.
October	Aristide Briand replaces Rene Viviani as French Premier.
October 12	Germans execute Edith Cavell.
Late Autumn	France recruits women laborers in earnest.

1916

January 24	Britain implements conscription.
February 21	Battle of Verdun begins (through December 18).
March	Clydeside Strikes in Scotland; Alexandre Ribot replaces Briand as French Premier.
April	Second Zimmerwald Movement Conference in Switzerland.
April 20	France implements policy of price control on vital necessities.
April 24–29	Easter Uprising in Ireland.
May 31–June 1	Naval Battle of Jutland.
June 4–October 10	Russian Brusilov offensive.
June 5	Start of Arab revolt against Turks in Hejaz; death of Britain's Lord Kitchener when his ship is torpedoed.
June 7–9	Anti-German riots in London following Kitchener's death.
June 12	Paolo Boselli replaces Antonio Salandra as Premier of Italy.

July 1–November 19	Battle of Somme.
November 7	Reelection of Woodrow Wilson as President of United States.
November 21	Death of Emperor Franz Josef of Austria-Hungary and succession of Archduke Karl.
December 2	Patriotic Auxiliary Service Act in Germany.
December 7	Lloyd George becomes Prime Minister in reconstruction of British government.

1917

January	Resumption of unrestricted submarine warfare by Germany.
January–February	"Turnip Winter" in Germany; food riots break out.
January 17	France initiates compulsory arbitration of wage disputes.
February 2	Britain introduces bread rationing.
March 16	Tsar Nicholas II of Russia abdicates his throne.
March 21–July 18	Germany launches spring offensive.
April 6	United States enters war against Germany.
April 7–9	Anti-German riots in London following German air raid.
April 16	Publication of infamous "Corpse Conversion Factory" propaganda in *The Times* (London).
April 16–29	Chemin des Dames offensive.
April 29	First mutiny by French army unit.
July 14	Resignation of German Chancellor Theobald von Bethmann-Hollweg and succession of Georg Michaelis.
July 31–November 10	Third Battle of Ypres (Battle of Passchendaele).
August	Third Zimmerwald Movement Conference in Stockholm; unrest in Turin, Italy, over lack of bread in stores.
August 1	Pope Benedict XV appeals for peace.
August 5	Act encouraging creation of nursing facilities for mothers in France.
August 6	Alexander Kerensky becomes head of Provisional Government in Russia.
August 14	China enters war on side of Allies.
October	Count Georg von Hertling replaces Michaelis as Germany's Chancellor.
October 24–November 10	Battle of Caporetto; Vittorio Orlando replaces Boselli as Italy's Premier.

November 2	Balfour Declaration supporting establishment of homeland for the Jews in Palestine.
November 7	Bolshevik overthrow of Provisional Government in Russia.
November 16	Georges Clemenceau becomes French Premier.
December 3	Lenin and the Bolsheviks sign armistice with Germany.
December 6	Finland declares independence from Russia.
December 9	General Edmund Allenby captures Jerusalem.

1918

January 8	Woodrow Wilson proposes his Fourteen Points as a basis for peace.
March 3	Russia signs Treaty of Brest-Litovsk.
March 21	Germany launches spring offensive.
May–October	Allied forces intervene in Russian Civil War.
July 16	Deposed Tsar Nicholas II and family are executed.
July 18–November 10	Allied counteroffensive against Germany.
Late September	Prince Max of Baden replaces Hertling as Germany's Chancellor.
October 3–4	Germany offers to make peace according to Wilson's Fourteen Points.
October 4	British and Arab forces occupy Damascus.
October 16	Austria-Hungary declares itself a federal state based upon nationalities.
October 28	German sailors mutiny at Kiel.
October 29	Turkey signs armistice with Allies.
Early November	Revolutionary unrest in Germany.
November 3	Austria-Hungary sues for peace with Allies.
November 7	Kurt Eisner declares Bavaria a Republic.
November 9	Abdication of Kaiser Wilhelm II of Germany.
November 11	Armistice is signed on the Western Front.

Preface

When Georg von Hase, a gunnery officer aboard a German battlecruiser, reflected upon his experiences in the great 1916 sea battle of Jutland against the British fleet, he began in a curious way. Rather than describing the principal naval actions preceding Jutland or condemning Britain for obstructing Germany's legitimate military and imperial aspirations, he recounted a seemingly unrelated episode from 1913. "Off the coasts of Albania," he explained,

> ships of almost every nation were lying at anchor. The commander of the German cruiser *Breslau* had invited the admirals and commanding officers of all nationalities to dinner. Next [to] the German commander sat the English admiral, and all around, between Germans and Englishmen, sat Italians, French, Russians, Spaniards, Turks, Greeks, and Albanians, in a motley assemblage. Toasts had been proposed and the political situations were being animatedly discussed in all possible languages. The English admiral and the German commander had seen each other furtively examining the members of this strange round table, and they exchanged their observations regarding the highly diversified types of people. Suddenly the English admiral raised his glass, gazed straight into the blue eyes of the German commander, and as their glasses touched, softly whispered, "The Two White Nations."

Clearly, von Hase, who was writing after the war in part to extol the honor of a defeated service, included this vignette to emphasize that British sailors respected their German counterparts, indeed regarded them as their only true equals among the varied navies represented that would, for the most part, fight in the Great War. But his specific evocation of racial terminology is revealing, not least for his exceptionally restrictive use of the term "white" in circumstances where it would have seemed to have a wider application.

This underlying current of racial attitudes is one of the themes we have chosen to address in this new second edition. The original volume served honorably enough in the seventeen years since its publication in 1995, but the profusion of new research on the First World War and identification of fresh perspectives has encouraged us to undertake a thorough revision of the text. In particular, we proceed from the explicit recognition that the conflict was an imperial war, and readers will now find expanded coverage of events in Africa, Asia, and the Middle East, as well as of imperial influences on events in Europe. Because several good source collections on America's participation in the war already exist, we have elected not to retrace that territory in this volume.

Nonetheless, in the final reckoning, the war was won and lost on the European continent, and we have therefore retained from the previous edition a focus on the major combatant nations and their respective populations, for the eventual military decisions in the field are inexplicable without reference to the social, political, and economic developments behind the lines. We also retain the conviction, nourished by years of teaching experience, that exposure to and analysis of original sources is one of the most effective and rewarding ways of enabling students to understand a particular historical era or problem. We hope that this revised volume will provide a convenient and accessible, yet wide-ranging and comprehensive, introduction to the First World War.

Although the first edition's four major sections have morphed into the second edition's eight chapters, the organization remains relatively straightforward. Thematic chapters explore different facets of the war, but within an overall chronological framework. The first chapter focuses upon the popular mood in the war's opening weeks, and while enthusiasm on the part of some people spoiling for a fight was not unknown, many of the sources point toward a sense of resignation and an acceptance of patriotic duty as the more prevalent attitudes.

Chapters II and III detail the specific military course of the conflict, both specifically in western Europe, as well as elsewhere around the globe. Readers will come to appreciate how civilian soldiers sought to adapt to military life, to prolonged and murderous campaigns, and to the challenges to imperial authority inherent in a conflict that called upon imperial nations to mobilize all of their resources, human as well as material. Some of the specifically newer technological aspects of industrialized killing feature in the fourth chapter, including machine guns, tanks, poison gas, submarines, and airplanes.

From the fifth chapter onward, the primary focus shifts behinds the lines. As prospects for quick victory at the front diminished, the domestic organization of the war effort in each nation assumed greater significance as a complementary "home front." Chapter V documents the increasing role of the state, including its intervention in the labor market, industrial production, and public health, and some of the unanticipated consequences, especially for gender roles. The sixth chapter explores the dilemmas of maintaining social order under duress, asking how nations defined unity and purpose as they struggled to keep the war effort going as strains and divisions mounted. Conceptions of duty and sacrifice, and of religious conviction, are among the relevant topics here, but so too are the increasingly divisive definitions of race or ethnicity. Chapter VII follows the themes of the preceding two sections to their logical conclusion in 1917–18, when dissent and/or exhaustion finally threatened to overwhelm the participants. It traces the repercussions, from the immediate and cataclysmic (as in Russia) to the more protracted (as in Ireland and India).

Finally, Chapter VIII follows the legacies of this catastrophically destructive war, for those who perished, those who were maimed, and those who mourned. How the war and its participants would be remembered and celebrated was neither obvious nor uniform, and the chapter addresses some of the varied efforts to make sense of the carnage. Whatever the perspective, however, it was clear that the world had indelibly changed as a result, a theme illustrated by the concluding selections.

Acknowledgments

We would like to thank the anonymous readers whose helpful comments and suggestions improved the final product. Wiley-Blackwell's exemplary staff of Tessa Harvey, Isobel Bainton, and Alec McAulay were a pleasure to work with at every stage of the process.

Every effort has been made to trace copyright holders and to obtain their permission for the use of copyright material. The publisher apologizes for any errors or omissions in the above list and would be grateful if notified of any corrections that should be incorporated in future reprints or editions of this book.

Map 1 The Western Front, 1914-18 from Herwig, Holger H. 2010. "War in the West, 1914–16." In *A Companion to World War I*, edited by John Horne, 49–65. Oxford: Blackwell.

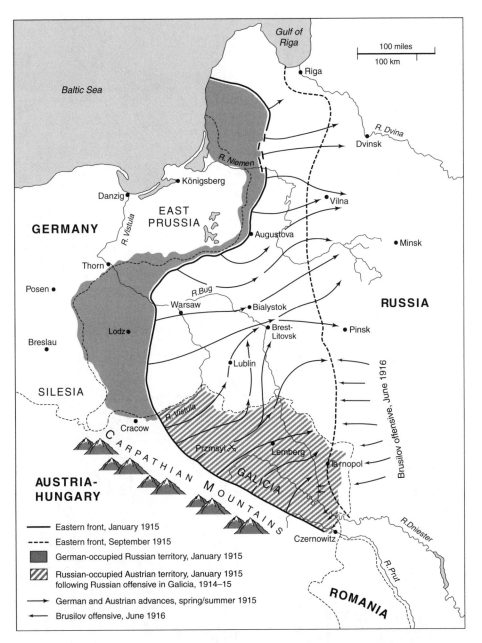

Map 2 The Eastern Front, 1914–17 from Showalter, Dennis. 2010. "War in the
East and Balkans, 1914–18." In *A Companion to World War I*, edited by John
Horne, 66-81. Oxford: Blackwell.

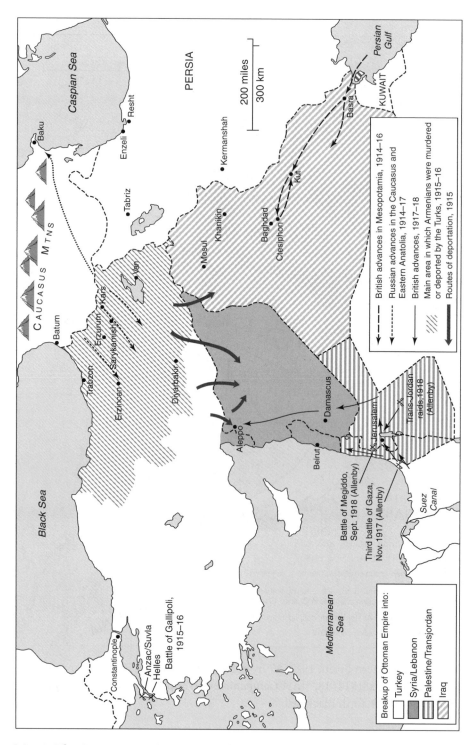

Map 3 The Ottoman Empire, 1914–18 from Trumpener, Ulrich. 2010. "The Turkish War, 1914–18." In *A Companion to World War I*, edited by John Horne, 97–111. Oxford: Blackwell.

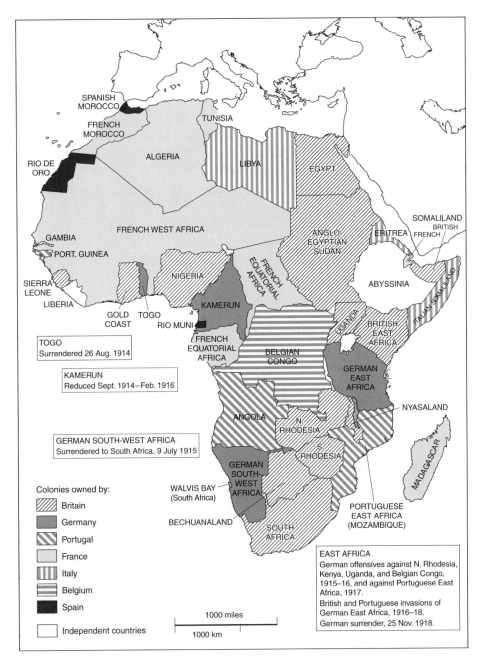

SPANISH
MOROCCO
FRENCH
MOROCCO
TUNISIA
RIO DE
ORO
ALGERIA
LIBYA
EGYPT
SOMALILAND
BRITISH
FRENCH
GAMBIA
PORT. GUINEA
FRENCH WEST AFRICA
ERITREA
ANGLO-
EGYPTIAN
SUDAN
SIERRA
LEONE
LIBERIA
NIGERIA
FRENCH
EQUATORIAL
AFRICA
ABYSSINIA
ITALIAN SOMALILAND
GOLD
COAST
TOGO
RIO MUNI
KAMERUN
UGANDA
BRITISH
EAST
AFRICA

TOGO
Surrendered 26 Aug. 1914

FRENCH
EQUATORIAL
AFRICA
BELGIAN
CONGO
GERMAN
EAST
AFRICA

KAMERUN
Reduced Sept. 1914–Feb. 1916

NYASALAND

ANGOLA
N.
RHODESIA

GERMAN SOUTH-WEST AFRICA
Surrendered to South Africa, 9 July 1915

S.
RHODESIA

MADAGASCAR

Colonies owned by:

	Britain
	Germany
	Portugal
	France
	Italy
	Belgium
	Spain
	Independent countries

WALVIS BAY
(South Africa)

GERMAN
SOUTH-
WEST
AFRICA

BECHUANALAND

SOUTH
AFRICA

PORTUGUESE
EAST AFRICA
(MOZAMBIQUE)

1000 miles

1000 km

EAST AFRICA
German offensives against N. Rhodesia,
Kenya, Uganda, and Belgian Congo,
1915–16, and against Portuguese East
Africa, 1917.
British and Portuguese invasions of
German East Africa, 1916–18.
German surrender, 25 Nov. 1918.

Map 4 Africa in World War I from Killingray, David. 2010. "The War in Africa"
In *A Companion to World War I*, edited by John Horne, 112–126. Oxford:
Blackwell.

I

The Mood of 1914

A century after its outbreak, the First World War remains a subject of abiding interest. As (arguably) history's first "total" war, it enveloped a multitude of nations, nationalities, races, and religions; produced new and more deadly weapons of destruction; altered traditional gender patterns; strengthened the power of the state; and unleashed revolutionary forces in Germany, Austria-Hungary, and Russia. In the four years of its duration, 1914–1918, some nine million soldiers succumbed to the fighting; many more were wounded and disabled. The total number of civilians killed is unknown but very high, especially in eastern Europe. The memory of war, for both surviving combatants and their families, lingered. Hailed by President Woodrow Wilson as the war to end all wars, one that would restore international and domestic stability and punish its instigator, Germany, the Great War instead ushered in decades of economic and political chaos, ultimately leading to dictatorship in Mussolini's Italy, Stalin's Soviet Union, Hitler's Germany, and a half-dozen east European states.

Perhaps the term "First World War" is misleading, because previous conflicts such as the Seven Years' War (1756–1763, known to Americans as the French and Indian Wars) and the Napoleonic Wars were truly intercontinental in scope, involving military action in the various European nations' colonial empires. In that case, the claim of the conflict of 1914–1918 to represent the first world war rests on the more slender thread of Japanese participation and the Allied conquest of Germany's African colonies. It was, in fact, not so much the geographic breadth of the war that distinguished it from earlier struggles, but rather its social, economic, and cultural scope that marked it as the "Great War," as contemporaries (who did not know it would be followed by another massive conflict) labeled it.

Empires, Soldiers, and Citizens: A World War I Sourcebook, Second Edition.
Edited by Marilyn Shevin-Coetzee and Frans Coetzee.
© 2013 John Wiley & Sons, Ltd. except sources 1 to 14. Published 2013 by John Wiley & Sons, Ltd.

One reason why the war proved so significant was because it did not conform to expectations. There had, of course, been extensive planning by military leaders throughout Europe before 1914 to prepare for a war; after all, such preparation was at the heart of their professional duty. Yet such efforts had focused on the intricate questions of quickly getting men into uniform and to the national frontier, as well as on strategic questions, such as the Germans' planned strike through Belgium (envisioned in the Schlieffen Plan of 1905) or the French Plan XVII to recover Alsace and Lorraine in a speedy thrust. Assuming that any war would be brief and decisive, military and government planners had given little thought to the equally vexing problems of mobilizing the domestic population for war. And so the various governments had to improvise; societies felt that improvisation all the more keenly, and as a result, the unanticipated social consequences of a seemingly endless total war were all the more profound. The lack of any prior comparable experience is one reason why the social history of the Great War proved so wrenching at the time and so fascinating in retrospect.

In 1914 as temperatures soared during one of the hottest summers on record in Europe, so too tempers flared. Lacking such conveniences as air-conditioning that twenty-first century Europeans take for granted, and sweltering in heavy conventional fashions, the peoples of Europe were put to the test by both the torrid climate and events. It is only in hindsight, however, that we can see they were poised on the brink of war, for at the time they appeared to be confronted with more immediate and pressing problems. Wherever one looked, nations appeared embroiled in internal conflicts of their own.

French politics throughout the nineteenth century had been notoriously contentious and unstable, as divisions persisted over the legacy of the Revolution, relations between the Catholic church and state, and the role of organized labor. On the eve of the war, nothing indicated that political life would grow any more settled. Bitter public debates broke out over electoral reform, taxation, and, above all, the introduction of longer terms of compulsory military service. Accordingly, France witnessed no fewer than six prime ministers in the two and one-half years preceding the war. Moreover, the assassination of the French Left's champion, Jean Jaurès, just days before the armies clashed in 1914, revealed that the Left's legitimacy still came into question

In Russia, despite the apparent monolithic authority of the tsar, political life was both restricted and unsettled. The autocracy still grappled with the impact of military defeat at the hands of Japan and the revolution of 1905, and although the regime had acquired some trappings of parliamentary government, no consensus existed for liberalizing reforms or reaching political stability. Political debate was not limited to proponents of autocratic reaction and their liberal critics, for after the turn of the century no European nation boasted more rapid industrialization than Russia. The world would soon witness the power of Russian factory workers, but even on the eve of the war, when St. Petersburg laborers launched a massive strike during the visit of the French president, the changing features of the Russian political landscape came into focus. That such changes were unfolding in a nation noted for its unresponsive, unwieldy bureaucracy and reactionary leadership provided further evidence of the growing polarization of Russian life.

The German domestic scene also betrayed signs of discord and discontent. Germany's narcissistic emperor, William II, fancied himself an authority on all aspects of foreign and domestic affairs. Nevertheless, he spent long stretches of time aboard the royal yacht, *Hohenzollern*, surrounded by an eccentric circle of sycophantic advisers and admirers. The nation's political system was wracked by ideological, religious, and regional divisions. In elections in 1912, the Socialists had won more seats than any other party, and the unease felt by Germany's propertied elites was only aggravated by this development and the growth of labor unrest. A small but boisterous clique of extreme nationalists, outraged by the Socialists' success and the parliamentary system's inertia, urged Germans to prepare themselves for battle against internal and external foes.

Celebrated as an exemplar of stability and consensus, even the British political system faced severe challenges, whether over the power and privileges of the House of Lords, the issue of female suffrage, Irish Home Rule, and the willingness and ability of British working men to bring the industrial system to its knees. Ulster intransigence, suffragette arson, and labor militancy all seemed to threaten the very ideal of peaceful compromise at the heart of British public life.

Although Italy would not enter the war until May 1915, it was no more united or prepared for conflict than its neighbors. A country in which over half the population still labored at agricultural pursuits in 1914, Italy lagged far behind its European counterparts in social programs and industrial legislation. Poor living conditions, low pay, and heavy taxation provoked further resentment toward the government among Italy's working and middle classes.

Whatever the issues specific to individual countries, however, Europe as a whole was vulnerable to the threat of war because of deep-seated economic, military, diplomatic, and political developments. Ironically, the very technology that brought the continent closer together—telegraph, telephone, steamship—helped in the end to tear it asunder. Eventually, long-term causes and short-term accidents combined to precipitate the war.

Tensions in Europe had been exacerbated by the imperial rivalries of the 1880s and 1890s, when the quest for raw materials, potential markets, military bases, possible destinations for the emigration of surplus populations, as well as for prestige, prompted the race for colonial possessions in Africa and the Far East. The psychological effect of the falling profits of the era—the so-called Great Depression (1873–1896)—renewed pressure from industrial and commercial interests in the various European countries for colonial acquisitions to ensure their nations' exclusive gain at their rivals' expense. Colonial expansion, contend contemporary critics and subsequent scholars, yielded only meager tangible returns, yet the imperial race aggravated the competitive nature of state relations and threatened the preceding decade's fragile diplomatic equilibrium.

It was partly the need to sort out differences between colonial rivals and minimize probable friction that prompted the emergence of long-standing alliance systems.

Certainly, the Triple Entente of England, France, and Russia served the dual purpose of protecting each country's colonial ambitions from those of its partners (tensions between Britain and France, for example, had escalated over the Fashoda incident of 1898), as well as precluding the easy hegemony of the competing alliance bloc—the Triple Alliance of Germany, Austria-Hungary, and Italy. Originally the advocates of alliance diplomacy presumed that such links afforded members a degree of flexibility and influence over the excesses of their partners; by 1914, however, the reverse was the case, for the alliances threatened to escalate any local conflict involving one pair of powers into a general European conflagration.

Moreover, diplomats found their room to maneuver constrained by military leaders who themselves were responding to the technological advances that had reshaped not just the conduct of war but also the very preparation for it. With mass armies of conscripts and unprecedented quantities of equipment and supplies, mobilization was bound to be protracted, subject to intricate timetables. Once the carefully coordinated mobilization of hundreds of thousands of men, horses, and weapons had begun, it was difficult to stop. Only a strong-willed diplomat, politician, or monarch would be willing to defy military advice and invite confusion by delaying war preparations in the hope of finding a peaceful solution in one of the periodic local crises that punctuated the pre-1914 period.

The most serious of these crises was triggered—literally—by the assassination in Sarajevo of the heir to the Austro-Hungarian throne, Archduke Franz Ferdinand and his wife Sophie, on June 28, 1914. The assassin, Gavrilo Princip, a teenaged Serbian nationalist, shot the imperial couple as a gesture of defiance on behalf of the Serbs of Bosnia-Herzegovina, a province of mixed Serb, Croatian, and Muslim Slavic populations that had been annexed by Austria-Hungary. European opinion was shocked by this brazen act, but it did not regard it as likely to culminate in a continental conflict. Over the course of the next few weeks this impression proved illusory. First, the Austro-Hungarian government was persuaded that the government of neighboring Serbia had plotted the assassination in an attempt to seize Bosnia-Herzegovina. Diplomatic pressure to elicit from Serbia concessions or a confession of complicity inevitably entangled Slavic Serbia's protector, Russia, in the crisis. The second significant factor was that both Austria-Hungary and Russia were authoritarian monarchies facing domestic agitation for reform and in danger of fragmenting into their constituent nationalities. Repressed nationalism was the potentially explosive issue, above all, that needed just a spark to engulf the continent and bring the multi-national empires to the brink of disintegration. One seemingly attractive way of forestalling such an erosion of imperial authority was to achieve a quick and convincing triumph, diplomatic or military, over an irresolute rival.

Russia's proclivities on this score were reinforced by Tsar Nicholas II's determination not to yield, as he felt he had humiliatingly been forced to do in the past; Austria-Hungary's resolve was meanwhile strengthened by strong German pressure not to capitulate. The public and secret intricacies of the alliance system ensured that if Germany and Austria-Hungary went to war against Russia, France and possibly Britain would intervene. Yet Germany's military leaders, recognizing the difficulty of simultaneously fighting a war on two fronts, had in the Schlieffen Plan sought to alleviate the difficulty by deciding on a rapid strike at France through Belgium, discounting the prospect that the violation of Belgium's neutrality would ensure British intervention.

On July 23, 1914, Austria-Hungary issued an ultimatum to Serbia that, if accepted, would have eroded the small country's sovereignty. Under the circumstances the Serb response was quite conciliatory but insufficient to preclude Austria-Hungary from declaring war on Serbia five days later. Russia responded by mobilizing, prompting Germany to do the same—and to declare war on Russia on August 1 and on France two days later. On August 4, after German troops had violated the Belgian frontier, Britain honored its treaty obligation to protect Belgian neutrality and entered the fray on the side of France and Russia, though strategic considerations for the safety of the English Channel had influenced the decision for war.

More than a concern for national honor brought Germany into the war, for a bitter economic and naval rivalry had pitted it against Britain for several decades. Germany's remarkable economic dynamism threatened Britain's industrial ascendancy, while Germany's ambitions for a colonial empire and fleet commensurate with its economic achievement deepened the antagonism between the two countries. A growing fear of encirclement by the modernizing French and Russian armies and of Socialist political gains and domestic tensions all influenced imperial Germany's elite in their decision to go to war.

By August 4 the Continent had plunged into an abyss. "The lamps are going out all over Europe," observed the British foreign secretary, Sir Edward Grey, on the evening of that long and somber day. "We shall not see them lit again in our lifetime." Grey's pessimistic assessment of the likely impact of the war was not, however, initially shared by all of his contemporaries. Some intellectuals anticipated the coming conflict as a spiritual release from the banalities of everyday life and as a transformation of the degeneracy inherent in modern culture through looking to a higher, common purpose. In part, these suppositions drew strength from the mistaken premise, shared by individuals in all countries, that the war would prove something of a sporting match, brief and glorious, possibly even concluded by Christmas. Indeed, the link between sport and war was not entirely fanciful; an English public-school education assumed that training in team sports served as excellent preparation for the exercise of command. Sporting organizations, such as football clubs, helped to attract war volunteers, and officers were known to lead men into battle kicking a football before them. In Germany, too, the *Turnvereine* (gymnastic associations) aimed to strengthen individuals and the body politic alike. The idea of war as the greatest game of all even became a staple of popular art. In Germany, such paintings or drawings depicted young, beautiful maidens handing flowers or beverages to soldiers departing by train to the front, or men, young and older, rushing to volunteer before they missed out on the adventure of a lifetime.

Some historians have suggested that fear of accelerating domestic disintegration and anarchy played a key role in persuading politicians to embrace the idea of war. On this reading, European leaders calculated that only the unifying pressure of war could hold their fissiparous societies together. Certainly, propaganda encouraged the notion of a community solidified in its newfound resolve to achieve victory. One British poster appropriately entitled "Are you in this picture?" depicted Britons from all social classes waiting in a long line to enlist in the army. Both the German slogan *Burgfrieden* (the internal peace of a fortress under siege) and the corresponding French concept of *Union sacrée* (Sacred Union) urged citizens, under pressure from external enemies, to put aside their differences and rally around the flag.

Yet this image of spontaneous, frenzied unanimity is incomplete and in some ways misleading. In fact, many European statesmen questioned the likelihood of national unity in a time of crisis and worried lest the outbreak of war only aggravate social unrest. To be sure, they harbored grave misgivings—unfounded in 1914—about the potential threat of the socialist parties. So if some Europeans looked to the war optimistically, others viewed it through less rosy spectacles.

As the combatants' lack of military preparation came to light time and again, the more guarded responses to the outbreak of hostilities gained credence. In underestimating the duration of the conflict, the opposing nations, each confident of victory, failed to take measures to ensure a steady supply of food for both military and civilian populations and to stockpile raw materials for weapons and munitions. The British presumption that they could continue to conduct "business as usual" typified the initial response throughout Europe. These inadequate preparations went unchallenged because Europeans looked in the wrong place for examples of what to expect once the shooting began. Their expectations of a brief conflict stemmed partly from the short, decisive campaigns of Prussia against Austria (1866) and France (1870–1871) or Japan against Russia (1904–1905) that suggested that one power could defeat another with relative ease. Instead, military planners should have taken their cue from the American Civil War, which dragged on for four years with staggering casualties.

⚭

War Comes to France

On the evening of August 4, 1789, the French National Assembly, by renouncing the estate system that had hitherto divided French society into three corporate orders, helped usher in the French Revolution. That momentous event, like the mobilization of the armies of the French Third Republic 125 years later, aroused apprehension as well as great anticipation. Similarly, the ideals of liberty, equality, and fraternity espoused by the French Revolutionaries found resonance with their fellow citizens in 1914. The First World War, like the Revolution of 1789, initially seemed to foster a spirit of cooperation, brotherhood, and common endeavor. The mood evoked by the mobilization of French troops is expressed here by three observers. The first is Mildred Aldrich, an American journalist, author, and friend of Gertrude Stein. She settled in France in 1898, moving into a cottage called "Hilltop" in a village on the outskirts of Paris in 1914 from which she wrote about the war and her experiences. The second is Félix Klein, a chaplain who ministered to the injured on and off the battlefield in France. Finally, one of the most penetrating analysts of the war was Marc Bloch. Born into a distinguished Jewish academic family (his father was a professor at the Sorbonne), Bloch was an ardent French patriot and a brilliant Medieval historian, who reflected on his military service as he convalesced from typhoid in 1915.

1. A Nation Suddenly United

July 30, 1914

It looks, after all, as if the Servian affair was to become a European affair, and that, what looked as if it might happen during the Balkan War is really coming to pass—a general European uprising. . . .

Well, it seems that the so-called "alarmists" were right. Germany has NOT been turning her nation into an army just to divert her population, nor spending her last mark on ships just to amuse herself, and keep Prince Henry busy.

I am sitting here this morning, as I suppose all France is doing, simply holding my breath to see what England is going to do. I imagine there is small doubt about it. I don't see how she can do anything but fight. It is hard to realize that a big war is inevitable, but it looks like it. It was staved off, in spite of Germany's perfidy, during the Balkan troubles. If it has to come now, just imagine what it is going to mean! It will be the bloodiest affair the world has ever seen—a war in the air, a war under the sea as well as on it, and carried out with the most effective man-slaughtering machines ever used in battle. . . .

France really deserves her revenge for the humiliation of 1870 and that beastly Treaty of Frankfort. I don't deny that 1870 was the making of modern France, or that, since the Treaty of Frankfort, as a nation she has learned a lesson of patience that she sorely needed. But now that Germany is preparing—is really prepared to attack her again—well, the very hair on my head rises up at the idea. . . .

The tension here is terrible. Still, the faces of the men are stern, and every one is so calm—the silence is deadly. There is an absolute suspension of work in the fields. It is as if all France was holding its breath. . . .

August 2, 1914

Well, dear, what looked impossible is evidently coming to pass.

Early yesterday morning the garde champetre—who is the only thing in the way of a policeman that we have—marched up the road beating his drum. At every crossroad he stopped and read an order. I heard him at the foot of the hill, but I

I.1 From Mildred Aldrich, *Hilltop on the Marne: Being Letters Written June 3–September 8, 1914* (Boston: Houghton Mifflin, 1915), 45–47, 49–54, 57–64.

waited for him to pass. At the top of the hill he stopped to paste a bill on the door of the carriage-house on Pere Abelard's farm. You can imagine me—in my long studio apron, with my head tied up in a muslin cap—running up the hill to join the group of poor women of the hamlet, to read the proclamation to the armies of land and sea—the order for the mobilization of the French military and naval forces—headed by its crossed French flags. It was the first experience in my life of a thing like that. I had a cold chill down my spine as I realized that it was not so easy as I had thought to separate myself from Life. We stood there together—a little group of women—and silently read it through—this command for the rising up of a Nation. No need for the men to read it. Each with his military papers in his pocket knew the moment he heard the drum what it meant, and knew equally well his place. I was a foreigner among them, but I forgot that, and if any of them remembered they made no sign. We did not say a word to one another. I silently returned to my garden and sat down. War again! This time war close by—not war about which one can read, as one reads it in the newspapers, as you will read it in the States, far away from it, but war right here—if the Germans can cross the frontier.

It came as a sort of shock, though I might have realized it yesterday when several of the men of the commune came to say *au revoir*, with the information that they were joining their regiments, but I felt as if some way other than cannon might be found out of the situation. War had not been declared—has not to-day. Still, things rarely go to this length and stop there. Judging by this morning's papers Germany really wants it. She could have, had she wished, held stupid Austria back from the throat of poor Servia, not yet recovered from her two Balkan wars.

I imagine this letter will turn into a sort of diary, as it is difficult to say when I shall be able to get any mail matter off. All our communications with the outside world—except by road—were cut this morning by order of the War Bureau. Our railroad is the road to all the eastern frontiers—the trains to Belgium as well as to Metz and Strasbourg pass within sight of my garden. If you don't know what that means—just look on a map and you will realize that the army that advances, whether by road or by train, will pass by me.

During the mobilization, which will take weeks,—not only is France not ready, all the world knows that her fortified towns are mostly only fortified on the map,— civilians, the mails, and such things must make way for soldiers and war materials. I shall continue to write. It will make me feel in touch still; it will be something to do: besides, any time some one may go up to town by road and I thus have a chance to send it.

August 3, 1914

Well—war is declared.

I passed a rather restless night. I fancy every one in France did. All night I heard a murmur of voices, such an unusual thing here. It simply meant that the town was awake and, the night being warm, every one was out of doors.

All day to-day aeroplanes have been flying between Paris and the frontier. Everything that flies seems to go right over my roof. Early this morning I saw two machines meet, right over my garden, circle about each other as if signaling, and fly off together. I could not help feeling as if one chapter of Wells's "War in the Air" had come to pass. It did make me realize how rapidly the aeroplane had developed into a real weapon of war. I remember so well, no longer ago than Exposition year—that was 1900—that I was standing, one day, in the old Galerie des Machines, with a young engineer from Boston. Over our heads was a huge model of a flying machine. It had never flown, but it was the nearest thing to success that had been accomplished—and it expected to fly some time. So did Darius Green, and people were still skeptical. As he looked up at it, the engineer said: "Hang it all, that dashed old thing will fly one day, but I shall probably not live to see it."

He was only thirty at that time, and it was such a few years after that it did fly, and no time at all, once it rose in the air to stay there, before it crossed the Channel. It is wonderful to think that after centuries of effort the thing flew in my time—and that I am sitting in my garden to-day, watching it sail overhead, like a bird, looking so steady and so sure. I can see them for miles as they approach and for miles after they pass. Often they disappear from view, not because they have passed a horizon line, but simply because they have passed out of the range of my vision—? becoming smaller and smaller, until they seem no bigger than a tiny bird, so small that if I take my eyes off the speck in the sky I cannot find it again. It is awe-compelling to remember how these cars in the air change all military tactics. It will be almost impossible to make any big movement that may not be discovered by the opponent. . . .

August 10, 1914

It is a week since I wrote you—and what a week. We have had a sort of intermittent communication with the outside world since the 6th, when, after a week of deprivation, we began to get letters and an occasional newspaper, brought over from Meaux by a boy on a bicycle.

After we were certain, on the 4th of August, that war was being declared all around Germany and Austria, and that England was to back France and Russia, a sort of stupor settled on us all. Day after day Amelie would run to the mairie at Quincy to read the telegraphic bulletin—half a dozen lines of facts—that was all we knew from day to day. It is all we know now.

Day after day I sat in my garden watching the aeroplanes flying over my head, and wishing so hard that I knew what they knew. Often I would see five in the day, and one day ten. Day after day I watched the men of the commune on their way to join their classe. There was hardly an hour of the day that I did not nod over the hedge to groups of stern, silent men, accompanied by their women, and leading the children by the hand, taking the short cut to the station which leads over the hill, right by my gate, to Couilly. It has been so thrilling that I find myself forgetting that it is tragic. It is so different from anything I ever saw before. Here is a nation—which two weeks ago was torn by political dissension—suddenly united, and with a spirit that I have never seen before.

I am old enough to remember well the days of our Civil War, when regiments of volunteers, with flying flags and bands of music, marched through our streets in Boston, on the way to the front. Crowds of stay-at-homes, throngs of women and children lined the sidewalks, shouting deliriously, and waving handkerchiefs, inspired by the marching soldiers, with guns on their shoulders, and the strains of martial music, varied with the then popular "The girl I left behind me," or, "When this cruel war is over." But this is quite different. There are no marching soldiers, no flying flags, no bands of music. It is the rising up of a Nation as one man—all classes shoulder to shoulder, with but one idea—"Lift up your hearts, and long live France." I rather pity those who have not seen it.

Since the day when war was declared, and when the Chamber of Deputies—all party feeling forgotten—stood on its feet and listened to Paul Deschanel's terse, remarkable speech, even here in this little commune, whose silence is broken only by the rumbling of the trains passing, in view of my garden, on the way to the frontier, and the footsteps of the groups on the way to the train, I have seen sights that have moved me as nothing I have ever met in life before has done. Day after day I have watched the men and their families pass silently, and an hour later have seen the women come back leading the children. One day I went to Couilly to see if it was yet possible for me to get to Paris. I happened to be in the station when a train was going out. Nothing goes over the line yet but men joining their regiments. They were packed in like sardines. There were no uniforms—just a crowd of men—men in blouses, men in patched jackets, well-dressed men—no distinction of class; and on the platform the women and children they were leaving. There was no laughter, none of the gayety [sic] with which one has so often reproached this race—but neither were there any tears. As the crowded train began to move, bare heads were thrust out of windows, hats were waved, and a great shout of "Vive la France" was answered by piping children's voices, and the choked voices of women—"Vive l'Armee"; and when the train was out of sight the women took the children by the hand, and quietly climbed the hill.

Ever since the 4th of August all our crossroads have been guarded, all our railway gates closed, and also guarded—guarded by men whose only sign of being soldiers is a cap and a gun, men in blouses with a mobilization badge on their left arms, often in patched trousers and sabots, with stern faces and determined eyes, and one thought—"The country is in danger."

There is a crossroad just above my house, which commands the valley on either side, and leads to a little hamlet on the route nationale from Couilly to Meaux, and is called "La Demi-Lune"—why "Half-Moon" I don't know. It was there, on the

6th, that I saw, for the first time, an armed barricade. The gate at the railway cross-ing had been opened to let a cart pass, when an automobile dashed through Saint-Germain, which is on the other side of the track. The guard raised his bayonet in the air, to command the car to stop and show its papers, but it flew by him and dashed up the hill. The poor guard—it was his first experience of that sort—stood staring after the car; but the idea that he ought to fire at it did not occur to him until it was too late. By the time it occurred to him, and he could telephone to the Demi-Lune, it had passed that guard in the same way—and disappeared. It did not pass Meaux. It simply disappeared. It is still known as the "Phantom Car." Within half an hour there was a barricade at the Demi-Lune mounted by armed men—too late, of course. However, it was not really fruitless—that barricade—as the very next day they caught three Germans there, disguised as Sisters of Charity—papers all in order—and who would have got by, after they were detected by a little boy's calling attention to their ungloved hands, if it had not been for the number of armed old men on the barricade.

What makes things especially serious here, so near the frontier, and where the military movements must be made, is the presence of so many Germans, and the bitter feeling there is against them. On the night of August 2, just when the troops were beginning to move east, an attempt was made to blow up the railroad bridge at lie de Villenoy, between here and Meaux. The three Germans were caught with the dynamite on them—so the story goes—and are now in the barracks at Meaux. But the most absolute secrecy is preserved about all such things. Not only is all France under martial law: the censorship of the press is absolute. Every one has to carry his papers, and be provided with a passport for which he is liable to be asked in simply crossing a road.

Meaux is full of Germans. The biggest department shop there is a German enter-prise. Even Couilly has a German or two, and we had one in our little hamlet. But they've got to get out. Our case is rather pathetic. He was a nice chap, employed in a big fur house in Paris. He came to France when he was fifteen, has never been back, consequently has never done his military service there. Oddly enough, for some reason, he never took out his naturalization papers, so never did his service here. He has no relatives in Germany—that is to say, none with whom he has kept up any correspondence, he says. He earns a good salary, and has always been one of the most generous men in the commune, but circumstances are against him. Even though he is an intimate friend of our mayor, the commune preferred to be rid of him. He begged not to be sent back to Germany, so he went sadly enough to a concentration camp, pretty well convinced that his career here was over. Still, the French do forget easily.

Couilly had two Germans. One of them—the barber—got out quick. The other did not. But he was quietly informed by some of his neighbors—with pistols in their hands—that his room was better than his company.

The barber occupied a shop in the one principal street in the village, which is, by the way, a comparatively rich place. He had a front shop, which was a cafe, with a well-fitted-up bar. The back, with a well-dressed window on the street, full of toilette articles, was the barber and hairdressing-room, very neatly arranged, with modern set bowls and mirrors, cabinets full of towels, well-filled shelves of all the things that make such a place profitable. You should see it now. Its broken windows and doors stand open to the weather. The entire interior has been "efficiently" wrecked. It is as systematic a work of destruction as I have ever seen. Not a thing was stolen, but not an article was spared. All the bottles full of things to drink and all the glasses to drink out of are smashed, so are counters, tables, chairs, and shelving. In the barber shop there is a litter of broken porcelain, broken combs, and smashed-up chairs and boxes among a wreck of hair dyes, perfumes, brillantine, and torn towels, and an odor of aperitifs and cologne over it all.

Every one pretends not to know when it happened. They say, "It was found like that one morning." Every one goes to look at it—no one enters, no one touches anything. They simply say with a smile of scorn, "Good—and so well done."

∞

2. We Shall Be without Fear

On August 3rd, Belgium is required—by an ultimatum—to facilitate the German operations over her territory; she refuses, and, in her turn, sees her neutrality violated. Then Germany officially declares War with France; England declares War with Germany; Austria declares War with Russia. From the Urals to the Atlantic, from the Balkans to the mountains of Scotland, with hundreds of vessels, with thousands of regiments, navies and armies are set in motion. In Serbia, in Belgium, in Russia, on the Algerian coast, towns are bombarded. And while on land the cannon already roar, the ironclads sail the seas, and the heavens are crossed by aeroplanes seeking news or carrying explosives.

Oh! that Saturday the 1st August, when the terrible seriousness of the situation was suddenly revealed to a people still but little anxious! That morning three whole classes, three hundred thousand men, receive individually the order for immediate departure. Heedless of all else, giving no backward glance leaving unfinished tasks begun, taking no precaution for the future, completely absorbed in the solemn present, they leave family, undertakings, business. *Veni, sequere me!* orders the Country, without further explanation, and, like those called in the Gospel, they follow; they go to the frontier, to battle, probably to die. The astonishing thing is that not one murmurs and many are enthusiastic; but the women weep, and the children they are leaving. In the streets, in the squares, in the shops to which they are already rushing for provisions, wives, mothers, sweethearts, make moan. At the stations, to which they have accompanied their men, they try, for their sake, to keep a brave front; but when they come back alone . . .

I.2   From Felix Klein, *Diary of a French Army Chaplain* (London: Andrew Melrose, 1915), 18–19, 24–27.

In the middle of the afternoon, at the summons of telegraph or telephone, all the town-halls, all the stations, simultaneously post up the order for general mobilization, which enjoins four millions of men, at the risk of their lives, to help the country in danger. And all answer: "Here we are!" and just consult their time-table to make sure of when they must start. . . .

Where, but a few weeks ago, could be found a more grievous spectacle than the first sittings of the new Chamber? And where, even in turning over the annals of many Parliaments, could be found a more admirable scene than that it offered on the 4th August; listening, silent as a tribunal of history, to the act of accusation drawn up, with proofs in hand, against those who had hurled twenty-five millions of men on to the fields of slaughter! And in this hot-bed of dissensions, quarrels, selfish desires, boundless ambitions, what trace remained of groups, of rivalries, of hates? Unanimous the respect with which the Presidential message was received; unanimous the adhesion to the Chief of the Government and his noble declaration: "It is the liberties of Europe that are being attacked of which France and her allies and friends are proud to be the defenders. . . . France did not wish for the war; since it is forced upon her, she will defend herself. We are without reproach, we shall be without fear. . . . "

And, without debate, with no dissentient voice, all the laws of national defence, with the heavy sacrifices they imply, are at once voted. The night of August 4th, just a hundred and twenty-five years ago, saw the end of Privileges; finer still this day of August 4th, 1914, which sees the end of our dissensions and our egotisms.

The fact is that we know ourselves no longer; barriers are falling on every side which, both in public and private life, divided us into hostile clans. A head committee is formed to guard the material and moral interests of the country without delay; to it the Government summons, side by side with those most technically competent, a representative of each party and the best known of its adversaries in the past—Briand, Delcassé, Millerand, de Mun, Ribot. In Belgium it is the same, or even better; the Catholic Government elects the chief Socialist Vandervelde as Minister of State to take his seat beside the venerable M. Woeste. With our friends no more than with ourselves, can political divisions reach the sublime level of patriotism. . . .

It is the same in private life, as I said. The relations between citizens are transformed. In the squares, in the streets, in the trains, outside the stations, on the thresholds of houses, each accosts the other, talks, gives news, exchanges impressions; each feels the same anxiety, the same hopes, the same wish to be useful, the same acceptance of the hardest sacrifices. Even the children say: "Papa is gone; he went to the War to prevent the Germans doing us harm."

The old proudly enumerate the sons, the nephews, the sons-in-law, the grand-sons they have with the Colours; their own age prevents them from going, so they have enlisted in the Civic Guard. The women talk of the anxiety they are feeling for the dear absent ones, of the applications they have made to be admitted as hospital nurses. They tell us familiarly of the precautions against famine they are taking, their fear that milk may fail for the quite little ones; above all, of the possible invasion.

For, next to the field of battle where the men they love are slain, what is most horrible for women in war is the idea of falling into the hands of the enemy soldiers; the thought that in the absence of husband, brother or son, the house may be invaded, the home outraged by victorious brutes.

A woman of the people, to whom I was speaking of the imminence of the War a few days ago, astonished me by her calmness, all the more because she was aware that her husband would go amongst the first. The explanation was not long delayed.

"Happily," she said to me, "Serbia is far from here!"

When she understood that there was a question of a repetition—no doubt with better chances, but perhaps on the same site—the terrible duel of '70, she quickly changed her note: "Oh! Monsieur, the Prussians here!"

August 6th

They are not here yet. Neither from within nor without do things take the same turn as in the Summer of 1870.

While our mobilization goes on with the most irreproachable coolness, calmness and order, Germany, who wished to take us by surprise, in the execution of her principal plan comes up against a moral and material obstacle which was the last to be expected. Her famous sudden attack is transformed into a sudden check. By one action she turns against herself the human race and the first chances of the struggle. She begins the war by a crime against a people's rights and by a military loss. The violation of Belgian neutrality and the attack upon Liége may bring about—O justice of history and Providence!—the fall of the German Empire; a fine opportunity for that great law which makes the crime bring forth its own punishment to manifest itself.

∽

3. On The Way to the Front

One of the most beautiful memories the war has given me was the sight of Paris during the first days of mobilization. The city was quiet and somewhat solemn. The drop in traffic, the absence of buses, and the shortage of taxis made the streets almost silent. The sadness that was buried in our hearts showed only in the red and swollen eyes of many women. Out of the specter of war, the nation's armies created a surge of democratic fervor. In Paris there remained only "those who were leaving"—the nobility—and those who were

I.3   From Marc Bloch, *Memoirs of War, 1914–15*, trans. Carole Fink (Ithaca, NY: Cornell University Press, 1980), 78–79. Copyright Carole Fink. Reprinted with kind permission.

not leaving, who seemed at that moment to recognize no obligation other than to pamper the soldiers of tomorrow. On the streets, in the stores and streetcars, strangers chatted freely; the unanimous goodwill, though often expressed in naive or awkward words and gestures, was nonetheless moving. The men for the most part were not hearty; they were resolute, and that was better. . . .

Very early on the morning of August 4, I left for Amiens. I went part of the long way between the avenue d'Orléans and the Gare de la Chapelle in a market gardener's wagon that a police constable had requisitioned for my use. Because I sat in the back, wedged between baskets of vegetables, the fresh and slightly acrid odor of cabbage and carrots will always bring back the emotions of that early-morning departure: my enthusiasm and the constriction that gripped my heart. At the Gare de la Chapelle, an aged, white-haired father made heroic but unavailing efforts to hold back his tears as he embraced an artillery officer. At Amiens I found an extraordinarily animated city, its streets predictably teeming with soldiers.

⟡

Russia: For the Tsar and Motherland

Russia's troops were the first to mobilize, but the process of preparing for war was no less chaotic as a result. The first selection, by an English clergyman, represents the view of a sympathetic, if sometimes bemused, foreign observer. W. Mansell Merry, a vicar of St. Michael's in Oxford, had accepted the invitation of the English church in St. Petersburg to serve as its chaplain during July and August 1914. Anticipating a restful summer abroad, Merry found himself engulfed in the maelstrom of war with little warning. The second extract is from the memoirs of a Russian general, Vasily Gurko, who commanded the 1st Cavalry Division at the outbreak of the war. An ardent proponent of military reform and a political moderate, Gurko was forced into exile following the October Revolution of 1917.

4. The View from St. Petersburg

It is a fact that the through-journey to England *via* Berlin is no longer guaranteed; it is also undeniably true that both the "*suisse*" and the "*dvórnik*" [groundskeeper or porter] at my own lodgings have been "mobilized" for possible service—but what about all the other rumours that are busily circulating?

I.4   From W. Mansell Merry, *Two Months in Russia* (Oxford: Blackwell, 1916), 74–76, 78–79.

The Baltic is mined, we hear, and full of German ships; the English fleet has sailed westward under sealed orders; the Japanese have asked to be allowed to help us "to the last ship and man," should we be drawn into hostilities; the Serbs have scored a victory over the Austrians in the first battle fought; and a German descent upon Hango is imminently expected. How much of all this is true? Unfortunately, the gentleman, from whom answers to all my questionings were to be forthcoming, is unable through pressure of business to return home for lunch, so curiosity has to go unappeased; his wife tells me that she and her husband have been at work on the telephone practically all night, with the gleaning of very little news that is definite as the result of their long and tiresome vigil. However, three facts are certain enough amid all the "mélange" of current gossip; that Russia realizes that no honourable escape is any longer open to her from the duty of championing her fellow-Slavs of Serbia against the aggressive designs of Austria, although even at this eleventh hour she is offering to stop mobilization if Vienna will acknowledge Serbian sovereignty; that, in the event of hostilities being forced upon her, the campaign will be the most popular on which she will have embarked since 1812; and that, with an almost pathetically confident positiveness, she is relying on the whole-hearted co-operation in her undertaking, not of France only—for that is a foregone conclusion—but of Great Britain as well, the traditional foe of tyrants and bullies, the defender of the down-trodden, the friend of humanity, liberty and justice. This evening my English host and I have engaged ourselves to dine with a mutual friend at his country-house at Párgolovo, a most picturesque little village of dátchas some half an hour's run from Petrograd by rail, and a very delightful and refreshing time do we spend alike in the enjoyment of the hospitalities of his comfortable bungalow, and in acquainting ourselves with the beautiful lake and woodland scenery of its surroundings. On the drive back to the station quite an exciting adventure befalls us. Our dróshky [carriage] is stopped in a dark and narrow lane by a huge crowd of "demonstrators," all carrying thick sticks and singing the National Hymn at the top of voices whose huskiness is readily traceable to the last public-house! The multitude close in all round, and one of their number, who acts as spokesman, requests us to inform him of our nationality, enquiring, moreover, why, on our hearing the strains of the Russian Anthem, we had not straightway uncovered our heads. My comrade, who speaks Russian like a native, replies chaffingly that we have not as yet heard anything approximately resembling the patriotic melody in question. This for the moment non-plusses our interrogator, who, evidently, has but little sense of humour. But he soon returns to the charge. "If," he shouts, "you do not tell us who you are and why you have kept your hats on, we shall upset you into the mud!" It is not always wise to rely too much on the sustained good temper of a Russian mob, so now the discretion of a soft answer is obviously the better part of valour. "Listen, all of you," cries my friend, standing up in the carriage, "we are both of us Englishmen born and bred, and if you'll start that hymn of yours again, and sing it properly, we'll stop here with our hats in our hands as long as ever you care to keep it up!" The effect of this little speech is electrical. The crowd breaks into uproarious cheering; their leader leans over and kisses again and again both the hands of the lately suspected stranger; the familiar hymn bursts out afresh—this time with considerable approach to recognisable tune—and we both join in it heartily, erect and bare-headed, until the roysterers have had their fill, and, with a final round of applause, send us galloping off into the gloom to catch our homeward train by the barest possible margin.

Friday, July 31st

All sorts of rumours reach us towards evening; that an English squadron is occupying the Belt; that twenty-nine Dreadnoughts are "hanging on to the tail" of the German fleet; that Germany and Austria are already anxious to make peace; with many other exciting and amusing "canards" of a similar breed. The weather has cleared towards sunset, and as we sit on deck, enjoying an after-dinner smoke, the broad, cobble-paved roadway that runs alongside down to the port is thronged and noisy with the tramp of ceaseless streams of reservists, naval and military; rarely, marching to the blaring, lilting strains of a brass band; more generally, trudging along, bundle on back or in hand, in sullen silence; the women-folk, many of them weeping as if their hearts would break, breathlessly struggling to keep pace with husbands, brothers, sons or lovers on either side, as company after company swings past. For two days past these sturdy sons of the soil have been collecting at their various depôts; some dazedly, ignorant of whys and wherefores, recognizing necessity perforce, and wondering why they should leave their farms so soon before harvest; others have deserted their burnt-up lands with a shrug—in many districts there will be no harvest in any case—and they bear the new caprice of fate with indifference. Shaggy, uncouth peasants, they herd sheepishly into the appointed rendezvous, and are there transformed into genial, swaggering soldiers, a little shy, perhaps, of their trim appearance, easily abashed by personal remarks, but restored to the verge of boastfulness by a hint as to the prowess they will doubtless exhibit against the Germans.

> It seems that some gigantic hand
> Behind the veils of sky
> Was driving, herding all these men
> Like cattle into a cattle-pen;
> So few of them can understand,
> So many of them must die.
>
> A. Noyes

The swiftness and completeness of this feature of the Russian mobilization is, considering the enormous difficulties of transport, little short of a miracle.

5. Russia's Popular Mood

Among the population after the mobilisation, as far as we could gather, the distinguishing characteristic was a calm and general desire to fulfil their duty and to bring as much help as possible to the affairs of the nation. Therefore there were no specially noisy demonstrations in the streets or in public gatherings, but everywhere could be felt the heightened spirit and mind and the understanding that Russia and her Allies had taken up arms in a just cause. There was no appearance of any kind of chauvinism or aggressiveness, or any kind of hatred to the enemy; but, on the other hand, everybody spoke out their firm conviction that in this just cause victory must be on our side.

Germany: For the Kaiser and Fatherland

In an effort to unite Germans of differing political persuasions behind the war effort, Kaiser Wilhelm II announced, early in August 1914, that he no longer recognized parties, only Germans. While fleeting, the *Burgfrieden*, as it came to be called, initially brought nationalists, liberals, centrists, and socialists together under the banner of patriotism for the Fatherland. Some Germans, like seaman Richard Stumpf, a Catholic sailor, enthusiastically greeted the war, justifying it as retribution against a haughty British nation that sought to outshine and outpace Germany both economically and militarily. Stumpf served on the German battleship *Helgoland* for the duration of the war. Socialists, on the other hand, struggled with the idea of supporting a war led by individuals whom they viewed as manipulative and exploitative militarists, nationalists, and capitalists. In 1907, socialists from various European nations had assembled in Stuttgart, Germany, to discuss how they might respond to a general European conflict. The second extract details the policy on militarism and international conflict adopted at that congress that would ostensibly guide socialist leaders in the event of war. The third source demonstrates the quandary faced by the German Socialist Party upon the war's outbreak and its eventual decision to join in the *Burgfrieden*. The symbol of the SPD's readiness to support the war was its acceptance of the financial measures necessary to fund the war effort, the so-called war credits voted by the German legislature. The last voice in this section is that of a young law student, Franz Blumenfeld, whose enthusiasm for the war appears more tempered and resigned than that of Seaman Stumpf.

I.5   From Vasilii I. Gourko, *War and Revolution in Russia, 1914–1917* (New York: Macmillan, 1919), 19–20.

6. A Just War against England

August 2

We are anchored at Wilhelmshaven Roadstead. We are about to go on war patrol today—real war patrol. Thus I wrote in my notebook on August 2.

Two rumors circulated everywhere at the time. One of them was that America was about to dispatch two billion dollars and two squadrons to our aid and the other asserted that Japan would give us moral support by demanding compensation for the war from Russia. The future was to prove both rumors to be nonsense. We got no newspapers or information until 5:30 that evening when the Executive Officer called us together again and set our minds at ease.

"The political situation," he began, "has deteriorated to such an extent that we must count on the outbreak of a war with England. All telegraphic communication with England has been cut off since four o'clock this afternoon. You must know what that means. Furthermore an English fishing boat was discovered cruising around Helgoland this afternoon. One of our cruisers the *Danzig* ordered it to leave. The boat refused and consequently *Danzig* took her into custody. It is certainly very suspicious that this Englishman was snooping around Helgoland. Hence you know now that we are facing a war with England."

All of us breathed a sigh of relief. The very thing for which we had so long waited and hoped, the thing we had yearned for and feared, had come true. There was no doubt that the real cause was jealousy over our economic progress. Germany had grown great, strong and wealthy. The quality of German goods had deprived England of a large part of the world market. The reasons cited by the English that they wanted to protect Belgian neutrality are ridiculous. Would she also have declared war on France if it had violated the Belgian border? However I don't wish to deal with events that occurred later. At that time Germany had not yet crossed the Belgian frontier.

I should like to add one more example to indicate how great the excitement was during those first days and how totally harmless incidents gave rise to the craziest rumors and suspicions. That evening while the starboard watch was busy painting camouflage, a great commotion arose suddenly and everyone ran to the top deck. There I heard that the *Oldenburg*, which lay next to us, had just fired five shots at English submarines. Some of the men insisted that they had seen and heard the shots quite distinctly. The next morning it turned out that none of our ships had fired. Twelve miles away, however, on the island of Wangerooge, a few blank shots had been fired!

I.6 From Daniel Horn, *War, Mutiny and Revolution in the German Navy* (Brunswick, NJ: Rutgers University Press, 1967), 24–27. Copyright © 1967 by Rutgers, the State University. Reprinted by permission of Rutgers University Press.

At that time there was a general panic about spies. It was alleged that here alone eighteen of them had been captured and shot. I did not believe it. Then there was also the fear of enemy aircraft. The searchlights of some of the ships and of the coastal fortresses were continually playing in the air because of aircraft reports. The next day the newspaper announced that a bomb had even been dropped on the town hall. Later on this, too, was repudiated.

That same night while we stood at battle stations, we received a wireless message that our light cruiser the *Augsburg* had bombarded the Russian naval station at Libau, set it on fire and was now engaged in battle with [Russian] cruisers.

On the following day the official *Norddeutsch Zeitung* published the news that the French had already crossed the border. In addition, one of their planes had bombed the main railroad track near Nuremberg. As a result, the Kaiser had declared war on France. We had expected this news. It was inevitable. The center of our interest still focused on England's attitude. Would she merely rattle her saber again and sic the others on us? The next day relieved us of these fateful doubts.

At that time I often wondered whether there were any objective reasons for England's intervention. As far as I could tell, the governments, scientists and labor leaders of both sides had tried very hard to establish friendly relations between the two countries. How long ago was it that the English war fleet was received with great honor at Kiel harbor? A few days! We were to pay them a return visit at this very time.

Bitter thoughts rise to my mind whenever I recall that the cause of it all was probably envy and petty trade jealousy. But then the Kaiser had told us that they were Germans like us, of the same race and of the same blood. Blood is thicker than water. And the English?—My country right or wrong! The pursuit of Mammon has deprived that nation of its senses. Can they actually believe that they can conquer a Germany which stands united behind its Kaiser with their soldiers whom they pay ten shillings a week? Can they believe that?

It is my opinion that they do not know what they are facing. They do not know our army and navy. They probably expect a repetition of the Boer War. One can forgive the French for going to war with us, the victors of 1870. And the Russians? They are an apathetic, stupid mob who do as they are commanded. That poor shadow the Tsar may not even know that he has broken his promises. Perfidious England, however, has stabbed us in the back with premeditation! This war is actually a racial conflict of the Germanic race against the Slavs, of culture against barbarism. Many prominent Englishmen understood this and have said as much. . . .

It was our captain, Kapitän zur See Lübbert, who told us of the English declaration of war on the evening of August 4. "We shall show them what it means to attack us," he cried. "Look at our wonderful ships all around.

They shall all fight to the last man and so long as they remain afloat. Down with our enemies! Death and destruction to all those who break our peace. Join with me in giving three cheers to our Supreme War Lord! His Majesty the Kaiser!"

$\mathcal{CD}$

7. The Socialist Alternative

Wars between capitalist states, generally, result from their competitive struggle for world markets, for each state strives not only to assure for itself the markets it already possesses, but also to conquer new ones; in this the subjugation of foreign peoples and countries comes to play a leading role. Furthermore, these wars are caused by the incessant competition in armaments that characterizes militarism, the chief instrument of bourgeois class rule and of the economic and political subjugation of the working class.

Wars are promoted by national prejudices which are systematically cultivated among civilized peoples in the interest of the ruling classes for the purpose of diverting the proletarian masses from their own class problems as well as from their duties of international class solidarity.

Hence, wars are part of the very nature of capitalism; they will cease only when the capitalist economic order is abolished or when the number of sacrifices in men and money, required by the advance in military technique, and the indignation provoked by armaments drive the peoples to abolish this order.

For this reason, the working class, which provides most of the soldiers and makes most of the material sacrifices, is a natural opponent of war, for war contradicts its aim—the creation of an economic order on a socialist basis for the purpose of bringing about the solidarity of all peoples. . . .

If a war threatens to break out, it is the duty of the working class and of its parliamentary representatives in the countries involved, supported by the consolidating activity of the International [Socialist] Bureau, to exert every effort to prevent the outbreak of war by means they consider most effective, which naturally vary according to the accentuation of the class struggle and of the general political situation.

Should war break out none the less, it is their duty to intervene in favor of its speedy termination and to do all in their power to utilize the economic and political crisis caused by the war to rouse the peoples and thereby to hasten the abolition of capitalist class rule.

I.7 From Olga Hess Gankin and H.H, Fisher, eds., *The Bolsheviks and the World War: The Origin of the Third International* (Stanford: Stanford University Press, 1940), 57–59. Copyright © 1940 by the Board of the Trustees of the Leland Stanford Junior University, renewed 1968. All rights reserved. Used with the permission of Stanford University Press. www.sup.org.

8. German Socialists Support the War

In today's session of the Reichstag the Social-Democratic "Fraktion" voted the war credits demanded by the Government. At the same time it outlined its position as follows:

We are face to face with destiny. The result of the imperialistic policy which introduced an era of competitive preparation for war and roused the antagonistic elements in the different nations is breaking over Europe like a tidal wave. The responsibility for this disaster rests upon the supporters of the imperialistic policy which we reject.

Social-Democracy has always done all in its power to fight this disastrous development, and up to the last moment has worked for the maintenance of peace by strong demonstrations in all countries, especially in close co-operation with our French comrades. Its efforts have been in vain.

Now we face the inexorable fact of war. We are threatened by the horror of hostile invasion. Today it is not for us to decide for or against war but to consider the means necessary for the defense of our country.

We must now think of the millions of fellow-countrymen who are drawn into this disaster without any fault of their own. It is they who suffer most from the horrors of war. Our warmest wishes go with all those, irrespective of party, who have been called to arms.

But we are thinking also of the mothers who must give up their sons, of the women and children who are deprived of the husband and father who supported them. For them the fear for their loved ones is mingled with the dread of need and of actual hunger. And this army of women and children will soon be joined by tens of thousands of wounded and crippled soldiers.

To help all of them, to lighten their lot, to ease their suffering, this we consider our urgent duty.

Everything is at stake for our nation and its development toward liberty in the future if Russian despotism stained with the best blood of its own people should be victorious.

It is our duty to ward off this danger, to protect the civilization and independence of our own country. Thus we carry out what we have always emphasized: In the hour of danger we shall not desert the Fatherland. In saying this we feel ourselves in accord with the International which has always recognized the right of every nation to national independence and self-defense, just as we agree with it in condemning any war of aggression or conquest.

We hope that the cruel experience of suffering in this war will awaken in many millions of people the abhorrence of war and will win them for the ideals of socialism and world peace.

I.8   From Ralph Haswell Lutz, ed., *Fall of the German Empire, 1914–1918*, 2 vols. (Stanford: Stanford University Press, 1932), 2:6–7. Copyright © 1940 by the Board of the Trustees of the Leland Stanford Junior University, renewed 1960. All rights reserved. Used with the permission of Stanford University Press. www.sup.org.

We demand that as soon as the aim of security has been achieved and our opponents are disposed to make peace this war shall be brought to an end by a treaty of peace which makes friendship possible with our neighbors. We ask this not only in the interest of national solidarity for which we have always contended but also in the interest of the German people.

With these principles in mind we vote the desired war credits.

✎

9. Thoughts on Mobilization

Freiburg, August 1st, 1914

If there is mobilization now, I must join up, and I would rather do so here, where there would be a chance of going to the Front quite soon, than in Travemünde, Hamburg or Bahrenfeld, where we should probably be used only to defend the Kiel Canal. And I can't think of anything more hateful than to be forced to sit at home doing nothing when there is war and fighting out there.

You must not imagine that I write this in a fit of war-fever; on the contrary, I am quite calm and am absolutely unable to share the enthusiasm with which some people here are longing to go to war. I can't yet believe that that will happen. It seems to me impossible, and I feel sure that things will go no further than mobilization. But if it does start then you will understand that I can't stop anywhere here. I know too that you are a dear, good, sensible little Mother, and would not wish that your sons should show cowardice in the face of great danger and stay prudently behind.

✎

Britain and the Empire Mobilize

The broad spectrum of popular reactions to the prospect and then the outbreak of war, ranging from apathy to apprehension to resignation to enthusiasm was no less prevalent within Britain and its empire than in the rest of Europe. In the British case, however, the situation was complicated by two concerns: first, the initial uncertainty whether the island nation would in fact intervene in a struggle between rivals on the Continent; and second, if it did fight, whether it could persuade a sufficient number of volunteers to join the armed services, given that it had not enacted a compulsory military draft. The first selection below is by Basil Thomson, who as the head of the London Metropolitan Police's Criminal Investigation Department (CID), was charged with monitoring threats to domestic stability and security, including those from foreign spies. If confusion,

I.9   From Philipp Witkop, *German Students' War Letters* (London: Methuen, 1929), 17.

ill-preparedness, and susceptibility to rumor seem the dominant themes from Thomson's perspective, others were confident that such energies could be channeled to positive ends, as in Coulson Kernahan's account of the vibrant collective patriotism that could be stimulated by a shrewdly managed recruiting meeting. A new sense of unity and cohesion, forged in the process of mobilization and superseding the class prejudices of the prewar era, is likewise a theme of the third selection by Donald Hankey. He was the son of the highly influential secretary to Britain's War Cabinet, Maurice Hankey, and like so many young men from a privileged position, served and died in combat.

Even in the war's earliest days the repercussions were felt across the oceans. Frederick G. Scott, a Canadian clergyman whose poems testified to the consciousness of both a common imperial endeavor and a nascent sense of Canadian nationality, could not remain aloof, and was drawn inexorably to the events in France. For the author of the fifth extract, the war came to him. It is a rarity, a firsthand written account in a predominantly oral culture. J.G. Mullen (probably a pseudonym) was a junior clerk in the Cameroons whose world was turned upside down by the announcement of hostilities. His recollections, published in 1916 in *The Gold Coast Leader* newspaper, detail the arrogance and arbitrary brutality of colonial rule and the inevitable movement of refugees, in West Africa no less than in Belgium or Eastern Europe.

10. Popular Hysteria

I think that we all had at the back of our minds a feeling that a European War on the great scale was so unthinkable that a way would be found at the eleventh hour for avoiding it. A staff officer in whose judgment I believed remarked that if this were so he would emigrate, because he knew that the day was only postponed until Germany felt herself better prepared for the inevitable war. There were, in fact, no illusions at the War Office. . . .

Who now remembers those first feverish days of the War: the crowds about the recruiting stations, the recruits marching through the streets in mufti, the drafts going to the station without bands the flower of our manhood, of whom so many were never to return soldiers almost camping in Victoria Street, the flaring posters, the foolish cry "Business as Usual"; the unseemly rush to the Stores for food until, under the lash of the newspapers, people grew ashamed of their selfishness; the silence in the 'buses, until any loud noise, like a motor back-fire, started a Zeppelin scare? Who now remembers the foolish prognostications of experts how the War would result in unemployment and a revolution would follow; the assurance of certain bankers that the War would be over in six months because none

I.10   From Basil Thomson, *Queer People* (London: Hodder & Stoughton, 1922) 33–34, 36–38, 40.

of the belligerents could stand the financial strain for longer? We have even forgotten the food-hoarding scare that followed the spy scare during the height of the submarine activity, when elderly gentlemen, who had taken thought for the morrow, might have been seen burying biscuit tins in their gardens at midnight for fear that their neighbours should get wind of their hoard and hale them before the magistrate.

I began to think in those days that war hysteria was a pathological condition to which persons of mature age and generally normal intelligence were peculiarly susceptible. War work was evidently not a predisposing cause, for the readiest victims were those who were doing nothing in particular. In ante-bellum days there were a few mild cases. The sufferers would tell you gravely that at a public dinner they had turned suddenly to their German waiter and asked him what post he had orders to join when the German invaders arrived, and that he, taken off his guard, had clicked his heels and replied, "Portsmouth"; or they would whisper of secret visits of German aircraft to South Wales by night and mysterious rides undertaken by stiff guttural persons with square heads who would hire horses in the Eastern Counties and display an unhealthy curiosity about the stable accommodation in every farm that they passed. But in August 1914 the malady assumed a virulent epidemic form accompanied by delusions which defied treatment. It attacked all classes indiscriminately, and seemed even to find its most fruitful soil in sober, stolid, and otherwise truthful people. I remember Mr. Asquith saying that, from a legal and evidential point of view, nothing was ever so completely proved as the arrival of the Russians. Their landing was described by eyewitnesses at Leith, Aberdeen, and Glasgow; they stamped the snow out of their boots and called hoarsely for vodka at Carlisle and Berwick-on-Tweed; they jammed the penny-in-the-slot machines with a rouble at Durham; four of them were billeted on a lady at Crewe who herself described the difficulty of cooking for Slavonic appetites. There was nothing to be done but to let the delusion burn itself out. I have often wondered since whether some self-effacing patriot did not circulate this story in order to put heart into his fellow-countrymen at a time when depression would have been most disastrous, or whether, as has since been said, it was merely the rather outlandish-looking equipment and Gaelic speech of the Lovat Scouts that set the story afloat.

The second phase of the malady attached itself to pigeons. London is full of pigeons—wood pigeons in the parks, blue rocks about the churches and public buildings—and a number of amiable people take pleasure in feeding them. In September 1914, when this phase was at its height, it was positively dangerous to be seen in conversation with a pigeon; it was not always safe to be seen in its vicinity. A foreigner walking in one of the parks was actually arrested and sentenced to imprisonment because a pigeon was seen to fly from the place where he was standing and it was supposed that he had liberated it.

During this phase a pigeon was caught in Essex which was actually carrying a message in the usual little aluminum box clipped to its leg. Moreover, the message was from Rotterdam, but it was merely to report the arrival of an innocuous cargo vessel, whose voyage we afterwards traced.

$$\mathcal{O}$$

11. Recruiting for War

Enthusiasm of any sort, but most of all perhaps when it takes the form of politics, patriotism or religion, is contagious. Mr. F. A. Atkins tells a story of a minister calling upon a man who had ceased to attend church. The man informed his caller that in his opinion religion was in no way dependent upon attendance at places of worship, and that he could be just as truly religious in his own room as in a chapel or church.

The minister rose from his seat without a word and walked over to the fireplace. With the tongs, he picked out the most red-hot and fiercely glowing piece of live coal he could find, and placed it by itself in the hearth. For two or three seconds the fire within the heart of the coal was undimmed. But five or six seconds had hardly passed before—though still burning warmly within—the outer surface of the coal had begun slightly to darken, to crackle, and to cool. In half a minute the thing had turned to a dull and sullen red, and before the minute was out, the once brightly glowing and live coal was black cinder and grey ash.

I am of opinion that this apt object lesson has a bearing upon recruiting as well as upon religion. The assembling together of men and women, with one object in view, and all with one thought in mind, is like the laying of coal by coal when making a fire. As the fire kindles, each separate coal, by giving out heat, causes the coals nearest to it to burn more brightly, and is in return the gainer in warmth and brightness by the warmth and brightness it has itself thus helped to generate and to diffuse. Soon there is no longer a mere collection of odd pieces of live coal, but a fire. The many have coalesced into a unit. So, too, with the units constituting a crowd. Each hearer who feels and responds to the spoken word, communicates in some strange way—the psychology of crowds deserves closely to be studied—his enthusiasm and his ardour to those around him. Some mysterious soul-electricity or personal magnetism which moves men and women poignantly is abroad. It acts and re-acts not only on each member of the audience but upon the man who thus holds them with burning words. He too is conscious of it, and is moved thereby to new effort, to loftier thoughts and nobler speech, until at last he holds and sways the mass of men and women as one person. He and they *are* one, and at one—one in vision, one in aspiration, one in intention, and willing therefore to be one in deeds.

The singly burning coals have become a fire. The crowd had before this ceased to be a mere gathering together of individual women and men. It had already become a unit, an integral part of the nation. But now it is a personality, *one* personality,

I.11   From Coulson Kernahan, *The Experiences of a Recruiting Officer* (London: Hodder and Stoughton, 1915), 28–31.

and more even than a personality, it is a passion, and one passion—the sacred and inextinguishable passion and fire of selfless patriotism . . . and the speaker stands down. His work is done. Thereafter there is no further need of words to urge men to their duty. Rather is there need of help to record their names, so fast and so continuously does the stream of recruits pour in.

Meetings where one hears such oratory and witnesses such response and such results are of course rare, and meetings may, I admit, be overdone; for at this stage of the war they are less necessary than at an earlier period.

In those early days of the war, and I fear the fact holds true also to-day, it was very difficult to make the British public awaken to the fact that this is a war which is *their* business, not merely the business of soldiers; and that if they, the public, did not make it their business, they not only might not have any business to which to attend, but might live to see their own homes burning, their own women and children treated even more brutally and inhumanly than the enemy had treated the women and children of France and Belgium.

Meetings, the purpose of which is to explain the cause of the war, no doubt serve an educational purpose, and the use and influence of such meetings cannot always be accurately estimated by the immediate results. At least they set people thinking, and possibly they set a good many people working; and so eventually assist recruiting—but the note we were instructed; and rightly, to strike at our meetings was as follows: We were to endeavour to fix the attention of audiences, not upon how the war came about, but upon the fact that no matter how it came about, the one fact to be realised now was that a war which would have to be fought to a finish was upon us, and that the only way to end that war was to send more men, and again more men, and yet again more men, to the front.

The recital at one gathering of Mr. T. W. H. Crosland's almost brutally realistic poem "Reveille" did more to bring this fact home to the hearers than all the speech-making. As the poem will be new to many readers I venture to reprint it here:

> I.
> Oh, it's war, war, war! Peep o' day and morning star
> Aghast, above a world that reels to war, war, war!
> We've cheerful songs a-plenty and we've sung 'em sweet and well,
> But the band has got new music from a shop not far from hell,
> And the words aint "lovey dovey" nor "snookey cow-boy coon,"
> But "Death and bloody slaughter," and the Devil's wrote the tune—
> Hold your chins up—sing it hearty—don't you shirk a single bar;
> For it's war, war, war!
> My bonny boys—it's war!
> II.
> Oh, it's war, war, war! No matter who you are
> You can either like or lump it, but all the same it's war!
> You bear ill-will to nobody, your soul's desire is peace—
> Well, stand upon your doorstep and bid the bugles cease:

You've been drilled and milled and hardened, you're spoiling for a fight—
Your chance is at your elbow! Wherefore put your caps on tight—
Chuck your chests out, grab your rifles, fling your blankets in the car,
For it's war, war, war!
My hefty lads—it's war!
III.
Oh, it's war, war, war! See 'em massing near and far;
Roaring, rumbling, tumbling, stumbling on to war, war, war!
The missus she looks scared like, she's forgiven you your sins,
The kids go down the alley beating rataplans on tins,
And waving bits of Union Jacks—the trooper's on the waves,
And now's the time for Englishmen to seek their honoured graves!
Oh, get busy! Up and at 'em—be you soldier-man or tar,
For it's war, war, war!
My dear young friends—it's war!
IV.
Oh, it's war, war, war! It may make us. It will mar
Many a man and many a woman—but it's war, war, war!
There's Drake and Blake and Nelson, and "Bobs" who pulled us through—
Now it's Kitchener and Jellicoe and George the Fifth and YOU:
The Lord help honest people and the foul Fiend take his own,
For you shall smash the Mad Dog's head and stamp his rabbles down,
And keep the old flag flying from Wick to Malabar—
Oh, its war, war war!
By Dad's best hat—it's war!

To say in effect directly yet not offensively, to each member of the audience; "Thou art the man!" is what is wanted in an appeal for recruits: and these stirring lines give a speaker several openings. To the pacifists we can emphasise the biting irony, the savage satire, of the lines addressed to the man whose "soul's desire is peace."

"Well, stand upon your doorstep and bid the bugles cease."

To the man in the street who is disposed to regard the war as a soldier's; somebody's, anybody's business except his own, one can say:

"There's Drake and Blake and Nelson, And Bobs who pulled us through—
Now it's Kitchener and Jellicoe and George the Fifth—and YOU."

This direct man-to-man appeal must, our chief insisted, be made at every recruiting meeting he organised. While on recruiting duty, as with soldiers on parade, each of us—myself, his honorary recruiting officer, the recruiting sergeant, an ex-company-sergeant-major of the Royal Garrison Artillery, and the clerical staff, down to the smartest cadet-orderly who ever wore khaki or stood at salute—was rigidly expected to obey orders.

While no martinet, and welcoming suggestions from any of us, he rightly insisted—as we were responsible to him, and he, and he only, was responsible to headquarters for the conduct of recruiting in his area—that nothing be done inside the office or out of it without his cognisance and approval. In the meetings under his control, little or nothing was left to chance. He spared no pains in selecting and sifting his speakers, rarely, if ever, putting up anyone entirely "on spec," but giving the men whom he had good cause to believe would come to the point, and would not "spread themselves" unduly, a hearing. If dissatisfied he unconditionally thenceforth cut them out.

Even in meetings in towns at a long distance from the recruiting office, and so necessarily organised by others, it was his rule, so far as was possible, not to call upon outside speakers. A few words, possibly, as chairman, or in proposing some resolution,were occasionally invited from someone well known in the neighbour-hood where the meeting was held; but the Chief preferred, at all events at the first meetings in any particular place, to put up his own speakers, generally the same three, each of whom had the lines upon which he was to speak laid down for him, and each of whose speech was quite different in subject and in style from the speeches of the other two.

One spoke entirely as a civilian. He addressed himself from the standpoint of the man in the street and the woman in the house, and showed how urgent it was that every able-bodied man who could come forward should enlist; another gave a straightforward and soldierlike statement of the facts, the rates of pay, terms of service, and the like, and showed how many and how unique are the advantages, physical and mental, offered by the Army; while the third struck the patriotic note, and made a direct appeal for recruits.

12. A British Student in Arms

The unprecedented had occurred. For once a national ideal had proved stronger than class prejudice. In this matter of the war all classes were at one—at one not only in sentiment but in practical resolve. The crowd that surged outside the central recruiting offices in Great Scotland Yard was the proof of it. All classes were there, struggling for the privilege of enlisting in the new citizen Army, conscious of their unity, and determined to give effect to it in the common life of service. It was an extraordinary crowd. Workmen were there in cord breeches and subfusc coats; boys from the East End in the latest fashions from Petticoat Lane; clerks and shop-assistants in sober black; mechanics in blue serge and bowler hats; travelers in the garments of prosperity; and most conspicuously well dressed of all, gentlemen in their oldest clothes. It was like a section cut out of the nation.

I.12   From Donald Hankey, *A Student in Arms* (London: Andrew Melrose, 1916), 25–29.

Men and boys of the working class formed the majority. They were in their element, shouting, singing, cheeking the "coppers" with as much ribald good humor as if the recruiting office had been a music-hall. But some of the other classes were far less at their ease. They had been brought up from earliest youth to thank God that they were not as other men, to set store by the innumerable little marks that distinguished them from "the lower classes." All these they were now sacrificing to an idea, and they felt horribly embarrassed. Even the gentleman, who had prided himself on his freedom from "the snobbishness of the suburbs," felt ill at ease. Of course he had been to workingmen's clubs; but there he had been "Mr. Thingumy." Here he was "mate." He told himself that he did not mind being "mate," in fact he rather liked it; but he fervently wished that he looked the part. He felt as self-conscious as if he had arrived at a dinner party in a Norfolk jacket. A little later on, when he sat, one of four nude men, in a cubicle awaiting medical inspection, he did feel that for the moment they had all been reduced to the common denominator of their sheer humanity; but embarrassment returned with his clothes and stayed with him all through the march to the station and the journey to the depot.

At the depot he fought for the prize of a verminous blanket, and six foot of floor to lie on. When he awoke the next morning his clothes were creased and dirty, his collar so filthy that it had to be discarded, and his chin unshaven. He perceived with something of a shock that he was no longer conspicuous. He was no more than the seedy unit of a seedy crowd. In any other circumstances he would have been disgusted. As it was, he sought the canteen at the earliest opportunity and toasted the Unity of the Classes in a pint!

All emerged from the depot clothed exactly alike, and meditated on the symbolism of clothes. They donned the gray shirt and ready-made khaki of the new era, and deposited the emblems of class distinction on a common rag-heap. Even the perfunctory manner of the Q.M.S. [Quartermaster sergeant] could not rob the occasion of an almost religious solemnity. It was the formal beginning of a new life, in which men of all classes, starting with something like equality of opportunity, should gain what pre-eminence they might by the merit of their inherent manhood or the seduction of their native tact. Henceforward all fared alike. All ate the same food, slept on the same floor in similar blankets, and in their shirts. Even the pajamas no longer divided them! All took their share in scrubbing floors and washing dixies; and until the novelty wore off even these menial and dirty jobs caught a certain glamour from the great ideal which they symbolized. Gradually all found their level. The plausible were promoted, found wanting, reduced, and replaced by the men of real grit and force of character. Mechanics joined the machine-gun section, clerks became orderlies, signallers, or telephonists. The dirtiest and most drunken of the old soldiers were relegated to the cookhouse. Equality of opportunity had been granted, and the inequality of man had been demonstrated. It was found that the best formula, after all, was that of St. Paul: "Diversities of gifts, but the same Spirit."

13. A Canadian Clergyman at War

It was on the evening of the 31st of July, 1914, that I went down to a newspaper office in Quebec to stand amid the crowd and watch the bulletins which were posted up every now and then, and to hear the news of the war. One after another the reports were given, and at last there flashed upon the board the words, "General Hughes offers a force of twenty thousand men to England in case war is declared against Germany." I turned to a friend and said, "That means that I have got to go to the war." Cold shivers went up and down my spine as I thought of it, and my friend replied, "Of course it does not mean that you should go. You have a parish and duties at home." I said, "No. I am a Chaplain of the 8th Royal Rifles. I must volunteer, and if I am accepted, I will go." It was a queer sensation, because I had never been to war before and I did not know how I should be able to stand the shell fire. I had read in books of people whose minds were keen and brave, but whose hind legs persisted in running away under the sound of guns. Now I knew that an ordinary officer on running away under fire would get the sympathy of a large number of people, who would say, "The poor fellow has got shell shock," and they would make allowance for him. But if a chaplain ran away, about six hundred men would say at once, "We have no more use for religion." So it was with very mingled feelings that I contemplated an expedition to the battle-fields of France, and I trusted that the difficulties of Europe would be settled without our intervention. However, preparations for war went on. On Sunday, August 2nd, in the afternoon, I telephoned to Militia Headquarters and gave in my name as a volunteer for the Great War. When I went to church that evening and told the wardens that I was off to France, they were much surprised and disconcerted. When I was preaching at the service and looked down at the congregation, I had a queer feeling that some mysterious power was dragging me into a whirlpool, and the ordinary life around me and the things that were so dear to me had already begun to fade away.

On Tuesday, August the Fourth, war was declared, and the Expeditionary Force began to be mobilized in earnest. It is like recalling a horrible dream when I look back to those days of apprehension and dread. The world seemed suddenly to have gone mad.

All civilization appeared to be tottering. The Japanese Prime Minister, on the night war was declared, said, "This is the end of Europe." In a sense his words were true. Already we see power shifted from nations in Europe to that great Empire which is in its youth, whose home is in Europe, but whose dominions are scattered over the wide world, and also to that new Empire of America, which came in to the war at the end with such determination and high resolve. The destinies of mankind are now in the hands of the English-speaking nations and France. In those hot August days, a camp at Valcartier was prepared in a lovely valley surrounded by the old granite hills of the Laurentians, the oldest range of mountains in the world. The Canadian units began to collect, and the lines of white tents were laid out. On Saturday, August 22nd, at

I.13   From Frederick George Scott, *The Great War as I Saw It* (Toronto: F.D. Goodchild, 1922), 15–17.

seven in the morning, the detachment of volunteers from Quebec marched off from the drill-shed to entrain for Valcartier. Our friends came to see us off and the band played "The Girl I Left Behind Me," in the traditional manner. On our arrival at Valcartier we marched over to the ground assigned to us, and the men set to work to put up the tents. I hope I am casting no slur upon the 8th Royal Rifles of Quebec, when I say that I think we were all pretty green in the matter of field experience. The South African veterans amongst us, both officers and men, saved the situation. But I know that the cooking arrangements rather "fell down", and I think a little bread and cheese, very late at night, was all we had to eat. We were lucky to get that. Little did we know then of the field kitchens, with their pipes smoking and dinners cooking, which later on used to follow up the battalions as they moved.

The camp at Valcartier was really a wonderful place. Rapidly the roads were laid out, the tents were run up, and from west and east and north and south men poured in. There was activity everywhere. Water was laid on, and the men got the privilege of taking shower-baths, beside the dusty roads. Bands played; pipers retired to the woods and practised unearthly music calculated to fire the breast of the Scotsman with a lust for blood. We had rifle practice on the marvellous ranges. We had sham battles in which the men engaged so intensely that on one occasion, when the enemy met, one over-eager soldier belaboured his opponent with the butt end of his rifle as though he were a real German, and the poor victim, who had not been taught to say "Kamarad," suffered grievous wounds and had to be taken away in an ambulance. Though many gales and tempests had blown round those ancient mountains, nothing had ever equalled the latent power in the hearts of the stalwart young Canadians who had come so swiftly and eagerly at the call of the Empire. It is astonishing how the war spirit grips one. In Valcartier began that splendid comradeship which spread out to all the divisions of the Canadian Corps, and which binds those who went to the great adventure in a brotherhood stronger than has ever been known before.

The dominating spirit of the camp was General Hughes, who rode about with his aides-de-camp in great splendour like Napoleon. To me it seemed that his personality and his despotic rule hung like a dark shadow over the camp. He was especially interesting and terrible to us chaplains, because rumour had it that he did not believe in chaplains, and no one could find out whether he was going to take us or not. The chaplains in consequence were very polite when inadvertently they found themselves in his august presence.

News from overseas continued to be bad. Day after day brought us tidings of the German advance. The martial spirits amongst us were always afraid to hear that the war would be over before we got to England. I, but did not tell the people so, was afraid it wouldn't. I must confess I did not see in those days how a British force composed of men from farms, factories, offices and universities could get together in time to meet and overthrow the trained legions of Germany. It was certainly a period of anxious thought and deep foreboding, but I felt that I belonged to a race that has never been conquered. Above all, right and, therefore, God was on our side.

14. The View from the Cameroons

It was on the night of the 11th August 1914, when news of a great war in Europe reached us at Mbua (a town in the South Cameroons, about nine weeks or more from Duala [Douala]) and that preparations were being made between the allied forces of the British and French for a war with the Germans in the Cameroons. Being a native of Cape Coast and a British subject employed in an English factory [a trading station], it occurred to me that I would fare badly at the hands of either the German soldiers or the natives should this news be authentic. The inevitable trend of events was evident if war really broke out, the natives being mostly canni- bals, would attack all aliens, irrespective of race or colour and eat their flesh before any assistance from the German Government could be obtained. My agent was stationed at Njassi, four days from Mbua, and until I heard from him, my sole duty was to remain at my place. There was hardly any signs of agitation noticeable in Mbua between the 12th and 14th August, but on the 15th the natives could be seen running hither and thither, with spears in their hands, removing their belongings to the bush, mysteriously disappearing and returning in a similar manner, with a seeming stern resolve to finally eradicate all foreigners. These wild ignorant people had long waited for this with wariness, and nothing could afford them a better chance than such an event. In a short time the whole country was thrown into a state of commotion so that by the 18th instant no woman or child could be seen in the town of Mbua except the men who appear and disappear concocting dangerous schemes, with surprising secrecy. Besides myself in Mbua there were the following clerks: two Kwitta [a coastal town in Ghana] clerks with 26 yard boys, five Cameroon native clerks with 30 yard boys and two Gabon clerks with 6 yard boys. I had ten yard boys. All these people were concerned with the safety of their stores and preparing some means of defence, should the natives attack us. On the 20th August I received a note from my boss intimating that he had been arrested by the German authorities, and his stores commandeered and, that sooner or later, a similar treatment would be meted out to me, so I closed up my accounts, and gave up myself to contemplation of the future. . . .

One by one all the traders removed from Mbua, so that by the end of August only three important stores remained, including mine. About the 11th September, I received another note from my boss intimating that he was being sent down to Ajoa, as a prisoner of war, by the Germans, and that I should follow at once. I dare not go, without the sanction of the German Government and I wrote to say so. On the 22nd September, however, a German official with three soldiers arrived to commandeer my store. This official first asked for the key of the safe which I handed to him. When I called his attention to the goods in the store, he said the best thing he could think of was to set fire to the goods, and put me inside to burn with them. "Dem be shit cargo, and I no get no time for count dem!" he said, and

I.14   From J.G. Mullen, "The View from the Cameroons," *Gold Coast Leader* (October 14, 16, and 28, 1916), as reprinted in *Africa* 78 (2008): 401–409.

then with a vehemence which alarmed me, this great German cursed me, the English, and everything connected with the English, and emphasised his words by kicking the breakable articles in the store. This caused me to giggle, but unfortunately he looked up and saw me in this act, and after that he administered heavy blows and kicks to me, he ordered the soldiers to bind me up, and keep me in custody. I soon found myself in the hands of these unscrupulous soldiers, whose cruelty was proverbial throughout South Cameroons. All day they goaded me to pain and anger. They were indeed painfully jocular; they tickled me, pelted at me with stones, ordered me to lick the dirty soles of their boots, and to do all sorts of un-nameable things. The officer stood by in calm indifference to my sufferings; my mute anger grew till I felt I must choke; an innocent person kept in captivity for the populace to stare at, might feel as I felt. These torments continued all day and the least reluctance on my part to comply with their requests was rewarded with whips and kicks. In addition to this, the cord with which I was bound gnawed into my flesh and inflicted a pain beyond description. I cried aloud in my agony for forbearance and the louder I cried out the more the soldiers jeered at me. Gradually I lost consciousness, and then all became still blackness. When I recovered consciousness, the German officer was bending over me, and I was unbound. My hands were very much swollen; this officer, after a short reproof full of venomous invectives handed me a passport to Ajoa, and ordered me to provision myself for the journey, I made up two loads and that very night I left Mbua with my boys. Great was my thankfulness to God for my wonderful deliverance from a torturing death, and from the hands of these wicked people, and as I repeated the "magnificat" the only song of thankfulness that I could think of at the moment I said my last farewell to Mbua. . . .

Three days from Njassi brought me to Dume, a large station situated on a hill, with walls which stood grim and forbidding. I arrived there on a Monday, and the crowd of people waiting to show their passports to a German Official, was thick and dense. I made several efforts to get through, but all was in vain. It can only be compared to a packed mass of humanity, which surged and swayed with the impatience of waiting. People were jostling and cuffing each other, gesticulating and shrieking in sharp piercing tones, in their mad and fruitless attempts to make way with their passports. No way in any given direction was possible and the more haste one made, the less he progressed. I followed closely at the heels of one tall man, a Kaka native, who, with majestic tread, and the strength of a giant, made way for himself by pushing the people right and left with an air of quiet unconcern. I kept close behind him, and indeed made good progress with him, but suddenly, my course was impeded by a Jaunde man, who sharply slapped me in the face, and said, "You be English shwine, *du sow.*". . .

I pushed my way as best as I could through the German Official inspecting passports, not without some trepidation though, for, as a British subject, I expected no more from the Germans, than contempt and reproaches and possibly 25 lashes. When I at length approached this Official with my passport, he cast a very severe and scatching [sic] glance at me, and asked—"Nigger, was ist du, und was machst sie hier jetzt?" ("Nigger, what are you, and what doest thou here now?")

"Massa, I be Cape Coast man," I blurted out.

"Cape Coast, Cape Coast," he said, "You zink I be fool? You member I no sabe you long time palaver? I say vat for country you be? Na you talk quick ich habe keine seit." Uncertain how to reply, I stood pinned to the ground racking my brain for a fitting answer. The word Cape Coast somehow seemed to rouse his ire and indignation, and I felt at a loss what to say next.

"Donner, wetter Himmel Gott, how much for town, du sow, mench shwine," the German roared, evidently annoyed at my delay in replying, and thereat he whacked me on the head with a cane which he jerked somewhere from his Office. I writhed in agony. It then occurred to me that the Germans in Cameroons were more conversant with the names of Accra and Sekondi out of the whole Gold Coast (towns at which the German-South Coast Express steamers called) and ports like Cape Coast or Saltpond etc., were utterly beyond their ken.

"Massa, I be Accra true born," I hazarded, avoiding in the meantime, the incisive cane, with which this great German aimed at my head. "Jah you be dem English schwine what make plenty big moff,"he said, and initialling the passport, he hurled it at me. As I stooped to pick it up, again came the cane on my back with such stunning aggressiveness, that I groaned like a bull. He then called a soldier to chase me out of the port, and for more than half a mile, this soldier chased me, hurling at me stones, pieces of wood, and even some raw cassada which he snatched from farmers. When all attempts to reach me proved futile, the soldier with menacing gestures, turned and went away. I had reason to be thankful that I had a pair of good legs to carry me far from these wicked people.

II

War on the Western Front

The first two months of campaigning in August and September 1914 conformed to expectations, at least insofar as they embodied a war of movement. In fact, much of that movement stemmed from the German General Staff's surprising decision to launch the major thrust of its attack upon French forces through neutral Belgium. In the first years of the twentieth century German military planners had struggled with the unpleasant fact that in any likely war they would be fighting on opposite fronts simultaneously—against the French to the west and the Russians to the east. Germany would be in danger of being crushed from both sides. Count Alfred von Schlieffen, the German Chief of Staff, was convinced that his best hope of success lay in concentrating his forces first on one front to crush an opponent quickly enough to then transfer those troops to defend against an attack from the other direction. Because Russia would take longer to mobilize, von Schlieffen reckoned it made more sense to concentrate on France first, so long as victory could be achieved in six weeks. If the French campaigns took any longer, Russia's overwhelming numerical superiority would tell against the diminished German defenders. How, then, to secure a decisive victory over France quickly enough became the critical question. In war games and operational plans undertaken before his retirement in 1905, Schlieffen's answer was a powerful right hook through Belgium, circumventing French defenses, and then sweeping in a wide arc, perhaps even west of Paris, to surround and destroy the off-balance French armies. That this violation of Belgian neutrality could bring Britain into the war was largely discounted. The British might abstain, it was thought, but even if they intervened, they would not field enough soldiers to sway the balance.

Schlieffen's successor, Helmuth von Moltke, nervous and pessimistic, worried that the proposed grand outflanking maneuver was too ambitious and scaled it back to

Empires, Soldiers, and Citizens: A World War I Sourcebook, Second Edition.
Edited by Marilyn Shevin-Coetzee and Frans Coetzee.
© 2013 John Wiley & Sons, Ltd. except sources 1 to 17. Published 2013 by John Wiley & Sons, Ltd.

release more troops to the eastern front (in part because the Russian army seemed capable to getting more men into the field more quickly in 1914 than it had a decade earlier). Nonetheless, the early German gains were spectacular enough, fueled by the rapid capture of Belgian fortifications around Liège. But as the German advance continued, its supply lines lengthened, while those of the French contracted. Moreover, gaps began to open between the two armies on the German right flank tasked with the longest marches, and communications suffered as well, adding to the strain on von Moltke, some 150 miles behind the front in Luxembourg. French commander Joseph Joffre, who began by launching a series of futile attacks from southeastern France, kept his composure, changed course, and concentrated what forces he could near Paris for the decisive battle. Over several days in early September near the River Marne, the French finally stopped the German advance and compelled both sides to move troops toward the Belgian coast in an ultimately unsuccessful effort to outflank each other. Even up to late 1914, an observer from the Napoleonic Wars would have recognized much of this conduct of war. Cavalry still cantered at the head of columns, soldiers trudged on foot, horse-drawn carts laboriously pulled supplies. But as the year drew to a close, war on the Western Front settled into a different and less recognizable mode: a prolonged and bloody stalemate.

That stalemate reflected the war's enormous emphasis on defense. Barbed wire, which had confined cattle on the U.S. Great Plains, proved effective in impeding the advance of fighting men. Machine guns used to deadly effect by imperialists in Africa and Asia now scored equal success against the soldiers of the European powers themselves. And the devastating bombardments of heavy artillery forced troops to burrow ever deeper into the soil merely to survive. By early 1915, parallel lines of German and Allied trenches stretched from the Belgian coast to the Swiss frontier.

Those trenches became a marked feature of the Western Front over the next three years and in their own peculiar way reflected the different nations' approaches to the war. The British, for example, appeared to rely on their alleged talent for improvisation. Because they persisted in viewing trenches as temporary, they reserved resources for offensive action instead. The French trenches, often squalid and uncomfortable, were little better. Many German emplacements, in contrast, exuded an air of permanence. Deeper and drier, they afforded relative comfort and protection from the incessant shelling.

Nevertheless, for trench dwellers of all nations, boredom became the other enemy, as soldiers filled periods of inactivity with mundane tasks such as delousing themselves and killing rats. Military leaders, however, knew well that offensive action kept morale high, and so, resolved to win the war promptly, they executed mass attacks on enemy lines. As casualties mounted, they grew only more determined to force a decisive breach through their opponents' trenches. As they saw it, the massive firepower now at their disposal offered an enormous advantage to the offensive, and they launched deafening bombardments before attacking.

Preliminary artillery fire negated any element of surprise, however. Furthermore, the constant shellfire devastated the once pristine countryside. The resulting pitted terrain between the trenches, a virtually impassable morass of mud, corpses, shell craters, and tangled wire, appropriately became known as No Man's Land. Strategists began to perceive a devastating contradiction between their initial dreams of a brief, glorious, and inexpensive victory and their soldiers' desperate attempts to win a few yards of blood-soaked ground at tremendous cost. They saw an appalling incongruity, a conflict that embodied remarkable technological innovation but that confined combatants to a primordial subterranean realm.

For much of 1915, the initiative in this sort of warfare lay with the Allies. Germany concentrated its offensive actions on the eastern front, partly to relieve pressure on beleaguered Austrian armies, partly because further significant victories over Russian troops seemed possible under the leadership of Paul von Hindenburg and Erich Ludendorff which had already proven so effective at Tannenberg. Moreover, because the German invaders occupied French and Belgian soil, there was strong public pressure for the Allies to push them back. But persistent heavy fighting, especially around Ypres and Loos in Belgium, achieved little and cost hundreds of thousands of casualties on both sides.

In 1916, both sides were ready to try again. Erich von Falkenhayn, Chief of the German General Staff, hoped to deliver a knockout blow to French troops, but not by achieving a breakthrough in enemy lines as conventionally understood, but by sucking French divisions into a murderous killing zone dominated by German artillery. By applying pressure to a sector the French could not afford to abandon (a salient or bulge in the lines around the town of Verdun), Falkenhayn sought to "bleed France white" and compel the demographically challenged French nation to sue for peace. The battle lasted from late February to late June and came to symbolize the slaughter of the entire war. France's Philippe Pétain mounted an impassioned defense, pledging that "they [the Germans] shall not pass" and forcing the Germans, by the inexorable logic of the campaign, to commit ever-larger numbers of their own troops. It was partly to relieve the pressure on the French that the British commander, the taciturn and relentless Sir Douglas Haig, committed the new armies that had been raised in the initial period of widespread voluntary enlistment before rising casualty totals staunched the flow of new recruits. Massive artillery bombardment (some 1.5 million shells) preceded the attack against German positions near the river Somme, but once again the superiority of the defensive was vindicated. German defenders emerged from their dugouts to cut down more than 20,000 British troops on the first day of fighting alone. In the end, both sides claimed to be waging a war of attrition, insisting that their opponent could not possibly continue to absorb such heavy losses (but without admitting the obvious, namely that neither could they maintain such casualties as well).

From the spring of 1917 the warring sides resembled two staggering boxers with the real question being which could retain his footing long enough to muster the strength for one massive blow. The Germans hoped to crush tottering Russia and transfer additional troops from the east for one final offensive in the west (which they managed in the spring of 1918). The Allies hoped to hold on through mutinies in the French armies in the wake of the disastrous April 1917 Chemin des Dames offensives and replenish their depleted ranks with fresh American soldiers once that country had entered the war. Despite some nervous moments, the Allies contained the German attacks, and then, with a significant and growing superiority in men and material, applied continuous pressure on German armies that could no longer withstand it. By October 1918 German forces were beaten all along the front, and a month later their defeat was registered in the armistice of November 11.

☙

Adapting to Trench Warfare

The First World War confounded expectations of a relatively quick and decisive conflict, and as it dragged on without any swift end in sight, it forced everyone, and especially the troops in the field, to come to terms with the unanticipated consequences of a murderous stalemate.

The following selections explore the experiences of ordinary soldiers on the Western Front. Inadequate preparation and the challenge of forging cohesive units from a diverse collection of draftees are the underlying themes of the first extract from the wartime memoirs of one of France's greatest historians, the medievalist Marc Bloch. He survived the war, only to see his country invaded a second time. Serving in the French Resistance during the Second World War, he was captured by the Germans and executed in 1944. The second piece, by an English artillery officer serving in the Ypres salient in 1915, illustrates many of the daily realities of the struggle: monotony and tedium, broken by attacks "over the top," the rhythms of attack and counter-attack, and the persistent threats from gas and artillery bombardment. Reactions to these stresses varied. Julian Grenfell, an Eton and Oxford-educated member of an elite Dragoon cavalry unit, exulted in war as an adventure and glorious sport, while Melville Hastings (who was not from a class that thought fox-hunting was ideal preparation for killing Germans) tempered his commitment to a just victory with the recognition that the German enemy was not so different after all. Grenfell died in May 1915 at the age of 27, Hastings a month before the war's end in 1918.

The remaining documents illustrate the diversity of British forces and the ways in which they were challenged to adapt to trench warfare. Scottish units, such as the Seaforth Highlanders, were forced to relinquish one distinctive marker of their identity (kilts) in favor of drab khaki uniforms. The subject of poet Siegfried Sassoon's "A Working Party" goes about his military duties in even greater anonymity while death comes without warning from an unknown and unseen enemy. Sassoon himself served with distinction and conspicuous bravery, but his enthusiasm for the war soured, and he was nearly cashiered after publishing a pacifist appeal in 1917. Only the intervention of his friend and fellow author, Robert Graves, saved his career and enabled Sassoon to be diagnosed with shell shock and invalided home. The seventh and eighth extracts detail the actions of Canadian units and reinforce the lesson that artillery dominated the battlefield. Those who did not absorb that lesson, and learn to appreciate the sounds and trajectories of different shells, had little chance of surviving. Snipers posed the other persistent, unseen danger; indeed, the career of the author of the seventh piece, Canadian infantryman John Erskine Lockerby, was cut short when his right arm was shattered by a sniper's bullet at Neuve Chapelle in 1915.

Surely even greater shock was experienced by the recruits from India whose units were transferred to the Western Front. The Allied effort rested in part on the backs of imperial recruits or conscripts, including laborers from China or South Africa, and soldiers from West Africa and India. We can begin to grasp what those Indian soldiers endured because all of their letters to family members at home or to wounded comrades convalescing in Britain first passed through military censors. Those censors were looking for evidence of Indian morale, and they either prepared reports quoting the letters they let through or withheld others as too damaging to the war effort. In reading these letters, we should bear in mind that the soldiers knew that their correspondence would be reviewed (hence the possibility of self-censorship) and that, in the cases where the soldiers themselves were illiterate, the actual text would have been written by a scribe (suggesting that certain turns of phrase might have been more formulaic than authentic). Despite these reservations, these letters provide insight into the experiences and aspirations of ordinary soldiers who would otherwise have left few traces in the conventional written historical record.

1. Life Different as Possible

Thus from August 10, 1914, to January 5, 1915, I led a life as different as possible from my ordinary existence: a life at once barbarous, violent, often colorful, also often of a dreary monotony combined with bits of comedy and moments of grim tragedy. In five months in the field, who would not have amassed a rich harvest of experiences?

Like everyone else, I was impressed by the total inadequacy of our material preparation as well as of our military training. In La Gruerie I installed wire without barbs. I have seen my trench showered with bombs to which we could respond only with rifle fire. I have ordered the ground dug with hand tools and intrigued with my colleagues to secure a few good full-size implements for my platoon. I saw—alas, right up to the end—the inadequacy of our telephone lines impede our communication with the artillery. Moreover, only experience taught me—and no doubt most imperfectly—how to dig trenches. Reflecting later on what we did during the first months of war, I realized that the corps of engineers knew little more about that problem than we did. Before Larzicourt, didn't our officers build

II.1   From Marc Bloch, *Memoirs of War, 1914–15*, trans. Carole Fink (Ithaca, NY: Cornell University Press, 1980), 159, 161–166. Copyright Carole Fink. Reprinted with kind permission.

for our battalion commander a shelter that was cleverly hidden in a cabbage field but totally lacking any direct communication with the front lines? Thus, in the event of an attack, our unhappy major, after having killed off all his quartermaster sergeants by sending them with his orders to the various companies, would have been forced to watch, like a powerless spectator, the combat he should have been directing. I saw progress occur slowly, with difficulty, but surely. By December we had more barbed wire and pointed stakes than we knew what to do with. I heard the noise of our artillery, so weak and intermittent during our first stay in La Gruerie, grow gradually to dominate the uproar of the enemy's cannon.

I was aware, especially at the start of the campaign, of some shocking negligence. When we were holding the trenches near Thonne-la-Long we had absolutely no idea what was in front of us. One day, when we thought we had made contact with the enemy, the French outposts were still in front of us. Our orders to leave Han-les-Juvigny arrived several hours late. At Larzicourt we worked under the supervision of the corps of engineers. On the first day we exerted considerable effort to dig trenches that, being visible from a distance, would have offered the enemy's artillery an invaluable target. The next day the engineers' captain, who was billeted in the village, examined our work, correctly judged it unacceptable, and made us start again; had he come the day before to direct our inexperienced efforts, he could have spared us both the painful fatigue and the discouragement of our wasted efforts. One of my men, a master carpenter from a town in the Ile-de-France, said, "If I were responsible for work like that, I'd soon have to close up shop." Wasn't he right?

I was by no means always satisfied with our officers. Often I found them insufficiently concerned with their men's well-being, too ignorant of their physical condition, and too uninterested to find out. The words "Let them cope"—that sinister phrase which, after 1870, no one should have dared utter again—were still too often on their lips. The officers' and platoon leaders' mess sometimes appropriated too large a share of the supplies. The officers' cooks played too important a role in the company. The quartermaster sergeants should have been kept under closer scrutiny. Obviously there may have been regiments to which my criticisms do not apply. I can only speak of what I have seen, and the range of my experience was necessarily very limited. When in quarters, the company officers did not assemble their men frequently enough. Reservists are no longer children; they always impressed me as eager for news, and its lack discouraged them. It was up to their officers to keep them informed of developments and to comment on them. I had a captain who understood admirably how to communicate with his troops; why didn't he do it more often? In fairness, I should add that at Vienne-le-Château we were forced to avoid meetings, which would be dangerous in a village under constant bombardment.

Our battalion, and then the sixth, were for the time commanded by a captain who was a coarse and contemptible individual. He knew only two ways to make his men perform: either by insulting them or by threatening them with a court-martial. I heard him vilify some men who two days earlier (September 10) had stood without flinching under the devastating cannon and machine gun fire that had covered the German retreat. Once he hit someone; but I believe that incident was hushed up. Our revenge was to watch the terrible fright that his features betrayed at the sound of shellfire. Promoted major, he had himself recalled on the pretext of general exhaustion, which no one believed. But my battalion also served under an officer whom I greatly admired. With a somewhat severe appearance as well as a brusque manner and speech, his thin, almost ascetic face revealed no trace of humor. Yet, though he made not the slightest effort to be popular, he possessed that mysterious quality of personal magnetism which transforms a man into a leader; his soldiers had faith in him and would have followed him anywhere. In my comrade M., a reenlisted noncommissioned officer who rose to second lieutenant, I found the charm of simple courage along with the happy combination of cool self-possession and personal warmth. It was he who produced the heroic reply—so much finer because of its obvious innocence of any literary pretension—when a panic-stricken soldier cried, "The Germans are only thirty meters away from us," "Well, we are only thirty meters away from the Germans."

A company or platoon is not made up of men equally intelligent, attractive, or brave. When I recall the comrades with whom I have lived, men I have commanded, the figures I evoke do not all seem pleasant. By knowing Corporal H., I learned just how far malingering could go (how far in this case would probably have been a court-martial if the lieutenant had not been so kind, perhaps too kind). When I remember the face of Corporal M., I cannot restrain a smile. He was a miner, stocky and rather heavy-footed, with a square face; his nose was adorned with a fine blueish scar of the sort that the carbon dust of the coal pit frequently imprints on workers' bodies. Though an indefatigable walker, he was unaccustomed to shoes, so he traveled the roads of Lorraine and Champagne barefoot. He was so careless and so stupid that it now seems to me I did little during the first six weeks of the campaign but hunt for him from one end of the camp to the other, to transmit orders he never understood. But I should not forget that the last thing I did not succeed in making him understand, on the morning of September 10, was that his place was not at the head of the platoon. When we went into action that day, he fell, whether killed or wounded I do not know.

During the month of August and the first days of September, D. was our joy. A peasant from the region of Baupaume, he had the most beautiful Picard accent. When we saw the first wounded along the route between Grand-Verneuil and Thonne-la-Long, we noticed that many had their arms in slings, leaving their unused coat sleeves dangling. D. thought they were all amputees, and we were never able to convince him that he was mistaken. Very coarse in his own language, he accepted the grossest insults from his comrades without flinching; only one expression infuriated him: "Shut your——." He absolutely insisted on having a "mouth." I also muse over our handful of cowards: K., who all but spat at me when I happened on him by chance in his shelter; V., who, miserable at finding himself at war, never referred to himself without saying, "Poor martyr!" But I prefer to remember the good chaps: P., of whose death I have just learned, a Parisian worker with pale complexion, who had the insatiable appetite of a man who has not had all he wanted to eat, who has frequently gone hungry, and who was restless, nervous, and quick both to anger and to rejoice; poor G., secretary of a miners' union, active and talkative, and with a truly generous heart; and T., also a miner, uneducated, as taciturn as G. was loquacious, of dark complexion and gloomy expression, calm in moments of danger and burning with an unquenchable hatred of Germans, whom he never referred to except as "those assassins." Who will ever record the unknown acts of heroism performed in La Gruerie by our dispatch runners? I can still see our first, T., by occupation a manual laborer from Pontoise, small and quick, full of pompous phrases. He trotted through the wood, which was being sprayed with bursts of fire; and when a bullet passed too close, he made with his hand the gesture one uses to chase away a bothersome fly.

Of all my comrades who fell in Champagne or in the Argonne, there is none I mourned more than F., who was the sergeant of my second half platoon. F.'s line of work was not one usually considered important. He ran a shop for a wine merchant near the Bastille. He had scant education and could barely read. Yet no one has done more to make me understand the beauty of a truly noble and sensitive soul. He rarely used coarse language, and I never heard him utter an obscenity. His men adored him for his kindly good nature, which rubbed off on them. His calm courage inspired their confidence because they knew he was prudent as well as brave. Remarkably attentive to the practical details of life, he was one of those of whom it was said he always knew which way was north. I still remember his return from one dangerous patrol he had undertaken with resolute courage, confiding his wallet to me as he left, and which he led with a truly remarkable equanimity. He came back carrying a can of food that he had found in an abandoned sack somewhere between the lines. He devoted himself to making life more agreeable for those of his men he thought were poor, and shared with them those small treats that are beyond price in the field. He had a lofty notion of loyalty among comrades, which he explained by saying, "When I was a recruit, I was in a squad where we got along well together." Unquestionably his main desire and his greatest effort was to ensure that his half platoon should "get along well together." When I lost him, I lost a moral support.

During my months in the field I sometimes saw men show fear. The look of fear I found very ugly. To be sure, I encountered it very seldom. Military courage is certainly widespread. I do not believe it is correct to say, despite occasional opinions to the contrary, that it is easily come by. Not always, to be fair, but often it is the result of effort, an effort that a healthy individual makes without injury to himself and which rapidly becomes instinctive. I have always noticed that by some fortunate reflex, death ceases to appear very terrible the moment it seems close: it is this, ultimately, that explains courage. Most men dread going under fire, and especially returning to it. Once there, however, they no longer tremble. Also, I believe that few soldiers, except the most noble or intelligent, think of their country while conducting themselves bravely; they are much more often guided by a sense of personal honor, which is very strong when it is reinforced by the group. If a unit consisted of a majority of slackers, the point of honor would be to get out of any situation with the least harm possible. Thus I always thought it a good policy to express openly the profound disgust that the few cowards in my platoon inspired in me.

I have finished gathering my memories. T., of whom I have just spoken, wrote me a letter the other day; because it is in pencil, it will no doubt soon fade away. In order not to forget his last sentence, I shall copy it here: "Vive la France, et vivement la victoire!" ("Long live France, and let victory come quickly!").

$$\infty$$

2. The Attack

June 16th

At 4.15 [a.m.] a whistle blew. The men in the front line went over the top, and we scrambled out and took their places in the front trench. In front of us was a small field, with grass knee-high, split diagonally by an old footpath. On the other side of the field was a belt of trees, known as Y Wood, in which lay the first Hun trench.

In a few moments flags went up there, to show that it had been captured and that the troops were going on. Another whistle, and we ourselves scrambled over the parapet and sprinted across the field. Personally I was so overweighted that I could only amble, and I remember being intensely amused at the sight of a little chap in front of me who seemed in even worse case than myself. Without thinking much about it, I took the diagonal path, as the line of least resistance, and most of my section did the same.

When I dropped into the Hun trench I found it a great place, only three feet wide, and at least eight deep, and beautifully made of white sand-bags, back and front. At that spot there was no sign of any damage by our shells, but a number of dead Huns lay in the bottom. There was a sniper's post just where I fell in, a comfortable little square hole, fitted with seats and shelves, bottles of beer, tinned meats, and a fine helmet hanging on a hook.

Our first duty was to change the wire, so, after annexing the helmet, I slipped off my pack, and, clambering out again, started to move the wire from what was now the rear, to the new front of the trench. It was rotten stuff, most of it loose coils, and the only knife-rests were not more than a couple of feet high. What there was movable of it, we got across without much difficulty, and we had just finished when we were ordered to move down the trench, as our diagonal advance had brought us too far to the right.

II.2   From Guy Chapman, ed., *Vain Glory* (London: Cassell, 1967), 167–173. Reprinted with permission of PFD www.pfd.co.uk on behalf of the estate of Guy Chapman.

We moved down along the belt of woodland, which was only a few yards broad, to a spot where one of our companies was already hard at work digging a communication trench back to our old front line. Here there was really no trench at all. One or more of our own big shells had burst in the middle, filling it up for a distance of ten yards and practically destroying both parapet and parados [back wall of the trench]. Some of us started building up the parapet with sandbags, and I saw the twins merrily at work hauling out dead Huns at least twice their own size.

There was a hedge along the back of the trench, so I scrambled through a hole in it, piled my pack, rifle, and other things, including the helmet, on the farther side, and started again on the wire. Hereabouts it was much better stuff, and it took us some time to get it across and pegged down. We had just got the last knife-rest across, when I saw a man who was placing sandbags on the parapet from the farther side swivel round, throw his legs into the trench, and collapse in a heap in the bottom. Several others were already lying there, and for the first time I realized that a regular hail of machine-gun bullets was sweeping over the trench.

I made a dive for my pack, but though I found that, my pet helmet had disappeared. Quite a string of wounded and masterless men had passed down the back of the hedge while I was working, and one of them must have thought it a good souvenir to take into hospital. . . .

The attacking battalions had carried several more trenches and we were told that two at least had been held, but our own orders were to consolidate and hold on to the trench we were in at all costs. We could see very little in front. There was a wide field of long grass, stretching gently upward to a low mound of earth several hundred yards away. This was the next line. Away on the right front was Bellewarde Wood and Hooge Château, both above us, but the latter was partly hidden by the corner of Y Wood. I had just filled a sandbag and placed it on the top of the parapet when I happened to glance down, and saw a slight movement in the earth between my feet. I stooped and scraped away the soil with my fingers and found what seemed like palpitating flesh. It proved to be a man's cheek, and a few minutes' work uncovered his head. I poured a little water down his throat, and two or three of us dug out the rest of him. He was undamaged except for his feet and ankles, which were a mass of pulp, and he recovered consciousness as we worked. The first thing he said was in English: "What Corps are you?" He was a big man, and told us he was forty-five and had only been a soldier for a fortnight.

We dragged him out and laid him under the hedge. There was nothing else we could do for him. He had another drink later, but he must have died in the course of the day. I am afraid we forgot all about him, but nothing could have lived there until evening.

The Captain was the next to go. He insisted on standing on the parados, directing operations, and got a bullet in the lungs. He could walk, and two men were detailed to take him down to the dressing-station. One came back, to be killed later in the day, but the other stopped a bullet *en route*, and followed the Captain.

When we had got our big Hun out, he left a big hole in the ground, and we found a dead arm and hand projecting from the bottom. We dug about, but did not seem to be able to find the body, and when I seized the sleeve and pulled, the arm came out of the ground by itself. We had to dig deeper for our own sake, but there was nothing else left, except messy earth, which seemed to have been driven into the side of the trench. The man helping me turned sick, for it wasn't pretty work, but I claimed a substitute, and between us we carted out a barrowful in wetter sheets and dumped it under the hedge. After that I had had enough myself.

About 5.30 a.m. the Huns started shelling, and the new communication trench soon became a death-trap. A constant stream of wounded who had come down another trench from the north, passed along the rear. The Huns made a target of the two traverses (unluckily including our own), from which the communication trench opened, and numbers of the wounded were caught just behind us. The trench itself was soon choked with bodies, as it was easier and as safe to pass over the open above it.

The shelling got worse as the day wore on and several more of our men went down. They plastered us with crumps, shrapnel, and whizz-bangs. One of the latter took off a sandbag from the top of the parapet and landed it on my head. It nearly broke my neck and I felt ill for some time after.

It was grillingly hot and the air was full of dust, but although we were parched up, we dared not use much of our water. One never knew how long it must last. I came off better than most in that respect, for I had taken the precaution of carrying two water-bottles knowing that one would never last me.

The worst of it was the inaction. Every minute several shells fell within a few yards and covered us with dust, and the smell of the explosives poisoned my mouth. All I could do was to crouch against the parapet and pant for breath, expecting every moment to be my last. And this went on for hours. I began to long for the shell which would put an end to everything, but in time my nerves became almost numbed, and I lay like a log until roused.

I think it must have been midday when something happened. An alarm was given and we manned the parapet, to see some scores of men retreating at a run from the trench in front. They ran right over us, men of half a dozen battalions, and many dropped on the way. As they passed, something was said of gas, but it appeared that nearly all the officers in the two front trenches had been killed or wounded, someone had raised an alarm of gas, and the men had panicked and run.

A lot of the runaways insisted on gathering by the hedge just behind us, in spite of our warnings not to do so, and I saw at least twenty hit by shrapnel within a few yards of us.

The Brigade-Major arrived, cursing, and called upon some of our own men to advance and reoccupy the trench in front. He led them himself, and they made a very fine dash across. I do not think more than twenty fell, and they reoccupied the trench and, I believe, the third also, before the Huns realized that they were empty.

In connection with this attack a rather amusing incident happened amongst ourselves. As soon as the man next me saw the attack commence, he yelled out:

"They're our own men. Come on, we can't let them go alone." He was over the parapet in no time and dragged me half-way with him. As soon as the "gallant lad" was seen, he was ordered back, and the order was repeated by nearly all the men who were manning the parapet. He told me afterwards that it was the funniest of sights as he looked back, a dozen heads projecting over the sandbags, all with their mouths wide open, and all with one accord saying: "Come back, you silly ass!" He came back rather crestfallen.

The interlude was really a welcome one, and useful, too, for we realized then that nearly every rifle was clogged with dirt and entirely useless. We set to work cleaning at once, and this kept us occupied amidst the constant bursting of the shells. Our own guns were practically silent, and we supposed they were reserving ammunition, which was not too plentiful at the best of times.

Soon the runaways began to return. They had been turned back, in some cases, at the point of the revolver, but when their first panic had been overcome, they came back quite willingly, although they must have lost heavily in the process. They crowded into our trench, and there was hardly room to move a limb.

It was scorchingly hot and no one could eat, although I tried to do so. All day long—the longest day I ever spent—we were constantly covered with debris from the shell-bursts. Great pieces fell all about us, and, packed like herrings, we crowded in the bottom of the trench. Hardly anything could be done for the wounded. If their wounds were slight, they generally risked a dash to the rear. Every now and then we stood to in expectation of a counter-attack, but none developed.

About 6.0 p.m. the worst moment of the day came. The Huns started to bombard us with a shell which was quite new to us. It sounded like a gigantic firecracker, with two distinct explosions. These shells came over just above the parapet, in a flood, much more quickly than we could count them. After a quarter of an hour of this sort of thing, there was a sudden crash in the trench and ten feet of the parapet, just beyond me, was blown away and everyone around blinded by the dust. With my first glance I saw what looked like half a dozen bodies, mingled with sandbags, and then I smelt gas and realized that these were gas-shells. I had my respirator on in a hurry and most of our own men were as quick. The others were slower and suffered for it. One man was sick all over the sandbags and another was coughing his heart up. We pulled four men out of the debris unharmed. One man was unconscious, and died of gas later. Another was hopelessly smashed up and must have got it full in the chest.

We all thought that this was the end and almost hoped for it, but luckily the gas-shells stopped, and after a quarter of an hour we could take off our respirators. I started in at once to build up the parapet again, for we had been laid open to the world in front, but the gas lingered about the hole for hours, and I had to give up delving in the bottom for a time. As it was it made me feel very sick.

A counter-attack actually commenced as soon as the bombardment ceased, and we had to stand to again. My rifle had been broken in two pieces, but there were plenty of spare ones lying about now. I tried four, however, before I could get one to act at all. All were jammed, and that one was very stiff. As we leaned over the parapet, I saw the body of a Hun lying twenty yards out in front. It commenced to writhe and finally half-sat up. I suppose the gas had caught him. The man standing next me—a corporal in a county battalion—raised his rifle, and before I could stop him, sent a bullet into the body. It was a rotten thing to see, but I suppose it was really a merciful end for the poor chap, better than his own gas, at any rate.

The men in the front trenches had got it as badly as we had, and if the counter-attack was pressed, it did not seem humanly possible, in the condition we were in, to offer a successful defence. One man kept worrying us all by asking what we were to do if the Huns did us in, whether surrender or run! Fortunately, our own guns started and apparently caught the Huns massing. The counter-attack accordingly crumpled up.

In the midst of it all, someone realized that the big gap in the parapet could not be manned, and four of us, including myself, were ordered to lie down behind what was left of the parados and cover the gap with our rifles. It was uncomfortable work, as the gas fumes were still very niffy and the place was a jumble of dead bodies. We could not stand up to clear them away, and in order to get a place at all, I had to lie across the body of a gigantic Hun.

As soon as things quietened down a bit, we had a chance to look around. Since the morning most of the branches of the trees in the wood had gone and many of the trunks had become mere splintered poles. Something else had changed also, and for a time I could not make out what it was. Then it suddenly flashed across my mind that the thick hedge at the back of the trench had entirely disappeared. It was right in the path of the storm of gas-shells and they had carried it away.

We managed to get some sort of parapet erected in the end. It was more or less bullet-proof, at any rate. At dusk some scores of men came back from the front line, wounded or gassed. They had to cross the open at a run or a shamble, but I did not see any hit. Then the Brigade-Major appeared, and cheered us by promising a relief that night. It still rained shells, although not so hard as before dusk, and we did not feel capable of standing much more of it.

☙❧

3. War is Like a Big Picnic

[Flanders] October 24th, 1914

[To His Mother]

I *adore* War. It is like a big picnic without the objectlessness of a picnic. I have never been so well or so happy. Nobody grumbles at one for being dirty. I have only had my boots off once in the last 10 days, and only washed twice. We are up and standing to our rifles by 5 a.m. when doing this infantry work, and saddled up

II.3 From Laurence Housman, ed., *War Letters of Fallen Englishmen* (London: Victor Gollancz, 1930), 117–119.

by 4.30 a.m. when with our horses. Our poor horses do not get their saddles off when we are in the trenches.

The wretched inhabitants here have got practically no food left. It is miserable to see them leaving their houses, and tracking away, with great bundles and children in their hands. And the dogs and cats left in the deserted villages are piteous. . . .

[Flanders] November 3rd, 1914

[To His Parents]

I have not washed for a week, or had my boots off for a fortnight. . . . It is all *the* best fun. I have never never felt so well, or so happy, or enjoyed anything so much. It just suits my stolid health, and stolid nerves, and barbaric disposition. The fighting-excitement vitalizes everything, every sight and word and action. One loves one's fellow man so much more when one is bent on killing him. And picnic-ing in the open day and night (we never see a roof now) is the real method of existence.

There are loads of straw to bed-down on, and one sleeps like a log, and wakes up with the dew on one's face. . . . The Germans shell the trenches with shrapnel all day and all night: and the Reserves and ground in the rear with Jack Johnsons, which at last one gets to love as old friends. You hear them coming for miles, and everyone imitates the noise; then they burst with a plump, and make a great hole in the ground, doing no damage unless they happen to fall into your trench or on to your hat. They burst pretty nearly straight upwards. One landed within ten yards of me the other day, and only knocked me over and my horse. We both got up and looked at each other and laughed. . . .

We took a German Officer and some men prisoners in a wood the other day. One felt hatred for them as one thought of our dead; and as the Officer came by me, I scowled at him, and the men were cursing him. The Officer looked me in the face and saluted me as he passed; and I have never seen a man look so proud and resolute and smart and confident, in his hour of bitterness. It made me feel terribly ashamed of myself. . . .

[Flanders] November 18th, 1914

[To His Parents]

They had us out again for 48 hours trenches while I was writing the above. About the shells, after a day of them, one's nerves are really absolutely beat down. I can understand now why our infantry have to retreat sometimes; a sight which came as a shock to me at first, after being brought up in the belief that the English infantry cannot retreat.

These last two days we had quite a different kind of trench, in a dripping sodden wood, with the German trench in some places 40 yards ahead. . . . We had been worried by snipers all along, and I had always been asking for leave to go out and have a try myself. Well, on Tuesday the 16th, the day before yesterday, they gave me leave. Only after great difficulty. They told me to take a section with me, and I said I would sooner cut my throat and have done with it. So they let me go alone. Off I crawled through sodden clay and trenches, going about a yard a minute, and listening and looking as I thought it was not possible to look and to listen. I went out to the right of our lines, where the 10th were, and where the Germans were nearest. I took about 30 minutes to do 30 yards; then I saw the Hun trench, and I waited there a long time, but could see or hear nothing. It was about 10 yards from me. Then I heard some Germans talking, and saw one put his head up over some bushes, about 10 yards behind the trench. I could not get a shot at him, I was too low down, and of course I could not get up. So I crawled on again very slowly to the parapet of their trench. I peered through their loop-hole and saw nobody in the trench. Then the German behind me put up his head again. He was laughing and talking. I saw his teeth glistening against my foresight, and I pulled the trigger.

⌀

4. All the World Over a Boy is a Boy, a Mother a Mother

At the Front [France], 1917

[To the Headmaster of Wycliffe College]
I see that many stay-at-homes want to keep the Anglo-German wound raw even after the peace of Berlin, 1917. The returned German prisoners will never second the motion. There are thousands of them round here. They are well fed and well clad and seem as happy as sandboys. Never once yet have I seen any British soldier attempt to ridicule or annoy any prisoner, nay, rather, he shows him all consideration. This is saying much, for we are all sorts and conditions of men, and the German prisoner knows it.

The art of remembering consists largely in discerning what to forget, and to the will belongs the undeniable power to erase the unworthy, and the acid to etch in what is worth retaining. Last night I heard a youngster offer to do another's gas guard rather than awaken him out of a very weary sleep. What I heard has been etched in and preserved with a cover of thick glass. A couple of mornings ago I reached out for my pot of jam. It was jamless. May the sun never shine on his rice garden! No, that is a mistake. I meant I will forget it.

I write this outside a German dug-out wrecked by one of our sixty-pounders. The explosion has thrown five men lifeless down the stairway. Their boy officer, a young Absalom, is suspended head downwards by one of his Bluchers from two viced beams in the roof. Get the harrowing details out of the mind; remember only the faithful service.

It seems to me that so many of our journals urge the remembering of the worthless, the forgetting of the worth remembering. "Remember the *Lusitania*,

II.4 From Laurence Housman, ed., *War Letters of Fallen Englishmen* (London: Victor Gollancz, 1930), 122–125.

remember Nurse Cavell." Rather keep them out of the mind. Heaven consists largely in thinking of mothers and wives and children and other things that are thus beautiful. Get the habit. Increase Heaven by thinking of the homely, fat but selfless Frau and the lad who hangs from the ceiling by his foot. Hell consists largely in thinking of our own nastiness. We cannot forget them even when forgiven, and so this Hell survives, but other people's nastiness we can forget quite easily. Forget the *Lusitanias*, the Louvains—there are paid servants of the State who will attend to these.

Kipling has it that "East is East and West is West and never the twain shall meet." Nowadays it is fashionable to put Germany in the place of the East. We are at war and must go on until Justice shall be triumphant. I hope, however, that humanity will not forever sanction these "Wallace Lines," war-jaundiced and fear-bred. All the world over a boy is a boy and a mother is a mother. One there was Who after thirty years of thinking appealed to *all* mankind, and not in vain.

German food and British food, examine them closely, they are the same. The same in terms of stomach, of ears, of eyes or of the immortal soul. A week since I was lying out in no man's land. A little German dog trotted up and licked my British face. I pulled his German ears and stroked his German back. He wagged his German tail. My little friend abolished no man's land, and so in time can we.

At the Front [France], Autumn, 1917

[To the Same]

Quite frequently, in raids and attacks, British soldiers meet Germans whom they have known before the war. A bird cage facing us in Sanctuary Wood was at regular intervals occupied by an expert sniper who had served with one of our number as a waiter in Broadway, New York. His cage was only about twenty yards away. He killed one or two of us every day. In the intervals he engaged with us in racy conversation. Near Wulvergem I found on a corpse a pay book which showed the man to have been a chemist in Leipzig. On several toilet boxes belonging to my sister, who before the war was a student at Leipzig University, I had often seen this man's name.

It is not to be wondered at that many a Fritz, who has lived amongst us for years, bears us far from bitter feelings. When a very green soldier, I was sent out at Armentieres to cover a party engaged in cutting down a patch of seeding chicory a few yards in front of our own wire. Being ordered to advance a hundred yards Fritzwards, I had paced but eighty-odd, when, to my astonishment, I found myself securely entangled in the wire of what was evidently an unlocated listening post. My rifle, wrenched from my hands, evidently collided with a screw stake, and a flare shot up *instanter*. Not fifteen yards away, sticking out from a hole sunk into the turf, were a rifle and the head and shoulders of a man. Of course I "froze" stiff. Seeing, however, no movement of the rifle, I began to think—though such seemed impossible—that I was undiscovered. It was impossible. He had seen me plainly. Perhaps he was a sportsman, and scorned to wing a defenceless man. He laughed heartily, called out "Hallo, Johnny Bull, you silly old——," and sank into the earth.

Yours truly likewised, plus rifle, but minus half a yard of tunic, and nearly a pair of pants. A very similar experience befell my friend a Captain of Canadian Infantry. Scouting alone in No Man's Land—a most unwise proceeding, by the way—he walked on to the levelled rifle of a sniper. Halting the Captain, the sniper ordered him to hands up and step back five paces. In the couple of minutes of conversation that ensued it appeared that my friend was in the hands of a Saxon, an Oxford graduate, and a man who—despite repeated requests not to be used on the British Front—had been sent against us. My friend was right-abouted and ordered to count fifty. At fifty-one he found himself alone and free. On the Roll of Honour of Oxford University is the name of a German who fell in defence of his fatherland. I have often wondered whether this hero and my friend's captor are different men, or just one and the same.

Behind the lines we use humanity of every hue, from heliotrope to mud and water. Even in the trench regiments colour strains are numerous. Some days ago in Belgium I saw three Chinese walking arm in arm with four French girls, and another carrying a bouncing boy with curls like a Teddy bear and a face which Day, Martin and Co. could not have made more black. The same night I saw two Jamaican negroes win 200 francs from a Canadian sapper, and two Japanese cheat a Russian out of 5 francs at cards. I was myself called "Bo" by a Chink, and offered a cocktail by two Canadian Indians, drunk to the wide, wide world. Whatever are we coming to, when these darned foreigners are allowed all the white man's privileges? In Canada, thank God, we have no black question, and we mean to have no Yellow one, but what about Britain equatorwards? All these blacks and yellows will require hats two sizes larger when they return home.

∽

5. War Diary of the Seaforth Highlanders

Rats were the bane of our lives in this area, and if ever there was a place infested with rats it was Authuille and the trenches in front of it, and if ever there was need for the "Pied Piper of Hamelin" to charm them into the neighbouring river it was here. Wherever you go you hear them squeaking or settling family quarrels. When you fall off to sleep they come frolicking around, run over your body or face, and generally give you the "jumps," completely banishing the sweet influence of Morpheus. A man when lying sleeping in a dug-out fully clothed has been known to find one up under his tunic, and they are such a nuisance that war is waged upon them wherever and whenever possible.

One worthy officer hailing not far from Kildonan is particularly noted for unfailing accuracy with his trusty stick, and last night he marshalled three or four others, and with two electric torches and good hefty sticks they sallied out. Woe to the unfortunate rat which had selected the same hour for his nightly peregrination,

II.5 From D. Sutherland, *War Diary of the Fifth Seaforth Highlanders, 51st (Highland) Division* (London: J. Lane, 1920), 43–44, 69–71.

for he never returned to his domicile. Dazzled by the brightness of the torch, he was utterly nonplussed as to the direction to make for safety and down came the unerring stick, and with a squeak his career of theft and mischief came to an end. A good dozen were accounted for, the major portion of the bag falling to the afore-said officer, who retired for the night with the consciousness of having earned a good night's repose. . . .

31st May, however, saw the end of our rest, and we took over a new sector in front of Neuville St. Vaast, relieving the South Lancs and Border Regiments, who had suffered severely here just previously. The preparations for the battle of the Somme had already begun, the Division we were relieving being with-drawn to refit and train, and our Division had to take over and hold a two-Division front.

What a change this entailed upon our kilted men. To prevent the Boche finding out that our Division had extended its front, the units of the 152nd Brigade had their kilts and Balmoral bonnets taken from them and had been fitted out with khaki trousers and field service caps, much to the disgust of the men, who, suspi-cious of some Sassenach plot to strip them forever of the kilt, grumbled very much and protested to their officers.

Neuville St. Vaast, standing in the midst of the labyrinth, is a village which will be forever famous in the annals of the French. This village was a summer resort for the richer people from the bigger towns around, and had a popula-tion of 1500, a number of fine houses, and was beautifully embowered in trees. I passed through Festubert about a year ago, but the destruction there was not nearly so complete as here. Not a vestige of a roof can be seen, not a gable or side wall of any house is complete. Everything that still stands is at most a fragment of wall, and most of the houses are only heaps of brick. The trees, fruit and ordinary, are in the same shattered condition. If not lying on the ground, cut down by shells, they are all scarred, bruised, and battered, branches lopped off, and tops shorn away; in fact, I looked about to see if I could see a perfect tree and could not find one; a vivid illustration of the terrific storms of bullets, shells, and fragments of shells that have time and again swept over this deserted village. And yet there is a considerable population living in this desolation—probably 500—but they are British soldiers, and live in the cellars, where they are still intact, or in dug-outs constructed by themselves. Walking along a sunken road in this terrible place, for nearly a mile there was practically a continuous line of little crosses on the slopes of the road, sometimes singly, sometimes in twos and threes, and sometimes in clusters of dozens and scores, showing the terrible toll this place has taken from the sons of France. To pic-ture a town at home of 1500 inhabitants wiped out of existence in this fashion, not a house, hotel, church, or hall left standing, the streets simply footpaths among the litter of brick, stone, and timber from the houses, the very paving-stones and setts turned up and scattered by huge shells, would help one to real-ize what poor France and Belgium have suffered in hundreds of their towns and villages.

6. A Working Party

Three hours ago he blundered up the trench,
Sliding and poising, groping with his boots;
Sometimes he tripped and lurched against the walls
With hands that pawed the sodden bags of chalk.
He couldn't see the man who walked in front;
Only he heard the drum and rattle of feet
Stepping along the trench-boards,—often splashing
Wretchedly where the sludge was ankle-deep.

Voices would grunt, "Keep to your right,—make way!"
When squeezing past the men from the front-line:
White faces peered, puffing a point of red;
Candles and braziers glinted through the chinks
And curtain-flaps of dug-outs; then the gloom
Swallowed his sense of sight; he stooped and swore
Because a sagging wire had caught his neck.

A flare went up; the shining whiteness spread
And flickered upward, showing nimble rats,
And mounds of glimmering sand-bags, bleached with rain;
Then the slow, silver moment died in dark.
The wind came posting by with chilly gusts
And buffeting at corners, piping thin
And dreary through the crannies; rifle-shots
Would split and crack and sing along the night,
And shells came calmly through the drizzling air
To burst with hollow bang below the hill.

Three hours ago he stumbled up the trench;
Now he will never walk that road again:
He must be carried back, a jolting lump
Beyond all need of tenderness and care;
A nine-stone corpse with nothing more to do.
He was a young man with a meagre wife
And two pale children in a Midland town;
He showed the photograph to all his mates;
And they considered him a decent chap
Who did his work and hadn't much to say,
And always laughed at other people's jokes
Because he hadn't any of his own.

II.6   From Siegfried Sassoon, *Collected Poems of Siegfried Sassoon.* Copyright © 1918, 1920 by E. P. Dutton. Copyright © 1936, 1946, 1947, 1948 by Siegfried Sassoon. Reprinted with kind permission of Barbara Levy Literary Agency, on behalf of the Estate of George Sassoon, and Viking Penguin, a division of Penguin Group (USA) Inc.

That night, when he was busy at his job
Of piling bags along the parapet,
He thought how slow time went, stamping his feet,
And blowing on his fingers, pinched with cold.
He thought of getting back by half-past twelve,
And tot of rum to send him warm to sleep
In draughty dug-out frowsty with the fumes
Of coke, and full of snoring, weary men.

He pushed another bag along the top,
Craning his body outward; then a flare
Gave one white glimpse of No Man's Land and wire;
And as he dropped his head the instant split
His startled life with lead, and all went out.

∽

7. A Canadian in the Trenches

Here I am again in the trenches in about the most unhealthy spot of the Ypres Salient with the shells screaming over in all directions. It is really wonderful what narrow escapes we have. This afternoon there were at least a dozen lyddite shells struck within a few yards of our machine-gun dugout, giving us a clay bath on each occasion, and a little piece of one of them grazed the sleeve of my tunic. But with all the shells we have had so near there has not yet been a man wounded in my section.

I shall try to give you a description of our march into these trenches a few nights ago. To begin with we were turned out of our billets about 4 a.m. and after a long day's marching, etc., we arrived at our dressing station just before dark. After a meal and two hours rest we started for the front line trenches, which, by the way, were held by the French. The part of the line allotted to us was exceptionally hard to approach on account of having to go almost parallel with the trenches, which meant advancing under fire for about 1 1/2 miles over fields simply dotted with shell holes and old disbanded trenches, many of which were blown to pieces by artillery. Every hole and ditch was absolutely full of water, and to make matters worse it began to rain hard and got so dark that you could scarcely see the figure two paces in front of you.

In addition to our ordinary pack, which is anything but light, we had to pack our machine guns and mounts and all kinds of ammunition. We got into single file about two paces apart (for the bullets were already beginning to come uncomfortably near) and turned off the hard road into the unknown fields, with a French guide to lead us, who only knew a few words of English. Our troubles then

II.7   From Private John Erskine Lockerby, "A Canadian in the Trenches," April 18, 1915, Canadian Great War Project.

started in right shape. We were loaded so heavily that it made us quite awkward, and every time one of us stepped into a hole, which was always full of water and, owing to the extreme darkness, impossible to escape, he simply fell with his load headlong into the filthy mire. We all began to wish we were at our destination, especially when our guide, after taking us around in circles, over ditches, through barbed wire entanglements, over old fallen trees, along muddy communication trenches and through ruined houses in which corpses had been lying unburied for months, announced suddenly that he had lost his way. It was well for him and perhaps us too, that we could not speak French.

All the way along at intervals of about five minutes, star shells would go up making the surrounding country as bright as day. Then would come a hail of bullets and every man (with any sense) would drop his pack and flop on his face on a dead cow or anything that happened to be in front of him, then get up when the light went out and start again on his weary way. Although it is more of a tragedy than anything else to fall head first into a hole of water about three feet deep, with a full pack on your back and your arms full of ammunition, it is quite impossible to keep from laughing at the victim when you get him pulled out, which is no easy job.

After due consideration the guide decided to leave us in an old ditch (where we were at least safe from the bullets) and go to look for our particular trench. After what seemed hours to us the guide came back and informed us that he had really discovered our trench. Then we started again over what proved to be the worst part of the whole road. We stumbled along in the darkness and there was everything from a "Jack Johnson" [British slang for a six-inch German shell] hole to a dead German's equipment to obstruct our way. I expected to step on a dead body any minute, but I found later that the numerous bodies, which have not been buried, are between our front lines and the Germans.

At about 3 a.m. after very fatiguing manoeuvring we finally arrived at our trench and relieved the French Gun Section who were beginning to grow desperate; they expected us at least six hours earlier, and consequently had nothing to eat for over twelve hours.

We mounted the guns immediately and took turns standing by them until daylight, when we had a better chance to rest. When day dawned it presented a gruesome sight. Hundreds of dead Germans were lying between our lines with all their equipment on, just as they fell in a charge made several months ago. Many of the French who were killed in these trenches during the winter are buried right here, some have hardly enough earth over them to conceal their clothing.

Necessity is certainly the mother of invention. One of our chaps made a banjo out of a tin biscuit box, and he can play it well. You know I was always fond of music, that is why I volunteer to pack it in and out of the trenches for him. When the shells start coming close we always get the banjo and have a little Grand Opera just to show the Germans (who are less than one hundred yards away) that we are quite unconcerned and enjoying life as usual.

I am really enjoying this trip in the trenches very much. The weather is beautiful now and the trenches are drying up fine. We are all more or less anxious, many of us from a sense of curiosity, to get a taste of real war, which is, as you know, a bayonet attack in the open.

❦

8. Report on the Afternoon's Actions

Promptly at 2 o'clock our artillery began bombardment as notified us by your operation orders. The bombardment appeared to be particularly effective in and about PETITE BOIS and along the whole line of the German front line trenches. The Bombardment ceased at 3.20 p.m. and was resumed at 3.30 p.m. when our trench mortars, machine guns, and rifles joined in. Smoke bombs were thrown and smoke was kepted [sic] up in some cases as long as 30 minutes. The fire from the mortars seemd [sic] to be well directed and effective.

The enemy replied with artillery of various dimensions, particularly Whizzbangs and H.E. and we had a good deal of our parapet blown in and both the POSSE and WATLING STREET communication trenches were smashed in several places particularly between the fire and support trenches.

Things quited [sic] down somewhat until about 5.20 when the enemy began a bombardment of our trenches apparently in retaliation for our demonstration, and an enormous number of shells, mostly high explosives, were directed along our line, and considerable damage was done to our front line trenches and communication trenches, and a few casualties resulted, among them Lieut. A. D. Carter, our Machine Gun Officer who was wounded. Our artillery was called and immediately responded and finally silenced the Germans.

Throughout the afternoon we were able to keep up communication with C and D Companies, but the phone lines to A Company were cut very soon after our demonstration began, and although our linesmen worked like Trojans they were unable to get the line working.

Those Germans at whom our men were able to get a close look, appeared to average 5 ft. 9 ins. in height and to be of rather slight build. This would seem to indicate they are rather young and would bear out a report contained in a recent Intelligence Summary that "Boyish voices were heard in the German trenches."

Many of the Germans were wearing stocking caps with a whire [sic] rim round the top and what looked like a tassel. Their uniforms were dark blue in colour with no noticeable facings or buttons. Many of our men claim to have seen a number of civilians among the German troops.

Reports were sent in to us and forwarded on to the effect that the top of the crater was boarded in and sentries were stationed behind an earth parapet can now be accounted for by the fact that sounds as men on boards would of course come from their parties passing up and down the communication trench which led to

II.8 From "Report of the Afternoon's Actions," October 13, 1915, Canadian 26th Battalion to 5th Canadian Infantry Brigade, Library and Archives Canada. Reprinted with permission.

the crater. The sentries apparently stood on the near edge of the crater looking out over the earth which had been thrown up all round.

It would appear that the Germans had expected an attempt to be made on this place as they had a mine underneath it which they sprung, fortunately for us, some seconds too late.

Later reports confirm the fact that their trenches were badly knocked about and throughout the action our riflemen had the best of exchanges.

Snipers posted on the flanks of our trenches reported doing some very creditable execution among the Germans and one—Sgt Ryder, who is quite a reliable, claims to have brought down 11. . . .

✐

9. Indian Units in France

Rifleman Amar Singh Rawat (Garhwal Rifles) to a friend (India), Kitchener's Indian Hospital, Brighton, March 26, 1915

I have been wounded in the head, but hope to get better soon. My fate now is very lucky [in] that I am alive while all my brethren have been killed. All those who have been wounded are saved and the rest are killed. Such a scene has been enacted as when the leaves fall off a tree and not a space is left bare on the ground, so here the earth is covered with dead men and there is no place to put one's foot. Up to now the war has been as follows—the Germans kept on firing from their trenches and we from ours. But on the 9th and 10th March we attacked the Germans. So many men were killed and wounded that they could not be counted, and of the Germans the number of casualties is beyond calculation. When we reached their trenches we used the bayonet and the *kukri* [curved Nepalese knife], and blood was shed so freely that we could not recognize each other's faces; the whole ground was covered with blood. There were heaps of men's heads, and some soldiers were without legs, others had been cut in two, some without hands and others without eyes. The scene was indescribable. If I survive I will tell you all. As regards those men who have been killed it is well, but if I get killed it does not matter, when so many of my brethren have been slain it would not matter about me, but my great scene has been enacted. I have heard that the Pandevs and the Kauris had a great war, but their battle could not have been so great as this one. I think the Germans have been shaken and that the war will end soon, because the whole world is being destroyed, no men are being left, some hundreds of thousands, nay millions; the whole world is being finished. Both sides are now taking a little breathing space. At first in Belgium the Germans thus treated the inhabitants—they cut off the hands and feet of little children and let them go; and also in the case of women they cut off one hand or one foot or blinded one eye. The whole Kingdom of Belgium has been destroyed, and half of France. But up to now we have escaped and we have stopped the Germans, and on both sides

II.9   From David Omissi, ed., *Indian Voices of the Great War: Soldiers' Letters, 1914–1918* (Basingstoke: Macmillan, 1999), 45–46, 50–51, 102. Reprinted with permission of Palgrave Macmillan.

fortified trenches have been constructed. We have been constantly fighting for six months, but we have not even seen the sun; day and night the rain has fallen; and the country is so cold that I cannot describe it. The produce of the country is nothing; beyond wheat they have no crops . . . In time of calamity these four things are tried—faith, fortitude, friend and wife.

A Sikh sepoy (59th Rifles) to his brother (India) from a hospital in England, April 5, 1915

In Europe our bodies are suffering great hardships, but God has saved my life. The Guru can preserve us in flames of fire. He will preserve us in this world of trouble. Then we shall return to the Punjab—if not, who knows where our future lies, here or elsewhere. This is the will of God Almighty. What is written in our destiny must be. When you write, let me know if the wounded arrive in India. What do you think of the war in India? Is there fighting in Waziristan [North West Frontier Province] or not? We have heard that the fort beyond Peshawar has been taken by the people of Tirah and that the Waziris have occupied the country beyond Bannu. Write and tell the truth.

Now hear what happened to us. On the 9th March, the General told the Lahore and Meerut Divisions that they were to make a grand attack and glorify the name of the Punjab throughout Europe. The attack came off on the 10th at seven o'clock in the morning. We fix bayonets and look towards the enemy. The enemy trenches are two yards off [sic]. They have been well built. In front is barbed wire and we are not expected to attack here. With a shout to our Guru we hurl ourselves forward. The enemy's bullets scorch our heroes, while machine guns and cannons spread their shot upon us. We leap the wire entanglements and overwhelm the enemy, killing some and capturing the rest. On the 10th we captured 1,050 Germans and took four lines of trenches defending the city of La Basseé. Here from the beginning the enemy have been very strong. On the 10th and 12th we took two miles of enemy positions. Next day at five o'clock the Germans attacked in eight lines. There was fine fighting on the battlefield. Eight lines of the enemy were destroyed. We also suffered great loss in killed and wounded. On that day no one took thought of his friend, and the slightly wounded man made his way back himself. If severely wounded, a man lay out in the battlefield. When the sun set in the evening, the rain began to fall. The wounded were picked up and sent back. The enemy attacked fiercely but were beaten back with great loss. We did not give up our trenches but pressed the enemy hard. They could not recapture their lost lines. From the 10th to the 25th the Germans lost 70,613 men.

In the hospital is rumoured that the remnants of five or six regiments will be returned to India. Only the strong man sees the battle and he will never during his life forget its taste. Those who returned to India wounded early in the war have not seen the real battle. Some lucky men have returned to India without having known the taste of battle. They returned smiling to their country. Now only the lame and halt with one leg and broken bones are sent home. No sound man can return. You will say "you have not told me about the battle." Well, I can't describe it—so many are killed and wounded. . . .

The German arrangements for the war are very good. They have many machine guns. Their little bomb guns [mortars?] throw bombs to a distance of 500 yards, and they spray vitriol acid [gas?] which burns our clothes and dries up our bodies. At night they send up star shells, and also make light with electricity [searchlights]. The war is a great sight at night. Here cannons are firing, there machine guns; here there are bright lights, there bombs hurl through the air. Bullets fly day and night incessantly drinking the blood of heroes.

Sant Singh (Sikh) in France? to his wife, September 18, 1915

We perish in the desert: *you* wash yourself and lie in bed. We are trapped in a net of woe; while you go free. Our life is a living death. For what great sin are we being punished? Kill us. Oh God, but free us from our pain! We move in agony, but never rest. We are slaves of masters who can show no mercy. The bullets fall on us like rain, but dry are our bones. So we have spent a full year. We cannot write a word. Lice feed upon our flesh: we cannot wait to pick them out. For days we have not washed our faces. We do not change our clothes. Many sons of mothers lie dead. No one takes any heed. It is God's will that this is so, and what is written is true. God The Omnipotent plays a game, and men die. Death here is dreadful, but of life there is not the briefest hope.

⟣

Commitment, Duty or Disillusion: German Students Assess the War

Among the early victims of battle in 1914 were a disproportionate number of young, recent university graduates. Their loss would be mourned as a "lost generation" in Britain and as a "slaughter of the innocents" in Germany. The literary memorials for these fallen students were the carefully edited volumes of their war letters published a decade after the conflict. The letters below are drawn from a collection assembled by Freiburg Professor Philipp Witkop, who hoped to remind the nation of their sacrifice and contrast their idealism and ethical concerns with their barbaric image abroad.

The first correspondent, Franz Blumenfeld, whom we have already encountered, was a 23 year-old law student whose fear of brutalization and incipient disillusion were already clear before his death in December 1914. The next three, Herbert Weisser (a student of architecture), Alfons Ankenbrand (theology), and Kurt Peterson (philosophy) were all killed in their early twenties in 1915. Although they embraced German culture, they did not necessarily gravitate toward Prussian-style militarism. The final author, Ernst Jünger, is the most complex. He enlisted immediately at the age of nineteen and fought in some of the bloodiest battles in Flanders and northern France, being wounded seven times. Throughout the conflict, he kept a journal detailing his frontline experiences that became the basis for his highly acclaimed *Storm of Steel* published in 1920. His subsequent work, *Copse 125*, from which this extract is taken, describes the fighting over terrain that had "not the least strategic importance, and yet at that time had a meaning for all Europe."

10. The Readiness to Make a Sacrifice

At the moment we are sitting in the train. Where we are going we are not told, but we take for granted that it is to Belgium. We are supposed to be in for a thirty hours' journey. Now we are north of Trèves, I think in the Eifel, in most beautiful country. The sun is shining too and everything looks so peaceful. The contrast to the desolation in Lorraine, with all the military activity and the incessant rain, is incredible. But even yet one can't realize the war in earnest, and I keep catching myself simply enjoying all the novel impressions.

You can't imagine the purely artistic, marvelous fascination of this constantly changing, unaccustomed picture. Last night, for instance, the scene round a big table in the living-room of a peasant's house in Lorraine: infantry and artillery all mixed up together in the wildest confusion, one in a helmet, another with his cap on the back of his head or half over his face, all more or less unshaved, smoking, eating, and sleeping. Round the walls one or two more; others sitting on the floor asleep. And in the midst of all this, two old peasant women busy cooking a little soup and making coffee, poor and humble and delighted with the few coppers which they afterwards got from the soldiers for all their trouble. I learn more about the people like this than from all my lectures and touring-companies.

In the train, September 24th, 1914

My dear, good, precious Mother, I certainly believe and hope that I shall come back from the war, but just in case I do not I am going to write you a farewell letter. I want you to know that if I am killed, I give my life gladly and willingly. My life has been so beautiful that I could not wish that anything in it had been different. And its having been so beautiful was thanks above all to you, my dear, good, best of Mothers. And for all your love, for all that you have done for me, for everything, everything, I want to thank you and thank you. Really you can have no idea how keenly I have realized just lately how right you were in your way of bringing

II.10   From Philipp Witkop, *German Students' War Letters* (London: Methuen, 1929), 17–21.

me up—I was not entirely convinced of the wisdom of some things before, for instance as regards the importance of physical training—how absolutely right and good.

But not only for the way in which you brought me up do I thank you, but for everything, everything—for the life you gave me, and above all for being just what you are. Oh, but you know, without this letter, and much better than I can write it, how I feel.

Then I want to write to you about something else, which, judging from bits in your letters, you haven't quite understood: why I should have volunteered for the war? Of course it was not from any enthusiasm for war in general, nor because I thought it would be a fine thing to kill a great many people or otherwise distinguish myself. On the contrary, I think that war is a very, very evil thing, and I believe that even in this case it might have been averted by a more skilful diplomacy. But, now that it has been declared, I think it is a matter of course that one should feel oneself so much a member of the nation that one must unite one's fate as closely as possible with that of the whole. And even if I were convinced that I could serve my Fatherland and its people better in peace than in war, I should think it just as perverse and impossible to let any such calculations weigh with me at the present moment as it would be for a man going to the assistance of somebody who was drowning, to stop to consider who the drowning man was and whether his own life were not perhaps the more valuable of the two. For what counts is always the readiness to make a sacrifice, not the object for which the sacrifice is made.

This war seems to me, from all that I have heard, to be something so horrible, inhuman, mad, obsolete, and in every way depraving, that I have firmly resolved, if I do come back, to do everything in my power to prevent such a thing from ever happening again in the future. . . .

October 14th, 1914 (in Northern France)

One thing weighs upon me more from day to day—the fear of getting brutalized. Your wishing you could provide me with a bullet-proof net is very sweet of you, but strange to say I have no fear, none at all, of bullets and shells, but only of this great spiritual loneliness. I am afraid of losing my faith in human nature, in myself, in all that is good in the world! Oh, that is horrible! Much, much harder to bear than being out-of-doors in all weathers, having to get one's own food, sleeping in a hay-loft—I don't mind any of those things. It is much harder for me to endure the incredibly coarse tone that prevails among the men here.

The sight of the slightly and dangerously wounded, the dead men and horses lying about, hurts, of course, but the pain of all that is not nearly so keen or lasting as one imagined it would be. Of course that is partly due to the fact that one knows one can't do anything to prevent it. But may it not at the same time be a beginning of a deplorable callousness, almost barbarity, or how is it possible that it gives me more pain to bear my own loneliness than to witness the sufferings of so many others? Can you understand what I mean? What is the good of escaping all the bullets and shells, if my soul is injured? That is how they would have expressed it in old days. . . .

∞

11. My Life is no Longer my Own

September 27th, 1914

This longing for productivity after having been for twenty years merely receptive, makes it hard for me to think that my life is no longer my own. Whatever I may do in the war cannot be called production. . . . But, on the other hand, one cannot stand by and see the German people and all that they have created during hundreds of years destroyed by other nations. The only lightning-conductor is burning hatred and contempt for those few men—if they can still possibly be described by that name—who have brought the war about. Those people are lucky who can hold the enemy's whole nation responsible and believe that they are aiming their rifles at the actual culprits. I personally cannot feel any hatred against individual Frenchmen—on the contrary, I regret every young life which will be cut off through my instrumentality. Also I cannot rejoice unreservedly in our victories; but do you know what I do thoroughly and boundlessly rejoice in? In the German character, which now has an opportunity of exhibiting itself in shining splendour; in the faultless functioning of the gigantic machine to which each individual can and does contribute; in the discipline shown by our troops in their treatment of the inhabitants of enemy country; in the eagerness with which each one works for the general good; and in the firm, unshakable sense of justice which is displayed on the German side on every occasion. The great strength of our noble people does not lie in wielding the sword, but in its sense of the high responsibility of making the best use of its gifts, and in its inner worth as the people of culture. Other nations can tear down and destroy in war, but we understand, better than any other, how to build up, and of this I have been certain only since the beginning of the war. Therefore I do not trouble much as to whether the war has a positive or negative end for us.

March 7th, 1915

Soon after our meeting at M. station, you wrote me a postcard in which you said that you tried to remove my "pessimistic view" of the war. At the end you added that you had perhaps misunderstood the reason of my low spirits. And really—I will make an attempt to explain at least one thing: in 1870 the soldiers went into battle saying to themselves: "If we don't get home we get heaven" (I have to express myself briefly). Very few take that view now; a great many don't consider the question at all; others do, and then it depends on what sort of a religion they have worked out for

II.11   From Philipp Witkop, *German Students' War Letters* (London: Methuen, 1929), 107–110.

themselves whether it is easier or harder for them to give up their young lives. Many abandon all claim on a future life after death—I am too young for that, and I did hope to survive in what I had created, and above all in the influence which I had exercised on the younger generation, in whom I should see realized all the results of my experience. Some men say: "I am married and the father of five children, therefore I make a particularly great sacrifice for the Fatherland." In their place I should say: "Thank God that I have a wife who has loved me and whom I have loved, and still more that I have five children who will continue to develop in accordance with my ideas and will justify my existence. Otherwise my position would have been merely receptive and would only have influenced my own and perhaps the previous generation—even the former very imperfectly." That was what depressed me, personally.

Then came the objective view: our nation was, as I believe, on the right road towards self-regeneration from within, though the powers which were to bring about this regeneration were very limited. Now comes the war, tears everything out of the process of being and developing, and deprives us of just what we most needed—the youth of the present generation, who were growing up with progressive ideas.

I also imagined beforehand, what I now find abundantly confirmed: that the notions which our parents, our books and our history lessons had given us of war are either entirely false, or at least incomplete and therefore misleading. We were given to understand that heroic deeds were of the essence and the most frequent result of war. But is that so? How many such actions are in any case simply brought about by the impulse of the moment, perhaps by the bloodthirstiness and unjust hatred which a nation's political views spread among all its members and for which they have to suffer?

☙

12. I Look upon Death and Call upon Life

Souchez, March 11th, 1915

"So fare you well, for we must now be parting," so run the first lines of a soldier-song which we often sang through the streets of the capital. These words are truer than ever now, and these lines are to bid farewell to you, to all my nearest and dearest, to all who wish me well or ill, and to all that I value and prize.

Our regiment has been transferred to this dangerous spot, Souchez [near Arras in northwestern France by the Belgian border]. No end of blood has already flowed down this hill. A week ago the 142nd attacked and took four trenches from the French. It is to hold these trenches that we have been brought here. There is something uncanny about this hill-position. Already, times without number, other battalions of our regiment have been ordered here in support, and each time the company came back with a loss of twenty, thirty or more men. In the days when

II.12   From Philipp Witkop, *German Students' War Letters* (London: Methuen, 1929), 72–73.

we had to stick it out here before, we had 22 killed and 27 wounded. Shells roar, bullets whistle; no dug-outs, or very bad ones; mud, clay, filth, shell-holes so deep that one could bathe in them.

This letter has been interrupted no end of times. Shells began to pitch close to us—great English 12-inch ones—and we had to take refuge in a cellar. One such shell struck the next house and buried four men, who were got out from the ruins horribly mutilated. I saw them and it was ghastly!

Everybody must be prepared now for death in some form or other. Two cemeteries have been made up here, the losses have been so great. I ought not to write that to you, but I do so all the same, because the newspapers have probably given you quite a different impression. They tell only of our gains and say nothing about the blood that has been shed, of the cries of agony that never cease. The newspaper doesn't give any description either of *how* the "heroes" are laid to rest, though it talks about "heroes' graves" and writes poems and such-like about them. Certainly in Lens I have attended funeral-parades where a number of dead were buried in one large grave with pomp and circumstance. But up here it is pitiful the way one throws the dead bodies out of the trench and lets them lie there, or scatters dirt over the remains of those which have been torn to pieces by shells.

I look upon death and call upon life. I have not accomplished much in my short life, which has been chiefly occupied with study. I have commended my soul to the Lord God. It bears His seal and is altogether His. Now I am free to dare anything. My future life belongs to God, my present one to the Fatherland, and I myself still possess happiness and strength.

∽

13. Here One becomes another Man

October 25th, 1914, near Dixmuide

It is Sunday. We are blessed with glorious sunshine. How glad I am to greet it once more after all the horrors! I thought never to see it again! Terrible were the days which now lie behind us. Dixmuide brought us a baptism of fire such as scarcely any troops on active service can have experienced before: out of 180 men, only 110 unwounded; the 9th and 10th Companies had to be reorganized as one; several Captains killed and wounded; one Major dangerously wounded, the other missing; the Colonel wounded. Our Regiment suffered horribly. It was complimented by the Division.

What experiences one goes through during such an attack! It makes one years older! Death roars around one; a hail of machine-gun and rifle bullets; every moment one expects to be hit; one is certain of it. One's memory is in perfect working order; one sees and feels quite clearly. One thinks of one's parents. Then

II.13   From Philipp Witkop, *German Students' War Letters* (London: Methuen, 1929), 149–150.

there rise in every man thoughts of defiance and of rage and finally a cry for help: away with war! Away with this vile abortion brought forth by human wickedness! Human-beings are slaughtering thousands of other human-beings whom they neither know, nor hate, nor love. Cursed be those who, while not themselves obliged to face the horrors of war, bring it to pass! May they all be utterly destroyed, for they are brutes and beasts of prey!

How one gossips with the sun after such a night of battle! With what different eyes one looks upon Nature! One becomes once more a loving, sensitive human-being after such soul-racking pain and struggle. One's eyes are opened to the importance of man and his achievements in the realm of culture. To war against war; to fight against it with every possible weapon: that will be the work which I shall undertake with the greatest eagerness if the Almighty grants me a safe and happy return! Here one becomes another man. My parents will receive me as a new-born child, maturer, simpler.

∞

14. Copse 125

I generally make some use of this favourite hour of the day, and this morning took a stroll to Copse 125; for it is as well to have a quiet look at the place where at any moment one may be thrown into the battle. Uncertainty of one's ground is a heavy handicap at such moments, and by doing away with it one gains a great advantage over the attack. As it "was shooting"—this expression is a good example of the impersonal way we accept the enemy almost like the weather—and as, too, I had plenty of time, I sat down half-way on a big tussock that had slipped down into the trench and had breakfast and observed the insects. Then I put up my knife that, like a backwoodsman, I find it convenient to carry in a sheath stitched in my breeches, and continued my pilgrimage to the ill-famed copse of which I have already been told so much.

I must say the sight of it is not very cheerful. Shell upon shell has torn up the chalk, over which in any case there was only a thin layer of black humus, and a white powder has settled over what miserable traces of the undergrowth remain, so that they look as pale and sickly as if they had grown in a cellar. Roots and torn-up beeches and severed branches are thrown together in a coil—often hanging over the battered trenches, so that one has to pass by on all fours. The mighty trunks of the timber-trees, if not levelled with the ground, are docked of their tops, stripped of their bark and sapwood; only the hard, battered core remains in an army of bare masts, as though devoured by some horrible cancerous disease. I tried to picture the scene to myself as we may so easily experience it—this petrified wood by night lit by Verey lights [flares], whose white shine turns the bleached undergrowth to a garden of ghostly flora, fixed and fabulous; and among the great bare poles, that

II.14   From Ernst Jünger, *Copse 125* (London: Chatto and Windus, 1930), 55–57, 99–100.

every moment throw their shadows at a different angle, flash after flash of a fight with bombs and machine-guns, fought with an insensate desperation that only this stark and epic landscape could inspire.

For here some awful spirit has struck out all redundancy and created a background worthy of a tragedy that far exceeds the pitch of any poet. Hence man has no choice but to become a bit of nature, subjected to its inscrutable decrees and used as a thing of blood and sinew, tooth and claw. To-morrow, perhaps, men of two civilized countries will meet in battle on this strip of land; and the proof that it must happen is that it does. For otherwise we should have stopped it long ago, as we have stopped sacrificing to Wotan, torturing on the rack, burning witches, or grasping red-hot iron to invoke the decision of God. But we have never stopped it and never shall, because war is not the law of one age or civilization, but of eternal nature itself, out of which every civilization proceeds, and into which it must sink again if it is not hard enough to withstand the iron ordeal.

For this reason those who seek to abolish war by civilized means are just as ridiculous as those ascetics who preach against propagation in order to usher in the millennium. They form the belated rearguard of an enlightenment that sought to dispose by the intellect of matters that draw their life from a depth beyond its reach. But they are the real pests of civilization though they have it always on their lips. Wherever they are left undisturbed at their work, there civilization emits the first scent of decay. May they ever be a laughing-stock to the youth of our land. The blood shall circle in it fresh and earthy as the sap of a wood in spring and beat with as manly a pulse as in the veins of our forefathers who made a saint of the Messiah. Rather than be weak and timorous, let us be hard and merciless on ourselves and on others. Because we think in this way that becomes us best we here have made ourselves its living example, and shall so continue till the end of the war and after. As long as we have a youth that stands for all that is strong and manly our future is assured. . . .

We have to employ other means to-day than in the days of Frederick the Great when the officer, with the whole battle on his own shoulders, took in his serried ranks at one glance. A leader of troops today sees very little of his men in the sea of smoke, and cannot compel them to be heroes if they prefer to live for ever in another sense. He must be able to rely on them; and he can only do so if he has trained them to take the initiative rather than to act as puppets who carry out movements at the word of command. They must certainly be schooled in an iron school if they are to be real men, but they must be taught to face death with a higher sense of their own responsibility than in former days.

We have to free ourselves more and more from drill in massed movements; for since the development of mechanical weapons the functions of massed troops devolve more and more upon individuals. The most essential task to-day is to educate the soldier so that he can stand on his own with a machine-gun without losing sight of the engagement as a whole. We shall be able to replace platoons by machine-guns, companies by tanks, cavalry regiments by air-squadrons, and to rely, indeed, entirely on the machine—but only if we can count upon a high grade of specialist. For as Xenophon said when he encouraged his infantry to withstand cavalry, "all that occurs in battle is done by men." It is men who win battles, and only the picked men who know how to wield the best weapons. The materialists—and the supporters of soul-deadening drill are among the worst and the most abandoned of them—must never be allowed to forget it. As soon as ever we can put into battle large bodies of men of the same type as the flying men whom I visited the day before yesterday, resolute, intelligent, bold, and capable of enthusiasm—as I confidently expect from the further development of our people—we shall no longer need what we understand to-day by drill. There will be so much of interest to learn that no time will be left for it. Obedience will, of course, still be the first duty of a soldier, but I must be greatly mistaken if such men are not most disposed of all to be obedient, seeing that they have the best of all foundations of it in their own convictions. A man who feels that an extreme responsibility rests upon him will always strive to do his best.

Humor and Morale

Amid the tensions and horrors of war, soldiers found release in humor and satire. *The Wipers Times,* its name drawn from the British army's derisive name for the hotly contested Belgian city of Ypres, was probably the best known of a wide variety of so-called trench newspapers published by frontline soldiers in the various armies. Produced beginning in February 1916 by a former printer, the newspaper was notorious for its irreverent attitude toward authority, with frequent caricatures of senior officers and government officials. The first poem is from that publication, the next two from a similar one, The *B.E.F. Times.* All three date from late 1916/early 1917, the height of the stalemate.

15. War

Take a wilderness of ruin,
Spread with mud quite six feet deep;
In this mud now cut some channels,
Then you have the line we keep.

Now you get some wire that's spiky,
Throw it round outside your line,
Get some pickets, drive in tightly,
And round these your wire entwine.

Get a lot of Huns and plant them,
In a ditch across the way;
Now you have war in the making,
As waged here from day to day.

Early morn the same old "stand to"
Daylight, sniping in full swing;
Forenoon, just the merry whizz-bang,
Mid-day oft a truce doth bring.

Afternoon repeats the morning,
Evening falls then work begins;
Each works in his muddy furrow,
Set with boards to catch your shins.

Choc a block with working parties,
Or with rations coming up;
Four hours scramble, then to dug-out,
Mud-encased, yet keen to sup.

Oft we're told "Remember Belgium,"
In the years that are to be;
Crosses set by all her ditches,
Are our pledge of memory.

II.15   From *Wipers Times*, December 25, 1916.

16. Ten German Pioneers

Ten German Pioneers went to lay a mine,
One dropped his cigarette, and then there were nine.

Nine German Pioneers singing Hymns of Hate,
One stopped a whizz-bang, and then there were eight.

Eight German Pioneers dreaming hard of Heaven,
One caught a Flying Pig, and then there were seven.

Seven German Pioneers working hard with picks,
One picked his neighbour off, and then there were six.

Six German Pioneers, glad to be alive,
One was sent to Verdun, and then there were five.

Five German Pioneers, didn't like the war,
One shouted "Kamarad," and then there were four.

Four German Pioneers tried to fell a tree,
One felled himself instead, and then there were three.

Three German Pioneers, prospects very blue,
One tried to stop a tank and then there were two.

Two German Pioneers walked into a gun,
The gunner pulled the lanyard, and then there was one.

One German Pioneer couldn't see the fun
Of being shot at any more, and so the war was done.

II.16   From *The B.E.F. Times*, April 10, 1917.

17. Rats

I want to write a poem, yet I find I have no theme,
"Rats" are no subject for an elegy,
Yet they fill my waking moments, and when star-shells softly gleam,
'Tis the rats who spend the midnight hours with me.

On my table in the evening they will form "Battalion mass,"
They will open tins of bully with their teeth,
And should a cake be sent me by some friend at home, alas!
They will extricate it from its cardboard sheath.
They are bloated, fat and cunning, and they're marvels as to size,
And their teeth can penetrate a sniping plate,
I could tell you tales unnumbered, but you'd think I'm telling lies,
Of one old, grey whiskered buck-rat and his mate.

Just to show you, on my table lay a tin of sardines—sealed—
With the implement to open hanging near,
The old buck-rat espied them, to his missis loudly squealed,
"Bring quickly that tin-opener, Stinky dear!"

She fondly trotted up the pole, and brought him his desire,
He proceeded then with all his might and main,
He opened up that tin, and then—'tis here you'll dub me "Liar!"—
He closed it down, and sealed it up again.

II.17　From *The B.E.F. Times*, April 10, 1917.

III

War to the East and South

The prevailing image of the First World War as one of immobile trench warfare in muddy and shell-torn Belgium and Northern France may obscure the fact that much of the war was fought under different circumstances in widely varying locales. Campaigns were waged in Eastern and Southern Europe, the Middle East, Africa, and Asia. Even if the number of troops involved in some of these theaters of operations paled in comparison to the massive armies mobilized on the Western and Eastern Fronts, no analysis of the course and consequences of the conflict can be complete without some consideration of events in these different areas.

Warfare on the Eastern Front differed from that to the west in significant ways. Instead of a single static line of trenches running from northwest to southeast dividing the British and French armies from their German opponents, with military action occurring like repeated seismic activity along this single fault line, battles in the east erupted around the multiple epicenters resulting from the region's fractured political geography. After all, the initial hostilities (at the end of July) preceded German and Russian action and sprang from Austria-Hungary's desire to punish Serbia. General Oskar Potiorek's punitive expedition fired the war's opening shots in shelling the Serbian capital of Belgrade. The Austro-Hungarian Chief of Staff, Franz Conrad von Hötzendorf, optimistically believed that his forces could simultaneously crush Serbia and confront Russia, but the Serbian soldiers, battle tested by their service in the Balkan Wars of 1912–1913 and ably led by Marshal Radomir Putnik, soundly defeated two Austrian incursions in August and November 1914. Only a third offensive in December pushed back the outnumbered and exhausted Serbians.

Empires, Soldiers, and Citizens: A World War I Sourcebook, Second Edition.
Edited by Marilyn Shevin-Coetzee and Frans Coetzee.
© 2013 John Wiley & Sons, Ltd. except sources 1 to 18. Published 2013 by John Wiley & Sons, Ltd.

At the same time, Hötzendorf's troops sought to defend Galicia and access to the Hungarian plain, while also thrusting into Polish Russia to occupy Warsaw. These ambitious plans were met by the southern flank of Russian forces, which were stretched thin by the determination of the Tsar's troops to launch a two-pronged invasion further north of German territory (East Prussia) and relieve pressure on the French forces who by now were absorbing the brunt of the German march through Belgium. German forces defending East Prussia initially withdrew under a panicky Max von Prittwitz (who was relieved of his command), but his successors, Paul von Hindenburg and Erich Ludendorff, capitalized on the superior planning of their staff officers and the lack of coordination between the two opposing Russian commanders, to inflict a devastating defeat at Tannenberg. Russian casualties numbered some 150,000, and with their armies temporarily turned back, Hindenburg's and Ludendorff's reputations as infallible saviors of the Reich soared.

Already a pattern was emerging. No combatant nation could concentrate upon just one opponent, but was forced to contend with varied threats. Even Germany could not simply fight on a single front against Russia but had continually to lend support to its weaker Austro-Hungarian ally. Campaigns and offensives were thus less predictable than in the west, and with greater potential for movement, outflanking operations, and breakthroughs. The relative fluidity of the front lines was also the result of the greater distances involved, and the consequent dispersal of firepower. With such long lines to cover, and without artillery grouped in the almost unassailable concentrations of the Western front, trenches were less elaborate and more easily breached in the east. Casualty totals, however, were equally horrifying. The Austro-Hungarian armies lost nearly two million men, killed, wounded, or captured, by March 1915, and the other countries involved "spent" men and munitions at an equally alarming rate. Most effective and destructive of all were the German forces. Most German military planners preferred to concentrate their troops on the Western Front, but the prestige of Hindenburg and Ludendorff ensured that their demands would not go unheeded.

In 1915, the Central Powers (as Germany and Austria-Hungary were known) achieved further successes, especially in Galicia. But one tactical victory after another did little in the short term to alter the broader strategic balance. Matters grew even more complex with the entry of Bulgaria on the German side in October 1915, and Romania on the Allied side the following year. Italy, which had stood aside from the Central Powers in August 1914 by arguing that its commitment to aid its fellow members of the Triple Alliance only counted if Austria was attacked, did an about-face in May 1915. The Italian government judged the Allies to be the likely winners and entered their ranks. The promise of territorial gains at Austria's expense was another incentive.

What ensued all around was a war of attrition. The Austro-Hungarians and Italians bled each other white in rugged alpine terrain and the valley of the Isonzo River. Only German intervention broke that stalemate (at Caporetto) and then only temporarily, as British and French divisions were hurriedly transferred to stabilize the front. Serbia's forces were driven out of the country altogether and the broken remnants limped to safety in Greece (which declared war on the Central Powers in

June 1917). Russia, whose troops were so woefully equipped that all too often unarmed soldiers were sent to the front to scavenge for weapons from fallen comrades, managed to improve the production and delivery of guns and ammunition in 1916. They were led in a massive June 1916 offensive against Austro-Hungarian troops in Galicia by General Alexei Brusilov. A particularly able officer, Brusilov recognized that concentrating men and artillery upon a particular point in the enemy lines rarely produced a breakthrough, because it forfeited surprise and enabled the enemy to bring up reserves to seal any ruptures. He decided to attack on a broader front after a brief bombardment, so that the enemy could not ascertain where the heaviest blow was likely to fall. The Austro-Hungarians, faced with strong pressure in several regions, stretched their reserves thin, and so Brusilov's troops broke through in spectacular fashion. They captured hundreds of thousands of prisoners and drove deep through the original lines. But the Russians, by attacking on a broad front, had too few reserves to exploit the opportunity, and they suffered perhaps a million casualties of their own.

Attrition cut both ways. The Russian war effort would collapse first, in 1917, and the country would sue for peace at the end of the year. The harsh treaty of Brest-Litovsk imposed by Germany in March 1918 would end Russia's external war, but not its internal agony. Nonetheless, in the race to disintegration, the Austro-Hungarians, and even the Germans, were not all that far behind.

Russia had also been engaged on another front against another empire, the Ottoman, whose eventual military defeat was the final blow to a tottering edifice, the so-called "sick man of Europe," whose demise had been widely predicted for decades. With a Turkish geographic and demographic core, the empire had begun a program of modernization under the Committee on Union and Progress, formed by energetic young Turkish military officers. They had engaged German military advisors, led by General Liman von Sanders, to reorganize the army, as well as German investment, to strengthen the economy, so there was strong German influence on the country's ruling elite as Europe teetered on the brink of war. Initially, the Ottoman Empire declared its neutrality, but traditional enmity toward Russia, the unwillingness of the Allies to offer major concessions for Ottoman entry into the war, the British seizure for the Royal Navy of two battleships being built for the Turkish fleet, and the German provision of two replacement warships, all precipitated Ottoman intervention on the side of the Central Powers in November 1914. As a result, much of the Middle East was now destined to become a battleground.

Those battles occurred in four different areas. First, heavy fighting soon began between Turkish and Russian forces in the Caucasus region. Initial Turkish gains were reversed by Russian armies led by General Nikolai Yudenich, and from that point on the Russians had the better of the action but without winning a decisive victory. Second, to deal a decisive blow was also the ambition of Britain's eloquent First Lord of the Admiralty, Winston Churchill, who enthusiastically advocated a naval strike to open a passage through the Dardanelles. Success in the venture would enable the Allies to move supplies to and from Russia, threaten the great Turkish city of Constantinople, aid the hard-pressed Serbs, and possibly persuade the Greeks to join the war effort. Naval power alone, however, could not force the issue. What was required was a coordinated amphibious assault, but this feat was beyond Allied comprehension or capabilities. An attempt by the fleet, basically on its own, to force through the Dardanelles in March 1915 was stopped cold by Turkish minefields and artillery. Delays in landing troops on the Gallipoli peninsula to support the campaign afforded Liman von Sanders the opportunity to reinforce the Turkish forces and fortify their defensive positions. Both sides fought bravely, and the men of the Australian and New Zealand Army Corps (ANZAC) earned a formidable reputation as a result, but they could make little headway. In the end, the Gallipoli campaign was notable more for the damage (temporary) to Churchill's ultimately illustrious career and the success of the Allied evacuation. The battles claimed upwards of 300,000 casualties on both sides. Many of these men fell victim to unsanitary conditions and disease.

A third campaign raged in Mesopotamia (in what today is Iraq) as the British sought to protect oil fields around Basra (the Royal Navy's switch from coal-burning to oil-burning warships made this imperative). From that base they launched an expedition toward Baghdad of British and Indian troops under General Sir Charles Townsend, but it was surrounded and besieged in the town of Kut-el-Amara. In one of the more dramatic defeats of the war, Townsend was forced to surrender in April 1916 with the loss of almost 10,000 men. Stung by this defeat, the British mounted a much larger expedition in 1917, which decisively outnumbered the Turkish forces and eventually captured Baghdad.

Particularly dramatic, certainly to those western Europeans nurtured on tales of the Crusades, were the actions in the fourth battleground, Palestine. British troops succeeded in repulsing Turkish incursions into Egypt and in defending the Suez Canal (the vital link to India), but were unable to break through Turkish positions in Gaza until General Sir Edmund Allenby took command in 1917. Combining an astute use of cavalry (in a way impossible on most other fronts), effective air support, and the assistance of Arab units recruited by T.E. Lawrence ("of Arabia"), Allenby's offensive drove the Ottoman forces backward and finally secured Jerusalem as a welcome "Christmas present" for the Allies in December 1917.

Allied successes in the region did not have the greatest direct military impact on the course of the war, but they did have long-term geopolitical significance. With the collapse of Ottoman rule, one empire was gone, but Britain and France seized the opportunity to extend their imperial authority in the Middle East. The 1916 Sykes–Picot Agreement embodied the desire of the two countries to carve up the region between them (basically stipulating French authority over Lebanon and Syria, British influence over Palestine and Iraq) even as it contradicted promises made to prominent Arab leaders such as Sharif Hussein of Mecca concerning independence. The conflict accelerated the development of Arab nationalism, while at the same time it also emboldened the British government, in the November 1917 Balfour Declaration, to indicate its support for the establishment in Palestine of a "national home for the Jewish people." Clearly, the war raised more issues in the region than it settled, and laid the course for the fractious years ahead.

Viewed from Europe, the remaining war zones seemed more peripheral, but developments there clearly pointed toward the future. German colonies in the Pacific, islands like the Marianas, Carolines, or Solomons whose names would reverberate in World War II, quickly fell victim to Allied sea power. The Japanese wasted little time in attacking German interests in China (Tsingtao) and laying the basis for an ominous extension of their own authority in that country. In Africa, where the first British shots of the war were fired, the Allies evicted the Germans without great difficulty from their West African colonies (Togoland, the Cameroons), quelled a limited Boer uprising in South Africa quickly enough to be able to then secure German South-West Africa (now Namibia), but foundered in their efforts to establish control over German East Africa (modern day Tanzania). The local German commander, Lieutenant Colonel Paul von Lettow-Vorbeck, waged a brilliant guerilla campaign in which his heavily outnumbered band of largely native troops (*askaris*) tied down over 100,000 Allied soldiers, some of whom would otherwise have been deployed on the Western Front.

Remarkably, Lettow-Vorbeck did not surrender until after learning of the November 1918 armistice in Europe. Yet if the overall military implications of the war in Africa paled beside those in Europe itself, its effects were felt across the continent in the first real signs of the erosion of European colonial authority.

✆

The Eastern Front

The Russian army's first disastrous campaign, which ended in the crushing defeat of Tannenberg, illustrated problems of communication and leadership that would continue to hamper its performance. General Gurko, who rose from a cavalry commander to Chief-of-Staff to the High Command, emphasizes the inability of his colleagues to see the bigger picture. Others, who lacked that broader perspective, were apt to praise the bravery of ordinary soldiers but to identify serious logistical issues that would have to be overcome for the troops to fight effectively. The second selection, for example, notes the prevalence of camels instead of motorized transport in what ostensibly was so modern a war. Its author was John Morse, an English businessman vacationing in Germany in July 1914 who determined to make his way home by way of Russia but interrupted his journey to experience the adventure of the conflict. Bernard Pares, another Englishman, first visited Russia in 1898 and made its study his life's work. He served as professor of Russian history at the University of Liverpool and as secretary of the Anglo-Russian Committee, which sought to promote better relations between the two nations. From 1914 to 1917 he was attached to the Russian army, and in 1917 to the British ambassador in Petrograd (as St. Petersburg was renamed shortly after the outbreak of the war). The third extract that follows is drawn from his memoirs of his stay in Russia. The fourth document, by General Anton Denikin, stresses the substantial progress Russia had made in armaments production by 1917, but notes the growing war-weariness that had set in by the third year of the conflict (and contrasts with the generally positive evaluation of morale by Pares in 1915). Seemingly endless suffering without real purpose is vividly evoked by Ladizhensky's poem, "War in the East," a further indication of the erosion of morale. Casualties mounted in persistent fighting in which armies attacked and advanced, only to be thrown back by effective counterattacks, at which point the cycle could begin again. This was the case in Serbia, a country whose population suffered dreadfully, as the Austrian offensives outlined in the sixth selection sputtered in harsh terrain against fierce resistance. The victims were not just those who were killed or wounded, but also those who were captured and confined in prisoner-of-war camps. The physical and psychological toll of captivity is relayed here from two perspectives. Edwin Dwinger, an Austrian cavalry officer-cadet, was only seventeen when captured and managed to keep this record of his experiences as a prisoner in Siberia. The final selection is by Elsa Brandstrom, daughter of the Swedish ambassador to Russia and a representative of the Swedish Red Cross, who visited prisoner camps to distribute aid and to determine whether minimal requirements of the prisoners were being met. She was widely known as the "Angel of Siberia."

1. Tannenberg

Fighting began on the morning of September 28th, and from the beginning the corps on the flanks met with some resistance, the Germans threatening an attack on their exterior, which was but poorly protected with cavalry. Probably this resistance was unexpected, for both corps, without half their troops having come into action, began to retire at the moment the two central corps were heavily engaged. On the front the battle had been going well for the Russian troops; a few thousand prisoners had been taken, and there was every possibility of a great victory. Things moved normally for some time afterwards and heavy losses had been incurred by both sides, when suddenly fresh German columns made their appearance, marching to strike a blow at both flanks of the Russian troops attacking in the northerly direction. It was reported at the same time that these enemy columns could turn both flanks of our forces, which, of course, would mean that both army corps would be encircled.

Headquarters of the central corps were entirely without information as to what had happened to the corps on the flanks. They were supposed to be holding in check any turning movement attempted by the Germans. In reality they were retreating and had altogether lost touch with the enemy. Probably it is quite natural to ask why General Samsonoff did not give orders to compel the flanking corps

III.1   From Vasilii I. Gourko, *War and Revolution in Russia, 1914–1917* (New York: Macmillan, 1919), 74–77.

to stop their retreat, to reattack and by a single frontal blow strike hard at the flank and rear of the German columns which were then beginning to surround the two corps in the centre. Failing this in any case he could have had given orders in due time to withdraw from a fight that was fast threatening to become unequal. . . .

The worse the organisation of communication, the more an army commander is disinclined to come close to the actual scene of the fighting and by personal super-vision counterbalance the failure to maintain communication between himself and the unit under his command. Again the tendency to generalise, which nearly every man possesses, will inevitably lead an army commander to imagine that an opera-tion happening before his eyes must be similar to that of the other areas where fighting is taking place, which he cannot see. The defeat or success of a unit under the immediate observation of the army commander may result in such orders being given to the whole army as would certainly meet the situation immediately within vision but might prove disastrous taking the battle altogether.

In the Battle of Tannenberg the preliminary success enjoyed by the troops under General Samsonoff's immediate observation was such an encouraging picture that final victory appeared a matter of certainty. Unfortunately, just at this time the retreat of the two flanking corps, of which Samsonoff was totally unaware, was lead-ing from hour to hour towards the catastrophe which was ultimately to overtake the corps in the centre. Every hour that passed brought confirmation of the fact that the 13th and 15th Corps were being more and more completely surrounded by the Ger-mans. General Martson set out for the scene of the frontal attack to issue orders for a gradual retirement, for the divisions to withdraw one by one. Simultaneously, Samsonoff set off in a different direction, presumably to get in touch with the other army corps of his army. But these measures were taken too late.

Disaster had already overtaken the 13th and 15th Corps; German turning col-umns had already penetrated their flanks and rear so deeply that only a portion of the transport and a comparatively insignificant number of infantrymen managed to escape from the ring of German masses which every minute became more con-tracted. The two army corps fell back slowly into the shades of Tannenberg Wood, absolutely helpless and unable to use their artillery. The result of this disaster was that the Germans captured, almost in full strength, two army corps with all their officers, and recovered possession of their own troops who had been captured earlier during the battle.

✑

2. Bad Things are Good Things under Adverse Circumstances

I have not yet mentioned the Bactrian camels which are used in thousands for Russian transport. During the winter the snow was so deep that the usual

III.2   From John Morse, *An Englishman in the Russian Ranks* (London: Duckworth, 1915), 252–256, 262–265.

indications of the roadways were completely buried; and even in the few cases where they could be discerned, it was most difficult to traverse them with either horse-waggons or motor-cars; indeed, the last-mentioned are useless in snow when it lies beyond a certain depth (though much depends on the power of the car); and guns, also, are impeded by the same cause.

Many persons think that the foot of a camel is peculiarly suited to traversing deserts, and is unfitted for progress over other kinds of ground. This may be true of the dromedary, or African one-humped camel; but it is not correct of the Bactrian, or two-humped camel, the species used by the Russians. This animal can keep its footing on the most slippery ground, and travel with facility over the deepest snow without sinking in to an appreciable depth. The Russians say that it will also go with speed over sand, rock and grass land, but founders in bogs and morasses. It carries a weight of 400 to 500 pounds, English; and proved to be very useful throughout the winter, until the thaw came, and three feet of mud succeeded six feet of snow; and then nothing on earth could drag itself through the miserable mire at a greater rate than a funeral pace.

But all the camels in the country were not enough to bring up the necessaries of the army; and the men, though fed and kept supplied with ammunition, were compelled to lack many things that would have increased both their comfort and their efficiency. Boots especially, and other wearing articles, were often badly wanted; and many of the men suffered greatly from frost-bites. My own feet were becoming very tender by the month of March, when the sun sometimes shone with sufficient strength to make the surface of the snow wet: and this added greatly to our troubles. It is essential to the welfare of troops that after marches they should have dry socks and a change of boots; otherwise they are almost sure to suffer from sore feet. It was the habit of the Russian infantry to take their socks off at night and dry them at the camp fires; but when in the presence of the enemy we were often forbidden to make fires; and at other times there was not sufficient fuel obtainable to supply the whole of our vast hosts: nor was there always a full supply of food, though it was the custom of the Russian soldiers to eat those horses and camels which were killed. There is but little difference between horseflesh and beef, and I have eaten it at scores of meals. I have also tasted camel's flesh; and have nothing to say in its favour. It is coarse, tough and flavourless.

The Germans having retired to carefully entrenched positions, from which we found it impossible to force them, a lull ensued; although occasionally attempts were made to surprise and assault some of the enemy's positions.

On the 5th March the Germans squirted liquid fire over one of these surprise parties which had got close up to their entrenchments, and was endeavouring to remove the wire-entanglements. It was the first time such a device had been reported; and there was some mystery concerning its nature. Some thought that boiling pitch had been used; others called it Greek fire. I do not think it was pitch, although I did not actually see it thrown. I examined the clothing of some of the men, who reported that the holes which were burnt smouldered, and were not easily put out. The fire came over them in a shower of sparks, and was not thrown by hand; but squirted out of a tube of some kind. The only actual injury that I could discover it did was in the case of one man who was badly burned about the face and probably blinded. It is astonishing what a number of devilish contrivances these dastardly Germans have invented and used in this war; and it is clear that they would resort to the foulest possible means, if this would give them the victory . . .

About this time I heard mentioned the poisonous gas which has since become notorious. The Germans, I believe, had not yet resorted to sending the horrid stuff in clouds against a position; but they fired shells which emitted it in considerable quantities, and caused some deaths, and many disablements, amongst the Russian troops. I saw some of the shells burst; and the gas, which gradually expanded to a small cloud with a diameter of about 30 feet, looked like a thick, dirty yellow smoke. The odour of it was horrible and peculiar and very pungent; and it seemed to be a very heavy vapour, for it never rose high above the ground—not more than 20 feet. It dispersed slowly. In my opinion the best way to avoid it would be to rush rapidly through it towards the point from which it had been discharged. Doubtless some of it lurks in the air; but not sufficient, I think, to have deleterious effects. The bulk of it rolls on in a low, dense cloud. That which was shot at us came from *percussion* shells, which do not explode in the air. These projectiles were usually fired at us in salvoes; so as to form a cloud of gas on the ground.

I went to see the bodies of two men who had been killed by one of these poison-shells. They looked as if they had been rolled in flour of sulphur, being completely covered, flesh and clothes, with a yellowish deposit. Some wounded men, and others who had first gone to their assistance, were similarly encrusted. Some of these were insensible; others were gasping for breath, and discharging froth from their mouths . . .

The Russian soldiers, like soldiers and boys all the world over where snow is to be found, had amused themselves by making snow figures in rear of the trench, mostly those of the Emperors, Saints and Generals. A shot struck one of these and threw the well-beaten, frozen snow to an immense height in the air. The shell did not burst, a circumstance of frequent occurrence, which seemed to show that the fuses were badly made, or fitted badly to the projectile.

When the riflemen at last came out of the trench for a fresh supply of ammunition, they were amazed to find me and my horse standing by their cart. They at first mistook me for an officer and saluted very respectfully; but my awkward replies to their salutations caused them to raise their lantern and examine me more closely. Then I was seized, and an officer began to interrogate me, and I produced my papers; but the officer was not so easily satisfied as my Cossack friends; and I was taken to the trench, and thrust into what the British call a "funk-hole," or small excavated resting-place. My belongings were overhauled, and the supply of food received from the Cossacks at once appropriated by the soldiers, who seemed to be very hungry. They were good enough to give me some of the tallow, and a piece of fat bacon. Fortunately I am as fond of grease as any Russian, and I fortified myself for what might happen by making a plentiful meal: indeed, I ate all they gave me, and drank a full measure of vodka on top of it. Bad things are good things under adverse circumstances.

The men had bales of straw in the trenches, and on them they stretched themselves to sleep—at least those close to me did so; but it was too dark to see much. I obtained some of the straw, and slept very soundly in my "funk-hole," though I had a suspicion that I might have very good cause to funk in the morning.

The soldiers were not unkind, whatever they thought of me. One of them awoke me in the morning by pulling me out of my hole by the legs. I thought this was a preliminary to shooting or hanging, but nothing so drastic happened. I was given a pint of strong tea without sugar and milk, but it was hot, and that was a great deal on a bitterly cold morning. With the tea I received a piece of the dirtiest bread I have ever eaten; and shortly afterwards a gun boomed from the enemy's position, and a shell fell in the advanced trenches. As it caused no commotion I suppose it did no harm. It gave the signal that it was getting light enough for the enemy to see; and our men stood to their arms; and soon afterwards began to "snipe," as the modern phrase has it.

Sometimes I took a peep along the little gutter-like cuts where the men rested their rifles when shooting over the edge of the trench. I did this with impunity so frequently that I grew bold, until a bullet came and knocked the snow and dirt over me. A few minutes later a rifleman was aiming along this very cut when a bullet struck his head and killed him instantly. It entered in the centre of his forehead, and came out behind, carrying away a large piece of the skull and letting his brains out. I was becoming used to such painful sights; and in two moments I had his rifle in hand and his pouch strapped round me, and was watching at the death-cut to avenge his fall.

I had brought my own rifle with me; but this and my cartridges were taken from me the previous night. My revolver was concealed in a pocket, and I thought it wise to keep it there for the present.

I could not see much to shoot at. Some of the enemy's trenches were a long way back; others, salient points, ran up to within fifty yards of our position. Occasionally I saw the spike of a helmet; but it generally disappeared before I could bring the sight of the rifle to bear upon it.

The Germans usually wore their spiked helmets, jocosely called "*Picklehaubes*," [*Pickelhaubes*] which much betrayed them when aiming from the trenches. Afterwards they became more cunning and wore their muffin-shaped caps when on duty of a dangerous character.

If I could not see the enemy they appeared to see me; for several bullets came unpleasantly close, and another man at my side was struck and badly wounded in the head. Then my chance came. I saw the spike of a helmet and about an inch of the top of it. It remained so still that I concluded the man was taking careful aim, an example which I followed, and fired. I saw the dirt fly up where the bullet struck the parapet, and the spike disappeared. I do not know if the bullet found its billet— probably not; I fired about twenty rounds at similar marks, sometimes seeing just the top of a spike, sometimes nearly the whole helmet; and then, turning rather quickly, I saw the officer who had arrested me the previous night watching me. He nodded approval; and I felt that I had "saved my bacon" if nothing else; and so it proved. I was no longer treated as a prisoner, and had evidently won the respect and goodwill of those who had witnessed my endeavours to trouble the enemy.

✐

3. Not a Beaten Army

The German method is to mass superior artillery against a point selected and to cover the area in question with a wholesale and continuous cannonade. The big German shells, which the Russian soldiers call the "black death," burst almost simultaneously at about fifty yards from each other, making the intervening spaces practically untenable. The cannonaded area extends well to the rear of the Russian lines, and sometimes it is the rear that is first subjected to a systematic bombardment, the lines themselves being reserved for treatment later. On one of my visits the divisional and regimental staffs were being so shelled that the former had to move at once and one of the latter was half destroyed; but meanwhile there was hardly a shot along the actual front. In this way confusion is created, and reinforcements and supply are made difficult. It is the wholesale character of these cannonades that make their success, for there is nowhere to which the defenders can escape. The whole process is, of course, extremely expensive.

When a considerable part of the Russian front has thus been annihilated, and when the defenders are, therefore, either out of action or in retreat, the enemy's infantry is poured into the empty space and in such masses that it spreads also to left and right, pushing back the neighbouring Russian troops. Thus the whole line is forced to retire, and the same process is repeated on the new positions.

When success in one district has thus been secured, the German impact is withdrawn and again brought forward at some further part of the Russian front. In other words, the German hammer, zigzagging backwards and forwards, travels along our front, striking further and further on at one point or another, until the whole front has been forced back.

The temper of this corps, as of practically all the others, is in no sense the temper of a beaten army. The losses have been severe; but with anything like the artillery equipment of the enemy, both officers and men are confident that they would be going forward. . . .

As large drafts of recruits had come in recently, we halted at the edge of a wood and the General gathered the men round him and made them a very vigorous little speech. He described how Germany and Germans had for several years exploited Russia, especially through the last tariff treaty, which was made when Russia was engaged in the Japanese War, and set up entirely unfair

III.3 From Bernard Pares, *Day by Day with the Russian Army, 1914–1915* (London: Constable, 1915), 245–247.

conditions of exchange. He said that the German exploited and bullied every-body; and that was a thing which the peasant could understand, often from personal experience. Then he got talking of the great family of the Slavs, of little Serbia's danger and of the Tsar's championship, of Germany's challenge and of Russia's defiance. Next he spoke of the Allies and of their help. And then he spoke of the regiment, which bears a name associated with the great Suvorov [renowned Russian general]; they were always, he said, sent to the hardest work, often, as now, to repair a reverse; and he spoke plainly and without fear of the recent retreat. Concluding, he told them a story of Gurko: some of his men had said that the enemy would have to pass over their bodies, and Gurko answered, "Much better if you pass over his."

⚭

4. The Russian Turmoil

In spite of all its defects, the Russian Army in March, 1917, was a formidable force, with which the enemy had seriously to reckon. Owing to the mobilisa-tion of industry, to the activities of the War-Industries Committees, and partly to the fact that the War Ministry was showing increased energy, our armaments had reached a level hitherto unknown. Also, the Allies were sup-plying us with artillery and war materials through Murmansk and Archangel on a larger scale. . . . At the same time new infantry divisions were beginning to deploy. This measure, adopted by General Gurko during his temporary ten-ure of office as Chief-of-Staff of the Supreme C.-in-C., consisted in the reduc-tion of regiments from four battalions to three, as well as the reduction of the number of guns to a division. A third division was thus created in every Army Corps, with artillery. There can be no doubt that, had this scheme been intro-duced in peace-time, the Army Corps would have been more pliable and con-siderably stronger. It was a risky thing to do in war-time. Before the spring operations the old divisions were disbanded, whereas the new ones were in a pitiable state in regard to armaments (machine-guns, etc.), as well as technical strength and equipment. Many of them had not been sufficiently blended together—a circumstance of particular importance in view of the Revolution. The position was so acute that in May the *Stavka* [high command] was com-pelled to sanction the disbanding of those of the Third Division which should prove feeble, and to distribute the men among units of the line. This idea, however, was hardly ever put into practice, as it encountered strong opposi-tion on the part of units already disaffected by the Revolution. Another mea-sure which weakened the ranks of the Army was the dismissal of the senior men in the ranks.

III.4   From General Anton I. Denikin, *The Russian Turmoil* (London: Hutchinson, 1922), 127–129.

This decision, fraught with incalculable consequences, was taken on the eve of a general offensive. It was due to a statement made at a Council at the Stavka by the Minister of Agriculture (who was also in charge of supplies) that the condition of supplies was critical, and that he could not undertake the responsibility of feeding the Army unless about a million men were removed from the ration list. . . . The elemental desire of those who had been given leave to return to their homes could not be controlled by any regulations, and the masses of these men, who flooded the railway stations, caused a protracted disorganisation of the means of transport. Some regiments formed out of Reserve battalions lost most of their men. In the rear of the Army transport was likewise in a state of confusion. The men did not wait to be relieved, but left the lorries and the horses to their fate; supplies were plundered and the horses perished. The Army was weakened as a result of these circumstances, and the preparations for the defensive were delayed.

The Russian Army occupied an enormous Front, from the Baltic to the Black Sea and from the Black Sea to Hamadan. Sixty-eight infantry and nine cavalry corps occupied the line. Both the importance of and the conditions obtaining on these Fronts varied. Our Northern Front, including Finland, the Baltic and the line of the Western Dvina, was of great importance, as it covered the approaches to Petrograd. But the importance at that Front was limited to defensive purposes, and for that reason it was impossible to keep at that Front large forces or considerable numbers of guns. The conditions of that Theatre—the strong defensive line of the Dvina—a series of natural positions in the rear linked up with the main positions of the Western Russian Front, and the impossibility of any important operations in the direction of Petrograd without taking possession of the Sea, which was in our hands—all this would have justified us in considering that the Front was, to a certain extent, secure, had it not been for two circumstances, which caused the *Stavka* serious concern: The troops of the Northern Front, owing to the vicinity of Revolutionary Petrograd, were more demoralised than any other, and the Baltic Fleet and its base—Helsingfors and Kronstadt, of which the latter served as the main base of Anarchism and Bolshevism—were either "autonomous" or in a state of semi-Anarchy.

✧

5. War in the East

> Dim is the twilight of raw winter's day,
> Hamlets lit up by a flash
> Stand out ablaze, then again die away.
> Hark! Cannons thunder and crash!
> All this is war. Crisp white snow on the ground,
> Long rows of trenches I see.

III.5   From V. Ladizhensky, *Poems Written during the Great War* (London: George Allen & Unwin, 1918), 63.

Real work of life, full of tasks fair and sound,
How far off you seem to me!
In the village near by the children play,
To guns accustomed their ear;
Out of the twilight the spent horses neigh,
Their trampling dimly I hear.
All this is war. If an answer you seek
To the question, What is war's aim?
I will say nought. Endless suffering shall speak,
Cruelty, torment, and shame.
I will say nought, but I will shed a tear
With the mother for her lad,
Or with the children in anguish and fear,
Homeless and hungry and sad.

6. Serbia's War

To gain a clear idea of the Balkan territory, draw a line from Venice to the mouth of the Danube, or, if the reader prefers, take the line of 45 N. parallel of latitude. Only the province of Moldavia, belonging to Roumania, will lie north of this. Draw another line from Naples to Constantinople, and, on the Balkan peninsula, only a very small piece of the Turkish Empire projects northward and this is distinctively Balkan; part of Albania, which is entirely Albanian, lies south of this, but Albania is classed with Greece.

The Balkans may thus be regarded as a rough oblong, with the Adriatic Sea and the Black Sea respectively on the west and east, or shorter sides of the oblong; Turkey occupying the greater part of the southern side; Austria-Hungary and Russia facing the northern side. Now divide this oblong into three equal parts by drawing a perpendicular line one third of the way from the western end, and dividing the larger eastern end in two by a horizontal line. The square western end will be Serb, the northern eastern end will be Roumanian, the southern eastern end will be Bulgarian . . .

It is one of the chief causes of trouble in the Balkans that the boundaries of territories do not agree with the boundaries of the lands occupied by those peoples. Much of northern Turkey is Bulgarian, much of southern Hungary is Serbian, much of eastern Hungary is Roumanian, and the Russian province of Bessarabia is Roumanian also.

The Serbian campaign, then, in a word, consisted of the conquest of this western square of the Balkans by the Austro-Germans and the Bulgarians. Since Roumania did not enter the war on the side of the Allies until later, it follows that Serbia, at the opening of the war, was almost entirely surrounded by enemies. Her defeat was certain from the beginning unless Russia and Roumania came to her assistance

III.6   From Francis Rolt-Wheeler and Frederick E. Drinker, eds., *The World War For Liberty* (Philadelphia: National Publishing, 1919), 129–133.

from the east and north and Greece from the south. Since Russia was too much occupied to do so, since Roumania could not make up her mind whether to join the Allies or the Central Powers and since Greece played battledore and shuttlecock with her promises and her allegiances, Serbia was deserted and left to her ruin. . . .

The operations in this theater of the world war were of a threefold character. There was the Serbian–Austrian campaign on the west side of the square; the Serbian–German campaign on the north side of the square; and the Serbian–Bulgarian campaign on the southeast side of the square.

The topography of Serbia, moreover, was not conducive to military movements upon the scale needed in the world war. Her mountains, though well adapted to guerrilla warfare, were not disposed in such a fashion as to make a single chain, defensible at a few passes, in such a way, for example, as the Carpathian Range protects Hungary. Moreover, the rugged nature of her country had an added disadvantage, that of transport. Roads were few and poor. Consequently, cross-country operations were extremely difficult.

Furthermore, and this was a crucial point in all the campaigns, owing to her lacking of sea-coast Serbia could only secure munitions through a neutral country and by one single railroad line, that running from Belgrade, through Nish, to Saloniki . . .

So far as military resources were concerned, comparisons are misleading. At the most, including reserve, the Serbs and the Montenegrins together could not muster more than 300,000 men. Austria could summon 1,000,000 men and could call on Germany for aid. Austria, as the invader, had the advantage of determining the point of attack; Serbia, defending, had but the choice of determining the general line along which the attack must be met. . . .

The [Austrian] advance began on August 14. The most important points for the Austrians to gain were the heights of the Tser Mountains, which separated their two largest armies. The Austrians stormed the heights. But, while the Serbians were inferior in numbers, they were far superior in fighting quality. Every soldier was a veteran of the two Balkan wars. They knew war, and modem war at that. The Austrian soldiers had never smelt powder. They broke at the first fire and ran.

The Austrian artillery tried to cover the retreat, but, without the support of infantry, the guns could not advance. The artillery did its best, men and oxen tried to haul the guns over mountain paths and rocky trails, but the Serbians, at home in such fighting, rushed over the rocks yelling, and charged among the batteries with bayonets and hand grenades.

In spite of this desperate resistance, the Austrian artillery gained command of parts of the Tser ridge. But there was neither time for profound intrenchment nor did the ground allow of it. Serbian control of the heights above the valleys absolutely precluded the formation of a continuous battle line. Superiority of artillery was of little use to the Austrians, the battles were too much broken up by the saw-toothed character of the country.

Fighting on the 17th and the 18th was much of the same character. At one point the Austrians advanced, at another they fell back. The important point, however, was that the Serbians absolutely prevented the union of the Austrian armies, which would have enabled the invaders to establish a solid, intrenched line on the Valievo plain.

On the 19th the Austrian batteries were dislodged from the heights they had won on the Tser ridge. This put all the controlling points in Serbian hands again. On August 20, the Austrians in the valleys were in a hopeless case. The Serbians swarmed down on them. The Austrians fled, leaving arms, ammunition, guns, provision, prisoners, wounded and everything else, fleeing panic-stricken for the Drina River which they had proudly crossed in force ten days before.

By the 21st only the Austrian army remained which had crossed to the north at Shabatz, over the Save. Three days sharp fighting disheartened this army also, and on August 24 the last Austrian trench was evacuated and the last unwounded Austrian soldiers retreated to their own country. The first Austrian invasion of Serbia had been an utter and a ghastly failure. Over 6,000 men had been killed, 4,000 prisoners had been taken, together with 40 guns, scores of machine guns and huge stores of ammunition. The Serbian losses had been heavy also, 3,000 dead and 15,000 wounded. It had been a costly, though a glorious victory. . . .

The Second Austrian invasion closely resembled the first. It began at the same points and resulted in the same tactics. Warned by the first defeat, however, the Austrian commanders contented themselves with making and holding small gains. The fighting was fierce and personal. Old wartimes seemed to have come again. Huge stones were rolled down the hills on advancing troops, soldiers hid behind trees to stab or shoot individually, men grappled and fought with knives and teeth. Again the invasion was stopped. All attempts to gain the Valievo Plain were fruitless, but Austria had effected a lodgement on the Serbian side of the Drina. It had cost her 150,000 men. Trench warfare at once commenced, as on the Aisne, with the resultant deadlock.

⚭

7. The Army behind Barbed Wire

We were brought for the first time since our capture into earthen barracks, horribly unhealthy, much-feared rectangular sheds dug deeply into the ground and covered with a flat roof. They were not even finished, for the walls were only partly covered with thin boards, and in many places the bare earth peeped out. At the ends were the doors, along the sides a couple of little windows already half covered by drifting snow, and in the centre was a long aisle leading from door to door. The remaining space was taken up by two tiers of plank beds made of pine-boards.

"By thunder," said Bruenn [one of the prisoners], "the veriest fox-holes, and so dark that a man can't even read his morning paper!"

III.7   From Edwin Dwinger, *The Army Behind Barbed Wire: A Siberian Diary* (London: George Allen & Unwin, 1930), 108, 120–121, 243–245.

We lay down together as before. Again twice as many were forced into one shed as there was actually room for. If we could only have moved about a little, could have nailed a few boards together for a table! For weeks we had been eating off the bare floor. In time our backs would become so crooked that we would no longer be able to look up at the sky. . . .

One morning the first of the doctors died, the younger of the two Germans, the one with the scarred face. The day before he had broken down at the side of a sick man and had not regained consciousness. Dr. Bockhorn raged, "Are we in a madhouse?" he roared. "Are we in hell?" During the past week he had aged ten years.

In front of the sheds the corpses began to accumulate in great heaps. We were not even given a barn to put them in, and the ground was frozen too hard to permit of their being buried, even if there had been anyone strong enough to dig the graves. They were simply thrown out on to the heaps of excrement where fat rats gnawed at them. . . .

In our barracks we had forty dead up to that time, and we had been able to take them all out. Pod [another of the prisoners] was still strong and kind. In those days, toward the end of January [1916], one hundred persons died daily in the whole camp.

On the preceding day as many had died in our shed as in the whole camp a fortnight before. Matters went rapidly downhill with us. The doors were scarcely opened even to throw out the dead. Once Pod had to lead a detachment to free the doors. It had not been possible to get out or in on account of the piles of dead. When he came back from this expedition, he looked so different that I scarcely recognized him. "Junker," he said, in a new, strange voice. "I liked being a soldier and did not shirk when my country called me. But I went in the belief that I was a soldier and should be treated like a soldier—not like a convict. . . .

To continue making entries in my diaries [from January 1918 onward] became increasingly difficult. At times my head seemed emptied of all thought and of the power to distinguish the association of ideas and events. Of certain events I could not write at all: to describe others the right words failed me . . .

Is it not possible, however, that the growing infrequence and increasing brevity of the entries in my diary witness more clearly than detailed entries could have done to the extent of our degradation and depression? Is not silence at times more eloquent than speech?

Frequently we used to say among ourselves: If an ordinary human being were placed among us for eight days he would certainly think he was in an asylum! If our life did not utterly destroy us, it was only because we were already completely blunted by all that had gone before. We no longer lived in the true sense of the word: we only waited . . . We could best of all have been compared with the hibernatory animals. Like them we were only conscious of one thing: the expectation of spring! For us spring meant—the return home.

In truth, our condition was such as to baffle description to one who had himself never experienced our lot. We became more restless and irritable with the passing of each day. The majority of us walked hourly in the barrack-yard—crossing it again and again, now lengthwise, now around the sides, forming circles, triangles, ellipses, in short, making a hundred different figures with the sole object of being tired out by evening in order to win the much hoped-for sleep. Others sat about all day long in silence. A chance remark sufficed to arouse their fury; the paltriest occurrence to earn their frantic enmity. Former friends no longer recognized each other. Sharp-tongued criticism was rampant. No matter whether one laughed or cried, slept or awoke, whatever one did was always wrong, and no one was any longer capable of putting things to rights. Every morning a couple of officers wearing their decorations went from one house to another—all these affairs of honour were eventually to be fought out at home with deadly weapons. If that had really taken place, not a single one of us would have been left alive; for each had been challenged one or more times to a duel with pistols or heavy sabres.

Days of furious irritability were succeeded by days of deathly apathy. Hopes for the future, longings for wives, children, sweethearts, the call of one's profession or work, and home-sickness, at times disappeared wholly and ceased to trouble us as much as the buzzing of a fly. Here and there among us a life sank into the depths, a spirit broke beneath the strain, destroyed by anger and the conflict with fate, eaten up with doubts about life and a gnawing fury—sank down beyond the help of all medical skill. Before one had time to be conscious of its approach, madness came to destroy in silence or in laughing, foaming frenzy, all that was human in a man.

✍

8. Among Prisoners of War

Though external conditions weighed heavily on the individual, though thousands fell victim to disease and the general wretchedness of existence, these sufferings were often far surpassed by the depressing mental and moral effect of captivity itself, a state of mind aggravated by that curse of captivity—enforced idleness.

Up to the Peace of Brest-Litovsk, neither Russia nor their own Government gave captive officers permission to work. During the first year, but only within the camp, captive privates were employed in looking after the sick, in cooking, carrying water, chopping wood and so forth.

Thus the prisoners were restricted to such occupations as they could invent for themselves in the isolation of the camp and with the limited material at their disposal. Each hoped to make his present activity of use to him in his trade or profession later on. All work was undertaken with an eye to the future in the homeland.

III.8   From Elsa Brandstrom, *Among Prisoners of War in Russia and Siberia* (London: Hutchinson, 1929), 117–123.

All prisoners looked upon their captivity as an unlucky but passing phase which they must get over as quickly as possible and turn to good account. Their confidence that it would be short gave them, at the beginning, buoyancy and desire to work. Later it led to repeated disappointments and finally to a hopeless distrust of everyone and everything, which poisoned their existence.

Time passed and for most of the prisoners their captivity stretched from over four to six years. With the change in outward circumstances during these various periods the mental condition also fluctuated. To deprive a civilized man of the support given him by society, family and custom is to try his moral strength to the utmost, while at the same time freeing him from all the restraints of education and convention. The very sharpness of the contrasts in these conditions roused in many inward conflicts seldom experienced in the ordinary routine of daily life. The more highly cultivated the prisoner, the more he suffered, but the better his chances of achieving a strength of will enabling him to rise above his surroundings, retain his self-respect, and even strengthen his character. The early stages of captivity often showed a marked development of individual character. There was leisure enough for collecting one's thoughts and for musing on the deeper problems of life. Isolation and enforced introspection brought out and matured the personality.

Intellectual hunger found expression in a strong thirst for knowledge and in a lively interchange of ideas. As a result there awoke in the prisoners that keen interest in study which characterized the early years of captivity. The prisoners' first difficulties were fundamental—the lack of books. In some camps all, even Russian, books and newspapers were forbidden on principle; in other places the prisoners were allowed to buy books in the nearest town. But foreign literature was scarce in out-of-the-way parts of Russia and at that time few knew the language of the country. Many of the camp commandants discouraged the learning of Russian, seeing in it a means of facilitating flight.

While some of the prisoners showed a thirst for learning, others had a desire to impart their knowledge. Thus arose the many lectures on the most varied subjects. Here the enforced separation of officers and men, alluded to above, was most unfortunate in that it hindered students from profiting by the teaching of the many university men among the officers.

Prisoners who had no taste for study tried to fill up their time with practical work. Thus there grew up in the camp a kind of home industry, primitive in character owing to the lack of raw materials and tools. A pocket-knife, a piece of wood, a little clay or, in its place, the daily black bread which strongly resembled it, was the only appliance. With the aid of these were fashioned cigarette-cases, boxes, buttons, paper-knives, frames and small ornaments. To what great practical use this capacity for work might have been put if tools and materials for tailoring and shoe-making had been supplied to the prisoners!

Among the captives were men with artistic gifts, painters, sculptors, actors and musicians. But the delight of the general company were the actors and, above all, the musicians, who succeeded by degrees in forming choirs and orchestras. It is certain that nothing helped so much as music to make the prisoners forget, for a time at least, the misery of their plight.

But these efforts at employment were only possible to the few. Many lacked the means as well as the elasticity necessary in order not only to surmount the constantly recurring difficulties, but also to enable one to do serious work in an environment continually swarming with people, and where neither by day nor night was there a moment's peace. With their health sapped, too, by disease and want, most of the prisoners soon lost all energy and desire for work.

The psychological effects of captivity made themselves more and more felt. A gnawing unrest, a despairing feeling of emptiness, of disgust at everything spreads everywhere. Like an evil spirit these feelings take possession of the prisoner, yielding only for a time to physical pain. They drive him out of the huts—to walk, anything to walk, on and on, round and round, now forming this figure, now that —anything to bring that weariness which leads to the longed-for, dreamless sleep. He seeks out comrades whose company he formerly found pleasant and stimulating, but his own irritability, like theirs, makes intercourse intolerable. Men formerly the best of friends can now scarcely bear the sight of one another, and a mere trifle, which otherwise would pass unnoticed, may now lead to blows. Everything gets on one's nerves. One is critical; one is annoyed because this man laughs, the other coughs, the third snores, the fourth talks too much and the fifth never speaks at all.

This excessive irritability makes the prisoners suspect a hidden motive behind the most harmless word and the alleged injury to one's self-esteem demands satisfaction. Hence the innumerable quarrels among the prisoners, which they register in detail with the firm intention of settling them at some future period. The merest trifles in their surroundings absorb their attention and take on gigantic proportions. Whether one should buy a cup or a jug, whether red or green is better, whether one's tin mug is still good—whether one should take his turn to-day to fetch his soup or whether he should leave it—these and such-like questions occupy the prisoner's mind for hours. He longs for solitude and freedom, but when he flees from the overcrowded barracks he runs into sentries and fences.

Only when a letter arrives from home are matters different—for a long time this gives him peace and restores his balance. But months and years might pass without a line from home reaching him, and sometimes these letters arouse the bitter feeling that those at home understood little or nothing of his agony. It could hardly be otherwise, since his letters had been written in moments of comparative calm and therefore could give the family no idea of his tortured spirit.

Periods of irritability give place to apathy and an unnatural craving for sleep. The thought of the future which had buoyed him up at first, the memories of wife and children, finally leave him as indifferent as if they concerned a stranger. A growing incapacity to see things in their true perspective makes his life a burden. He is inaccessible to reason, and nothing can penetrate his stony indifference.

Every prisoner had to fight such periods of irritable unrest and paralyzing depression; the one more, the other less. For some few among them the stain was too great, one day the brain gave way—madness was the end, raving and ungovernable, or shy and quiet.

But the struggle *could* be crowned with success, and under its influence men have developed a ripeness of character rarely achieved in ordinary life.

∽

War in the Mediterranean

Campaigns on the Italian front were dominated by the twelve battles between Italian and Austro-Hungarian troops along the Isonzo River. The first eleven were largely inconclusive, but the twelfth (October–December 1917) led to a rout of the Italians at Caporetto, as described below by Thomas Nelson Page. Page, from a prominent Virginian family, was American ambassador to Italy during the period he describes. The other dramatic episodes in the Mediterranean theater were the Allied landings at Gallipoli that intended, but failed, to knock Turkey out of the war, and the ultimately successful efforts to wrest control of Palestine. Perspectives on Gallipoli are afforded by three participants: Major John Gillam (an Australian supply officer), the war diarist for a New Zealand cavalry unit (that spent more time with shovels digging trenches than with sabers riding horses), and Mehmed Fasih (a 22 year-old Turkish lieutenant who participated in the stout resistance to the Allied invasion). The final selection, by British officer O. Teichman, details the dramatic atmosphere of modern warfare in the ancient setting of the Holy Land.

9. The Italian Front

Caporetto lay on the western bank of the Isonzo, where it skirts the foot of Monte Nero, towering above its surrounding mountains. The Italians held Monte Nero; but to the south, a little distance, in the angle of the Isonzo, the Austrians had never been dislodged from the Tolmino–Santa Lucia bridge-head on the western bank. Several roads converged on Caporetto down the valley, and thence through the gradually diminishing mountains ran a good road, and a newly constructed railway directly to Cividale, a dozen or more miles away, and so on to Udine, the headquarters of the Supreme Command. When the great disaster befell, Caporetto, as the first town of importance taken and mentioned in the despatches, gave its name to the event; but the German-Austrian drive, while it converged on Caporetto, covered a wider front than that represented by the little town on the highway to Udine. The enemy were quick to avail themselves of everything to their

III.9   From Thomas Nelson Page, *Italy and the World War* (New York: Scribner, 1920), 11, 303–309.

advantage. The bridge-head on the west side of the Isonzo was a good *point d'appui* [point of assembly] for their project. Monte Nero and the Bainsizza, Monte Santo and the Carso, could not be carried by assault; but, if flanked, they might fall.

The British and French had for some time had on the Isonzo front each an auxiliary artillery force. The British had had something over a hundred guns; the French had had something like three-fourths of that number. After his success at Bainsizza and San Gabriele, Cadorna considered his position impregnable, and as the British and French needed all the guns they could get on their own fronts, they took away most of their artillery. The British left only about thirty, and the French left perhaps ten or a dozen guns.

At the same time the Germans reinforced the Austrians with a number of Divisions, perhaps eight or ten, which rumor quickly increased to twenty-two. They also aided the Austrians essentially with the new tactics and methods devised by Ludendorff, who came to give his personal aid in the projected offensive.

The Italians were accustomed to fighting the Austrians and the Hungarians and Jugo-Slavs; but they had not been pitted hitherto, at least in Italy, against the Germans, and the latter had a great reputation there, especially for organization, persistence, and military skill. Also they had new tactics unfamiliar to the Italians. Of all of these facts the Germans were prompt to avail themselves.

It was known that the offensive was on the cards, and the presence of the German divisions, multiplied by rumor, created some anxiety in Italy when the offensive opened on the Isonzo front, especially in view of the sentiment disclosed in a Defeatist circular of the secretary of the Socialist organization denouncing the war and sent secretly throughout the country. But the news from Cadorna was reassuring, and the Minister of War, General Giardino, a gallant and capable commander, made a speech in the Chamber on the afternoon of the 24th of October, in which he declared that the army was sound to the core, and that he could assure the country that it was the solid and secure bulwark of Italy. It was his maiden speech, and he received one of the greatest ovations ever tendered in the Chamber to a Minister. The body voted that the speech be printed in large numbers and circulated throughout the country. That night the enemy broke through the Italian lines at Caporetto. It was a tragic climax to a lofty and patriotic speech.

In the light of facts now known, the importance of Caporetto appears quite obvious. It was undoubtedly supposed to be securely protected, but unfortunately something was wrong and, like a bolt from the blue, the disaster came with all its fell consequences.

All sorts of explanations have been given for the tragedy of Caporetto; many theories, some by no means reconcilable, have been advanced and numerous reasons assigned. And possibly, there were sundry reasons taken in combination, rather than one or two only which led to the tragic result and came so near destroying Italy and wrecking the Allied Cause.

The Italian Government must know all the reasons and their several relations thereto; but it is a great question whether all will be disclosed in our time. It may be asserted, though, as quite certain that those usually assigned have not the relation to the climax generally attributed to them. Only one thing is certain: that when Italy awoke to the realization of the situation into which she had been brought, and of the fate that impended over her, she gathered herself together and, utilizing every force within her reach, with every energy left within her stricken soul, she applied all her might in one supreme effort to extricate herself from the slough into which she had been flung, and succeeded. It was a supreme effort, and she has a right to feel proud of its success; for it was the decisive action of her national life, and it saved herself and possibly saved the Allies. At least eventually Peace was hastened by Austria's collapse under her final assault.

The causes that led to the disaster of Caporetto have been adverted to. The antecedent situation as a whole, with the relative bearing on it of different causes, is somewhat obscure.

First and foremost, the soldiers in all that region—as in all the sectors of the front—were tired; worn by constant labor and by even more exhausting vigil—they were, in fact, worn down. Month after month, winter after winter, they had been kept at it with little respite or relief. In winter in snow and sleet, rain and mud; in summer in sun and dust—ever toiling, ever watching, ever on a strain; they had fought and won ridge upon ridge, mountain after mountain, with infinite courage, giving up their lives, pouring out their blood like water, in assault after assault, with more to follow; yet they were apparently no nearer the goal of their aim than before their comrades had died by the thousand. There appeared to be no end to it. And the times when they were not fighting were more burdensome than when the fighting was going on. They were tired out; bored out with it all. If they got a *congedo* [furlough], it was days in a cattle-car to get home, and as many to get back. And they knew that their enemies—the Huns: Austrians, Hungarians, Croats—on the other side felt the same way. The prisoners and deserters told them so. The pickets, when they fraternized, said the same. When would it end? The food was so scarce; the prices were so high; the *sussidio* [allowance] so inadequate. When would it end? Why did not it end and let them come home? There were those who said it could be ended if the authorities would agree. The Priest thought so; the Socialists said so. In fact, the Holy Father had said so in Rome. The Priest said he had written a letter to say so. This was the burden of many letters that they received, and often the letters did not come. Were they forgot, or were the letters held by the Censors' office?

They agreed—those who became disaffected—that the time might come when the men would have to do as they were doing in Russia—at least, were said to be doing there —refuse to fight any more, and stop the whole war.

As we have seen, in the month of August and later on, the militarized Turin workmen who had been rounded up and arrested were sent en masse, fresh from the suppressed revolt at Turin, to the Caporetto sector to be taught a lesson. Instead of being taught, they gave lessons—in Defeatism. Some were deeply infected with the theory of Sovietism. They were all against the continuance of the war and of the actual regime. The fierce revolt in Turin was the proof of it. They were followed to the front by their newspaper. The *Avardi* was the Voice of the Future inveighing against the Present, and proclaiming the duty of sabotage against the war. The Secretary of the Socialist organization had sent a circular to all the Socialist Communes, urging them to disobey all the decrees that looked to the continuance of the war. All conspired to confuse the ideas of the plain soldier, who reasoned that when the Socialists agreed with the Priests, as they were doing back at home, they must be right. The new contingents from the Turin factories were not only imbued with this as a theory, they were ready to put it into practice. To some extent they did put it into practice. They deserted as occasion offered, and took through the lines with them exaggerated stories of disaffection. They also took with them definite information as to the location of the defenses and batteries; of telephone stations, etc.

On top of this came to the soldiers there the growing conviction that they were being treated unjustly; that they were being kept at the front longer than others, and that back of the front, where there were better rations and better barracks, towns and cafes and women, the streets swarmed with men who, they considered, were favored and pampered and spared the hardship of the trenches, at the expense of those at the front. It was, they felt, unfair—unjust—outrageous. They were put upon and abused. They talked about it—growled about it—sneered about it —wrote and sang songs about it. . . .

Amid all the stories, inextricably tangled and confused, of the reasons for its happening and of the way in which it happened, the physical military fact of the manner in which the break came appears to be that the Germans, finding themselves held up in France, and believing that should sufficient strain be thrown against her, Italy would give way and thus open a possible break in the Allies' defensive line, came down to render the Austrians the necessary aid to overwhelm Cadorna's hard-fought Right on the Isonzo. And having come, Von Ludendorff introduced his new system of hammering to pieces the first line; then of capturing it under cover of the moving barrage which, in a region where every foot of road and every possible approach were known to the assailants, would prevent the arrival of reinforcements from the rear. Having effected this, the plan was facilitated by what was termed the method of infiltration, which demanded a certain amount of individual thought and independence from the men who according to plan would penetrate the Italian lines, and when there form groups or units for capture, holding and, under favoring conditions, for further progress. . . .

So sudden and swift was the penetration of the front that, according to the report current at the time, the Commander of the Division (Twenty-fourth) holding the front above Caporetto was surrounded and caught in his headquarters before he knew of the break in his line. On parts of the line of the advance the fighting was as fierce as in any battle of the war. Regiments were wiped out in their desperate efforts to save their positions. Regiments of the *Bersaglieri* [crack Italian light infantry renowned for their marksmanship], as ever, stood their ground and fought till exterminated. Elements of the Twenty-fourth Division fought with a valor sufficient to redeem the reputation of the Division from the stain brought on it. But the valor of the now flanked and isolated commands was unavailing. Within a few hours the flood of the assailants had poured through the passes and were, if not in the plain, on the commanding points above it where they were able with their barrage to prevent the arrival of reinforcing Italian troops. In places the most dire of misfortunes that can befall an army—a panic—appears to have seized on some of the retreating troops; in others the Italians fought with surpassing courage to hold up the pursuit to give the disorganized elements time to escape, and those still unshaken time to retire.

Success begets success, and in nothing so much as in military action. With success, the Austrian and German forces acquired new powers, and in a region which was as well known to the Austrians as to the Italians, they were able to press the retreating Italians irresistibly, pushing them into ever-increasing confusion and disorder, and rendering vain the efforts made by the Staff and the still unshaken troops to stem the ever-rising tide and sweep back the overwhelming flood.

⟣⟢

10. Gallipoli

May 3rd, 1915

I hear that there was an armistice declared for the purpose of burying the dead of both sides. It lasted about two hours, during which both Turks and our men sat on their respective parapets watching each other with interest while parties were out in front, mixing freely with each other, clearing away their own dead. It was an extraordinary situation. One of the Turks picked up two of our live bombs which had fallen short and had failed to explode, and was making back to his trench with them, when his officer, spotting him, called him back and made him hand the bombs back to our men, and apparently gave him a good cursing in strong Turkish. A short time after, both sides are back in their trenches, and if a head should appear over the parapet of either side it is in danger of being promptly blown off.

At dinner I express the thought that I wished Turkey would throw over the Germans and become our allies. Our Tommies and theirs were so near this morning, and, by God! they would fight well side by side. I say that Turkey is the most valuable asset to have on either side. If she were our ally the Dardanelles would be open to the Allies, and the Central Empires would be utterly defeated in a year. As an enemy she will cause the war to drag on Lord knows how long, providing we are unsuccessful in forcing the Straits. I am "howled down" and am told that Achi Baba will be ours in a month's time, and once ours, Turkey is finished. But

III.10   From Major John Graham Gillam, *Gallipoli* (London: George Allen & Unwin, 1918), 72, 135–137.

strolling up to the top of the cliff after dinner, I take a long look at Achi. Ours in a month? I wonder. I turn, depressed and pessimistic, into my house of biscuit-boxes, and bless the man who invented sleep. . . .

June 18th

This morning Asia's guns have not worried us so far, but the batteries in front of Achi Baba are very active, and are worrying the troops in the valley very much. The sound of bursting shrapnel reminds me of the spit and snarls of angry cats. Our artillery is quiet. Rumour says that another enemy submarine has been accounted for, but the one that came in yesterday morning is still at large, and consequently our Fleet is unable to come and help us. At two o'clock H.M.S. *Prince George* is sighted off Imbros, surrounded by twelve destroyers and preceded by seventeen mine-sweepers. It was a very impressive sight to see all these destroyers and sweepers jealously guarding the great ship from submarine attack.

She takes up a position opposite the Asiatic coast, well out from the mouth, and then opens fire with all big guns on the Turkish batteries on Asia in position opposite Morto Bay. We enjoy seeing the pasting that she gives them, her big guns rapidly roaring away and belching forth spurts of flame and buff-coloured smoke. Everybody imagines that every Turkish gun must be knocked out. After four hours, she leaves with her retinue of smaller ships. Half an hour after, one big gun on the Asiatic side opens fire on to "V" Beach, and simultaneously a heavy Turkish attack on our left starts, supported by a tremendous bombardment from Turkish artillery. The fight lasted all night, and ended about six in the morning. Their infantry left their trenches very half-heartedly, and our machine-guns accounted for a heavy toll of enemy casualties.

June 19th

We gave way at a part of our line last night, but regained the ground later in the early morning, and our line was still intact, and as we were. We lost heavily, but Turkish losses were enormous.

Captain Usher, my Staff Captain, was killed this early morning in the trenches by shrapnel, and I feel his loss awfully. He was always so charming to me. It's the "good-uns" that go, as Wilkie Bard says. I am sure this war is too terrible to last long; it is simply wholesale butchery, and humanity will cry out against it soon.

At 11.30 an exceptionally heavy shell came over from Asia (a high explosive) and fairly shook the earth. Two minutes after, two more came, and every living soul rushed for cover. Then for three hours they pasted us: over they came, one after the other, with terrific shrieks and deafening explosions, throwing chunks of hot jagged-edged metal whizzing in all directions. All the mules and horses, as far as possible, were got under cover, and men rushed to their dugouts. Carver, Way,

Davy, Foley, Phillips, and I were under cover of the cliff in our "bivvy," which cannot be called a dugout, as it is simply a wide platform cut in and built up on the side of the cliff and in the line of fire, between the 60-pounder battery, twenty-five yards to our west, and the Asiatic battery. The 60-pounders soon opened fire, and then a duel began; and after one or two have pitched first over our "bivvy" into the sea, and one or two just short, we get nervy and decide to quit. Phillips and Davy made the first dash down the cliff, and the others said they would wait for the next shell. It came shrieking along, burst, and I got up and made a dart down the slope. I was down to the bottom of that cliff in thirty seconds, and found myself with the Divisional Ammunition Column people, and all amongst boxes of high explosive. Ammunition Column Officers are there, but I begin to think it would have been safer up in the "bivvy," where the others still were, for they did not follow me. After a lull in the firing, I went up to the cliff, and half-way up they popped off again, and I was fortunate in finding a very safe dugout belonging to Major Horton, and he invited me in with Major Huskisson, Major Shorto, Poole, and Weatherall. And while shells still come over, first bursting on the beach, then in the sea, then on the top of our cliff, and then on the high ground on the back of the beach, we have lunch.

⌒⌒

11. The ANZAC Experience

On our arrival at Gaba Tepe [Gallipoli area] (Anzac),we were joined by our 15th squadron plus the 50 men who had been detailed and bodyguard to the C. in C. The regiment was consequently about 540 strong when it took over the trench work. . . .

The work in the posts consists of observation and sniping. . . . usually working in pairs in a small area of the trench. Periscopes and periscope rifles are used in the day time, especially on exposed faces but it is on order that at night time the ordinary rifle must be used direct over the sand bags or dirt which form the parapet. If the ground is at all favourable night sentry posts are pushed out in front of these main posts which really resemble redoubts more than ordinary . . . trenches. On two of our posts we have an all round defence.

These posts which were occupied in the first instance by the landing parties and which were immediately put in a state of defence had to be converted later into more permanent works. Naturally the subsequent work in the strengthening of these posts had to be re-sited and improved with the result that the squadron on duty, in addition to finding men for observation and sniping had the greater part of its personnel deepening the existing trenches, traversing and recessing (mostly with sandbags), cleaning the fields of fire and giving men timely cover from . . . fire. . . .

III.11   From "Daily Trench Life for Otago Mounted Rifles Regiment," *Australian Imperial Force Unit War Diaries 1914–1918. New Zealand Units.* Reprinted with permission of The Australian Army History Unit and The New Zealand Defence Force.

The posts being self-contained and the personnel being engaged in the fort, men who are cooking and sleeping were constantly in the road of the men who were working. To meet this a small picquet resting place has been arranged close to and in the . . . entrance to the different works. . . .

On the Alarm sounding in the bivouac every group goes to its previously arranged fighting station, either in the forts or in the connecting works.

The regiment is bivouaced between the outpost and the sea (the sea is about 200 yds from the outpost line). The flat ground (about 150 yards) cannot be used on account of Turk snipers and shell fire—so that the bivouac is on the steep slope of the hills which form the posts and in all cases the men live in "dug-outs"— which are narrow . . . but which give little head cover (except for the head itself) the trunk and the body hang liable to shrapnel.

The bivouac area is very restricted but it was chosen in the first instance to give shelter from gun fire from the high trenches on Walker's Ridge. After we had been in this position the battery from Anafarta opened out and we found that we were just in the safety angle from this gun fire also.

Unaimed bullets from Quinn's Post to Walker's Ridge are continually dropping on the bivouac . . . but we have been remarkably free from the effects of all fire in the bivouac.

The guns from Anafarta shell us almost daily. . . .

Our water and stores are brought into our bivouacs by the Indian Mule Transport Corps. Our communication trench does not allow the mules entry— consequently we need to wait for darkness and fetch the stores along the beach. The evening, although constantly firing at the times of this supply trains passage, has inflicted no damage to speak of.

The water ration is $\frac{1}{2}$ gallon per man per diem, and this seems to be enough— although it is supplemented by sea-water—for body-cleansing and for washing clothes. The use of sea-water can only take place after dark on acct. [account] of snipers. . . .

The rations at present seem ample and of a very good quality and they consist of:

1 lb. biscuit or bread	3 oz. cheese
1 lb. meat—preserved or fresh	3 oz sugar
¼ lb ham	5/8 oz. tea
¼ lb bacon	$\frac{1}{2}$ lb dried vegetables (or fresh) (fresh onions and potatoes on issue now) . . .

The general health of the men is very good. Diarrhea has been constantly treated by our surgeon but enteric is unknown at present.

The site of the camp, which is clean fresh ground and the proximity of the sea-beach where men can bathe, may account for part of the immunity from disease . . .

Prevalence of flies in large numbers has to be combated—especially where men live in a very restricted are, but well-covered latrines, incinerators depots for empty meat and jam tins and such precautions have done much to keep the bivouac healthy.

Latrines have been dug and used by squadrons, in different squadron areas, with urine pits alongside. The troops (for the first time in my experience) take a pride in keeping and using these conveniences.

Shallow and narrow trenches, across which the men could straddle, proved to be the best and these required to be dug every second day—where each man defaccating [sic] immediately covered his excreta with earth.

Deep, narrow trenches, by way of keeping paper from blowing about were not so good, in that the men always seemed to prefer one place in these latrines and a uniform depth of trench was not maintained. . . .

No disinfectants of any sort have been used. Earth alone doing this work, with splendid results.

From the foregoing diary it will be seen that this regiment—trained for nine months as Mounted men—have been engaged almost exclusively in digging Fire and Communication trenches, opening up roads to bivouacs, occupying and fighting in outpost (trenched) positions, in throwing bombs, in sapping and countersapping, erecting barbed-wire entanglements and other works of a like nature. Most of this work has been done after dusk and before dawn (which including the moonlit nights) and has generally meant about 5 hours nightly.

This work has all been done at close quarters to an enterprising enemy, whose markmanship was good and who could always anticipate the opponent's move easily.

✍

12. The Turkish Defense

November 4, 1915—Thursday

13:30 hours—Am summoned by Battalion. Go. Commander wants me to pin-point enemy machine-gun on *Adana Slope*. Proceed to observation-post. It is in an underground chamber with a hole of 50 centimeters in diameter in center of ceiling. Its walls are at least a meter-and-a-half thick. Embrasure [from where machine-gun fires] is one-and-a-half meters long. A ladder enables one to climb up to the hole.

Climb up, install large observation-periscope there and get to work. It is getting progressively darker and there is some light rain. These conditions affect visibility and render observation difficult. Enemy trenches form a spur pointing at us. Our trenches are glaringly exposed from the rear [i.e. they do not provide cover from the rear]. Enemy seems to have only one line of trenches. However, on the right

III.12   From Mehmed Fasih, *Lone Pine (Bloody Ridge) Diary of Lt. Mehmed Fasih, 5th Imperial Ottoman Empire, Gallipoli, 1915* (Istanbul: Denizler Kitabevi, 2001), 56–61. Reprinted with permission.

they have two lines. The areas behind their trenches are visible. Fairly high mounds of earth have been piled up. This soil probably comes from the saps the enemy has been digging. A few large loop-holes can easily be spotted. From time to time, green flames spout from these. Shortly following each flash, one can see dust rising from our sand-bags. The enemy machine-gun on Gültepe [Rose Hill] in action. . . . Our machine-gun has now also opened fire. Its shots are slightly short [of target]. Tell them to lengthen the range slightly. They adjust their fire. Due to increasing darkness, can't tell whether they are now on target. . . .

Last night enemy grenades damaged covered communication trench we had just repaired. Request a machine-gun from Battalion. Alas! . . . Battalion Commander is busy. Having a dug-out, equipped with a door, built for himself. A land-slide in this area would turn many of our men into "pastirma" [dried beef flavoured with thick protective paste made of garlic, cumin, and other spices] . . . All very fine, but where are the resources for such work? Battalions, regiments, divisions are housed in mansions. But what about officers and men in front lines? . . . [They remain] in utter misery. . . .

20.30 hrs—Firing intensifies to our left. It spreads to entire front. Run out to trenches. Our soldiers are blazing away. Our left wing is really getting it. Enemy raining grenades. Thank God, they are not falling inside trenches. Enemy makes extensive use of flares to illuminate both our rear and front-lines. We benefit from this light as much as he does. His grenades are really pouring in. Tour trenches . . . Fear we shall reap the whirlwind.

21:00 hrs—From our left comes the "Allah! Allah!" rallying cry of our soldiers, followed by noise, then silence. . . . Suddenly, intense firing erupts. . . . Our 77th Regiment is apparently carrying out a probe [to test enemy reactions]. From time to time, feed information back to Battalion Commander. He passes it on to Regiment. Grenades continue pouring-down on rear.

21:30 hrs—Firing eases up. A few men from the 125th Company come over to find out what is going on. I tell them. Then inspect trenches. My men are performing their duties. Noncoms also. Am delighted. . . .

01:00 hrs—Am sleepy. Have not slept for two nights. However, must stay awake tonight. This is important. On 28 May 1915, enemy had launched his offensive after midnight. Hunt lice for a while, then stretch out. Unwittingly, fall asleep. . . .

November 5, 1915—Friday

05:30 hrs—Tour trenches. Am delighted by hard work and sense of duty of my company. Return to my place. Have tea and smoke water-pipe. Extreme calm prevails. The odd dumdum bullet continues to ring out in gullies. Yet, in comparison with last night's uproar it now is very quiet. Glorious daylight bathes everything. . . . Oh, for the bitter-sweet memories of days which have now become fantasies of our imagination! . . .

06.13 hrs—First enemy grenade just lobbed at us. Still, they are few . . . And have now stopped. Only the screeches of dumdums rise from gullies.

06:30 hrs—Hear artillery fire on our right. No grenades. Infantry fire and occasional machine-gun burst continue.

06:53 hrs—Grenade hits patio in front of my dug-out. No casualties. But fragments rattle on tin roof which extends there. Hearing this noise, enemy is under impression there might be something important in area. Thus, within two minutes, a second grenade follows. This time, one of my sergeants gets in the way. As he approaches with some orders, he is wounded in throat. . . .

08:00 hrs—Reach reserve positions and take all necessary measures [to settle in]. Battalion Commander calls me to accompany him on tour of trenches.

He points to a lovely spot and comments, "We shall relax here with our water-pipe. . . .

We start our tour.

The trenches have been properly dug. We go to positions on the eastern slope of Hulusidere [Hulusi Gully]. The trenches in this sector protect the rear of our present positions. As we proceed, I notice a group of first-aid men gathered around a stretcher. From inside the trench, ask them what is going on. "It is Sergeant *Nuri*, from 5th Company," they reply. "Dead or wounded?", I ask. "Dead!" comes the answer. Climb out of trench and join them.

Oh, my God! . . . What further tragedies are you going to make me witness? . . .*Nuri* has injuries to his chest, head, an arm and both legs. Both head and chest are ripped open. His hair is all mussed up, his uniform soaked in blood. He is pale. His mouth is partially open. One can see his white teeth between his lips. His eyes are half-open, staring at the sky. The purity of his handsome features is still evident. His hands are locked together on his chest. . . . He seems to be reproaching those who destroyed him. I can't stand it any more. What sorrow! . . .

"Are you going to continue roaming in places where you have no business and can't protect yourself?" This child was responsible for drilling the Battalion's replacements. He had absolutely no business in the front-lines. However, during lunch breaks, he would not stay put. He would come by: to open an embrasure here, fix a path there, bring up ammunition—roaming around to see what he could do to be of help. . . .

He had come all the way from *Erzurum* [main garrison town near Turkey's border with the Caucasus] to fight this war . . .

The loss of such a soldier upset me greatly. Have already witnessed so many deaths and tragedies. But none affected me to this extent. As a matter of fact, very few upset me any more. This is one of them. . . .

I send the remains to the cemetery while I collect a burial party. Obtain permission of Medical Corps to bury him in the officer's plot in the olive grove at *Karaburun* [Black Point] gully. Pick a spot under a fine olive tree, on the rim of the gully, and have the men dig his grave. In this place lie many of our martyrs, of whom *Nuri* is now one. We place his body in the grave so his head will be under the branches of the tree, while his feet point towards the opposite slope of the gully.

Gather many branches of olive and laurel trees and pile them around the body of the sergeant I appreciated so much. As I gaze at his face, my sorrow overwhelms me so that when I throw into the grave the first handful of earth, I break down.

Allow my tears to flow freely and, terribly upset, address *Nuri*, "Oh my son! It is awfully difficult for me to put you to rest in this soil. As I contemplate you there, my eyes can see nothing else." All those present were now crying, as I was. One of his comrades tells us that when they had arrived at the front together, *Nuri* had said, "I implore God to allow me to become a martyr." O *Nuri*! If that was so, you certainly achieved your wish in a big way!

We bury *Nuri* . . . It was God's will that I would be the one to bury his remains. Who knows who else I will be burying? After the last shovel of earth, I conduct our religious rites. As I recite the opening verse of the "Koran", with all the compassion, conviction and eloquence I can muster, I again find it most difficult to control myself. Warm tears stream down my cheeks. As everything must, this also ends.

∽

13. Palestine Campaigns

During the next two weeks we remained camped in the olive grove outside Ludd with all the horses belonging to our Brigade, while the latter was fighting in the hills to the north. It was hard work for our men in the plain, as each had six horses to groom, water, feed and exercise, and, as usual, the old septic-sore trouble made its appearance again. We sent up supplies daily to our Field Ambulance, and for the time being lived in comparative comfort in the olive grove. At this time railhead was near Gaza, and one had to send a considerable distance in order to fetch remounts, reinforcements or new equipment. In this Palestine campaign it always seemed that the private soldier required a good deal of initiative apart from fighting, owing to the lack of communications and the great area over which at this time our force was spread. I remember sending two A.S.C. drivers with orders to proceed to Gaza, a distance of 42 miles across country, via Yebna, Burka, Beit Duras, Mejdal, and Deir Sineid, in order to bring up some fresh wagons [sic], with remounts and drafts. At that time there was no road properly connecting these places, and the men had instructions to water wherever it was possible and to make their own arrangements en route. For some reason or other we suffered very much at this time from a match famine; the former were not required for smoking, as we had had no tobacco ration for a considerable time, but the question of fire for kindling purposes was becoming acute. When we had had this trouble at Latron there was always

III.13   From Captain O. Teichman, *Diary of a Yeomanry M.O.: Egypt, Gallipoli, Palestine and Italy* (London: T. Fisher Unwin, 1921), 202–207, 237–245.

the holy fire in the monastery of the Penitent Thief which could be utilized; this fire was said to have been burning continuously for some thousand or more years, and an Australian Light Horse trooper was heard to remark that it was about time someone blew it out! We were now well into the rainy season, and our olive grove became a bog, and most of the roads in the vicinity became impassable for wheels, which had a bad effect on the arrival of our rations. We felt this ration shortage particularly at the time, as reinforcements kept arriving from Gaza to be attached to the Field Ambulance without any warning, having expended their own three days' rations en route. Owing to the large number of dead horses and camels in the vicinity of Ludd, the jackals, as usual, made the night hideous with their shrieks and laughter. The old town of Ludd was of considerable interest, especially the early Christian church of St. George. On December 10th we heard that Jerusalem had surrendered, and the Jews and Greeks living in Ludd were hilarious in their rejoicings. On the following day the Fifty-fourth Division, who were fighting in the north, to the west of our line, were attacked, but drove the enemy back; this was followed by heavy artillery fire on both sides. During our stay in the olive grove Fritz visited the neighbourhood of Ludd daily, and we witnessed some good air fights. On one occasion a motor-lorry was entering Ludd from Ramleh; the two drivers were buying oranges at a neighbouring stall, and while so doing some natives commenced to loot the contents of the lorry. Fritz came over, dropped his bomb, and killed the natives, obviously a just punishment for the latter.

One morning the Third Australian Light Horse Brigade in their camp at Surafend suffered considerably, having eighty horses killed while at water. The Anzac Receiving Station, which had been at Ramleh, was moved at this time, and we now had to send back 42 miles to Deir Sineid for our medical stores. The camels did not do well in the wet weather, and most mornings one was informed by the sergeant in charge of these animals that another one had "passed away" in the night. After being about ten days in this camp we found that a Turkish long-range gun was beginning to drop an occasional shell at the end of our plantation, and therefore we moved to a more salubrious and drier position on the sand, closer to the Ludd road. Reports received from our Brigade in the line stated that things were fairly quiet, except for sniping, and casualties were not numerous. A rumour was current that 40,000 Bulgars were on their way down to our front. On December 13th we received an interesting summary of intelligence compiled by Desert Mounted Corps Headquarters. This told us all about the surrender of Jerusalem, and of the fighting which had recently been going on outside the Holy City. The Turkish newspapers stated that as a result of the Russian peace 40,000 Turkish troops were on their way down to Palestine from the Caucasus. On December 15th the whole of the Brigade led horses and transport, together with a comparatively small number of officers and O.R.'s [Other Ranks], left Ludd for Deiran; as we rode out of the former town we could see the Fifty-fourth Division heavily engaged a few miles to the north. We took the road through Ramleh, crossing the Jaffa–Jerusalem road, and for the first mile or so our route lay amongst wheat and olive groves; a little later we found ourselves riding through miles and miles of orange groves, heavily laden with fruit. These were the famous Jaffa oranges, and appeared to be cultivated most carefully. There were numerous nurseries where the trees could be seen in various stages, and a wonderful system of irrigation had been installed in the grove, consisting of large reservoirs, pumping engines, iron water-pipes and cement channels, the latter bifurcating in all directions in order to carry the water to every single tree. The earth was of a rich red colour, and the countryside also supported lemon groves, vineyards and almond fields. It seemed to us indeed a land of peace and plenty. Homely looking white farm-houses, with red-tiled roofs, peeped through the foliage, and cleanly dressed, fair-skinned European Jews came out of their houses as we passed. The largest oranges, of superb quality, were being sold at forty for a shilling, but there appeared at that time to be no objection to our men picking as many as they liked without payment. When one looked at these large orange farms and the cheerful well-fed European inhabitants, one could not help thinking with some amazement of the stories which had been circulated in the East, describing how the Turk had maltreated all but the Mohammedan population in Palestine. After riding for miles through these delightful surroundings, through air heavily scented with almond and orange blossom (we noted that the orange-tree flow-ered and bore fruit at the same time), the lane which we were traversing led out on to some open grassy country about half a mile west of the important Jewish settlement Deiran (Hebrew, Rehoboth).

Here we each pitched our camp, and began to hope that the personnel of our various units would soon join us, when they were relieved on the hills, and enjoy the luxuries of this fertile plain. In the distance we could see excellent grazing for our horses, and across the down-like land to the south lay the raised town of Yebna and the villages of new and old Akir. That night several of us walked into Deiran, where we repaired to the "hotel" Kliwitzky, an excellent restaurant, kept by a Russian Jew. We had not sat down to a meal at a table with a tablecloth for many months, and here we enjoyed a most excellent five-course dinner, served up in a spotlessly clean way. Dinner was followed by two sorts of port wine, made by the Jews, which was very much appreciated. The village of Deiran appeared to be pop-ulated by Jews from nearly every European country, who controlled the extensive orange, wine and almond trade in this fertile district. The houses were well built and the inhabitants seemed prosperous. There was an excellent water supply and pumping station, the water being laid on to every house, a thing which seemed to us hardly conceivable in Palestine. While at dinner, many Jews came in and were anxious to inquire from us how things were going, especially those whose vine-yards and orange groves were north of Jaffa and still in the hands of the Turks. On the following day we visited the village again, and were very struck, in the daylight, with its picturesque aspect. With its large number of cypress-trees and white houses it reminded one of an Italian scene. We were delighted to find the Field Cashier, generally a very elusive person, whom we had not seen for many months, installed in the town hall. It was quite a strange feeling to be in a place again where money was of some use. We found Desert Mounted Corps Headquarters established in a very fine house, owned by the mayor, in the upper part of the village, and were allowed to study the large flag maps which showed the position of every unit on the Palestine front, including those belonging to the enemy. It seemed wonderful to us how the Intelligence people always managed to know where the various enemy units were situate, including those which were some way behind his front line. Between our camp and the village was a mighty winepress, in the central yard of which we found ample water for our horses. In one of the buildings connected with the winepress it was possible to utilize the numerous vats as baths for the men. During this time we only suffered from one shortage, that of wood. We sent our native camel-drivers out to scour the neighbourhood, but with little success. There were naturally strict orders against cutting down trees, as these were all fruit-bearing. Eventually the only way we could obtain sufficient wood was to steal it from the supplies of wood captured on the railway near Ludd; these were carefully guarded, but still there were ways of obtaining it. The weather was now very wet, and the mortality amongst the camels and native camel-drivers increased. Although we had no tents, we were able to keep ourselves fairly dry with our bivouac sheets by digging into the side of the hills. South of our camp lay the Yebna-Mughar plain, where the Sixth Mounted Brigade made their famous charge. Standing on the Mughar Ridge and looking down on the plain beneath, it seemed almost inconceivable why the Turkish machine guns on the summit, aided by about 2,000 infantry, were unable to repel the yeomen's charge about a month previously. During these days we used to evacuate our casualties due east cross-country to Junction Station.

Owing to the state of the road it became necessary to use eight mules for one light ambulance waggon [sic], and it took them almost a day to complete the journey one way. . . .

May 2nd

The position was now a curious one. We had captured Es Salt, Divisional Headquarters were in that town, two Australian and our Yeomanry Brigade were disposed around it, and the enemy was attacking us from Ammam [sic—Amman] and Howeij. The infantry division had, after heavy casualties, failed to open up the road through Nimrim, El Haud and Howeij to the Shaib Valley. The track we had come up by had been closed by the enemy, who had drawn a sort of net round us. It had been hoped that by the time we had captured Es Salt it would have been possible to open up communication with the Jordan Valley by the Jericho road, which was a good one and capable of carrying heavy transport. Our intervening position on this road, between Ammam and Howeij, prevented the enemy to a certain extent from getting supplies and ammunition, although they were able to get a certain amount of both by circumventing us to the south-east. It was evident that the enemy would do his best to join hands with the Ammam force, and by so

doing annihilate our Division. At 9 a.m. it was decided by our Divisional General
in Es Salt that the Howeij bridge and position must be forced and the road opened
to the Jordan Valley. Rations for men and horses were finished, but there was still
some grazing, and we had managed to seize a few cattle belonging to the natives.
The two Australian Brigades being already busily occupied, one of them holding
off the Turkish Ammam force, it fell to our Brigade to attempt the task of taking
Howeij hill. On walking a short distance along the road above the Wadi Shaib
[a dry stream bed], one could see a few miles away the position which we were to
attack a steep grassy hill some 300 feet high, with a large open valley before it, lined
by a number of guns, whose shells were falling on the road below. Orders were
issued to the Gloucester Yeomanry to advance on the right of the road and take up
a position a few hundred yards from the bridge. The Sherwood Rangers and the
Worcester Yeomanry were ordered to attack the hill on the left of the road and, if
successful, open up the latter to Jericho. After leaving our horses in the bivouac in
the valley we were a very small force, and taking with us only the Hotchkiss gun
pack-horses, we proceeded under the cliffs of the Wadi Shaib for a short distance,
but soon discovered that we should be under observation the whole way to our
objective. Accordingly, we struck east for some four hours, climbing up and down
the mountain sides, and crossing many beautiful glens and streams bordered by
masses of giant oleanders, hollyhocks and roses, until we eventually reached a high
position whence we could see our objective, the guns on which were shelling the
troops on the right-hand side of the valley. The Turks had several 5.9 guns in
action, our only artillery being the little mountain mule battery, which was in
action behind the Gloucesters. One could not help feeling that our attack was
doomed to failure; we were two regiments, far below strength, about to cross an
open valley and then ascend a grassy hill, which was so steep that it would be difficult to obtain a foothold. However, the order had been given and the attack must
be carried out. We had been unable to keep our Hotchkiss guns with us, as some
hours before the ascent had been so steep that one horse had slipped and gone
hurtling down to the valley below, and the rest were unable to get any further. As
we took a breather for ten minutes preparatory to the attack, sitting amongst the
most beautiful flowers, under a cloudless blue sky, one realized what a waste it
would be that very soon many of us would be lying dead in the valley below, never
able to enjoy the beauties of nature again. During this brief interval the Turkish
cavalry were seen on a ridge to our left, and the order was given to advance. As we
descended the hill in very open order and began to cross the valley, we were met
with very heavy H.E. and shrapnel fire, which apparently came from behind the
Howeij hill. Every rock, behind which we naturally took cover as we advanced,
seemed to be marked, the second shell killing two of our officers and casualties
resulting in every part of the field. A little later, rifle fire broke out, but we were
unable to see a single one of the enemy, and, as one of our men remarked, they
could have kept us off that steep hill simply by rolling stones down on to us. My
first batch of casualties I collected in a cave, and then with some difficulty slid
them down a steep grassy bank some 100 feet to the stream below; this we found

was the Wadi Shaib, and we established a dressing station in a little stone water-mill. Unfortunately, as more wounded were collected there, the Turks noticed the concentration and dropped a shell on to the roof of the mill, and even at this moment a badly wounded man burst out laughing when his companion was covered with flour. Meanwhile our attack was progressing, but it soon became evident that no live man could ever reach the top of Howeij hill. The mill being now untenable as a dressing station, we transferred our wounded with some difficulty through the mill-stream, which was four feet deep, to the opposite side. We had only got our small cavalry stretchers, but these proved invaluable over the rocky ground, and by relays the wounded were carried through some fields to the main road just behind the barricade held by some Gloucester stalwarts. Although we had some more men wounded while our stretcher parties were ascending to the road, as soon as we were identified as stretcher parties the enemy ceased to shell us. The road having been reached, we placed our wounded in some of the German motor-cars, driven by Germans, and evacuated the former to Es Salt. On returning to collect our last wounded from the mill under Howeij hill, we found that the remains of our regiment and the Sherwoods had been forced to retire, as the task before them was absolutely impossible. The whole attack was doomed to failure, and the veriest tyro [inexperienced soldier] standing on the opposite hill would have realized that such a small body of men would be unable to take the position, which was so strongly held. We were unable to collect our dead, but managed eventually to bring all the wounded in under cover of the well-grown barley. On returning along the road some 3 miles towards our old bivouac, a few final shells fell amongst us from the Howeij hill as we straggled along. It had been a sad and tiring day, a forlorn hope doomed to failure from the first, and we had nothing to show except casualties. Australian Brigades had co-operated and tried to get through in our vicinity, but we were unable to see them during the day. At night our rations had given out, but we were able to make a fairly decent meal out of goats and green figs. A message was read from an official source saying that Es Salt must be held at all costs, and that reinforcements for the Turks were fast approaching from Ammam.

May 3rd

It appeared that we were completely cut off, owing to the nature of the ground and the Turkish reinforcements. During the morning, rifle and gun fire seemed to come from all directions, and later on Fritz bombed us up and down the Es Salt–Shaib Valley. An uneasy feeling prevailed, especially as it became known that large reinforcements were on their way from Damascus, via Ammam [sic], and some fighting took place on the Ammam [sic] road between an Australian Brigade and Turkish infantry during the afternoon. Our mounted patrols, who were high up on the hill on the opposite side of our valley, reported the presence of some Turkish cavalry regiments on the mountains a few miles away. At 6 p.m. secret orders were issued to each regiment that it was to make the best of its way to the Jordan Valley, which sounded like a general *sauve qui peut* [every man for himself]. Our Second-in-Command had a short time before managed to reconnoitre a fresh track towards the west, and it devolved upon him to act as guide to the Brigade. At 6.30 p.m. part of a donkey convoy of biscuits, which had been some days en route, managed to get through to us, escorted by a few Indian cavalry and yeomanry, a troop of which had been cut up. The Turkish hospital at Es Salt was now full of wounded from our two Divisions (Anzac and Australian Mounted), and the question was how to get them and our prisoners through the enemy's cordon down to the Jordan plain. The wounded men were tied on to horses and camels and sent down the only partially opened track under escort, before the main body moved. They were attacked, chiefly by irregulars, and had to fight their way through: it must have been an awful journey for the badly wounded, especially when their horses were stampeded by some Bedouin, who suddenly opened fire on them. At 7 p.m. we called our mounted patrols down from the opposite hills, and an hour later, after making up large camp fires, we left our bivouac and proceeded along the highroad on the right of the Wadi Shaib. It was our regiment's duty to do rear-guard, and when the usual halts, owing to the blocking of the road by someone in front, took place one felt very uncomfortable, as it was expected that the enemy, as soon as they found our camp empty, would charge down the road. Before reaching the barricade across the road, near the Howeij bridge, our column turned right-handed and struck a track across very broken country, which was particularly difficult to negotiate in the pitch dark.

May 4th

By 2 a.m. our Brigade had assembled in a cup-shaped depression on the top of the mountain, where commenced the Arsenyat track towards the Jordan. At 5 a. m. we were aware of other Australian Brigades on neighbouring hills, and the descent commenced. Each Brigade and regiment fought a rear-guard in turns, as the Turks were now pursuing us, at the same time picketing the hills on either side in order to protect the unit whose turn it was to go first; the latter then picketed the next hills and allowed the regiments which were following to pass through. The Turks, who had got wind of our intention, and were out in considerable numbers and with machine guns and mountain guns on the various peaks, tried to hinder our retreat. Most of the way it was a gallop across very rocky ground and down descents where in quieter moments one would probably have led one's horse. Every now and then, as one came round a corner, one would find oneself under fire from some little mountain gun, the explosions of whose shells had a very small range and did not do much harm. Our outposts on the heights kept off the enemy infantry to the last moment, and then came scuttling down to join our main body. Our wounded we had to tie on to horses and get them along as best we could. As the sun rose Fritz came

over and added to our discomfiture by bombing us as we descended the narrow
ravines. Much equipment was lost, and the tracks in our wake were strewn with
tin hats, sun-helmets, ammunition, dead horses, etc., but on the whole it was
said the retirement was carried out according to plan. As we descended one felt
the awful Dead Sea atmosphere again a great contrast from the clear mountain
air which we had been living in for the last few days. My last casualty we picked
up just before debouching into the plain, and it was an uncomfortable sensation remaining behind while attending to him and tying him on to a horse, as
Fritz was still overhead and the enemy, who were following our retreat, were
still busy. However, our Brigade Commander was the last to leave the hills, and
would not gallop into the plain until he had seen his three regiments clear. As
our small party eventually made its appearance in the open, we were met by a
salvo from the Turkish guns, but by galloping in extended order we managed to
put about 4 miles between us and the hills in a very short time. Our escape
from the hills to the plain was facilitated by the Sixtieth Division, who diverted
the enemy's attention to a large extent by attacking Shunet Nimrim and the
hills on the right of the Arsenyat track. After watering in the Nimrim brook,
close to the spot where it flows into the Jordan, we crossed the latter river by
the pontoon bridge, and after a long ride over the dusty plain eventually arrived
at our old bivouac below Tel El Sultan, behind the Wadi Auja outpost line.
With the exception of the prisoners captured by our force, some of whom had
been killed by the fire from their own guns as they were driven before us into
the plain, the whole thing had been a costly failure. It had been a gamble on the
fall of Nimrim and on the assistance of the Arabs which did not mature, consequently a quick retirement had to be undertaken in order to prevent further
disaster. We now heard of the experiences which our Third and Fourth
Brigades had had when they were pushed up east of Jordan towards the north.
When they had passed the line held by the Imperial Camel Corps west of
Jordan, on the opposite bank, and were engaged with the enemy, the latter,
crossing the river from the western side by a pontoon bridge, had attacked
them in the rear. Two batteries which accompanied these Brigades had suffered
heavily while in the foothills, and had to abandon seven of their guns. Some of
our dismounted men whom we had left in camp a week ago had been called
out with various oddments in order to strengthen these Brigades, and they told
us how the enemy cavalry had pursued them during the retreat. It now
appeared that the whole of our sudden move had a political meaning. On
April 23rd a Meccan force of 7,000 rifles were said to have captured Madeba
(18 miles south-west of Ammam), and it was reported that the Arabs east of
Jordan, including the Beni Sakhr tribe, were ready to side with us. Hence the
hurry and rush from Jaffa to Jericho in order to clear up the Es Salt–Madeba–
Ammam triangle, as it was said that it only needed a spark from the British
mounted troops to set the whole country ablaze and finally destroy the Hedjaz
Railway. But the result had been a fiasco; one wondered whether the whole
thing had not been a German or Turkish ruse. Had the Meccans ever taken

Madeba? Was the message sent through native sources merely in order to lure our troops on while large reinforcements were coming down the railway line to Ammam [sic]? A few days later we read the following "official" in the *Egyptian News*:

> Between April 30th and May 4th a mixed force of cavalry and infantry carried out a successful operation east of Jordan. The enemy, who were holding a strong position defending the Ghoraniye–Es Salt road, about Shunet Nimrim, were contained by our infantry, whilst the cavalry, moving rapidly northwards up the east bank of the Jordan, entered Es Salt from the north and west. Three hundred and thirty prisoners, including 33 Germans, were taken, and much valuable war material, including six motor-lorries and a motor-car, was destroyed. During the night of the 3rd–4th May we withdrew to the plain on the east bank of Jordan, and on the night of the 4th–5th May our troops returned to their positions on the original bridge-head. During the operation our total captures amounted to 46 officers and 885 O.R.'s and 29 machine guns.

This somewhat bald narrative did not quite coincide with our experiences, and few of us would have described the operation, at any rate the part we saw, as "successful." It was said that most of the machine guns captured had been found packed in cases at Es Salt, where they had been left. We wondered what the native population of Es Salt would think when the next raid took place and we occupied the town again. We were afraid that the chits on which we had requisitioned for goats and sheep would not be honoured by the Turkish commander!

For the next week we remained in the same position, our Division suffering considerably from Fritz's visits, one Brigade sustaining as many as eighty casualties in four days. An attack was daily expected on the Auja outpost line, west of Jordan, at that time held by the Imperial Camel Corps, and our regiments took it in turn to provide working parties and reinforcements. Several Indian Cavalry Brigades arrived in the valley, and were amalgamated with the yeomanry regiments in a proportion of two to one. We were taken out of the Fifth Mounted Brigade, which had been temporarily re-formed, and the latter now became a composite brigade, consisting of the Gloucesters and two native cavalry regiments. Every day the heat seemed to increase, and yet we were not really into the summer yet. Scorpions, tarantulas, mosquitoes, flies, dust and thorns, and the oppressive heat will ever remain in one's memory when one thinks of the old Jordan Valley. In the evening we used to climb the hills on our left and get a view over the Wadi Auja towards Redhill, held by the Turks. On these walks one saw a certain amount of animal life, including vultures, who nested amongst the rocks, rock-pigeons and hares. On May 10th we received orders to rejoin the Twentieth Corps, with Headquarters at Jerusalem.

Africa and Asia

From the perspective of the great powers, the campaigns in Africa and Asia raised not only issues of distance, communication, and supply, but also of race and colonial authority. These potentially volatile questions, often avoided or discussed in vague or allusive ways, are confronted head-on by Sol Plaatje. Plaatje, an exceptionally talented linguist, was one of the premier black South African journalists and writers of his generation. He was also the first general secretary to the South African Native National Congress (the forerunner of today's African National Congress), which was founded in 1912 to mobilize opinion of support of political rights for South Africa's people of color. The second document, from the memoirs of a white South African medical officer, details some of the daily realities of campaigning in Africa. A broader perspective on the African contribution to the war is deployed in the third selection, a December 1918 petition by the South African Native National Congress to Britain's King George V, outlining exactly how the native population had proven its worth and why the racially discriminatory system in South Africa must be reformed.

Threats to the imperial order in Asia were thrown into sharp relief by Japanese incursions in China. Since 1898, Germany had maintained a concession around the Chinese port of Qingdao (referred to as Tsingtau by the German administration), which came under attack from Japanese forces in October 1914. Jefferson Jones was an American reporter from the *Minneapolis Journal* who accompanied the Japanese troops and recorded these impressions of the battle. The capture of Tsingtao and sections of Shandong province were the prelude to a determined effort by the Japanese to extend their own influence within China. Japanese military and political leaders had watched with dismay the imperial ambitions of the European powers in their own backyard and believed that exploitation of China's resources was essential to Japan's own ascendancy to great-power status. To that end, in January 1915, Japan dictated the 21 demands reprinted below to the Chinese republican government. Still emerging from revolution and torn by strife among warlords, China was in no position to reject them all. In May 1915 it agreed to a pared-down list of thirteen demands.

14. The Use of Native Troops

The Natives and the Cape coloured Afrikanders were not alone in tendering loyal offers of service to the Government. The Indians of Natal and other coloured residents likewise offered their services to the Government, besides subscribing liberally according to their means to the various war funds. The St. Helenians of

III.14   From Sol Plaatje, *Native Life in South Africa* (London: P.S. King, n.d. 1916?), 279–283.

Capetown passed the following resolutions, which Mr. S. Reagon, the secretary, forwarded to the Government:—

(1) That this meeting of St. Helenians expresses its unswerving and devoted loyalty to His Majesty King George and His Governments.

(2) That it expresses its full confidence in the Union Government in the present crisis through which the Empire and Union are passing, and congratulates General Botha, and expresses its deep appreciation of his practical patriotism in having taken command of the Union Forces in the field.

(3) That the services of the Association and its members be hereby offered to the Union Government in whatever manner they may be of assistance to ensure the triumph of the Empire and for the maintenance of law and order.

Shortly after the outbreak of the present war, Dr. Abdurahman offered the Government the services of the 5,000 coloured warriors recruited through the A.P.O., and General Smuts replied that the offer was under consideration. Meanwhile the A.P.O. recruiting agency had been continuing its work, and no fewer than 13,000 coloured men had sent in their names and addresses and signified their intention to take the field. So Mr. Fredericks, the secretary of the A.P.O., wrote once more to General Smuts, on October 23, offering the services of these men in the name of the Coloured People's Organization. This offer brought forth the following definite reply, which is couched in identical terms to the one sent on the same date to Dr. Rubusana, who wrote offering the services of 5,000 Natives: —

Department of Defence, Pretoria, November 6, 1914.

Sir,—With reference to your letter of the 23rd ult., I beg to inform you that the Union Government greatly appreciates the offer of service of the Cape coloured people.

I am, however, to refer you to the provisions of Section 7 of the South African Defence Act, 1912, and to state that the Government does not desire to avail itself of the services in a combatant capacity of citizens not of European descent in the present hostilities. Apart from other considerations, the present war is one which has its origin among the white peoples of Europe, and the Government is anxious to avoid the employment of coloured citizens in a warfare against whites.

No doubt the Government of British South Africa was actuated by the loftiest motives in rejecting voluntary offers of service from citizens of non-European descent; but it is clear that such a reply at such a time ought not to please many people in Great Britain who had to offer the cream of British manhood to defend their portion of the Empire, and then to offer in addition more men to lay down their lives for the safety of the Colonies, including South Africa, a land with thousands of able-bodied and experienced warriors who are willing to defend their own country. For the same reason this decision ought not to please our French Allies, who, besides sacrificing men and money on the battlefields of Continental Europe, must provide more men and money to guard their colonial possessions in different parts of the globe. This decision ought not also to cheer any one in Belgium, where fathers and mothers and their children are separated and starving, a nation living practically in exile, or in bondage, its brave monarch sojourning in foreign territory. On the other hand, if there is any one place where this decision of the Government of British South Africa would be hailed with the liveliest satisfaction, it is certainly Berlin, and that particularly after the bitter experiences of German troops in encounters with native African troops, both in Continental Europe and in East and West Africa.

Similarly this decision of the South African Government ought not to please the Boers themselves, inasmuch as, finding the request for volunteers amongst the whites failed to secure sufficient men, the Union Government had perforce to resort to coercion, in that some 300 Boers who refused to enlist for service in the expedition to German South West Africa were fined or imprisoned. This course, which is practically conscription, would have been unnecessary had the Union Government accepted the offered service of the 18,000 and more volunteers whom it curtly rejected.

The coloured people, judging by the letters that many of them have sent to the Press, felt humiliated to find that during the Empire's darkest hour a Government to which they pay taxation is publishing decisions that ought to wound the feelings of the Allies' sympathizers and give satisfaction to the enemy.

It is just possible that the Government refused the offer of the coloured people in deference to the wishes of a section of the white people of the Union; but judging from the African Press, that section, although somewhat noisy, was an infinitesimal one. This section, as is shown from the extract below, also discussed the voyage of the Indian troops to Europe. The *East Rand Express*, a paper published in one of the most important suburbs of Johannesburg, said:

COLOURED TROOPS AND THE WAR

The news that Great Britain intends to employ Indian native troops against the Germans has come as a shock to many South Africans. We can but hope the news is incorrect. In our opinion it would be a fatal mistake to use coloured troops against the whites, more especially as plenty of whites are available. From the English standpoint there is probably nothing offensive in the suggestion. Most Home people do not seem to see anything repugnant in black boxers fighting whites, but they have not had to live in the midst of a black population. If the Indians are used against the Germans it means that they will return to India disabused of the respect they should bear for the white race. The Empire must uphold the principle that a coloured man must not raise his hand against a white man if there is to be any law or order in either India, Africa, or any part of the Empire where the white man rules over a large concourse of coloured people. In South Africa it will mean that the Natives will secure pictures of whites being chased by coloured men, and who knows what harm such pictures may do? That France is employing coloured troops is no excuse. Two blacks in any sense do not make a white. The employment of native troops against Germany will be a hard blow on the prestige of the white man.

15. A Doctor in Damaraland

April 17, 1915

Our scouts tell us the Germans are concentrating along a front from Earibib to Tsaobis. They know we have over 30,000 men, but they say we are not to be feared, for our men are only "dissipated farmers and swineful fat-bellies.". . .

April 22, 1915

There are several Ovampos working in the camp. They belong to a wild Bantu tribe inhabiting the Portuguese border, and have not been subdued by the Germans. Our authorities are alive to the fact that these men, who have offered their services as drivers, may be German spies, although they profess to have a great hatred for them. These Ovampos have a peculiar custom of extracting the central incisor teeth top and bottom. The lateral incisors are then filed to a point, which gives them a very uncanny and ferocious expression.

   Today we have received definite orders to move out from Swakupmund on the 26th. This is very good news, for the place and delay have got on a good many nerves. Sand has blown into the wheels of the army, with resulting friction, and there has been a good deal of petty quarrelling, in which the medical service has figured largely. . . .

May 28, 1915

There has been a good deal of talk about mines since we have been here. To delay our advance, the Germans relied almost entirely upon this mode of fighting. On the line of advance to Karibib, in the bed of the Swakup, and along the road from Biet to Otjimbingwe, dynamite was placed in great quantity. Not only were these mines put in places where we were likely to go, such as drifts in riverbeds, or near wells, but the Huns also laid traps for us. A favourite ruse was to put a mine in a riverbed, and then near it to put up a notice, such as "Wasser 3 kilos." In these places we never found the water, but generally the mine. Another trick was to place a stick of dynamite above a house door, so that when the door was opened an explosion occurred. As soon as our men discovered this kind of practical joke, everybody was to be seen entering houses by the windows.

   The number of mines the Germans laid was very great. In one place alone between seventy and eighty were taken out. At Tsaobis we slept within a few yards of a large one which was subsequently accidentally exploded by a native. It was cunningly placed between the well and the river, and hundreds of people must have walked over it. By putting down so many the enemy defeated their own object, for our men became very quick at finding and avoiding the places where

III.15   From H.F.B. Walker, *A Doctor's Diary in Damaraland* (London: Edward Arnold, 1917), 52, 137–140.

they were. Later on, too, when so many failed to explode or did so little damage, we became more or less indifferent about them. In all only nine men lost their lives in this way, which was due in great measure to two causes, the first being the straggling, scattered way in which our troops moved, so that very few were near when a mine did explode; and, secondly, for some inexplicable reason the mines generally failed to explode at all, or only exploded after nearly everybody had passed, as in the case already mentioned, where an artillery column passed over safely, and the harmless water-cart and its driver, following far behind, were blown up. . . .

The Germans employed both contact and observation mines, using the latter only at very important points where they hoped to do great execution. I only heard of observation mines at two places, Biet being one; the other was the narrow neck of beach between the sand-dunes and the sea just south of Swakupmund, the only way our troops could approach the town from Walfisch. Contact mines were arranged in various ingenious ways, the commonest being exploded by connecting an innocent-looking peg or stump to a detonator consisting of sulphuric acid and a mixture of chlorate of potash and picric acid. These chemicals were in separate glass phials, and when the peg was touched the phials were broken and the resulting explosion fired the dynamite beneath. Another kind consisted of a small wooden box with a hinged lid, which was buried in the sand, with the lid propped open a little bit. As soon as any weight was placed on the sand-covered lid, the box closed and an electrical contact was made which fired the dynamite.

If anything, I think the mines encouraged our men to fight rather than the reverse. They considered it a very unsportsmanlike way of fighting. On one occasion in the Swakup, when the troops were very much done up and discouraged, a mine exploded, destroying the eyesight of one man and partially that of another. The effect on the troops was magical; every man forgot his fatigue and thought only of revenge. From the German point of view, too, the indiscriminate scattering of dynamite about could only be considered foolish; for it had no military significance, and only irritated their enemies. On one or two occasions our troops were made so angry by these pinpricks that they were with difficulty restrained from putting Germans to death who happened to be in their hands at the moment.

16. Petition to King George V

It would scarcely be necessary to recite the active part played by ourselves—Your Majesty's subjects—in the prosecution of the Great War, but the occasion and the purposes of this Memorial justify such a recital:—

(a) It will be remembered that up till August 1914 the National Congress had a Deputation of its men in London to petition Your Majesty to exercise the right of

III.16 From "Petition to King George V from the South African Native National Congress, 16 December 1918."

veto against the Natives Land Act 1913, and at the outbreak of hostilities in Europe, Congress prompted by a sense of loyalty to Your Majesty's Throne and the British Empire made representations to the Governor-General of the Union of South Africa informing His Excellency that the Bantu people were prepared to render every assistance in the defence of Your Majesty's Throne and Empire, which pledge was greatly appreciated by His Excellency, the Governor-General and High Commissioner of South Africa.

(b) We offered 5,000 strong men to go and fight the Germans in South-West Africa, but we regret to say that the offer was refused by His Excellency the Governor-General's Ministers of the Union of South Africa on the ground that this war was waged between white people only, whereas we were as vitally affected by the results of the war as any white subjects of Your Majesty.

(c) Thousands of our men went to German South West Africa as drivers and to assist in the Railway construction into that Territory for military purposes.

(d) It will be significant to everyone that during the trying and provocative times of the Rebellion in this country, we remained perfectly quiet and passive, without causing the slightest embarrassment to the Union Government, when difficult circumstances offered dangerous and ill-advised temptations to an oppressed people.

(e) 17,000 of our men took part in the campaign in German East Africa under the Right Honourable Lieutenant-General J.C. Smuts, Minister of Defence of the Union, and there participated in fighting and transport capacities—many of which died with malaria fever and suffered severe hardships and privations.

(f) We heartily responded to the call of your Majesty's Imperial Government and the Army Council, for 25,000 men to do manual work in the French docks, and behind the trenches in Flanders. Our men braved the oceans and endured the hardships of European cold weather, all under new and rough war conditions; 615 of our men sank in the S. S. *Mendi* while in the service of Your Majesty and the Empire. Owing to circumstances beyond our control, but we believe them to be due to the Union Government's political prejudices, the South African Native Labour Overseas Contingent was demobilised against our wish and much to our despairing regret, while we were still prepared to send more men to assist in the World-wide war of Justice, Freedom and Liberty.

(g) For a period of four years and since the commencement of hostilities our countrymen steadfastly maintained the supply of labour in the Gold Mines on the Rand, thus affording a continued output of gold and the availability of cyanide for purposes of war: coal Mines and Harbours and all other industries necessary for the prosecution of the war were adequately supplied with the labour of our people, which was indispensable.

(h) While our men were engaged in the various theatres of war, in non-combatant capacities as already shown, those of us remaining at home gave contributions in money and kind according to our means, towards the support of the various War Funds. Chiefs gave cattle, mealies [cornmeal] and curios—all of which have been gratefully acknowledged by Your Majesty's representatives in this country.

(i) Your Majesty will no doubt recognise that all the assistance given by us in this Great War was entirely voluntary and made without any coercion or inducements. There was no promise of pension or bonus to our men and no provision made for their dependents out of the Governor-General's Fund or any other War Funds.

∞

17. The Fall of Tsingtao

War from a grandstand seat! I had never before heard of the possibility of witnessing modern warfare—the attack of warships, the fire of infantry and battery, the reconnoitering of airships over the enemy's lines, the rolling up from the rear of reinforcements and supplies—all at one sweep of the eye, yet after watching for three days the siege of Tsingtau, from a position on Prince Heinrich Berg, one thousand feet above sea level and but three miles from the besieged city, I am sure there is actually such a thing as a theater of war.

On October 31, the anniversary of Mutsuhito's accession to the throne of Japan, the actual bombardment of Tsingtau began. All the residents in the little Chinese village of Tschang-tsun had been awakened early in the morning by the whirr of the German Taube [reconnaissance plane] as it made its usual inspection of the headquarters of the Japanese staff officers . . .

A great black column of smoke was arising from the city and hung like a pall over the besieged. At first glance it seemed that one of the neighboring hills had turned into an active volcano and was emitting this column of smoke, but officers who stood about enlightened onlookers by explaining that the oil tanks in Tsingtau were on fire.

As the bombardment of Tsingtau was scheduled to start early in the morning, we were invited to accompany members of the staffs of the Japanese and British expeditionary forces on a trip to Prince Heinrich Berg, there to watch the investment of the city.

When we arrived at the summit there was the theater of war laid out before us like a map. To the left were the Japanese and British cruisers in the Yellow Sea, preparing for the bombardment of Tsingtau. Below was a Japanese battery, stationed near the Meeker house, which the Germans had burned in their retreat from the mountains. Directly ahead was the city of Tsingtau with the Austrian cruiser *Kaiserin Elisabeth* steaming about in the harbor, while to the right one could see the German coast and central forts and redoubts and the entrenched Japanese and British camps. . . .

"Gentlemen, the show has started," said the British captain, as he removed his cap and started adjusting his "opera" glasses. No sooner had he said this than the

III.17   From Jefferson Jones, *The Fall of Tsingtau: with a Study of Japan's Ambitions in China* (Boston: Houghton Mifflin, 1915) 70–76, 78–79.

report of guns came from all directions, with a continuous rumble, as if a giant bowling-alley were in use.

Everywhere the valley at the rear of Tsingtau was alive with golden flashes or the flashing from discharging guns, and at the same time great clouds of bluish-white smoke would suddenly spring up around the German batteries, where some Japanese shell had burst.

Over near the greater harbor of Tsingtau could be seen flames licking up the Standard Oil and Asiatic Petroleum Companies' large tanks. We afterwards learned that they had been ignited from the huge shells that had been turned upon the tanks from the Japanese guns, and the bursting tanks had thrown burning oil on to the naval buildings and wharves adjoining.

The warships in the Yellow Sea opened fire on Iltis Fort, and for three hours we continually played our glasses on the field, on Tsingtau, and on the warships. With glasses on the central redoubt of the Germans, we watched the effects of the Japanese fire until the boom of guns from the German Fort A, on a little peninsula jutting out from Kiaochow Bay, toward the east, attracted our attention there. We could see the big siege gun on this fort rise up over the bunker, aim at a warship in the sea, fire, and then quickly go down again. And then we would turn our eyes toward the warships in time to see a fountain of water, two hundred yards from the vessel, where the shell had struck. We scanned the city of Tsingtau. The one hundred and fifty-ton crane on the greater harbor, which we had seen earlier in the day, and which was said to be the largest crane in the world, had disappeared and only its base remained standing. A Japanese shell had carried away the crane. . . .

But this first day's firing of the Japanese investing troops was mainly to test the range of the different batteries. The attempt also was made to silence the line of forts extending in the east from Iltis Hill, near the wireless and signal stations at the rear of Tsingtau, to the coast fort near the burning oil tank on the west. In this they were partly successful, two guns at Iltis Fort being silenced by the guns at sea.

On November 1, the second day of the bombardment, we again stationed ourselves on the peak of Prince Heinrich Berg. From the earliest hours of morning the Japanese and British forces had kept up a continuous fire on the German redoubts, in front of the Iltis, Moltke, and Bismarck forts, and when we arrived at our seat for the theater of war, it seemed as though the shells were dropping around the German trenches every minute. Particularly on the redoubt of Tai-tung-chen was the Japanese fire heavy, and by early afternoon, viewed through field-glasses, this German redoubt appeared to have an attack of smallpox, so pitted was it from the holes made by bursting Japanese shells. By nightfall many parts of the German redoubts had been destroyed, together with some machine guns. The result was the advancement of the Japanese front line several hundred yards forward from the bottom of hills where they had rested earlier in the day.

It was not until the third day of the bombardment that those of us stationed on Prince Heinrich observed that our theater of war had a curtain, a real asbestos one that screened the fire in the drops directly ahead of us from our eyes. We had learned that the theater was equipped with pits, drops, a gallery for onlookers, exits, and an orchestra of booming cannon and rippling, roaring pom-poms, but that nature had provided it with a curtain—that was something new to us . . .

The fourth day of fighting at Tsingtau was undoubtedly the most severe of the siege.

With two guns on Iltis Fort already silenced, and with the Japanese force pressing the Germans hard in front of their redoubt walls, the Tsingtau garrison practically gave up the defense of their seacoast forts, and, with the exception of an occasional shot from Iltis, the battleships in the Yellow Sea were free to bombard Tsingtau at will.

Then it was that the Japanese, already famous for their military science, put into use, probably for the first time since naval warfare began, the wireless, as a means of marking the shots from the guns at sea. At the rear of the Japanese lines, a naval lookout had been erected, and there behind a bomb-proof shelter were entrenched several marines with horned telescopes focused on the Tsingtau forts. As soon as a shell landed, one of the marines would telephone the exact location of the bursting shell to the wireless station near Lauschan and immediately the message would be relayed to the warships standing out at sea. In this way gunners on the Japanese and British warships knew, a moment after each shot, whether the great shells were finding their marks in the German forts.

∞

18. Japan's Twenty-One Demands

Group I. The Japanese Government and the Chinese Government, being desirous of maintaining the peace of Eastern Asia and of further strengthening the friendly relations existing between the two neighboring nations, agree to the following Articles:

Article I. The Chinese Government agrees that when the Japanese Government hereafter approaches the German Government for the transfer of all rights and privileges of whatsoever nature enjoyed by Germany in the Province of Shantung, whether secured by Treaty or in any other manner, China shall give her full assent thereto.

Article II. The Chinese Government agrees that within the Province of Shantung and along its sea border no territory or island or land of any name or nature shall be ceded or leased to any third Power.

Article III. The Chinese Government consents to Japan building a railway from Chefoo or Lungchau to join the Tsinan-Kiaochow Railway.

Article IV. The Chinese Government agrees that for the sake of trade and for the residence of foreigners certain important places shall be speedily opened in the Province of Shantung as treaty ports, such necessary places to be jointly decided upon by the two Governments by separate agreement.

III.18   From Jefferson Jones, *The Fall of Tsingtau: with a Study of Japan's Ambitions in China* (Boston: Houghton Mifflin, 1915) 186–190.

Group II. The Japanese Government and the Chinese Government, since the Chinese Government has always acknowledged the specially favorable position enjoyed by Japan in South Manchuria and Eastern Inner Mongolia, agree to the following Articles:

Article I. The two contracting Powers mutually agree that the term of lease of Port Arthur and Dalny and the term of lease of the South Manchuria and Antung–Mukden Railways shall be extended to the period of ninety-nine years.

Article II. Japanese subjects in South Manchuria and Eastern Inner Mongolia in erecting buildings for the purpose of trade and manufacture or for farming shall have the right to lease or own land so required.

Article III. Japanese subjects shall be free to reside and travel in South Manchuria and Eastern Inner Mongolia and to engage in business and in manufacture of any kind whatsoever.

Article IV. The Chinese Government agrees to grant Japanese subjects the right of opening all mines in South Manchuria and Eastern Inner Mongolia, such mining places to be jointly decided upon by the two Governments.

Article V. The Chinese Government agrees that in respect of the two following subjects mentioned herein below the Japanese Government's consent shall be first obtained before action shall be taken:

(a) Whenever permission is granted to the subject of a third Power to build a railway or make a loan with a third Power for the purpose of building a railway in South Manchuria and Eastern Inner Mongolia.

(b) Whenever a loan is to be made with a third Power pledging the local taxes of South Manchuria and Eastern Inner Mongolia as security.

Article VI. The Chinese Government agrees that if the Chinese Government in South Manchuria or Eastern Inner Mongolia employs advisers or instructors for political, financial, or military purposes the Japanese shall first be consulted.

Article VII. The Chinese Government agrees that the control and administration of the Kirin–Changchau Railway shall be handed over to the Japanese Government to take effect on the signing of this agreement, the term to last for ninety-nine years.

Group III. The Japanese Government and the Chinese Government, seeing that Japanese financiers and the Hanyehping Company have close relations with each other at present, and also desiring that the common interests of the two nations shall be advanced, agree to the following Articles:

Article I. The two contracting Powers mutually agree that when the opportune moment arrives the Hanyehping Company shall be made a joint concern of the two nations and they further agree that without the previous consent of Japan, China shall not by her own act dispose of the rights and property of whatsoever nature of the Hanyehping Company, nor cause the said Company to dispose freely of the same.

Article II. The Chinese Government agrees that all mines in the neighborhood of those owned by the Hanyehping Company shall not be permitted without the consent of the said Company, to be worked by other persons outside of the said Company, and further agrees that if it is desired to carry out any undertaking which it is apprehended may directly or indirectly affect the interests of the said Company the consent of the said Company shall first be obtained.

Group IV. The Japanese Government and the Chinese Government with the object of effectively protecting the territorial integrity of China agree to the following special Article:

The Chinese Government agrees that no island, port, and harbor along the coast shall be ceded or leased to any third Power.

Group V.

Article I. The Chinese Central Government shall employ influential Japanese as advisers in political, financial, and military affairs.

Article II. In the interior of China, Japanese shall have the right to ownership of land for the building of Japanese hospitals, churches, and schools.

Article III. Since the Japanese Government and the Chinese Government have had many cases of dispute between the Japanese and Chinese police to settle, cases which cause no inconsiderable misunderstanding, it is for this reason necessary that the police departments of important places (in China) shall be jointly administered (by Japanese and Chinese) or that the (Chinese) police department of these places shall employ numerous Japanese for the purpose of organizing and improving the Chinese police service.

Article IV. China shall purchase from Japan a fixed ratio of the quantity of munitions of war (say fifty per cent or more), or Japan shall establish in China a jointly worked arsenal, Japanese technical experts to be employed and Japanese material to be purchased.

Article V. China agrees to grant to Japan the right of constructing a railway connecting Wu-chang with Kiu-kiang and Nan-chang. Also a line between Nan-chang and Hang-chow, and a line between Nan-chang and Chao-chow.

Article VI. China agrees that in the Province of Fu-kien Japan shall have the right to work mines and build railways and to construct harbor works (including dockyards), and in case of employing foreign capital Japan shall be first consulted.

Article VII. China agrees that Japanese subjects shall have the right to propagate religious doctrines in China.

IV

Combat in the Machine Age

As the first conflict in which nearly all the major participants had undergone significant industrialization, the First World War was marked by the persistent application of new technology to the battlefield. The inability of any nation to break the prevailing stalemate only intensified the commitment to develop and refine weapons that could give one side or the other a decisive edge. Of the new instruments of destruction, poison gas was surely among the most harrowing. Developed and used first by the Germans, chemical warfare debilitated its victims by either suffocating them or, more commonly, by damaging or burning their lungs. The use of chlorine gas for military purposes was the brainchild of Fritz Haber, a German chemist, Nobel Prize winner, and head of the prestigious Kaiser Wilhelm Institute in Berlin. After secret tests, German troops released chlorine gas for the first time in combat on April 22, 1915, in Belgium, near Ypres. The unfortunate victims, first French and Algerian soldiers, then Canadians, reeled in terror, and those who survived the assault abandoned their positions. German soldiers understandably hesitated to follow up their advantage, however, given the primitive state of gas masks and the gas clouds' notorious dependence on unpredictable atmospheric conditions such as wind and humidity. Aware of the demoralizing impact of chemicals on opposing armies, the Germans flirted with the idea of using zeppelins to drop gas bombs on Allied civilians but abandoned the plan for fear of retaliation by the French. The British and French produced their own gas shells for use at the front, and by 1917, chemical warfare had escalated further with the introduction of mustard gas. Although the quality of gas masks improved, they never afforded absolute reliability or protection. Thus gas became a permanent nuisance rather than a decisive way to break the stalemate.

Empires, Soldiers, and Citizens: A World War I Sourcebook, Second Edition.
Edited by Marilyn Shevin-Coetzee and Frans Coetzee.
© 2013 John Wiley & Sons, Ltd. except sources 1 to 15. Published 2013 by John Wiley & Sons, Ltd.

A second weapon with the potential to do so was the tank. Its ability to win campaigns by ripping through the enemy's frontlines and rampaging in his rear, disrupting the flow of supplies and reinforcements, was demonstrated again and again in the Second World War. In the Great War, however, tanks were less influential. They were relatively primitive, underpowered, slow, and prone to mechanical breakdown. They had difficulty negotiating the terrain churned and blasted by artillery barrages. Moreover, commanders habitually deployed tanks primarily in infantry support rather than concentrating them in specific armored formations as the Germans were to do so effectively in the *panzer* divisions of the next war. Though hardly an unqualified success, by 1918 the tank had taken its first halting steps toward future dominance.

The war at sea proved something of a stalemate as well, despite the tremendous sums that Germany and Britain had invested before 1914 in their respective navies. The British Admiralty, knowing that only its ships could protect the nation from starvation or invasion, pursued a cautious policy, while the German high-seas fleet, all too aware of Britain's numerical superiority, spent much of the war in port. The one major clash between the two rival armadas, the Battle of Jutland, erupted in May 1916, with inconclusive results. Three British battlecruisers (ships with the size and armament of battleships, but whose armor protection was reduced to allow increased speed) went to the bottom and although the Germans inflicted more damage than they sustained, the British retained their control of the North Sea. The Royal Navy could thus maintain a blockade of German ports, stifling the flow of imported raw materials and foodstuffs upon which war production and civilian morale depended.

From Britain's perspective, if the main German fleet remained bottled up, commerce raiders such as the cruiser *Emden* constituted only a temporary irritant. A more sinister threat to the commercial lifelines on which Britain depended came from Germany's submarines, or U-boats. The submarine's potential for destruction was impressive and its frequent ability to escape could be terrifying, but the early U-boats (from the German for "undersea boat") were still primitive vessels. They could not remain submerged for long, and on the surface of the water they were vulnerable. To preserve the element of surprise, submarine commanders often attacked without warning; sometimes the victims were civilians. In any event, submarines had no space to take on prisoners or extra manpower to provide prize crews for captured ships. To be truly effective, therefore, submarine warfare had to be ruthless or "unrestricted," shooting first and asking questions later. The danger was the threat this posed to neutral shipping and innocent civilians and the likelihood, therefore, of inflaming public opinion around the world against Germany. From February to September 1915 Germany waged such intensified warfare, and on 6 May 1915 a U-boat torpedoed and sank the British luxury passenger liner, the *Lusitania,* bound from New York. Although the *Lusitania* was likely carrying contraband, its sinking, and the killing of some 1200 passengers and crew (including more than a hundred Americans), seemed further evidence of German brutality. Germany curtailed its submarine commanders' initiative during 1916, only to resume unrestricted warfare in January 1917 in a desperate attempt to deprive Britain of the imports it needed to continue the war. That decision was an important factor in American entry into the war on the Allied side in April 1917. It also failed to bring any corresponding military benefits. For a time during the summer of 1917, it appeared that the heavy toll of merchant shipping exacted by German submarines might hamstring Britain's war-making powers. By introducing the convoy system, in which defenseless merchant ships were grouped together with naval escort, however, Britain ameliorated its losses and nullified the one naval weapon that might have swung the tide of victory to the Germans.

With the land war at a stalemate, the naval war dragging on, and popular support for the conflict waning, the war in the air offered a ray of hope. Here, speed, technological mastery, and romantic heroism combined to present the prospect of decisive resolution. The aerial dogfights recalled the jousting matches of knights from an earlier era and stood in sharp contrast to the squalid, faceless struggles below. In reality, however, the planes were frail and unsuitable as heavy bombers, and they never made a definitive contribution to ending the war. Even the larger German zeppelins failed to resolve the conflict, despite the initial terror that their raids provoked, for they proved no match for protective barrage balloons, nimbler fighters, and, occasionally, strong winds. Although no evidence exists that the big bombers seriously jeopardized civilian morale (some initial panic in London to the contrary), military planners perpetually feared them. In truth, it was fighter pilots, rather than bombers, who garnered public adulation and respect, although the remarkable exploits of a handful of exceptional pilots do not typify the air war as a whole. Aces such as Germany's Baron von Richthofen, France's René Fonck, and Canada's Billy Bishop might shoot down as many as eighty enemy planes and inspire a sort of reciprocal chivalry among their adversaries, but the airman's daily contributions derived primarily from the less spectacular work of observation and reconnaissance.

Combat in the machine age took a terrible toll, and not just among those who were killed or maimed. An increase in the number of cases of men who, while not wounded, were rendered physically or mentally incapacitated as a result of military service, fueled fears among the more conservative elements of European society that the war was not accentuating the ideals of masculinity but rather having the opposite effect, of effeminizing its participants. Disease and moral decay had been prominent themes in the medical literature and social commentary before 1914, so physicians, officers, and politicians were challenged to diagnose the inability of many men to return to the front. In some cases, that inability was interpreted as behavior verging on cowardice and defined as malingering. The response was harsh discipline, for many military physicians believed that malingering was more prevalent in units with poor morale and lax discipline. One alternative was to diagnose the problem as a physical result of the noise and concussions of modern combat, hence the term *shell shock*. Another, slowly evolving, alternative was to recognize that psychological damage could be the result of exposure to the horrors of war before one's eyes rather than to the percussive force of shells and noise. In later conflicts, such as the Vietnam and Gulf Wars, battle-induced hysterical behavior would be more sympathetically known as combat stress syndrome.

Technology and the Battlefield

Although artillery fire was the great killer on the battlefield, it was the machine gun that so often lent defenders a decisive advantage in actions great and small. In the first selection, two British experts identify the reasons why the machine gun was superior to the coordinated rifle-fire upon which the infantry had relied in previous conflicts. Two examples of the introduction of new technology on the battlefield, both designed to evoke terror and facilitate a breakthrough, were poison gas and tanks. The second extract details the response of Canadian troops at Ypres, who were among the first victims of German chlorine gas, while the third is a letter home to his mother by a Canadian soldier, Howard Clouston, later published in a Quebec newspaper in October 1918. Tanks feature in the fourth document, by one of the preeminent early theoreticians of armored warfare, British officer J.F.C. Fuller. His writings would attract greater attention in Germany than in his native England, and Heinz Guderian and others would develop his doctrines and employ tanks with devastating effect in the early stages of World War II.

The last two selections explore the psychological and physical impact of industrialized killing. Charles Myers, a noted British psychologist and lecturer at Cambridge, was the first to coin the term "shell shock" for the debilitating stress he observed among some veterans, and here he outlines the principal features of his diagnosis. The sheer desolation of combat zones is related by Lieutenant Paul Jones in his letters to his father. Jones, a classic public school boy, fine athlete, and Balliol College (Oxford) man, was prevented by his poor eyesight from serving with the infantry in the front lines as he had wished. Unhappy with being relegated to service in the Supply Corps, he eventually managed to secure a position in the Tank Corps and with it the combat experience he felt was his duty to endure. Like so many correspondents in this book, he was killed in action, on July 31, 1917, near Ypres.

1. The Dominance of the Machine Gun

Machine-gun fire is *concentrated* infantry fire.

For machine-gun fire has special characteristics that are entirely its own. It can be concentrated like a jet of bullets on a single oval area, or by the traversing of the gun on its pivot it can bring a sweeping fire to bear over a wide front. Thus the machine gun gives to a small group of men the power of either keeping up a low deliberate fire or delivering sudden gusts of fire, turning it rapidly on a diversity of targets or directing it upon one narrow space of ground, or again sweeping the

IV.1   From F.V. Longstaff, *The Book of the Machine Gun* (London: Hugh Rees, 1917), 179–183.

front with a rain of bullets that produce the effect so well suggested by the French technical expression, *feu fauchant*—a "mowing-down" fire.

The fact that only a few men are engaged in operating a group of guns, and that each gun is fired from a fixed support, with mechanical control of elevation and direction, gives a further special character to its fire. *There is less scope for the errors introduced into infantry fire by the human element.* Nerves and excitement are to a large extent eliminated. A body of infantry soldiers firing the same number of bullets will include a wide diversity of temperaments. As each man reloads and brings his rifle to the shoulder he will have to take a new aim; and experience shows that there are few men who, in the excitement of battle, fire with anything approaching the steadiness of fairly good shot on the rifle range. No matter how good the general discipline of the men may be, and no matter what earnest and well-directed efforts their chiefs may make to exert control, the firing tends to become excited, the bullets go high. As the range diminishes and the crisis of the fight approaches this tendency increases in a marked degree.

The machine gun, *because it is a machine*, and because it is aimed by one man, delivers an ideally controlled fire. . . .

It is quite certain, therefore, that the machine gun has at least the fire power of fifty rifles. It is probable that the estimate might be safely doubled. We arrive thus at the conclusion that the probable fire power of a section of two guns is equivalent to the condensed fire power of two platoons of infantry.

And this condensation is the more remarkable if we take into account the fact that the machine guns require only a front of a few yards, while a hundred rifles deployed in the firing-line in the first stage of an attack may cover nearly an eighth of a mile.

Hence we have another characteristic advantage of the machine gun. It is easier to conceal it from view and to secure for it effective cover against fire.

Again, firing from a fixed support it not only keeps its target and range better than even the best-trained platoon of riflemen, but it has a longer effective range than the rifle fired from the shoulder.

But this is not all. Its fire is more effective. One cannot judge the effect of fire in battle by merely counting up the hits made on paper targets on a rifle range. We have seen that the human element must be kept in mind with reference to the men who are firing. But there is also the moral effect on the men who are being fired at. On the range there is no such factor in the fire effect on the targets. But in battle it is all-important.

As is so often the case in discussing military problems, we are reminded of Napoleon's saying that in war the moral is to the physical as ten to one. In fire effect, not on targets, but on men, the moral effect is everything. One does not win battles by shooting down or bayoneting every opposing man, nor is a campaign decided by the complete destruction of the enemy in the literal sense of the world. Fire is intended to kill or disable a number of the enemy, and to do this in such a way that those who remain will be "demoralized"—that is, reduced to such a condition that they will no longer be steady disciplined soldiers, but will cease to shoot straight, and be so shaken that they will give way before the final rush with the bayonet. . . .

The machine gun supplies the means of delivering this sharp blow. Its gust of destructive fire has a peculiarly nerve-shaking quality. Those who have to face it and witness its devastating effect on their comrades have the uncanny feeling that they are up against a machine, not merely fighting with other men. And the effect is all the more demoralizing when the machine itself is invisible and there seems to be no possibility of doing anything to put it out of action. To this we must attribute the well-recognized fact noted in so many accounts of the action of the guns in battle, namely, that men seldom fail to remark the peculiar rattling reports of the machine guns, . . . and are heartened and encouraged by hearing it on their own side, and depressed by recognizing it as it dominates the crackle of rifle fire from the attacking line, which they are trying to hold back. The machine gun has thus some share of the moral effect that belongs to artillery in action.

The machine gun, properly mounted and in the hands of duly trained men, should be as mobile as infantry in the actual fire fight. Modern machine guns have all been improved in the direction of lightening both the gun and its mounting. In moving from position to position in action the gun is light enough to be carried or dragged along the ground by one or two men. The guns are far more mobile than artillery, and compared to the field gun, with its wheeled carriage and its teams of horses, the machine gun presents an infinitesimal target, and of such small height that it can generally be moved under cover.

⌀

2. Gas Warfare

Passing through Ypres we drove on to Wieltze, intending to walk into the salient to see that desolate, dreary, shell-shattered area where no birds sang. As we walked to the edge of the village, where we had left the car, we noticed a peasant planting seeds in the garden in front of his little house. The earth had all been dug and raked smooth by a boy and a couple of children. To our "How do you do," he replied: "It is a fine day," looking up at the sun with evident satisfaction.

As we tramped along towards St. Julien our attention was attracted to clouds of greenish-yellow smoke ascending from the part of the line occupied by the French. We wondered what the smoke could be coming from in such volume close to the firing line. We seated ourselves on a disused trench and looked about us. An aeroplane flying low overhead dropped some fireballs which seemed to be the signal for the beginning of a violent artillery bombardment. Rising along the French line we could see this yellowish-green cloud ascending on a front of at least three miles and drifting, at a height of perhaps a hundred feet, towards us.

IV.2   From George G. Nasmith, *Canada's Sons and Great Britain in the World War* (Toronto: John C. Winston, 1919), 193–197, 199–200.

"That must be the poison gas we have heard vague rumours about," I remarked. The gas rose in great thick clouds as if it had been projected from nozzles, expanding as it ascended. Here and there brown clouds seemed to be mixed with the general yellow-green ones.

"It looks like chlorine," I said, and the captain agreed that it probably was.

The cannonade increased in intensity. About five minutes after it began a hoarse whistle, increasing to a roar like that of a railroad tram, passed overhead.

"For Ypres!" we ejaculated, and looking back we saw a cloud as big as a church rise up from that ill-fated city, followed by the sound of the explosion of a fifteen-inch shell. Thereafter those great shells succeeded one another at regular intervals, the sound of each crash following the great black cloud. . . . The bombardment continued to grow in volume. In a field not two hundred yards away numerous "coal boxes" exploded, throwing up columns of mud and water like so many geysers. Shells of various calibres, whistling and screaming, flew over our heads from German batteries as well as from our own batteries replying to them. The air seemed to be full of shells flying in all directions.

The gas cloud gradually grew less dense, but the bombardment redoubled in violence as battery after battery joined in the angry chorus.

Across the fields we could see guns drawn by galloping horses taking up new positions. One gun we saw unlimbered not three hundred yards from us, when within two minutes a German shell exploded, apparently not twenty feet away from it, and the gun was quickly moved to another position.

Occasionally we thought that we could hear heavy rifle fire and machine-gun fire, but the din was too great to distinguish much detail. The expression commonly used at the front "Hell let loose" was the only term at all descriptive of the scene.

By this time our eyes had begun to run water and become bloodshot. The fumes of the gas had reached us, irritated our throats and lungs and made us cough. We decided that this gas was chiefly chlorine, with perhaps an admixture of bromine, but that there was probably something else present responsible for the irritation to our eyes.

The Canadian artillery had evidently received a message to support, for down to our right the crash of our field guns along the hedges added to the uproar. Along the road from St. Julien came a small party of zouaves with their baggy trousers and red fez caps. We stepped out to speak to them and found that they belonged to the French Red Cross. They had been driven out of their dressing station by the poison gas and complained bitterly of the effect of it on their lungs. Shortly afterwards the first wounded Canadian appeared—a Highlander, swathed in white bandages, sitting on a little donkey cart driven by a peasant.

We could scarcely credit what followed.

Coming across the fields towards us we saw men running, dropping flat on their faces, dodging into disused trenches and keeping every possible bit of shelter between themselves and the enemy while they ran. As they came closer we could see that they were French Moroccan troops, badly frightened. Some of them lay down in a nearby trench and lit cigarettes, only to start up in terror to run on again. Some of them even threw away their equipment after they had passed us. It was now quite evident to us that the Moroccan troops had given way before the gas attack. . . .

At last we reached Vlamertinge and entered the building occupied by the Canadian field ambulance. Lying on the floors were scores of soldiers with faces of a blue or ghastly green colour, choking, vomiting and gasping for air in their struggles with death.

The faint odor of chlorine gas hung about the place. These were some of our own Canadians who had been poisoned, and I felt, as I stood and watched them in agony that the nation, which had planned in cold-blood the use of such a foul method of warfare, should not be allowed to exist as a nation among nations, but should be taken and choked in turn until in humbleness and on bended knees it, too, craved for mercy.

At midnight we arrived home, gray and ghastly from the effects of our experience with the poison gas and its consequences upon our men. . . .

3. Gas at the Front

There have been two chief ways of using gas. In the early days of the war it was always "cloud gas". This was a cloud liberated from compressed gas cylinders, and could only be used when the weather conditions were just right, with the wind in the right direction and blowing with the correct velocity. It was a suffocating gas, could be seen coming, had a strong smell, and immediately irritated eyes, nose and throat, with choking. It was quite deadly. This form has not been used for two years, on account of its disadvantages. A variation of the same gas is to shoot over cylinders full of the gas. These break when they strike. These do not need good weather conditions, and the wind is not nearly as important a factor. This is still used.

The more common method now is to fill shells with compressed gas or liquid, with just enough explosive to smash them open. They may be fired right along with other shells and need no special transportation facilities to bring them up to the guns, and of course can be sent to just where they want to fire them. They may use only a "tear gas," which makes the eyes water, or a "sneezing gas." Both these make the soldier unable to carry on for a time.

The real devilish gas is "Mustard Gas." This is a heavy liquid, which evaporates slowly and may lie on the ground or on clothes a long time, and so be tracked in on boots or carried into dugouts. Of course when a shell of it breaks a certain amount is sprayed around and part evaporates at once. The mischief of it is, that it has only a faint smell, that of course could be easily missed, and it does not develop its deadly work for some time after it has attacked the man. In about three hours, his eyes become sore, some hours later vomiting sets in, with sore throat and chest.

IV.3 From Captain Howard Clouston, "Gas at the Front," Canadian Great War Project [originally written to his mother and then published in *Huntingdon Gleaner*, Huntingdon, Quebec, on October 10, 1918].

In from perhaps 24 to 48 hours blisters appear wherever the gas struck him, especially in the armpits or between the thighs. These blisters become very sore burns, which are hard to heal and are liable to make boils. The skin is stained deeply around them. If he got a good dose (which is very small) he may die in a few hours from the way the gas has eaten into and inflamed the linings of the throat and lungs, or may die in a few days from a pneumonia, which starts on the chest inflamed, or he may die from the extensive burns received by the stuff being spattered over him, although he had his gas mask on all the time and his chest and throat are all right.

It is quite common for those afflicted to have a sore throat, and lose their voices for 2 or 3 weeks, others have severe vomiting as their worst feature. A certain number have nervous conditions in [sic] some of these are hard to get rid of; many are quite easy. A simple one is to have a man think his voice is gone and he may recover it in a few minutes when he is talked to and reasoned with.

Of course, means are being devised all the time to meet this infernal gas. For example, they have chemicals at the door of dugouts in powdered form and they wipe their feet in this. The sentry will not let a man in with it spattered on his clothes, and all means are used to recognize the shells and warn and treat the soldiers immediately. The respirator, which is a wonder, put [sic] protects the face and lungs if it is worn. The one disadvantage is, that such shells are not as good as cloud was (before respirators were made) for a rush attack. About the only satisfaction is, that while the Germans started this gas business, it is being done now more effectively by our side and they suffer worse.

✍

4. Tanks at Ypres

From the tank point of view the Third Battle of Ypres is a complete study of how to move thirty tons of metal through a morass of mud and water. The area east of the canal had, through neglect and daily shell fire, been getting steadily worse since 1914, but as late as June 1917 it was still sufficiently well drained to be negotiable throughout, by the end of July it had practically reverted to its primal condition of a vast swamp; this was due to the intensity of our artillery fire.

It must be remembered at this time the only means accepted whereby to initiate a battle was a prolonged artillery bombardment; sufficient reliance not as yet being placed in tanks on account of their liability to break down. The present battle was preceded by the longest bombardment ever carried out by the British Army, eight days counter-battery work being followed by sixteen days intense bombardment. The effect of this cannonade was to destroy the drainage system and to produce water in the shell-holes formed even before the rain fell. Slight showers fell on the 29th and 30th, and a heavy storm of rain on July 31.

IV.4   From J.F.C. Fuller, *Tanks in the Great War* (New York: E.P. Dutton, 1920), 120–123. Reprinted with permission of David Higham Associates Limited.

A study of the ground on the fronts of the three attacking corps is interesting. On the IInd Corps front the ground was broken by swamps and woods, only three approaches were possible for tanks, and these formed dangerous defiles. On the XIXth Corps front the valley of the Steenbeek was in a terrible condition, innumerable shell-holes and puddles of water existed, the drainage of the Steenbeek having been seriously affected by the shelling. On that of the XVIIIth Corps front the ground between our front line and the Steenbeek was cut up and sodden. The Steenbeek itself was a difficult obstacle, and could scarcely have been negotiated without the new unditching gear which had been produced since the battle of Messines. The only good crossing was at St. Julien, and this formed a dangerous defile [narrow passage].

Zero hour was at 3.50 a.m., and it was still dark when the tanks, which had by July 31 assembled east of the canal, moved forward behind the attacking infantry.

Briefly, the attack on July 31, in spite of the fact that there are fifty-one recorded occasions upon which individual tanks assisted the infantry, may be classed as a failure. On the IInd Corps front, because of the bad going, the tanks arrived late, and owing to the infantry being hung up, they were caught in the defiles by hostile artillery fire and suffered considerable casualties in the neighbourhood of Hooge. They undoubtedly drew heavy shell fire away from the infantry, but the enemy appeared to be ready to deal with them as soon as they reached certain localities and knocked them out one by one. On the XIXth Corps front they were more successful. At the assault on the Frezenberg redoubt they rendered the greatest assistance to the infantry, who would have suffered severely had not tanks come to their rescue. Several enemy's counter-attacks were broken by the tanks, and Spree farm, Capricorn keep, and Bank farm were reduced with their assistance. On the XVIIIth Corps front at English Trees and Macdonald's Wood several machine guns were silenced; the arrival of a tank at Ferdinand's farm caused the enemy to evacuate the right bank of the Steenbeek in this neighbourhood. The attack on St. Julien and Alberta would have cost the infantry heavy casualties had not two tanks come up at the critical moment and rendered assistance. At Alberta strong wire still existed, and this farm was defended by concrete machine-gun emplacements with good dug-outs. The two tanks which arrived here went forward through our own protective barrage, rolled flat the wire and attacked the ruins by opening fire at very close range, with the result that the enemy was driven into his dug-outs and was a little later on taken prisoner by our infantry.

The main lessons learnt from this day's fighting were—the unsuitability of the Mark IV tank to swamp warfare; the danger of attempting to move tanks through defiles which are swept by hostile artillery fire; the necessity for immediate infantry co-operation whenever the presence of a tank forced an opening, and the continued moral effect of the tank on both the enemy and our own troops.

The next attack in which tanks took part was on August 19, and in spite of the appalling condition of the ground, for it had now been steadily raining for three weeks, a very memorable feat of arms was accomplished. The 48th Division of the XVIIIth Corps had been ordered to execute an attack against certain strongly defended works, and, as it was reckoned that this attack might cost in casualties from 600 to 1,000 men, it was decided to make it a tank operation in spite of the fact that the tanks would have to work along the remains of the roads in place of over the open country. Four tanks were detailed to operate against Hillock farm. Triangle farm, Mon du Hibou, and the Cockcroft; four against Winnipeg cemetery, Springfield, and Vancouver, and four to be kept in reserve at California trench. The operation was to be covered by a smoke barrage, and the infantry were to follow the tanks and make good the strong points captured.

Eleven tanks entered St. Julien at 4.45 a.m., three ditched, and eight emerged on the St. Julien–Poelcappelle road, when down came the smoke barrage, throwing a complete cloud on the far side of the objectives; at 6 a.m. Hillock farm was occupied, at 6.15 a.m. Mon du Hibou was reduced, and five minutes later the garrison of Triangle farm, putting up a fight, were bayoneted. Thus one point after another was captured, the tanks driving the garrisons underground or away, and the infantry following and making good what the tanks had made possible. In this action the most remarkable results were obtained at very little cost, for instead of 600 casualties the infantry following the tanks only sustained fifteen!

From this date on to October 9 tanks took part in eleven further actions, the majority being fought on the XVIIIth Corps front by the 1st Tank Brigade. On August 22 a particularly plucky fight was put up by a single tank. This machine became ditched in the vicinity of a strong point called Gallipoli, and, for sixty-eight hours on end, fought the enemy, breaking up several counter-attacks; eventually the crew, running short of ammunition, withdrew to our own lines on the night of August 24–25.

Of the attacks which were made with tanks in the latter half of September and the beginning of October, the majority took place along the Poelcappelle road, the most successful being fought on October 4. Of this attack the XVIIIth Corps Commander reported that "the tanks in Poelcappelle were a decisive factor in our success on the left flank"; and their moral effect on the enemy was illustrated by the statement of a captured German officer who gave as the reason of his surrender—"There were tanks—so my company surrendered—I also."

It is almost impossible to give any idea of the difficulty of these latter operations or of the "grit" required to carry them out. Roads, if they could be called by such a name at all, were few and far between in the salient caused by the repeated attacks during the battle. This salient had a base of some 20,000 yards and was only 8,000 deep at the beginning of October, at which date the enemy could still obtain extensive observation over it from the Passchendaele ridge. The ground in between these roads being impassable swamps, all movement had to proceed along them, consequently they formed standing targets for the German gunners to direct their fire on.

5. Shell Shock

During the previous month [November 1914] I saw for the first time one of those cases of "functional" mental and nervous disorder, which afterwards proved so plentiful and came to receive the name of "shell shock." This patient was a man near whom several shells had burst, in his endeavour to disentangle himself from barbed wire during retirement over open ground. Immediately after one of the shells had burst in front of him, his sight, he said, became blurred. Another shell which then burst behind him gave him a great shock—"like a punch on the head, without any pain after it". The shell in front cut his haversack clean away and bruised his side, and apparently it burned his fingers. This man was found to be suffering from "functional" contracted fields of vision, loss of smell and taste, and slight impairment of visual acuity. Two other cases, respectively due to a shell blowing in a trench, and blowing the patient off a wall, were characterized by similar "functional" symptoms and by well-marked loss of memory. The second of these three cases was the first in which I attempted successfully to restore the patient's memory by means of slight hypnosis. . . .

After a man has been buried, lifted or otherwise subjected to the physical effects of a bursting shell or other similar explosive, he may suffer solely from concussion (which should be termed "shell concussion"), or solely from mental "shock" (so-called "shell shock"), or from both of these conditions in succession.

If "shell shock" occurs, it will give rise to one or more of the following groups of mental symptoms, namely, (i) hysteria, (ii) neurasthenia, (iii) graver temporary "mental" disorder.

But "shell shock" and these three groups of accompanying symptoms . . . do not depend for their causation on the physical force (or the chemical effects) of the bursting shell. They may also occur when the soldier is remote from the exploding missile provided that he be subject to an emotional disturbance or mental strain sufficiently severe. Apart from the effects of complicating concussion (or, in its milder form, "commotion"), there are no mental signs in "shell shock" pathognomonic of the *physical* effects of an exploding shell on the central nervous system, which enable us to distinguish them from the *physical* effects following on a purely mental disturbance, where the tolerable or controllable limits of horror, fear, anxiety, etc., are overstepped.

A shell, then, may play no part whatever in the causation of "shell shock": excessive emotion, e.g. sudden horror or fear—indeed any "psychical trauma" or "inadjustable experience"—is sufficient. Moreover, in men already worn out or having previously suffered from the disorder, the final cause of the breakdown may be so slight, and its onset so gradual, that its origin hardly deserves the name of "shock." "Shell shock," therefore, is a singularly ill-chosen term; and in other respects, . . . it has proved a singularly harmful one. . . .

IV.5   From Charles S. Myers, *Shell Shock in France, 1914–1918* (Cambridge: Cambridge University Press, 1940), 11–12, 25–26, 37–40. Reprinted with permission of Cambridge University Press.

Recent strain. Long-continued fear, horror, anxiety, worry, previous "shell shock," persistent "sticking at it," exposure and fatigue are the most important factors under this head. There can be little doubt that insomnia, dyspepsia and constipation are also important predisposing factors. Adequate sleep is difficult to obtain in the trenches, and even when "in reserve," men may have to be employed in night-working parties; the regularity of the bowels, the state of the teeth and digestion are also prone to suffer in trench warfare.

Psycho-pathic predisposition. A large number of cases, especially of those who break down merely under the stress of warfare, occur in "nervous" (psycho-neurotic) subjects who have previously suffered from mental conflicts and malad-justments, from "fits" in childhood or from other "nervous" attacks or breakdown. But even those who start with the strongest "nerves" are not immune from "shell shock," if exposed to sufficiently often repeated, or to incessant, strain, or if sub-jected to severe enough shock. Of "nervous" subjects, however, two types must be recognized, the good and the bad: the former, often a highly intelligent person, keeping full control over his unduly sensitive nervous system; the latter, usually of feebler intellect, having little hold over his instinctive acts to escape danger, the emotions which impel him to them, and the resulting conflicts.

Discipline and self-control. If two units be exposed to the same conditions of shell fire at the same moment, the number of cases of "shell shock" is found to be very appreciably greater in the less disciplined unit. The one will have been taught to take safe shelter individually; the other, with less self-control and esprit de corps, will herd together in insecure places, the shells falling on which may cause grave bodily injuries to some, and "shell shock" to others from the effects upon them of these sights. There can be no doubt that, other things being equal, the frequency of "shell shock" in any unit is an index of its lack of discipline and loyalty. . . .

It is hardly surprising, then, that the very recognition of the term "shell shock" as a disease is liable to promote its frequency. Like all emotional disorders, "shell shock" is of a highly contagious nature; it may be rife in one unit, while rare, because regarded as a disgrace, in another.

CD

6. Picture of Desolation

August 23rd, 1915

Excessively busy days these—out sometimes from nine in the morning till about ten at night, often missing meals perforce. A few days back I was in the city whose name practically sums up the character of British fighting—Ypres. Never have I seen such a picture of desolation. Not a house standing; only skeletons of build-ings, shattered walls, and gaping window openings, from which all vestige of glass has long since disappeared. The Church and the Cloth Hall are simply piles of

IV.6 From Paul Jones, *War Letters of a Public-School Boy* (London: Cassell, 1918), 138, 160–161.

debris. To walk along the streets is like a kind of nightmare, even when the Boches are not indulging in a spell of hate against the place. Talk of Pompeii—why, this puts it quite among the "also-rans." What a pathetic spectacle to see a whole city in ruins! Stupefaction and sadness at the wholesale destruction is my impression of this melancholy ruin of an historic town.

Having seen my rations delivered to our regiments, I and my companions (two Hussar officers) visited a battery of 5-inch howitzers at work not far off, through the medium of a friendly Artillery officer. Their headquarters have been amazingly lucky in not being hit up to date. They told us that there was going to be great "strafing" that night, that the Boches were very good gunners, but that the Germans and the French sometimes became quarrelsome and loosed off at each other like fury for a short time, both sides doing very little real damage. As we were chatting a long whistle-blast betokened the presence of a Taube [a German airplane], and our companions quickly dragged us out of sight into a dug-out, lest the enemy airman should spot men about and send back the range. You must understand that the guns are so concealed that it is almost impossible to see them even when you know where they are located. After the aerial visitor cleared off, we had a great tea, with all the ground about us shaking to the reverberation of the battery discharges. Presently a long-drawn-out screech in the distance, and a fearful crash in the middle distance. "That's Percy again!" said the Artillery officer. We found that "Percy" is the name for a German 17-incher, which frequently drops shells ten miles behind our lines. The smallest crater made by his shells would accommodate a locomotive engine with ease. "Percy" is no doubt "some gun," as the Yankees would say. It was a curious sensation to walk about the fields with shells from both sides flying over one's head. Some gas shells had been discharged that day, and the air in places was quite heavy with the odour of them—not unpleasant to smell, but most mephitic, and apt to make your eyes water. . . .

October 25th, 1915

There is no greater mistake than to suppose that the function of the horse has vanished in modern war. On the contrary, even in the transport, horses are quite as much used as motors. Horse transport is not confined to roads, and can pass much more easily than motor vehicles over rough ground. When you get up near the front, where the roads are badly cut up, horse transport is not only desirable but essential. Of course, the motor is absolutely invaluable for speedy transport. But on the whole one can say that, except for motor-buses, which sometimes take the men right up close to the trenches, and except for the ammunition park—a collection of powerful and very speedy lorries loaded up with munitions, which has always to be in readiness to dash up to the front in view of an emergency—except in these cases, it is safe to say that motor transport ends some miles from the actual fighting-line, and all the remaining transport is horsed. True, motor-cars containing Generals on inspection, Supply officers, etc., go all over the place, often right up behind the firing-line. Also there are the motor machine-gun cars, and the armoured cars, which are fighting units proper. But don't for goodness' sake imagine that the horse is done with in modern war because of the advent of the motor.

What the motor has done is to alter the whole face of things because of the extraordinary rapidity with which it enables you to fling troops or supplies up to the Front or transport them from point to point. But for the effective use of motor vehicles you need pretty good roads. You will remember how in the earlier months of the War, ourselves, the Germans and the French effected big troop movements simply by motor transport. You will recall the occasion on which the French flung a force across the suburbs of Paris and attacked the Boches on the right, thus beginning the movement known as the Battle of the Marne. Then there was the occasion when Hindenburg attacked the Russians in October, 1914, feinting at their left and striking at their right at Tannenberg with a force of armoured cars, cavalry, and infantry conveyed in motors. Neither of these movements could have been achieved before the advent of motor transport. As this war progresses, the need for really capable and cool-headed motor drivers will steadily increase. But it will be none the less invaluable to know how to manage a horse—whether to ride it, drive a wagon, or ride—and-drive in a limber. One of our limber horses is a grey captured from the Germans last year. He is a very good worker and doesn't seem to mind being a prisoner in the least.

The Naval War

The first sea battle between elements of the British and German fleets took place off the northwestern German coast at Heligoland Bight on August 28, 1914. Stephen King-Hall, son of an admiral, was a junior officer serving on the light cruiser HMS *Southampton* when his squadron caught a group of German cruisers and sank three of them. These losses only accentuated the German naval commanders' habitual caution in the face of British naval superiority and ensured that German warships usually remained in port. That inactivity spurred the growing disenchantment among German sailors detailed in the second source by Seaman Richard Stumpf (contrast his attitude with the confident Anglophobia he expressed at the beginning of the war [document 6 in Chapter I]). When the two fleets finally met in full-scale action in 1916 at the battle of Jutland, no one was better placed to observe the action than Georg von Hase, the gunnery officer of the German battlecruiser *Derfflinger*. One of the fleet's finest ships (its gunnery champion) and part of a squadron ably and aggressively led by Admiral Franz von Hipper, the *Derfflinger* was in the thick of the action.

Hase provides a classic account of the seminal big-gun duel between surface fleets amidst the rolling waves and enveloping mist of the North Sea. Increasingly, however, the naval weapon upon which Germany pinned its hopes was the submarine, not the battleship. Submarine warfare involved solitary hunters relying upon stealth, and these aspects are illustrated by former U-boat commander Baron Spiegel von Peckelheim.

7. Battle at Sea

At 11.30 we seemed very close to the action, and the firing was so heavy that it seemed almost as if we were in the middle of the fight, except that no shells could be seen.

At 11.40 a number of destroyers, which turned out to be British, steamed out of the mist, evidently retiring from something, and a moment later we sighted the *Arethusa* on our port bow in action at close range with the German light cruiser *Mainz*.

Our squadron at that moment consisted of the *Southampton*, *Birmingham*, *Nottingham*, *Lowestoft*, *Liverpool*, and *Falmouth*, disposed in quarter line, and as soon as the *Mainz* saw us she ceased fire on the sorely tried *Arethusa* and very wisely fled like a stag.

At 10,000 yards the squadron opened fire, and the German replied with a straggling fire from her after 4.1-inch guns. Most of her shots fell short, but a few hummed over us.

It was very peculiar hearing the moaning sob, and realizing that a lump of steel full of explosives had just gone by. I examined myself carefully to see if I was frightened, and came to the conclusion that on the whole I was excited and rather anxious.

The *Mainz* was now under the fire of about fifteen 6-inch guns, and suddenly there were two yellow flashes amidships of a different nature from the red jabs of flame from her own guns, and I realized she had been hit twice.

A most extraordinary feeling of exultation filled the mind. One longed for more yellow flashes; one wanted to hurt her, to torture her; and one said to oneself, "Ha! There's another! Give her hell!" as if by speaking one could make the guns hit her.

Though she was being hit, she was not being hit enough, as at the range of 10,000 yards in that mist it was nearly impossible to see the splashes of the shells and thus control the fire. Also she still had the legs of us.

To our dismay, the mist came down, and for five minutes we drove on without sight of her.

Down below, in complete ignorance of what had been happening, the stokers forced the boilers until our turbines would take no more, and, the safety

IV.7   From Stephen King-Hall, "Battle at Sea," *A North Sea Diary, 1914–1918* (London: Hazell, Watson and Viney, n.d.), 54–56.

valves lifting, the steam roared up the exhaust pipes at the side of the funnels with a deafening roar.

Suddenly—everything happens suddenly in a naval action with ships moving at 30 miles an hour—we came on top of the *Mainz* only 7,000 yards away, and the range decreasing every moment.

Something had happened to her whilst she was in the mist, for she was lying nearly stopped.

It is now almost certain that she was torpedoed forward by a destroyer, though it will never be known which destroyer flashing past her in the mist launched the blow which permitted us to overtake her.

When the destroyers found themselves being harried by light cruisers, the traditional foe of the destroyers, they had lashed out viciously with their torpedoes and fired some thirty.

An eye-witness told me that the sea was furrowed with their tracks: I think he was being cynical. At all events, one got home on the *Mainz*, and we closed down on her, hitting with every salvo.

She was a mass of yellow flame and smoke as the lyddite detonated along her length.

Her two after-funnels melted away and collapsed. Red glows, indicating internal fires, showed through gaping wounds in her sides.

At irregular intervals one of her after-guns fired a solitary shot, which passed miles overhead.

In ten minutes she was silenced and lay a smoking, battered wreck, her foremost anchor flush with the water. Ant-like figures could be seen jumping into the water as we approached.

The sun dispersed the mist, and we steamed slowly to within 300 yards of her, flying as we did so the signal "Do you surrender ?" in International Code. As we stopped, the mainmast slowly leant forward, and, like a great tree, quite gradually lay down along the deck.

As it reached the deck a man got out of the main control top and walked aft—it was Tirpitz junior.

I have a photograph of him standing, a solitary figure, on the extreme end of his ship.

Her bridge was knocked to pieces and there was no one to read our signal, which signal seems incongruous in 1918, but the last precedent was years old in 1914.

Nevertheless, as we watched, a flag fluttered down from the foretopmast head; it had been lowered by the boatswain.

The feeling of exultation was succeeded by one of pity as I looked at this thing that had been a ship.

Through glasses I could see that her deck was a shambles, a headless corpse, stripped to the waist, hung over the forecastle side. This was indeed war, and the first realization of war is like one's first love, a landmark in life.

The hundred or so survivors in the water were wearing lifebelts and raising their hands, shouting for help. We were debating what could be done when we were roused from the contemplation of our handiwork by the sudden outbreak of firing to the northward.

ℂℂ

8. Rusting at Anchor

Today, on [April] 13, the same old thing happened again. Something was going on at sea. Early that morning three or four torpedo boats came into port in a sorry state. One of them was missing her forward mast, her bridge hung crooked and her bowplates were completely smashed in and bent. She had mounted a sail on her starboard side to prevent the water from leaking in. Some bow damage was evident on the other three boats. But all of them came in under their own power.

This incident stirred up a good deal of discussion. We were agreed that the boats must have had a fight with enemy ships. How else could they have lost a mast? We also remembered that a prize crew from our ship which had gone out with the torpedo boats four days ago had not returned. We knew that they had captured and seized as prizes twenty merchant ships. (Today I learned that they were Dutch fishing boats.) The crew included two officers, one reservist steersman, three petty officers, five stokers and six sailors from our ship.

At the ungodly early hour of four in the morning we were wakened to pull in the torpedo nets and to clear the ship for departure. The steam in our engines was set for a speed of 30 kilometers or 16 sea miles per hour. We waited expectantly for something to happen. After breakfast we made preparations which could only point to a battle. All hands were dressed in battle clothes, i.e., their best blue uniforms. The rest of the clothes were packed in the seabags and stowed away. At the same time we stored the tables and benches from the crew's quarters in a safe place. The officers' cabins were emptied and the chests placed in the storage compartment between decks. For a change the men were glad to do this work. The entire squadron was to be ready to sail out at eight o'clock that morning. Gradually we gathered all our ships. [We were surrounded] by heavy and light cruisers and a whole forest of thin tall masts of the torpedo boats. There were five flotillas of eleven ships each. We all sat around waiting for the order to sail out. By eight o'clock, however, we were still at anchor. Then it was announced that we would leave at ten. Only the devil knows why we lay there as though we were paralyzed. By noon we gave up all hope for action. The only thing which made this entire mess bearable was that we did not have to perform our regular duties. Since the sun was smiling down from the sky, we lay down on deck and lazily joked about the navy.

To put it bluntly, I no longer care if we get to fight or not. Once again our principal interest is food, extra rations and shore leave. Nothing has changed. The men

IV.8   From Daniel Horn, *War, Mutiny and Revolution in the German Navy* (Brunswick, NJ: Rutgers University Press, 1967), 81–83. Copyright © 1967 by Rutgers, the State University. Reprinted by permission of Rutgers University Press.

often express the hope that there will be no battle. For whom should they allow themselves to be killed? For the wealthy? After the war we will receive the same treatment as in the past and we shall be the ones who have to suffer and pay for it. I ought to add at this point that these statements are caused by our discontent at our inactivity. Should it ever come to a fight, all of us would be eager and raring to go. The adage, "idle hands make the devil's mischief," sums up the situation quite well. One can get used to anything but it is extremely difficult to be kept waiting all the time in the knowledge that our tremendous power is being wasted. The atmosphere is strained and embittered. One can sense it among the officers and the men. Happy songs and joyful games are no longer in evidence. We are virtually at each other's throats. The happy spirit of camaraderie has vanished and has been supplanted by deep depression. No wonder all of us wish to leave the ship. Whenever there is a call for volunteers for the submarines or for [the naval infantry brigade in] Belgium, everyone steps forward. We are very envious of those few who have already departed. Formerly none of us wanted to leave and we were all afraid lest we be transferred. But now? Some time ago the Chaplain held a sermon on changing values. He could well have cited this as an example.

$$\infty$$

9. Jutland

And so the battle went on. Huge columns of water, from 80 to 100 meters in height, rose where our shots fell; they were almost twice as high as the enemy's masts. Our joy at being passed over did not last long. The mistake had been detected by the other side and we were now often covered with well-aimed salvos. I again examined the gun turrets of our opponent on which I had directed my glass and saw that the guns were now aimed directly at us. At the same time I suddenly made a discovery which filled me with surprise. At every salvo which the enemy fired I clearly saw four or five projectiles approaching through the air. They looked like long, black points. They gradually became somewhat larger and suddenly— boom—they reached us. They exploded on impact with the water or the ship with a deafening roar. Finally, I could quite plainly see whether the shells were going to fall in front of us or pass over us, or whether they were going to honor us individually. Impact on the sea always raised a huge column of water. Some of these water columns up to half their height were poisonous, greenish yellow in color, and doubtless produced by lyddite shells. They lasted fully 5 or 10 seconds before they collapsed. They resembled giant fountains in comparison with which the famous jets of Versailles were mere child's play. . . .

How did things seem to be going with the enemy at this time? At 6 p.m. his rear ship, the *Invincible*, was blown into the air. I did not see her, as my attention was fully absorbed in directing the fire against the second ship. It was also impossible to

IV.9 From George von Hase, "The Two White Nations," in *The Battle of Jutland, 31 May–1 June 1916, Monograph ©1* (Newport, RI: Naval War College, 1920), 19–20, 22–23, 27–29, 32.

hear the noise of the explosion, which must have been great, owing to the internal uproar in our own ship and the noise made by the exploding enemy shells in our vicinity, though we were able to hear the report of the enemy salvos as a dull roar when our own guns were silent for a moment. . . .

With the English ships, the northwest wind carried the smoke of their guns past their ship to windward. In this way the view of the English was often obstructed and their firing made difficult. But as the conditions of visibility were still more unfavorable toward the east than toward the west, the English battlecruisers had decided to take up a position which was tactically unfavorable. We were but little disturbed by the smoke from the enemy's guns, as it was sufficient with our stereoptical range finders if the range taker could see merely a little bit of the top of the mast.

At 6.17 p.m. I again took the second battle cruiser under fire on the port hand. I supposed that it was the same ship, the *Princess Royal*, at which I had already been firing. As a matter of fact it was the *Queen Mary*, the third ship in the enemy line. . . .

The *Queen Mary* and the *Derfflinger* waged a regular gunnery duel above the torpedo battle raging between us, but the poor *Queen Mary* had a hard time of it. In addition to the *Derfflinger*, the *Seidlitz* was also firing at her. The gunnery officer of the *Seidlitz*, Lieut. Commander Foerster, was one of our ablest gunners, who had been tested in all the previous engagements of the ship and was cool-blooded and of quick decision. The *Seidlitz* had only 28-centimeter guns on board. These projectiles could not penetrate the thickest armor of the *Queen Mary*. But each ship had thinly armored portions, the perforation of which by the 28-centimeter shell, could produce great damage. . . .

From 6.24 p.m. on, each one of our salvos had landed on that ship. The salvo fired at 6 hours 26 minutes 10 seconds p. m. fell after the terrific explosion had begun inside the *Queen Mary*. At first a yellowish red flame appeared in the fore-part of the ship. This was followed by an explosion, which in turn was succeeded by a much more violent explosion amidships, which hurled black pieces of the ship into the air, and immediately thereafter, the entire ship was shattered by a terrific explosion. Enormous clouds of smoke were developed. The mass fell together amidships; the smoke covered everything and rose higher and higher. Finally, nothing remained where the vessel had been but a thick black cloud of smoke. At the water line this cloud of smoke was of small extent but it broadened as it leaped into space and seemed almost like a huge pine tree. The column of smoke, according to my estimate, was from 300 to 400 meters in height. . . .

At 7.40 p.m. enemy small cruisers and destroyers started an attack with torpedo boats. We were steering a course north-northeast at the time; that is, about six points to starboard. The visibility was now quite poor, so that it was difficult to see the English ships. We fired at the small cruisers and torpedo boats. At 7.55 p.m. we turned to the east, and at 8 o'clock the entire battlecruiser squadron moved off in echelon on a southerly course as the torpedo boats attacked us. In this way we avoided the enemy's torpedoes very successfully. At 8.12 p.m. we again turned toward the enemy. During this time we had fired only occasionally with the main and secondary batteries. At 8.15 p.m. we received a heavy fire. All about us were flashes of light. We could make out the ship's hull only indistinctly, but everywhere I could see along the horizon were enemy ships. . . .

I continued to fire at the large ships. I no longer had any idea what ships they were. At 8.22 p.m. we turned into a southwest course, but in the poor conditions of visibility and the confusion of battle now prevailing, I had no longer any correct grasp of the tactical conditions. At one time it flashed through my mind, "May it not be German ships that we are firing at?" Then the visibility, which varied from minute to minute but which on the whole was gradually growing worse, became somewhat better, and one could clearly recognize the typical English contours and the dark gray color of their paint. I am of the opinion that our light gray paint is better than the dark color of the English. Our ships disappeared much more quickly in the thin mists which were now drifting from east to west. . . .

Meanwhile, we were receiving heavy and well-placed rapid fire from several ships simultaneously. It was obvious that the enemy could now see us much better than we could see him. To those who have ever been at sea this statement will seem ambiguous. As a matter of fact, however, the differences in visibility at sea in weather of this kind vary greatly. Persons on board a vessel enveloped in mist can make out a vessel silhouetted against a clear horizon much more distinctly than the latter can make out the vessel enveloped in mist. The position of the sun plays an important part in visibility conditions. In misty weather the ships which have their shaded side toward the enemy are much more plainly visible than those on which the light shines.

Thus it was that the battle became an unequal, bitter struggle. Several heavy hits fell with terrific force on our ships and exploded with a terrible report. The entire ship trembled in every joint at the impact of the shell. The commanding officer frequently swerved out of line to avoid the hail of shell. It was no easy firing. . . .

The *Derfflinger* herself now presented a pretty bad appearance. The masts and all the rigging were badly damaged by fragments of explosion, the antennae hung down in wild confusion so that we were able to use our wireless only for receiving. It was therefore impossible to send any regular messages. A heavy shot had torn away the armor plates of the bow, leaving an enormous hole at least 6 by 5 meters in size just above the waterline. Water continuously flowed in through this hole when the ship pitched.

⟋⟍

10. Adventures of the U-202

Noiselessly we slipped closer and closer in our exciting chase. The main thing was that our periscope should not be observed, or the steamer might change her course at the last moment and escape us. Very cautiously, I stuck just the tip of the

IV.10   From Baron Spiegel Von Und Zu Peckelsheim, *The Adventures of the U-202* (New York: Century, 1917), 50–57, 172–173.

periscope above the surface at intervals of a few minutes, took the position of the steamer in a second and, like a flash, pulled it down again. That second was sufficient for me to see what I wanted to see. The steamer was to starboard and was heading at a good speed across our bows. To judge from the foaming waves which were cut off from the bow, I calculated that her speed must be about sixteen knots.

The hunter knows how important it is to have a knowledge of the speed at which his prey is moving. He can calculate the speed a little closer when it is a wounded hare than when it is one which in flight rushes past at high speed.

It was only necessary for me, therefore, to calculate the speed of the ship, for which a sailor has an experienced eye. I then plotted the exact angle we needed. I measured this by a scale which had been placed above the sights of the periscope. Now I only had to let the steamer come along until it had reached the zero point on the periscope and fire the torpedo, which then must strike its mark.

You see, it is very plain; I estimate the speed of the boat, aim with the periscope and fire at the right moment.

He who wishes to know about this or anything else in this connection should join the navy, or if he is not able to do so, send us his son or brother or nephew.

On the occasion in question everything went as calculated. The steamer could not see our cautious and hardly-shown periscope and continued unconcerned on its course. The diving rudder in the "Centrale" worked well and greatly facilitated my unobserved approach. I could clearly distinguish the various objects on board, and saw the giant steamer at a very short distance—how the captain was walking back and forth on the bridge with a short pipe in his mouth, how the crew was scrubbing the forward deck. I saw with amazement—a shiver went through me—a long line of compartments of wood spread over the entire deck, out of which were sticking black and brown horse heads and necks.

Oh, great Scott! Horses! What a pity! Splendid animals!

"What has that to do with it?" I continually thought. War is war. And every horse less on the western front is to lessen England's defense. I have to admit, however, that the thought which had to come was disgusting, and I wish to make the story about it short.

Only a few degrees were lacking for the desired angle, and soon the steamer would get into the correct focus. It was passing us at the right distance, a few hundred meters.

"Torpedo ready!" I called down into the "Centrale."

It was the longed-for command. Every one on board held his breath. Now the steamer's bow cut the line in the periscope—now the deck, the bridge, the foremast—the funnel.

"Let go!"

A light trembling shook the boat—the torpedo was on its way. Woe, when it was let loose!

There it was speeding, the murderous projectile, with an insane speed straight at its prey. I could accurately follow its path by the light wake it left in the water.

"Twenty seconds," counted the mate whose duty it was, with watch in hand, to calculate the exact time elapsed after the torpedo was fired until it exploded.

"Twenty-two seconds!"

Now it must happen—the terrible thing!

I saw the ship's people on the bridge had discovered the wake which the torpedo was leaving, a slender stripe. How they pointed with their fingers out across the sea in terror; how the captain, covering his face with his hands, resigned himself to what must come. And next there was a terrific shaking so that all aboard the steamer were tossed about and then, like a volcano, arose, majestic but fearful in its beauty, a two-hundred meter high and fifty-meter wide pillar of water toward the sky.

"A full hit behind the second funnel!" I called down into the "Centrale." Then they cut loose down there for joy. They were carried away by ecstasy which welled out of their hearts, a joyous storm that ran through our entire boat and up to me.

And over there?

Landlubber, steel thy heart!

A terrible drama was being enacted on the hard-hit sinking ship. It listed and sank towards us.

From the tower I could observe all the decks. From all the hatches human beings forced their way out, fighting despairingly. Russian firemen, officers, sailors, soldiers, hostlers, the kitchen crew, all were running and calling for the boats. Panic stricken, they thronged about one another down the stairways, fighting for the life-boats, and among all were the rearing, snorting and kicking horses. The boats on the starboard deck could not be put into service, as they could not be swung clear because of the list of the careening steamer. All, therefore, thronged to the boats on the port side, which, in the haste and anguish, were lowered, some half empty; others overcrowded. Those who were left aboard were wringing their hands in despair. They ran from bow to stern and back again from stern to bow in their terror, and then finally threw themselves into the sea in order to attempt to swim to the boats.

Then another explosion resounded, after which a hissing white wave of steam streamed out of all the ports. The hot steam set the horses crazy, and they were beside themselves with terror—I could see a splendid, dapple-gray horse with a long tail make a great leap over the ship's side and land in a lifeboat, already overcrowded—but after that I could not endure the terrible spectacle any longer. Pulling down the periscope, we submerged into the deep.

When, after some time, I came again to the surface there was nothing more to be seen of the great, proud steamer. . . .

"Poor devils," I thought, "I understand how you feel over your beautiful, fine ship, but why didn't you stay at home? Why do you go to sea when you know what threatens? Why do you or your governments force us to destroy your ships wherever we can find them? Do you think we are going to wait until our own women and children starve and let you keep your bread baskets full before we defend ourselves? You have started it. You are responsible for the consequences. If you would discontinue your inhuman way of carrying on the war, then we would let your sailing ships and steamers pass unmolested, when they do not carry contraband. You have wanted war to the knife. Good, we have accepted your challenge."

The Aerial War

The ability of pilots to soar among the birds in powered flight fired the popular imagination, but so too did the prospect of destruction raining down from the sky. Perhaps this latter concern was more acute in Britain, whose civilian population, thanks to the supremacy of the Royal Navy, had not been accustomed to being threatened by direct harm in wartime. German Zeppelins and aerial bombers punctured that assurance of immunity. The first source, from a parliamentary debate about British aerial defenses, is a strong condemnation of the inadequacy of those defenses by William Joynson-Hicks, an ardent Conservative MP for Brentford and future Home Secretary, who persistently worried over undue alien influences and other threats to national security. His concerns are to some extent reiterated in the second document, an account of Folkestone's experience with air-raids. One should bear in mind that as a town on England's southern coast (near Dover), Folkestone was more vulnerable than communities further inland. It is also striking how the minimal damage (and popular unease) from the random Zeppelin attacks contrasts with the more destructive and better organized raid by Geman bombers. That very superiority of the aircraft over the dirigible is emphasized in the Irish MP for Clare West, Arthur Lynch's, response to Joynson-Hicks. Just what an airplane was capable of in the hands of a skilled pilot can be grasped from the memoirs of one of the very best, Germany's Oswald Boelcke. It was Boelcke, above all, who formulated the tactics for fighter squadron combat, and many of Germany's best pilots (including Manfred von Richthofen) trained under him. It is all the more ironic that Boelcke died at the age of 25 in October 1916 after a mid-air collision with another plane from his own squadron. With 40 confirmed kills, he was, at that point, Germany's greatest ace. In other theaters, however, such as the Middle East, a pilot's career was less glamorous, and revolved around reconnaissance missions and close support of the ground troops rather than perpetual aerial dogfights.

Lieutenant-Colonel John Tennant describes many of the pilot's duties in the desert in the final extract.

11. Zeppelin

The powers of the Zeppelin are increasing very strongly. I want the House to realise how much Zeppelins have improved, and therefore how much our defence ought to improve concurrently. Four years ago the Zeppelin had a radius, out and home, of 250 miles. Two years ago it had a radius of 350 miles. To-day it has a

IV.11   From *Hansard's Parliamentary Debates*, February 16, 1916, vol. 80, cols. 86–89. © Crown Copyright material reproduced with the permission of The Controller HMSO.

radius of over 450 miles, and there is every reason to suppose that within a short time the Zeppelin will have a radius of at least 600 miles, out and home. This time they went not merely to the East Coast, but got right into the middle of the country. Our defence against Zeppelins must come under three heads. It can either be by gunnery, by aeroplane, or by a strong offensive over on the other side of the water. I leave out of the question defence by Zeppelins of our own because we have not got them. In that matter the responsibility lies very heavy on the shoulders of the right hon. Gentleman who was First Lord of the Admiralty at an earlier period. Think what the benefit would have been if we had three, four, or five large airships of the Zeppelin type able to patrol our East Coast whenever there was a chance of Zeppelins coming over, and able to meet them there! If we had had four or five Zeppelins we should not have had these raids carried out so successfully as they have been. . . .

Let us look at the position. We had these six Zeppelins over here, and it is no good shirking the facts. We have to deal with the facts as they are, to see what ought to have been done and what was done on the 31st January. These Zeppelins came over our East Coast. It is well known where they came. They came in daylight. They were seen, not merely by scores but by hundreds of people, coming over, as they nearly always do come over, flying low down. It is essential, I understand, for the Zeppelins to cross the coast rather low after drifting across the sea in order that they may pick up the landmarks and see where they are and then direct their course to whatever position is required. These Zeppelins came over flying not more than two or three thousand feet high. I do not think anyone will deny that. That was a height at which any anti-aircraft gunnery of any pretensions to use could have got them down. What was the truth in regard to the matter? Either the guns were not fired or the guns were no use. . . .

I will not mention places, but I have a great deal of information in regard to what happened when the Zeppelins came over. There was one gun, a big gun, at one place where the Zeppelins came over on the East Coast, flying at a height of not more than about 3,000 feet. This gun stood, more or less, on end and fired at the Zeppelin. It missed it, but the effort of firing was such that the gun rolled over and it fired no more. I ask the right hon. Gentleman (Mr. Tennant) whether that is true or not. I want to go further. I want to ask him, or perhaps I ought to ask the First Lord of the Admiralty, because I think he is responsible, what is the condition of our anti-aircraft corps at the present time? It was started eighteen months ago, and a very large number of men volunteered, men of the keenest intelligence and determination, who gave up their positions in order that they might serve their country in this anti-aircraft corps. They have been given guns and they have been practising from time to time on the East Coast. . . . This is the position of this particular corps on the 31st January last, which had control of about 3,000 square miles of our land—a force which the Crown rely upon to bring down Zeppelins if they come over, and which we were entitled to rely upon, because everyone knew of their existence. They had ten maxim guns, which were used in the Boer War, mounted. Maxim guns fire rifle bullets, and you might as well fire a pea shooter at an elephant as to fire maxim guns at a Zeppelin with any hope of bringing it down. In September last year, when things became critical in regard to Zeppelin raids, they were provided with certain 1-lb. pom-poms and also $1\frac{1}{2}$-lb. pom-poms. Of these pom-poms three were new at the time of the South African War, and five were reconstructed last year. They were guns which Sir Percy Scott turned out of London because they were not good enough for London, and so they were sent down to the East Coast, although the East Coast is the place where, as everybody knows, we ought to attack the Zeppelins. The First Lord of the Admiralty will agree with me in that, because in the last speech he made in this House he said quite frankly that we must have local defences as well as coast defences, and he entirely agrees that we should extend the circle of our defences as far as possible, and, if you can and when you can, catch your Zeppelin as he approaches your shores. That is the view of the First Lord of the Admiralty. It is my view, and it is the view of everybody. We should catch the Zeppelins on the coast. But how can you expect to catch them on the coast if you arm your men with guns of the calibre I have mentioned? Now I think the hon. Member is answered who asked me why the guns did not fire. They were there, but they were no use. They did fire some of them, it is only fair to say that. If the right hon. Gentleman wants to know I can tell him that these guns were fired numbers of times during previous Zeppelin raids. They have been in action again and again, but they are no earthly use whatever. Is the country to be palmed off after eighteen months of war with defences of that kind? Surely that question hardly needs elaborating? At the end of eighteen months, after raid after raid has taken place, this is the condition of affairs. Are you going to end it?

∞

12. Air Raids

[Incident Occurred on May 25, 1917]

An aeroplane cruised about over the town rather low down, but we had become so familiar with the spectacle of flying machines that one hardly even associated it with the war, and certainly nobody would regard it as an ominous sign. Complete tranquility was the predominant note of the closing day, and there was nothing to warn us of the tragedy that was about to burst upon us. Yet only a few minutes journey away nearly a score of German aeroplanes of the most recent design and construction were racing towards Folkestone at top speed, laden with bombs ready to be hurled amongst the hapless populace. . . .

IV.12   From John Charles Carlile, *Folkestone during the War, 1914–1918: A Record of the Town's Life and Work* (Folkestone: F.J. Parsons, n.d.), 96–99.

At first some of the inhabitants laboured under the impression that the town was being bombarded from the sea, but the unmistakable whirr of powerful aeroplanes, heard between the explosions as the machines were passing directly overhead, informed them that the attack came from the air. It was a racking, nerve-testing experience. In the principal zones of devastation the horror of it all was enhanced by the cries and moans of the wounded, the noise of falling masonry, and the crash of broken glass as windows were rent into a million atoms. Sixty or more were killed instantaneously, before they had time to realise what was happening; others, less fortunate in a way, were injured beyond recovery, and many others maimed for life.

A ghastly, horrible business of death and mutilation truly! The sights which met the gaze of those who hastened to the grim task of removing the bodies and remains and succouring the wounded baffled description. Human trunks were cleft in two or more pieces, heads were blown from bodies, and there were fragments of bodies and limbs in whose case identification was more a matter of surmise than anything else. Yet, in spite of this heartrending holocaust, the military value of the raid was practically nil. One bomb hit the railway. This fell between the up and down lines at the Central Station but it did not explode, and the damage was quickly repaired. Obviously the object of the German aviators was to wreck the railway and the Harbour, but in this they signally failed, although it must be admitted that their aim was far from being discreditable, bearing in mind the great height at which they flew. Many civilians were killed and a greater number injured, but from a military point of view the achievement was of insignificant, if any, value.

The enemy aircraft had approached the town from the west in well-observed formation, the leader of the fleet being somewhat in advance by himself. Not a few people who happened to be out of doors gazed at the oncoming Gothas with keen, undisturbed interest, mentally remarking, "What a fine spectacle!" and failing to realise that they were enemy raiders until bombs dropping in the heart of the town startled them into an accurate appreciation of the deadly character of the aerial visitation. As the aeroplanes neared Folkestone they broke from their formation and spread out fanwise, some deviating so that their course lay over the golf links, their objective being probably the military encampment at the foot of Castle Hill (Caesar's Camp), others taking a line over the railway, and some diverging seawards, evidently in the hope that their bombs would strike the Harbour and perhaps sink some of the transports there. But the German crews, being at the great height of 14,000 feet or so, failed, with the slight exception already recorded, to hit their targets.

The total number of bombs dropped in the borough, including those which fell into the sea not far from the beach, was fifty-one. Of these thirty-one exploded or partially exploded, fourteen which fell on land did not explode at all, and six dropped into the sea, some a short distance from the Victoria Pier. Others were dropped at Shorncliffe and Hythe, and yet others near the Railway further up the line. A fast train from London was on its way to Folkestone at the time, but the driver, sagaciously apprehending the danger of the situation, slowed down with the object of letting the aeroplanes get well in front. With regard to the bombs which were discharged in Folkestone and the immediate district, a military expert in explosives who visited the town stated that only a few fully exploded, including that which fell in Tontine Street and one which fell at Shorncliffe Camp. But some of the others "exploded sufficiently" to cause enough damage to life and property. One hardly likes to imagine what the total extent of the disaster would have been had all the bombs completely exploded.

∽

13. The Importance of the Airplane

The question of Zeppelins has been put forward, and the First Lord has regretted that we have not proceeded to build Zeppelins in this country. I would venture to say that the great salvation of this country in this War has been that the Germans have thrown themselves so determinedly into the construction of Zeppelins, because, having devoted so much of their constructive ability and their engineering genius to the perfection of Zeppelins, they have been less energetic than they might have been in the construction of aeroplanes. No greater mistake could be made than that, at this hour, so belatedly, this country should recognise certain advantages in Zeppelins, and should now proceed to follow suit and start factories for the building of imitation Zeppelins. The Zeppelin is a slower instrument than a first-class aeroplane. The Zeppelin does not rise so quickly as the best type of aeroplane; and remember that one aeroplane is capable of bringing down a Zeppelin, and that the time, money, skill, and labour devoted to the construction of one Zeppelin would be sufficient to turn out a whole fleet of the best kind of latest type aeroplanes. So that instead of now so belatedly attempting to follow the Germans in this line of Zeppelin building, a successful policy would be, I think, to devote the utmost energy to the construction of the latest type of aeroplanes, fast aeroplanes, fast-rising aeroplanes, aeroplanes of great power and aeroplanes carrying fighting guns.

Lately we have had considerable alarm and considerable discussion on the question of German aeroplanes. The Fokker is one machine, and one would think it was something suddenly sprung like a bolt from the blue, a surprise to our experts, as if it were something following a new device, and something entirely beyond their own reach. As a matter of fact, it is nearly twelve months since the Germans first began to recognise the great value of the aeroplane as an arm in this War. All their engineers were instructed to devote their energies to the devising of new types and to the adoption as far as could be of the best qualities of the existing types, in order to produce a superior kind of aeroplane, and the Fokker has been the result.

IV.13   From *Hansard's Parliamentary Debates*, February 16, 1916, vol. 80, cols.150–152. © Crown Copyright material reproduced with the permission of The Controller HMSO.

Over eight months ago the Germans were beginning to build aeroplanes which were showing their superiority over the aeroplanes of the Allies at the front. In all these questions where the Germans have gained any superiority at all it has not been because they have shown any great inventive genius in these matters or produced the original bright idea which is truly the work of genius. Their skill and superiority, where it has existed, has been in adopting and adapting the ideas of others, but they have adapted them. The result was that eight months ago they had a fast aeroplane carrying two engines and able to rise more quickly and fly more quickly than any of the aeroplanes possessed by the Allies. The first aeroplane of very high power produced in this War was the product of the Russians—the Sikorski. The Germans had nothing of the kind. When the first Sikorski fell within their lines, it was submitted immediately to their experts and photographs were taken and reproduced of the parts and details, and those were sent into every workshop in Germany, and even every private engineer and every head of every workshop was invited by the Government to study those details and to reproduce them if he found they were of the best kind, and, if not, to suggest any improvement which the Germans could adopt. So that, although the initiative has arisen either in this country or in France, and though at the beginning of the War, as the aeroplane was an invention of an English-speaking nation, this country and France had a great advantage, yet in the progress of the War the Germans have in some respects acquired the upper hand over the Allies. While I say that, I believe that in the personnel the Allies are still superior, and that the flying men of England and of France are superior to those of Germany. But in the mechanical part, and particularly in the adaptation of what has been useful, even though invented in other countries, the Germans have shown superiority over this country, and the Government has not yet waked up to the vast importance of the part which aeroplanes could play in this War if a fleet of aeroplanes were provided of sufficient magnitude and sufficient power. If the question be asked, "Has the Government done its best?" is there any man, even on the Front Bench, who can truthfully answer, "Yes, the Government has exerted the full power of its ability"? The Government has not yet fully recognised the immense part which aeroplanes could play in this War if they were regarded less as an appendage of the naval or military forces, and were regarded as a distinct fighting arm. If, in fact, aeroplanes were regarded in this new kind of service somewhat as the Cavalry is in regard to military service, that is to say, if it were regarded as possible that this country could build not merely dozens of aeroplanes or hundreds of aeroplanes, as the Under-Secretary has said, but thousands of aeroplanes if necessary, so that the country would have a fleet whose superiority would be such that in no part of any one of its fronts would any hostile aeroplane be able to show itself above the horizon. I say that that is an ideal well within the possibilities of attainment by the Government, and to that they should bend their energies; that is to say, to build the Cavalry of the air and to recognise that that Cavalry of the air could be brought to such a pitch of perfection or of sufficiency that it would become one of the decisive factors in the termination of this campaign.

✑

14. A Superior Pilot

December 31, 1915

Day before yesterday I had a fight with a very keen opponent, who defended himself bravely. I was superior to him and forced him into the defensive. He tried to escape by curving and manœuvring, and even tried to throw me on the defensive. He did not succeed, but I could not harm him either. All I did accomplish was to force him gradually closer to earth. We had started at 2,800 and soon I had him down to 1,000 meters. We kept whirring and whizzing around each other. As I had already fired on two other enemy craft on this trip, I had only a few cartridges left. This was his salvation. Finally he could not defend himself any more because I had mortally wounded his observer. Now it would have been comparatively safe for me to get him if I had not run out of ammunition at the 800-meter level. Neither of us was able to harm the other. Finally another Fokker (Immelmann)[Max Immelmann, another famous ace] came to my rescue and the fight started all over again. I attacked along with Immelmann to confuse the Englishman. We succeeded in forcing him to within 100 meters of the ground and were expecting him to land any moment. Still he kept flying back and forth like a lunatic. I, by flying straight at him, wanted to put a stop to this, but just then my engine stopped and I had to land. I saw him disappear over a row of trees, armed myself with a flashlight (I had nothing better) and rode over on a horse. I expected that he had landed, but imagine my surprise! He had flown on. I inquired and telephoned, but found out nothing. In the evening the report came that he had passed over our trenches at a height of 100 meters on his way home. Daring of the chap! Not everyone would care to imitate him. Immelmann had jammed his gun and had to quit.

January 8, 1916

On the 5th of January I pursued two Englishmen, overtook them . . . and attacked the first one. The other did not seem to see me; at any rate he kept right on. The fight was comparatively short. I attacked, he defended himself; I hit and he didn't. He had dropped considerably in the meantime, and finally started to sway and landed. I stayed close behind him, so he could not escape. Close to H. he landed; his machine broke apart, the pilot jumped out and collapsed. I quickly landed and

IV.14 From Oswald Boelcke, *An Aviator's Field Book* (New York: National Military, 1917), 91–96, 101–105.

found the 'plane already surrounded by people from the nearby village. The Englishmen, whom I interviewed, were both wounded. The pilot, who was only slightly wounded, could talk German; the observer was severely wounded. The former was very sad at his capture; I had hit his controls and shot them to pieces. Yesterday I visited the observer at the hospital; the pilot had been taken away in the meantime. I brought the observer English books and photographs of his machine. He was very pleased. He said he knew my name well.

On the afternoon of the 5th, I made another flight, but everything was quiet. I landed and rode to the city to eat with the rest, because it was getting cloudy again. Just imagine my luck! I was hardly in when a squadron of ten planes appeared. I hurried back again and arrived just as they were dropping their bombs on our field. All the helpers were in the bomb-proofs. I howled as if I were being burned alive. At last someone came. I had to take an 80-horsepower machine, because Immelmann, who had remained behind, had already taken my 160-horsepower machine. But with the 80-horsepower machine I could not reach the enemy in time. Then I saw one somewhat separated from the rest. One Fokker had already attacked it, and I went to help him, for I saw I could not overtake the rest. When the Englishman saw both of us on top of him, he judged things were too hot for him, and quickly landed at V., both of us close behind him. The Englishman was alone, still had all his bombs, was unwounded and had only landed through fear. . . .

January 15, 1916

On the 14th, that is, yesterday, it was ideal weather for flying. So I went up at nine o'clock to look around. As it was getting cloudy near Lille, I changed my course to take me south of Arras. I was up hardly an hour, when I saw the smoke of bursting bombs near P. I flew in that direction, but the Englishman who was dropping the bombs saw me and started for home. I soon overtook him.

When he saw I intended to attack him, he suddenly turned and attacked me. Now, there started the hardest fight I have as yet been in. The Englishman continually tried to attack me from behind, and I tried to do the same to him. We circled 'round and 'round each other. I had taken my experience of December 28th to heart (that was the time I had used up all my ammunition), so I only fired when I could get my sights on him. In this way, we circled around, I often not firing a shot for several minutes. This merry-go-round was immaterial to me, since we were over our lines. But I watched him, for I felt that sooner or later he would make a dash for home. I noticed that while circling around he continually tried to edge over toward his own lines, which were not far away. I waited my chance, and was able to get at him in real style, shooting his engine to pieces. This I noticed when he glided toward his own lines, leaving a trail of smoke behind him. I had to stop him in his attempt to reach safety, so, in spite of his wrecked motor, I had to attack him again. About 200 meters inside our positions I overtook him, and fired both my guns at him at close range (I no longer needed to save my cartridges). At the moment when I caught up to him, we passed over our trenches and I turned back. I could not determine what had become of him, for I had to save myself now. I flew back, and as I had little fuel left, I landed near the village of F. Here I was received by the Division Staff and was told what had become of the Englishman. To my joy, I learned that, immediately after I had left him, he had come to earth near the English positions. The trenches are only a hundred meters apart at this place. One of the passengers, the pilot, it seems, jumped out and ran to the English trenches. He seems to have escaped, in spite of the fact that our infantry fired at him. Our field artillery quickly opened fire on his machine, and among the first shots one struck it and set it afire. The other aviator, probably the pilot, who was either dead or severely wounded, was burned up with the machine. Nothing but the skeleton of the airplane remains. As my helpers did not come till late, I rode to D. in the Division automobile, because I had to be with the King of Bavaria at 5:30. From D. I went directly on to Lille. King and Crown Prince both conversed with me for quite a while, and they were especially pleased at my most recent success. Once home, I began to see the black side of being a hero. Everyone congratulates you. All ask you questions. I shall soon be forced to carry a printed interrogation sheet with me with answers all filled out. I was particularly pleased by my ninth success, because it followed so close on the *Pour le mérite* [popularly known as the "Blue Max," it was the Kingdom of Prussia's highest military order].

☙

15. In the Clouds above Baghdad

These records are no place for technical details, but the lay reader may not know that an aero-engine can only run a certain number of hours without overhaul; in our case it was usually a hundred hours. It was impossible to forecast for how long this full power would be required by the Army; economy in the use of machines was therefore essential. The conditions on the Western Front were different. There an aeroplane could be replaced in a night; a wire was sent and a new pilot and machine would arrive next morning. A pilot did six to nine months at the Front, after which, if he survived, he returned to England for a spell of other work. In Mesopotamia there were a few reserve machines at Amara and Busrah [Basrah] which could be flown up in, say, a couple of days by pilots sent back from the front; outside these the nearest source of supply was Egypt, three weeks away! There was no certainty of any relief owing to high demand elsewhere, and a fresh man from England might take anything up to eight or ten weeks to reach us. The Mediterranean route had been closed, so troops and material came half-way round the world, via the Cape, with perhaps long delays at Durban and Bombay. It frequently

IV.15   From John E. Tennant, *In the Clouds above Baghdad* (London: C. Palmer, 1920), 59–63.

happened that reliefs went sick at one of these places, or even after getting so far as Busrah, and never reached us at all. The overworked, feverish individual, anxiously carrying on with visions of England, Home and Beauty, would, after an extra whiskey-and-soda, resign himself to his fate, and with the sympathy of his fellows go off again on reconnaissance "for the millionth time," still praying that his luck might hold till perhaps some day fresh blood reached the Squadron. It can be understood then how necessary it was to husband our resources, and in these opening days of action there was the greatest difficulty in restraining eager pilots. Work there was work for three squadrons, but in December, 1916, the Western Front absorbed new units ere they were hardly formed. We had to manage as best we could.

It was common in the great deeds perpetrated in France for the best part of a squadron to be put out of action before nightfall. Here in this far land, where, without aerial observation, shot might as well not be fired; where maps were insufficiently accurate for troops to march by; and where, unless guarded and forewarned by the Air unit, men might walk into unknown and ambushed *nullahs* [gullies]; it would have been a sorry tale to tell G.H.Q. that there could be no flying on the morrow because of casualties to-day. The risks had to be taken and we backed our luck; it never failed. A feature of the country that considerably promoted the efficiency of close co-operation was the fact that a good pilot could generally land by the unit itself, give them their accurate position and inform the commander of the situation personally. It was done on many occasions.

On this first day of fighting, enemy aircraft made another attempt to come out, but was met over Kut by D. H., who chased it down on to its own aerodrome in a steep nose-dive; whereupon, taking steady aim, he dropped a bomb which dropped only ten yards from its tail as soon as it had landed.

In the evening a message came through that Lieuts. Chabot and Browning had been forced to land in front of our cavalry with a main strut shot away. For the benefit of the fresh air I flew out with a spare in order to get them back. The sun was setting as I arrived over the rearmost patrols, retiring by troops to their positions for the night; I could see Arab horsemen, showing up well in their flowing garments, hovering about on the flanks; I could also see the damaged aeroplane being dragged back by the cavalry. The ground was very broken, and it was necessary to land among the rear party, who were retiring steadily in open formation. As I came low one of the horses took fright, threw its "sowar" [rider] and bolted, dragging the rider over the stony ground; he must have been killed. Events moved rapidly. It had been my intention to land, hand them the strut to take back to the machine, and clear off without stopping my engine. But the engine unfortunately stopped as I landed. A "sowar" galloped up and took the strut while I endeavoured to start the engine single-handed. The last few "sowars," thinking I was about to start, were retiring past me to the right and left, occasionally turning round to fire back at the "Buddoos" (Arabs), who were blazing off their old "bundooks" and spitting up the sand all round. It was rapidly growing dark, and the situation was unpleasant; in a moment I should be alone with these howling savages all round. As I was exerting my best strength to start the propeller, a British officer fortunately came galloping back. Major Seeker, of the 14th Hussars; he had been an aerial observer in France. I leapt into my seat and he started me off, thereby saving an awkward situation. The damaged aeroplane was never recovered; the cavalry dragged it five miles, but to do so had to hack off its wings; the machine had to be left outside protection on account of a deep nullah filled with water; when the engine was regained it had been damaged beyond repair by Arabs.

That night of the 14th/15th December, Captain Herring went out on a moonlight reconnaissance to trace any move the enemy might contemplate under cover of darkness. He discovered that the Turkish pontoon bridge had been dismantled, and was being towed in sections further up-stream by a steamer. As a result of the continual bombing the steamer repeatedly slipped her tow, and the pontoons drifted down into the banks; the steamer went ashore herself several times. The pilot twice returned to Arab Village to replenish his bombs, and the same thing happened again. As a result the steamer accomplished nothing for six hours. Captain Herring dropped twenty-four bombs during the night from a height of from two to four thousand feet, under continuous rifle fire. The day broke to find the enemy without communication between their forces on either bank, and the pontoons were not collected or the river bridged till later in the day. It was an achievement of great magnitude for one individual.

V

Mobilizing the Home Front

Preparing citizens to make sacrifices during wartime, not just on the battlefield but in hearth and home, forced governments eventually to take draconian measures. Governments expanded their power to an unprecedented degree with the enactment of emergency legislation that suspended basic civil liberties in the name of national security. Germany and France revived mid-nineteenth-century siege laws, while Italy, Austria-Hungary, Britain, Australia, and Canada passed legislation allowing them greater latitude to ensure their citizens' compliance. Private letters from soldiers to their families were censored, suspected spies and enemy aliens rounded up and sent to internment camps or deported. New government agencies sprang up to deal with issues of labor and production, food supply and distribution, as well as transportation and engineering. But because few had foreseen just how costly and drawn out this war would prove, states were ill-prepared for the conflict and their extension of authority and efforts at regulation were, as a consequence, often haphazard, inconsistent, and unprecedented.

Poor planning and insufficient resource management led inexorably to economic dislocation, especially food shortages and, eventually, to rationing in Germany, France, and England. Italy fared no better. By the end of 1916, food shortages had become a way of life, and between 1917 and 1918, the government also resorted to rationing. Although intended to provide a basic minimum caloric intake for citizens, rationing in fact did not solve the problem of food shortages. Those who needed food the most, such as working-class children and pensioners on fixed incomes, still found sustenance difficult to obtain, for the government allocated the best food to male workers. Britain and France seem to have suffered the least privation, compared with Russia, Austria-Hungary, and blockaded Germany. In Austria, the number of hunger

Empires, Soldiers, and Citizens: A World War I Sourcebook, Second Edition.
Edited by Marilyn Shevin-Coetzee and Frans Coetzee.
© 2013 John Wiley & Sons, Ltd. except sources 1 to 22. Published 2013 by John Wiley & Sons, Ltd.

strikes climbed from 40 percent of all strikes in 1916 to 70 percent the following year. Beginning in the spring of 1915, Russian women agitated against shortages and sky-rocketing prices. In Italy in 1917, severe bread shortages sparked protests in Milan and Turin.

Food prices throughout Europe had begun rising before the war, but individuals who could afford it increasingly turned to paying black-market prices for basic necessities. Government subsidies to soldiers' families failed to stem burgeoning infant mortality and disease and the declining birthrate. In desperation, politicians began preaching frugality and thrift, not to mention ingenuity, as the best way to endure home-front hardships. Small "war gardens" were planted, and cookbooks instructing working-class wives on the principles of nutrition and stretching the family food budget proliferated.

For women, the war imposed special burdens. Whether employed in the industrial or agricultural sectors or engaged in domestic service, women still bore principal responsibility in the "traditional" female sphere and on the home front. They endured the burdens of domestic life, such as standing in seemingly interminable lines for scarce food, especially meat, eggs, and sugar. And although the conflict offered them avenues into the workplace, European women remained disenfranchised and earned inferior wages. During the first few months of the war, unemployment actually rose for women in industries such as textiles and clothing that supplied civilian markets.

But as the war ground on and casualties mounted, industrialists and governments realized the potential pool of labor that women represented and began to train them for skilled positions left vacant by male employees now serving in the military. Beginning in 1915, women gained access to occupations from which society had formerly excluded them. In 1916, the French government adopted a policy by which women, many of whom had never worked before or who had labored in more traditional areas (such as textiles), replaced male workers called to the front. French women, spurred by the chance to earn crucial extra income, accounted for one-quarter of personnel in war factories; their numbers had quadrupled to some 1.6 million. The German government also sought to offset loss of male labor by recruiting women for positions in war industries in 1917, offering them special incentives such as higher pay and factory housing. Because government supplements for soldiers' families were meager and housing extremely expensive and difficult to come by, such incentives had instant appeal. German women worked in engineering, metallurgy, and chemical production in numbers six times greater than on the eve of the war, and British women flocked to munitions factories. Russian women assumed prominence in the transport and utility industries, and in Vienna, women constituted 54 percent of the city's streetcar workers by 1918.

Many women who worked in the factories did so out of necessity, to provide for themselves or, their husbands at the front, for their families. Financial incentives, however, masked the realities of the industrial workshop. On the factory floor, women encountered discrimination by men who envied their ability to learn difficult skills rapidly and who feared that they would take jobs from their brethren at the front. Some men, especially French munitions workers, went so far as to accuse women of indirectly contributing to the bloodbath at the front by freeing up males for military service. Even clothing provoked clashes: the overalls that many women wore to protect themselves from the dirt and dangers of the workplace drew ridicule from men who resented the "masculine" attire.

The blurring of gender lines in the workplace and at the front, with the service of female nurses and ambulance drivers, underscores the turmoil of the war years. Yet in other respects, the war actually reimposed traditional values. In Great Britain, for example, some historians have argued that organized feminism lost much of its prewar momentum and returned to the notion of innate differences between men and women. Some suffragettes such as Millicent Fawcett and her organization, the National Union of Women's Suffrage Societies, relinquished the idea of pacifism, supported Britain's entry into the war, and implored women to take up their traditional duties of caring for children and destitute women so as to maintain domestic order. Feminists in France, too, embraced the war effort but with the expectation that after the war, the government would reward French women with suffrage and employment opportunities. In Germany, the Federation of German Women's Associations *(Bund deutscher Frauenverein)*, an umbrella organization comprising a broad spectrum of women's groups led from 1910 until 1919 by Gertrude Bäumer, was swept up in the initial frenzy of the war and eagerly volunteered its members' assistance for the Fatherland. Likewise, Russian feminists called on women to do their patriotic duty for Mother Russia and extracted educational and employment opportunities for them from the tsarist government.

Male domination persisted, however, in the inequities of women's legal status. In France, Germany, and Italy, the Civil Codes reinforced the *paterfamilias:* men continued to maintain custody of their children and, to a large extent, fiscal control over their wives. Germany became an exception: wives could administer any money that they themselves earned.

The fiscal, psychological, and social impact of the war on widows proved equally unsettling. For the first time in their lives, many women found themselves required to manage their own affairs and those of their children. The loss of their husband's income, coupled with paltry widows' pensions, wreaked havoc on their already shattered lives. In Germany, for example, widows of privates, corporals, and sergeants received a meager allowance of approximately 33 to 50 marks (roughly $8 to $12) monthly, plus 9 marks per child. In Italy, widows of low-ranking soldiers received between 630 and 1,900 lira per year, depending on the number and age of their children. Widows sought to comprehend why their male-dominated governments abandoned them after they had urged their husbands and companions into battle, where their men had died for the cause. Although in some cases a widow might reclaim rights denied to her in marriage, such as property and child custody, by and large she retained an ambiguous place in the traditional family hierarchy. Some nations subjected widows to yet other traumas. Italian law, for example, imposed a strict ten-month mourning period on all widows. Failure to comply suggested disrespect for the deceased spouse and resulted in the forfeiture of the woman's dowry or inheritance from her deceased husband.

While women demonstrated their determination and dexterity in the factories, pronatalist movements throughout Europe were less impressed by women's functions in the public sphere and reminded them that their ostensible first duty as mothers and patriots was procreation. Declining birthrates before the war, coupled with the loss of men in combat, renewed fears about the shrinking of future generations. Demands for the strengthening of familial bonds revived. For example, when in 1915 and 1916 the French birthrate fell to a record low, the government promoted romantic liaisons through suggestive postcards that appealed to both sexes. One postcard, captioned "Frenchmen, this is what you are defending," featured a wife and grandparents seated around a small infant in a crib, with a map of France in the background. The card portrayed traditional images of men as fathers and warriors and women as procreators and protectors of hearth and home. Another postcard applauded the sexual prowess of soldiers and the biological function of women. Entitled "A good thrust," the card depicted three male babies dangling swaddled from a bayonet, with a soldier's cap and leave card nestled in the lower corner.

Germany had also long fretted over its declining birthrate and, like France, promoted domesticity for women, but through legal means. The German government intended to deny women the right to use contraceptives, although condoms for men remained permissible. Germany also sought to outlaw abortion unless a woman's life or health depended on the procedure. The government would have implemented these measures had the November revolution of 1918 not intervened. Even in Britain, pronatalist sentiments surfaced as couples continued to produce fewer children and as married women constituted a large share (about 40 percent) of the wartime workforce. The fear that gender roles would fall into a permanent muddle and that female babies would continue to outnumber males led to calls, especially by extremist groups, for women to produce offspring rather than machine guns.

In assessing the impact of the war on women, some scholars have suggested that by permitting access to paid employment and occupational choice, the war proved a liberating experience for them. According to this line of argument, women gained satisfaction from their contribution to the war effort, while men were forced to concede, however grudgingly, that female workers in fact could perform many tasks once segregated by gender. Yet the war merely accelerated a trend of women's entering the workplace that actually began before the conflict, although it did redistribute women into new work classifications. In fact, the upsurge in female employment in war-related industries proved transitory. After the war, women workers were displaced as economies readjusted to peacetime and soldiers returned home to resume their jobs.

One could also point to the concession of female suffrage during the war by Denmark (1915) and the Netherlands (1917), both neutral, and in Britain (1918) and Germany (1919) as proof that the position of women improved. But women's right to vote was often subject to special restrictions. In Britain, the government granted woman suffrage in conjunction with introducing universal manhood suffrage, but only to women over thirty. Men could vote at age twenty-one. Under the Weimar Constitution, German women obtained sexual equality, although the document left the civil rights and duties of both men and women ambiguous. French women, on the other hand, were denied the vote until after the Second World War.

The State

The first extract below is by John Hobson, a prominent exponent of the New Liberalism in England and a trenchant critic of imperial expansion. Here he voices the apprehension that in a war ennobled as a struggle to preserve liberty in the face of arbitrary state power (as in the case of tiny Belgium against Prussianism), the means to which an intrusively organized Britain was resorting to achieve the otherwise laudable end (victory) were no longer justified. Similar sentiments about the unintended consequences of total mobilization were not confined to intellectuals, however, as evidenced by the reflective letter to his mother by Captain John Crombie of the elite Gordon Highlanders. The erosion of the German civilian government's power in the face of the encroaching influence of the military authorities is a principal theme of the third document. Its author, Albrecht Mendelssohn-Bartholdy (who counted among his distinguished ancestors the famous philosopher Moses Mendelssohn and composer Felix Mendelssohn-Bartholdy), was a committed liberal who had directed the Institute for Foreign Policy in Hamburg. The fourth source illustrates the old adage that in war the first casualty is journalistic freedom. Governments intent on maintaining morale were as concerned about the control of information as the control of production, and the following catalog of prohibited topics indicates how intrusive censorship could be.

The dictates of military efficiency could justify intrusion into various aspects of private life, including drinking behavior (British pubs, for example, found their hours curtailed by the government) or sexual activity. During the Franco-Prussian war of 1870–71, the equivalent of an army corps (over 33,000 men) had been incapacitated in German military hospitals with venereal disease. The fifth source, a report in the prestigious British medical journal, *The Lancet,* details the reasons why rates of infection rose during wartime and the efforts by the German authorities to prevent a recurrence on a similar scale after 1914.

The final two selections explore the aspects of governmental action in Russia. Prince Georgi Lvov headed the All Russian Union of Zemstvos and was a key figure in the subsequent Provisional Government. Established in 1864 as representative institutions for local government, the *zemstvos* would serve as one focus for organizing popular support for the war effort. Here, late in 1915, in a speech to a congress of representatives from the zemstvos, Lvov reviews the difficult challenges the All Russian Union had faced and the real successes it had achieved. More ominously, however, his speech also touches on the widening gap between the Russian state and its people. Traditionally, one way to promote that bond had been through education, but the war disrupted education as much as other areas of civilian life. School buildings were destroyed or requisitioned, whole regions were overrun and students forced to seek refuge, and other needs often took priority. The selection below, by three contemporary experts on the subject, notes the emergence of new antagonisms and the erosion of some entrenched attitudes, including the prospect (ephemeral as it turned out) that religious prejudice might be mitigated by a spirit of universal sacrifice.

1. The War and British Liberties

Liberty as a True War Economy

Even if the defence of the British democratic State, founded on the maintenance of the free moral personality of its citizens, were adjudged unsound, the attempt suddenly to transform our worse policy into the better German policy for the purposes of war, would be exceedingly unwise. The addition of, at the most, a few hundred thousand unwilling men to the fighting forces of the nation is a poor compensation for the moral and intellectual shock of a sudden reversal of the forces which have moulded the entire course of British history. And when I call it a poor compensation, I do not mean merely in the long run, I mean also for the immediate practical work which Britain has in hand, the winning of the war and the attainment of some settlement which afterwards will give a prospect of security. For though the full havoc of this intrusion of the spirit of Prussianism into our British life is not realized at once, the culmination of the long series of attacks on personal liberty in this striking and widespread example will do more to undermine the confidence in the Government and the moral support given to the purposes and conduct of the war than any other action that could have been taken. For that confidence and moral support have been evoked and sustained by the appeal to the judgment, will, determination, and voluntary co-operation of men's minds. They have responded lavishly with their work, their money, and their lives, because they were trusted. Conscription has been a rude formal withdrawal of this faith. It says, in effect, "You have sent out your sons, husbands, and brothers in millions to toil in the trenches and to risk and lose their lives: you think you have been liberal in your patriotic sacrifice of those near and dear to you. But, after all, you are unprofitable servants, you have not done nearly as much as you ought to have done. So, having drained you dry of all your voluntary services, we will extort the rest by force." The effect is to damp the ardor and depress the spirit of the people. They feel it to be a cruel and an unjust accusation. It begins to stir a spirit of criticism in those who hitherto had cheerfully accepted the statements of their rulers as to the national needs of life and money for the conduct of the war. Suspicions begin to spread, questionings as to the necessity of these new enlargements of our forces, the wisdom of their wide dispersal over many fields of precarious and unsuccessful action, doubts regarding the solidarity of the Government, and the discretion and disinterestedness of the ruling classes who are so dissatisfied with the extent of the people's voluntary sacrifices. I am not at all concerned with the validity of such doubts and suspicions. I merely cite them as examples of the sort of moral damages which in such a country as ours are the natural and necessary result of the sudden introduction of the Prussian method. Our militarists may reply that they care nothing, provided that they get the men, the munitions, and the money. But

V.1   From J.A. Hobson, "Liberty as a True War Economy," *The Nation*, July 29, 1916.

this is a foolish and short-sighted reckoning. History shows that the consent and the moral support of the people are essential to the successful conduct of a war, and that what the men and women at home are thinking, feeling, and suffering does act with direct and great force upon the *moral* of every army.

In other words, the collective strength of the nation, wielded by the State for the defence of its existence, is not enhanced but diminished by a sudden abandonment of normal liberty and a reversion to the distinctly lower principle of physical coercion. For what it gains in the sum of physical resources, the number of formal fighting men, is lost, and more than lost, by the weakening of that very factor of moral consent and spiritual conviction which constitutes the will to win.

It has been admitted that some losses of civil liberty are necessary in a State at war. It may not be easy, or possible, to draw any exact lines as to the particular encroachments upon normal liberty that are justified and those that are not. But when the determination of the limits of such interference is removed from all effective control either of the legislature or the civil courts, to be exercised by the arbitrary will of the military authority or by special tribunals relieved from the ordinary rules and safeguards of civil procedure, all sorts of excesses are to be expected.

⟨℘⟩

2. The State as the Supreme God

[France] March 2nd, 1917

The Union of Democratic Control [a leftwing pressure group dedicated to making the conduct of foreign policy more open and responsive to popular opinion] was the only sensible Socialist organisation before the war, and a very good one. I don't know what its Peace ideas are, but as a matter of fact I am quite in agreement with Snowden [Philip Snowden, a prominent Labour party politician, pacifist, and its first Chancellor of the Exchequer in the 1920s] and that lot. Their trouble to my mind is, that they have such an irritating way of putting their opinions, not that the opinions are wrong in themselves. Anyhow when you think of it, the moral situation is damnable—we can only beat Germany by assuming her mentality, by recognising the State as the Supreme God whose behests as to military efficiency must be obeyed, whether or no they run counter to Christianity and morality. We call their use of gas inhuman, but we have to adopt it ourselves; we think their policy of organising the individual life contrary to the precepts of freedom, but we have to adopt it ourselves; we profess to shudder at the Zabern incidents [a town in annexed Alsace where the German garrison abused local civilians with apparent impunity], but what of our treatment of conscientious objectors? Oh! There are stacks of incidents, and the only hope is that we can drop it after the war. I agree I can't suggest an alternative, but I also agree with Ramsay Macdonald [future

V.2   From Laurence Housman, ed., *War Letters of Fallen Englishmen* (London: Victor Gollancz, 1930), 80–81.

Labour Prime Minister who adopted antiwar stance], that it shows that the way to defeat German militarism was not by fighting it—not the best way at least. And I don't believe we shall stamp out German militarism at the end of it; you can't change a nation's morality by military conquest, I am sure. But of course one must admit that if we had not fought them, what else were we to do? I suppose at this stage of the world's history one could not expect anything else. It is an interesting question.

3. Germany's Government at War

In the War the Government overreached itself . . . and it may also be said that the War brought out flaws and false pretensions in the Government which had long existed without causing much comment. It is difficult, if not impossible, to say whether that is primarily or mainly due to the peculiar German situation in 1914, or whether it is an innate corollary to war on the great scale in any case and everywhere. No doubt the constitutional arrangement by which, on the outbreak of war and almost automatically, the executive power is transferred from the civil to the military authorities, did much to raise reasonable doubt as to public administration in the minds of the public, and to make restive and critical those who had, before the War, been patient and long-suffering about public affairs, almost to the point of criminal indifference. Throughout Germany, including Bavaria, in spite of her special prerogatives of sovereignty, the military districts became the administrative districts, in some cases including the territories of several of the smaller central and northern states. The Emperor, as Supreme War Lord, was represented by the general-in-command *(Kommandierender General)* of the district, or, to be more precise, the lieutenant-general-in-command, for the general-in-command himself had to go on active service, and in his place it was usually a retired general who was called upon to reënter service and become the regent of the district. Nor was he a representative official only; he wielded an almost unlimited power in the case of civil administration and political rights generally, as well as in military matters. The conception of his office was essentially different from that of the Cabinet Minister or Secretary of State or Civil Governor *(Regierungspräsident)* whose functions were to be fulfilled by him. It was not service which was expected of him, but command. He was the military commander, *Militärbefehlshaber*, and as such had to exercise civil executive power in its entirety. Civil servants remained at their posts, at least those who had not been called to the colors, and except for the courts of law, the independence of which was strictly maintained, worked under military orders. In addition to this, the general-in-command had a whole staff of officers and officials of military rank. Most of them were retired on grounds of age or

V.3 From Albrecht Mendelssohn-Bartholdy, *The War and German Society* (New Haven: Yale University Press, 1937), 108–110. Reprinted with permission of Carnegie Endowment.

disability; and, in the later stage of the War, they were officers who had been wounded or contracted some illness which prevented them from doing active service. It was pure chance if any of these men who formed the government of a district and who, of course, were practically exempt from either ministerial or parliamentary censure or control, was either trained in administration of any kind, or was able to master the technique of civil government by sheer energy of will and quickness of intellect. Many of them were unable to do so, and some of them were unwilling, having their own ideas about the unnecessary fuss trained civil servants used to make about their work, thinking how easy it was for a businessman, or an officer, or any other man with ordinary common sense to administer, if not strict law, then at least a sound measure of equity to everybody concerned.

The people had thus more occasion and likewise perhaps a better opportunity of getting in touch with the authorities and of judging of their impartiality and efficiency. They had to ask all kind of permissions to do things which needed no special permit in times of peace. They volunteered information which they thought was essential; and during the final few months of the War the spy mania gave the information departments of the *Generalkommando* a lot of trouble. People were forced to go to the censor for *imprimaturs* for newspaper items or general literature, and to obtain leave to hold meetings, and so on. Favor or its opposite began to play a rôle it had never played before in administration; and where in peacetime businessmen (and idle men too) had often grumbled about there being too much *Gründlichkeit*—pedantic thoroughness—in the Civil Service or the courts of administration when dealing with petty cases, it became quickly the reverse under the new régime. Decisions were speedy, and, as must be the case with summary decisions, arbitrary; and suspicions of favoritism and petty corruption—there was hardly a case of gross corruption on the part of the military authorities during the whole of the War—grew rife.

Apart from that, some ill will was inevitable in the case of civil servants who were displaced, or who had to carry out orders where they had given them before. It was galling to a man who thought of his work as being a wholly necessary part of an organization that had been perfected through a long period of laborious effort and was admired throughout the world for its honesty and efficiency, to be told that any officer incapacitated for military service, or his non-commissioned subaltern with hardly a full command of German grammar (not to speak of the language of the law), could replace him at a moment's notice. The public—even those who were inclined to be opposed to military supremacy over the civil service—were apt to heap ridicule on those who had believed themselves indispensable for the maintenance of law and order, and who had been suddenly put out of court without any very terrible consequences. Bureaucracy must believe in the necessity of its labors. With this belief shattered, let alone the loss of public favor, it can hardly do its work as it should be done.

On the whole, it was more the system than the men who worked it which made the thing go wrong, and caused the aftereffects with which Germany has had to battle since the War. To my personal knowledge, which was acquired from contacts with two or three *Generalkommandos*, superior military commanders were almost without exception well-intentioned men, and in most cases very anxious to continue the administrative routine of the civil service with the least possible change and to observe the letter as well as the spirit of the law. Incompetence was chiefly noticeable in the censor's office, and in the censorship of private correspondence. The latter should have been left to the public prosecutor's office, and the former might have been entrusted to almost any civil servant versed in literature and newspaper editing rather than to officers or laymen who used their rank as reserve officers to offer voluntary service as heads of information bureaus, as railway station superintendents, commanders of prisoners' camps, and censors. In one of the districts which came to my special notice during the War the owner of a cheap bazaar who had risen to the rank of *Kommerzienrat* and captain in the militia by reason of his officious patriotism, succeeded in wrecking the domestic peace of his town by a few months' tenure of the censor's office; for he read private letters and used their contents to make those who had written or received them both suspect and suspicious. These were, happily, isolated cases. But even if there had been none at all, the system would have led to deplorable results in the end. It was bound to destroy the quiet relation of mutual respect and trust between the civil service and the public which forms one of the firmest bases of public order in a modern community.

✑

4. Censorship

A Memorandum for the Press   *Secret*

I

The Military Command, in referring to the "Prohibition of Publications about Troop Movements and Means of Defense," issued by the Chancellor, turns in this eventful time to the press as that organ whose works are being spread far beyond the confines of the Reich.

The history of late wars is rich in examples of how easily inadvertent reports may disclose to the enemy the marching up of the country's forces and thereby give the course of the war a turn destructive to the Fatherland. . . .

If the press is conscious of its heavy responsibility and the consequence of its reports, it will not light-heartedly become an ally of our enemy. It will give thanks

V.4   From Ralph Haswell Lutz, ed., *Fall of the German Empire, 1914–1918*, 2 vols. (Stanford: Stanford University Press, 1932), 1:178–181. Copyright © 1940 by the Board of the Trustees of the Leland Stanford Junior University, renewed 1960. All rights reserved. Used with the permission of Stanford University Press. www.sup.org.

to the War Command when the latter informs it as to what publications would be injurious to the Fatherland. By refraining unselfishly from every report of a military character it will spare the military and naval authorities the necessity of taking legal action against it, the strictest enforcement of which in cases of violations of this prohibition is demanded by interests of state.

The War Command will in its turn do everything to satisfy the legitimate demand of the nation for news. If these reports will have to be at first rather meager, it will be best for the realization of the patriotic effort of the press if it enlightens the nation about the reasons for and the necessity of secrecy and reminds it of its duty. . . .

II

It is impossible to say beforehand all that which in case of war should be kept secret in the interest of the Fatherland. Tact and insight of the representatives of the press will enable them to form a judgment from the following statements in what matters silence is being dictated until further notice.

Measures the disclosure of which could be injurious to the Fatherland and be of value to the enemy:

1. Formation of troops for the protection of boundary, coast, and islands. The guarding of harbor entrances and mouths of rivers.
2. Measures for the protection of railroads, canals, buildings, etc., and the formation of troops assigned for it.
3. The appearance of our own airships or aëroplanes.
4. Data as to the course of mobilization, the calling of reserves and the Landwehr, and the arriving of ships.
5. The placing of new troop formations and their description.
6. The arrival of detachments in the border districts for the preparation of the quartering of troops.
7. Building of ramps at railroad stations in the border districts by railroad troops and civilians.
8. The establishment of warehouses in the border districts and the purchasing of provisions by the military and naval administrations.
9. The shipment of troops and military authorities, of artillery, munitions, mines, and torpedoes from the garrisons, and the direction of their journey.
10. The journeying or marching through of troops of other garrisons and the direction of journey or march.
11. Arrival of troop divisions from the interior at the border and the naming of the station of their disembarkment and their quarters.
12. Strength and kind of troops advancing toward the frontier.
13. Naming of border districts where there are no troops or from which troops have been withdrawn.
14. Names of the higher leaders, where used, and possible changes in command.

15. Information as to departure and arrival of the higher military authorities at Great Headquarters.

16. Journeys and destination of Princes and other personalities, accompanying the army, as well as the place of their stay upon arrival at the front.

17. Delays of railroad shipments through accidents or the depreciation of railroads and bridges.

18. Work being done on fortresses, coast and inland defenses, in government or private shipyards and other establishments, entrusted with military consignments.

19. The making ready of rolling stock and laborers for purposes of the army or the navy.

20. The launching and damaging of warships.

21. Place of stay and movements of warships.

22. Arrival and sailings of ships of commerce.

23. The preparation and erection of barriers and supplying of ships with mines.

24. Changes of sea code and the extinction of lighthouses.

25. Damaging of ships and their repairs.

26. The garrisoning of places of naval information.

27. Making ready, equipping, and impressing of ships of the merchant marine for naval purposes; change of their crews.

28. The preparing of docks.

29. Publication of letters from people belonging to the army or navy without the consent of the military authorities at home.

30. Publication of lists of losses prior to their release by the military authorities.

The above refers to the allied armies and navies. Publications concerning them in the above sense are forbidden even in the eventuality of an outbreak of war. What countries are to be regarded as "allies" will be announced.

What other information the publishers should be able to find out after the outbreak of war through their foreign correspondents about the armies and navies of our enemies may be published only after the military authorities shall release such publications, since otherwise it will be easier for the enemy to draw conclusions as to our countermeasures. However, in order to utilize in time all reports from abroad, the publishers who come in possession of such reports would earn the praise of their country if they wire them—giving the source of the information— immediately to Great Headquarters in Berlin, in case the information deals with army affairs, or to the Admirals Staff of the Navy in Berlin, in case of naval affairs. The expenses entailed hereby will be borne by the Army and Navy Administrations.

It is desirable that none of these statements under II of this memorandum be published.

As far as is possible every publisher in the Reich has received a copy of this memorandum.

The publication of a forbidden military report in one paper does not absolve other publishers from the observance of the secrecy injunction of the Chancellor.

Supplement to the Memorandum for the Press

It must be emphasized that the attitude of the press and its observance of the rules laid down in the "Memorandum for the Press" so far deserves and finds full appreciation. In spite of that it must be noted that certain papers use now and then a language which is not adapted to the importance of the time. This circumstance forces the War Command, in order to supplement the "Memorandum for the Press," to formulate the following regulations, the observance of which during the duration of the state of war is urgently recommended. The War Command is convinced that the hitherto patriotic attitude of the press is evidence that the press endeavors also in the future to prevent unintentional injuries to our great cause.

1. A questioning of the national sentiment and determination of any German, any one party or newspaper is highly detrimental, because it impairs the impression of German unity and energy.
2. German victory means liberation for many foreign peoples from Russian despotism and English world-hegemony, and does not signify oppression. It would be injurious to our cause if German papers should express a contrary view.
3. The language used against the enemy countries may be harsh. However, an insulting and belittling tone is no sign of power. The purity and greatness of the movement which has gripped our nation demands a dignified language.
4. The foreign policy of the Chancellor, conducted upon instructions from His Majesty the Kaiser, must in this critical moment not be interfered with or hindered by covert or overt criticism. To doubt its firmness injures the prestige of the Fatherland. Confidence in it must be strengthened, and, like the confidence in the military leaders, it too must not be shaken.
5. Demands for a barbaric conduct of war and the annihilation of foreign peoples are repulsive. The army knows where severity and leniency have to prevail. Our shield must remain clear. Similar clamors on the part of the inciting press of the enemy are no excuse for a similar attitude on our part.

May 14, 1915

Military considerations demand that the press should refrain from discussing the question whether the German Colonial Possessions will be retained or lost or whether any territories outside of Europe might be acquired from foreign powers. Lectures discussing this topic in public are not desirable. Such lectures must not be reported nor should the papers express their own attitude.

May 14, 1915

It is highly desirable that the German press, when arguing the causes which brought about the war, should point to Serbia as the decisive factor. German war literature (for instance, the very title of a whole series of publications, *"The German War"*) has greatly helped persons in Austria who, in good faith or with malicious intent, wish to make it appear that Austria has been made the victim of Germany in the war. All polemics must be avoided, but it must be stressed that the aim of the war is to preserve Austria, an aim which is greatly in the interest of Germany. This will serve to counteract or, at least, to weaken from the very beginning the malicious agitation which is expected to break out in Austria after the war.

∞

5. War, Prostitution, and Venereal Disease in Germany

The present war has revived the problems of prostitution and venereal disease in an acute form, and, thanks to recent advances in the diagnosis and treatment of venereal disease, the energetic measures adopted in certain of the belligerent countries have given far better results than could have been obtained a few decades ago. But venereal disease remains a greater drain on the fighting forces than any other infectious disease, and the problems associated with it are still far from being solved. . . .

The Causes of the Growth of Venereal Disease in War Time

The axiom enunciated many years ago, . . . that the incidence of venereal disease rises steadily during a war, and is therefore directly proportional to its duration, is founded on many different factors. Recruits drawn from country districts, where neither prostitution nor venereal disease is known, find the temptations of a garrison town irresistible; the women, the money, and the time unoccupied by military duties all help to lower the rustic's moral sense. Destitution is another common cause, many a previously virtuous woman being driven by dire poverty to maintain life by prostitution. And in the case of both men and women separation from wife or husband, and the resulting loneliness and deprivation of an intercourse which has become second nature, lead to the establishment of extra-marital, promiscuous relations. War brings in its wake a code of morals so utterly at variance with the accepted standard of peace that many men successfully posing as models of probity at home run amuck when constrained only by a so-called military law. It is particularly in hostile, occupied territory that the licentiousness of the German soldier has been given free rein, to judge only by German sources of information. . . . In Poland the distress is so great that the bulk of the women still living there have been driven to prostitution as the only means of existence. In the Balkans the conditions in this respect are little better. Terrible as the fate of these

V.5   From "War, Prostitution and Venereal Disease: The Position in Germany," *The Lancet*, September 23, 1916, 567–568.

women is, it is safe to say that their sufferings would not have attracted the attention devoted to them by the German military authorities were it not for the ill-effects of this state of affairs on the health of the German Army. . . . In a small village about 135 men of the "Landsturm" contracted gonorrhœa which was traced in every case to the same source, a girl aged 13.

The German Campaign Against Venereal Disease

Germany has found it necessary to take the gloves off in the fight against venereal disease and to disregard many of the niceties and qualms respected before the war. Well disciplined as the German nation undoubtedly is, the restrictive measures put into force by the higher command would have roused serious opposition were it not for the plea of urgent necessity. As it is, a discussion has already been started in the German medical press on the feasibility of continuing after the war measures which have been found so effective at present; and the opinion is held in many quarters that after the war Germany will not tolerate the moral dragooning submitted to now.

In June 1915, v. Hindenburg issued his now notorious order which aimed at a drastic suppression of venereal disease. Briefly, this order threatened with imprisonment for from two months to one year any woman who cohabited with soldiers or civilians in spite of the knowledge that she was suffering from venereal disease. Prostitutes who failed to register as such with the police were also liable to a year's imprisonment followed by banishment from the occupied district.

Preventive Measures in Berlin

The war had not lasted long before the authorities in Berlin realised that energetic measures would be necessary for the restriction of prostitution in an aggravated form. The Chief of Police issued three orders in succession, beginning with the warning that the already existing regulations in connexion with prostitution would be strictly enforced, and that all provocation to immorality would be suppressed. In his second order he forbade all registered prostitutes to attend public places of entertainment, and in his third order he gave 24 hours' notice to barmaids and the like to quit. Thus, in one day about 700 women lost their employment and had to seek work in other and less exposed occupations. Much was done to find employment for these and other women left dependent on themselves by mobilisation.

Much has also been done for the German soldier. In Brussels, for example, a special institution has been organised for the comfort and entertainment of the 4,000 Germans of the railway service in which, as might be expected, the incidence of venereal disease is extraordinarily high. On the lines of communication and in many towns reading-rooms and entertainments have been provided as counter-attractions; and whenever it has been feasible billeting on private houses has been avoided. When on the march soldiers are not put up in towns or densely populated districts, and when it is impossible to avoid quarters in a town the soldiers' leave is restricted. An educational campaign among soldiers has been conducted with great thoroughness, but it has been found that a whole sheaf of printed warnings is incomparably less impressive than the demonstration . . . of a severe case of venereal disease. The treatment of venereal disease by quacks has been practically stamped out by certain army commanders, and penalties attached to the concealment of venereal disease have been most conducive to early detection and treatment.

Control of Prostitution

Judging by the recent utterances [of] authorities . . . , the belief is prevalent in Germany that extensive extra-marital sexual intercourse is an inevitable evil; the moral regeneration of the nation is not practical politics, and every effort should be concentrated on rendering irregular relations as harmless to their patrons as possible. In other words, the dangers of venereal disease from prostitution must be reduced to a minimum, and this aim naturally raises the old arguments for and against brothels under medical supervision. . . .

Prophylaxis of Venereal Disease

The decline of venereal disease in the German Navy during the last decades has been largely attributed to compulsory prophylactic measures. These were not compulsory in the army before the war, but in some commands they have subsequently been enforced, and the soldier who contracts venereal disease and is found to have omitted the ritual of prophylaxis is punished.

The æsthetic aspect of this system of prophylaxis seems to have been lost sight of under the stress of war, the suppression of venereal disease at whatever cost being the first thought of the military authorities. Even Germans who before the war were vehemently opposed to the system of prophylaxis and the moral degradation entailed, seem to have come round to the view that nothing short of this unsavoury measure can be expected to check the spread of venereal disease. Many of them now admit that individual prophylaxis is the most powerful weapon against venereal disease yet known. . . . Though the law still penalises the sale of anticonceptional remedies in Germany, her leading military authorities not only countenance but recommend their employment as preventives of venereal disease. It has been calculated that the decline in the birth-rate due to anticonceptional remedies is to a certain extent compensated for by the relative immunity to venereal disease secured by these remedies. And the decline of the birthrate traceable to venereal disease itself is far from negligible, for it has been estimated that gonorrhœa has reduced the annual number of births in Germany by 200,000 and syphilis by 70,000. Before the war some squeamishness was felt by the medical profession with regard to recommending condoms; as preventives of conception they were viewed with disfavour by the authorities. But this property of the condom has almost been lost sight of during the war. . . . Every facility is given the German soldier to provide himself with this and other devices, and printed leaflets describing their mode of application are distributed broadcast by the military authorities to the soldier. In some commands the soldiers are equipped with small outfits containing calomel or sublimate ointment and solutions of silver nitrate, and it is even reported that these packets have become so popular as to be sent to soldiers as "Liebesgaben an den tapferen Feldgrauen" [gifts for our brave soldiers in field gray].

6. The Russian State

Gentlemen: at the very start of the war, when Russia was confronted with problems that were beyond the administrative capacities of our governmental machinery, and when the unprogressive methods which had become firmly and deeply rooted proved themselves bankrupt in the face of those unexpected, feverish demands of history which suddenly overwhelmed us,—we, men of the zemstvo, went to work without any hesitation for the good of the state.

We knew that life itself would summon us to this work. To us, the call did not come as a surprise. Recall to your minds the modest proposals made to us at the beginning of the war, that we should take part in the relief of the sick and wounded soldiers, and compare them with our expectations at that time and the present state of affairs. We do not fight, and we do not now have to fight, for the right to take part in the activities of the State. Life itself is giving that right to us, and we have gradually gone ahead in our work, from rendering hospital service to supplying the wants of the army in the trenches, furnishing it with ammunition, preparing shells, constructing lines of defense, and so on. Hospital, commissary, artillery, engineering services, every branch of the life of our army at the front and in the rear, has become near and dear to us. We have actually been welded together with the army. National in its objects, the war has become truly national in the manner of its conduct as well. . . .

Gentlemen, this national war has turned upside down all the old notions, traditions, and old standards. In reality, we have no longer those old divisions and cells among which the component parts of the body politic had been distributed and artificially maintained. All distinctions between the nationalities composing our State, all party differences, are obliterated. The age-old distribution of functions among the different elements of the State is changing. It is true that the force of habit still makes them hold on to the old forms, but the new demands are more

V.6 From Frank Golder, ed., *Documents of Russian History, 1914–1917* (Gloucester, MA: Peter Smith, 1964), 146–149.

powerful than force of habit, and we all feel that life itself is seeking, and finding, a fresh channel for its mighty current. . . .

For us, no peace is possible. No yoke will be accepted by the Russian people. For them, there can be only one issue of this war—complete victory. We are now retreating, yes, but we know that we shall again advance. We are fully aware that our valiant army and our heroic people are conquering, even while retreating. Their valor and their self-sacrifice give strength also to our own spirit, the spirit of the rear. And it is our sacred duty to uphold this spirit, this courage, and to organize for a conquering spirit in the rear. But we must not for an instant forget that the future of our national existence, of our great country, hinges not only upon the issues of the war, but likewise upon the things that happen in the course of the war. We are fully aware that the loftier the ideal we are aiming at, the longer and harder must be the road we have to travel, and the more we shall require endurance and patience.

Our country is longing not only for the resumption of peaceful existence, but for the reorganization of that existence. Never before has the need of solidarity among all the forces of our country, probably, been felt as keenly as at this time. Never before has this unity, which was proclaimed from the heights of the throne as the pledge of a victorious issue, been needed as urgently as now.

We are happy to see how deep this unity has gone among the masses of the people, a unity that has actually welded together all the nationalities of the empire into a single unit with the army. To our regret, however, we fail to observe solidarity between the ruling powers and the people, and this we are bound to declare emphatically to these powers, for that is the only thing that still obstructs our organization of victory.

∽

7. Russian Education

Apart from the external difficulties which beset the normal course and development of secondary education, the War itself rapidly affected the internal life of the secondary schools.

The rich and varied information contained in the answers sent in by parents and teachers from all over the country to an inquiry published in November 1914 in a number of educational periodicals makes it possible for us to obtain some knowledge of the effects of the War upon the psychology of pupils in the secondary schools.

"War, as may be expected, produced a stronger impression upon children living in towns than upon those living in the country, and among the former a stronger

V.7   From Paul Ignatiev, Dimitry Odinetz, and Paul Novgorotsev, *Russian Schools and Universities in the World War* (New Haven: Yale University Press, 1929), 72–77, 83–84. Reprinted with permission of Carnegie Endowment.

impression upon children living in large cities than on those living in small provincial towns." The senior pupils of secondary schools were now often compelled to think about complex problems which under normal conditions would have been beyond their grasp. The more mature among them, those belonging to the better educated social groups who had more of an opportunity to follow world events and to observe the reaction of them upon their elders, were prone to such valorous discussions as the responsibility for the War, the relative merits of Germany, France, Great Britain, and Russia, the respective values of the civilization of those countries. They drew plans for the defeat of the enemy, drafted conditions to be embodied in the future peace treaty, and remodeled the map of Europe. But generally speaking, the pupils of secondary schools reacted to the War in a manner similar to that of the pupils of elementary schools. This is of course particularly true in the case of the junior pupils.

"My boys are in a state of perpetual war," writes a mother. "The roof of the new attic is their favorite position. . . . Their games are full of hatred and violence." "The games of my boys," writes another mother, "have undergone a complete change. Travels, boats and buildings have now given place to war, the siege of fortresses, the mining of bridges, of fortifications and ramparts. In response to the news of the capture of Tsing-Tao they at once proceeded to the erection of the fortress, its noisy capture and destruction, and then came a triumphant procession with songs and banners through all the rooms, their faces radiant." An exhibition of children's drawings held in Moscow fully supported the view as to the popularity of military subjects.

The spirit of animosity toward the enemy was as common among the pupils of the secondary schools as it was among those in elementary schools. When a mother reports that her boy, eleven years old and a pupil in a gymnasium, "builds prisons for Germans and erects gallows on which to hang them," she gives a vivid illustration of one of the fundamental conditions of the state of the children's minds at that time. "My son, now in the sixth year in a gymnasium and one of the best students in his class," writes another mother, "continues to dwell each day on the destruction of traitors. His eyes flash when he hears the news of the sinking of a German cruiser or of some other loss suffered by the enemy. Among the children the hatred of Germany is growing day by day. Today, for instance, they have decided to petition the school authorities for the removal of their German teacher and the discontinuance of their German lessons." The children of the junior year of one of the *real* schools [*Realschule* were German secondary schools designed to prepare students for tracks other than university study] were asked in 1914 to write a paper on the topic, "My wishes for the New Year." A great many of them replied with bad wishes for William. "I wish William and his sons would become ill." "I want to strangle, to hang William." Perhaps the kindest of them was the following: "I should like to make William a prisoner and put him in jail as an ordinary citizen, and not to hang him, as Grigoriev suggested." . . .

Even M. Kasso in August 1914 issued an ordinance to the effect that "pupils of Jewish religion from schools that have been closed owing to war conditions may, in the course of the current school year, be admitted into other schools, even if the latter have no vacancies for Jewish pupils, provided that the interests of Christian children are not thereby prejudiced."

The necessity for making such modifications in existing regulations, which admitted equality of responsibility but not the equality of rights, furnished an excellent example of the serious practical defects of these regulations, patently obvious even to their supporters. But under the restrictions imposed by M. Kasso, the position of Jewish children whose fathers were at the front was in no way improved. The children of a Jew, if he were killed or wounded, might enter a school only within the quota and, what is more, not on the basis of the marks obtained in examination, but, under M. Kasso's regulation, by lot.

Later, in May 1915, the new Minister, Count Ignatiev, permitted children of Jewish fathers, who had distinguished themselves or had been killed or wounded, to enter the schools not by lot, but by position on the list of marks; they were still admitted, however, only within the Jewish quota.

At the end of July 1915, at the instance of the Minister of Education, the Government sanctioned the unrestricted admission to the schools of Jewish children whose fathers were serving in the army. The new Minister, so far as we can judge from his whole action and the views he expressed, was unable to approve of the disabilities from which the Jews had hitherto suffered in this respect. Owing to general political conditions, however, even his influence was sufficient only to modify the existing regulations, not to secure their complete repeal.

The other amendments of the regulations made toward the end of the school year by the Ministry were still less important. They related chiefly to the conditions under which the final examinations might be taken. But even here small changes were indications of a new policy. Former Ministerial ordinances had shown marked distrust of the school boards, and had entrusted the fundamental control of the school to the authorities of the educational districts and of the headmasters.

The Economy

The Austro-Hungarian war effort was hampered by bureaucratic inefficiency and nationalist and ethnic rivalries, which magnified the economic disruption felt by each of the combatants. In the first document below, David Mitrany, a Romanian-born academic, analyzes the specific stages of the Empire's seemingly inexorable slide toward discontent, defeat, and revolution. Maintaining adequate standards of living was one crucial challenge that governments had difficulty in meeting, and the problem for Germany was made worse by Britain's indirect action against civilians by means of naval blockade. In the autumn of 1914, the German government convened a commission, chaired by Paul Eltzbacher, a prominent lawyer, to examine the country's food supply. The commission's optimistic conclusions were misplaced, but the report's introduction outlines some of the probable features of a war over food.

What this general stance meant for the realities of daily life is illustrated in the letters of Anna Pöhland, a working-class wife from the northern port city of Bremen, to her husband Robert at the front. Plagued by shortages and inequities of distribution, Anna was resourceful and intelligent in managing to feed her family. Her letters testify to the persistence of class tension and the demise of the *Burgfrieden*. The situation was no better in the capital of Berlin, and underlay the sharp critique of capitalism by the Socialist party deputy Emanuel Wurm. His charges were answered by one of the Berlin city government's municipal councillors, but he could not refute the idea of "defective supply." The fifth extract is taken from an investigation by the physiology department at the University of Glasgow into the welfare of forty Scottish working-class families in that city and to compare the results with a similar survey undertaken four years earlier. To compensate for diminished purchasing power and the scarcity of certain ingredients, especially meat and sugar, families were advised by wartime cookbooks, such as that by Mae Byron, to practice strict economy and extract maximum caloric value from unfamiliar sources.

8. Economic Exhaustion in Southeastern Europe

The Four Stages of Economic Exhaustion

The evolution of the economic situation during the War shows for every group of objects, whether actually used in the conduct of war or in everyday life, a growing and parallel exhaustion. That process of exhaustion passed in almost every case through four phases, each of which had its own peculiar characteristics. The first phase lasted from the outbreak of the War until the beginning of the first winter of war. During that time the disturbance caused by the conflict in economic life was violent in the extreme. It showed itself first in the undermining, for various reasons, of certain branches of production. A first reason was the sudden calling up of workers; many undertakings which were not engaged on war work thus had to close their doors, simply because they did not see whence they could get the necessary labor. At the same time the usual markets were utterly upset; exports were almost wholly cut off, and at home trade in anything but necessaries was at first at a standstill. Again, many industries were

V.8   From David Mitrany, *The Effect of the War in Southeastern Europe* (New Haven: Yale University Press, 1936), 157–161.

faced at once with a lack of raw materials, not necessarily because there was a shortage of them, but because the available supplies, having been requisitioned for military purposes, were not to be had at all, or only at exorbitant cost, for private needs. The conditions of the money market further contributed to that disturbance. The raising of the bank rate from 5 to 6 and then to 8 per cent had a discouraging effect on industry; so had the moratorium proclaimed at once at the outbreak of the War, as it impeded the free use of bank deposits. Moreover, the immediate cessation of all public works also reacted upon industry; and the complete suspension of all private railway traffic as long as the mobilization lasted, that is till the end of August, had, like the sudden departure of the workers, a bewildering effect both on industry and on agriculture.

The abrupt disturbance caused through these circumstances lasted, however, no more than a few weeks. By the end of August industry was already recovering from the first shock. Indispensable skilled workers were being released from military service, and women began to take the place of the absent men. The loss of foreign markets was made up for by fresh demand at home, especially from the army, which absorbed almost everything that any industry could produce. Private industries suffered at first, because private demand was disturbed, while the army seemed to have everything in excess. They began to recover as soon as it became clear that the needs of the army could not be satisfied by the few firms which had been producing war material already before the War, and that as large a number of industrial undertakings as possible would have to be enlisted for the production of military supplies. A few months passed, of course, before the readjustment could be made; during that period the army was insufficiently supplied, though in a decreasing measure. The exhaustion of available supplies was not fully overcome till the spring of 1915. During that phase one can distinguish thus three periods. The first was characterized by profusion in the army and shortage in private industry; the second, during the autumn of 1914, on the contrary by profusion in industry and shortage in army supplies; while a state of balance was reached only in the spring of 1915, a period which marked the second phase of war economics. During that first period began the process of inflation; at first it passed almost unnoticed, but later it had an enormous influence on the whole process of exhaustion. At the time one had the impression that the revival in industry had brought with it easier conditions in the money market.

With the spring of 1915 began the second phase. It had all the appearance of a time of economic prosperity. Industry was in full activity, and the needs of the army were being satisfied with relative ease. According to normal economic standards a steady demand and a tendency toward rising prices are the tests of a good situation. During that second phase industry enjoyed an almost limitless demand at continually rising prices. Profits were great, new fortunes were rapidly made, and all means and resources were thrown into the process of reproduction so as to exploit those favorable conditions. Little notice was taken at the time of the loss in the internal value of the money thus gained. More and more factories were being placed in the service of the army. A few special materials were getting short, but

were replaced with substitutes; coal and iron were still sufficient. The textile industry was working at full speed and the shortage in cotton did not begin to make
itself felt until the second half of 1915. Agriculture, especially in Hungary and in
the regions which lay outside the battle zone, reached in 1915 nearly the harvest of
normal years, notwithstanding the loss of men and animals.

The real nature of that flushed prosperity was not then realized. It had its
roots in fact in the enormous increase of the currency in circulation. By that means
ready money was always available for the immense orders of the army, and the
prices paid for them could be ever higher. . . . This effect was perhaps more powerful in Austria and Hungary than in the Western states. As the blockade and other
restrictive measures had closed most of the avenues through which money went
abroad, the currency was continually coming back into circulation within the
country. Inflation and the consequent rise in prices were thus the means through
which the necessary sacrifice and limitations were imposed upon the population,
and also the means for drawing upon the capital resources of the nation for purposes of war. What on the surface, therefore, appeared as a flourishing state of
economic life, in reality was a creeping process of destruction of capital values.
"Capital resources which were meant to be placed in the service of production
were used up for military ends; they were gradually destroyed and could never
again serve the ends of production." This phase of fictitious prosperity was also
relatively the easiest for the army. Of the three levels of exhaustion—shortage,
lack, and want—only the first was felt at all so far, and even that not generally. It
was pointed out with relief that the disturbed conditions which had prevailed at
first had been overcome, and that the production of war material had reached a
very high level.

Gradually, however, certain ominously dark spots began to appear on the horizon. Among the first and the most serious was the institution of a closer blockade,
in March, 1915. By the autumn a number of raw materials were running short,
though not all of them. A severe shortage only began to be felt in 1916—in wool,
cotton, leather, iron; coal only in the winter of 1916–1917; animals and special
metals by the spring of 1917, when the army also began to have difficulties with
man-power. "If 1915 was a year, if only in appearance, of a flourishing economic
state, 1916 was a year of growing shortage, 1917 a year of transition from shortage
to want, and 1918 a year of extreme want." Taken as a whole, one can identify 1917
with the third phase of war economics. It was characterized by the struggle against
exhaustion, which in truth was often no more than a struggle for postponing
exhaustion. The supply of corn had become so inadequate that the Monarchy had
to be helped by Germany; the worst was for a time warded off by exploiting the
occupied territories. The replenishing of the army ranks was also getting difficult.
A special office was set up behind the front to weed out every likely man for military service. This led to a shortage of labor and, therefore, to a growing use of
prisoners of war. In the textile as well as in the munition industries only substitutes
were available as raw materials; the quality was bad, but at least the quantity could
still be made up.

Exhaustion began to creep in also in the spirit of the people. It was evident in the feverish atmosphere of the parliamentary bodies, and in a declining enthusiasm for the War. Extreme radical sentiments and slogans began to appear instead, and the people listened with increasing approval to those ideas and men who were least in sympathy with the War. Common sense demanded at that juncture an effort to end the War. The leaders of the Monarchy made indeed the well-known overtures for peace, but they failed. War had assumed the nature of an elemental phenomenon which could not be stopped at will at any given moment.

During 1918 it became logically clear that exhaustion could no longer be avoided. The supply of food was utterly inadequate, and only desperate efforts could keep it even at that low level. In certain regions the shortage had become chronic and was marked by occasional famines. The mortality rate rose rapidly, especially among elderly people and children. "No one will say it, yet everyone knows that they died of hunger." The shortage of food reacted on the production of coal. By the winter of 1917–1918 hundreds of thousands were already living in dark and unheated rooms. The lack of coal in its turn reacted on the production of munitions. At a joint Ministerial Council the head of the General Staff complained that the supply of munitions had fallen to the disastrous level of the autumn of 1914. People were going about in torn and patched clothes that offered scant protection against the weather. The shortage of fats was so acute that all sorts of experiments were tried, such as the attempt to extract fats from wild chestnuts and from rats. Even paper had become so short that the Government instructed all official departments and public institutions to surrender those parts of their archives which were not indispensable.

Nor did the army fare much better. July and August, 1918, were months of real hunger. For days on end the troops saw neither meat nor fats. Sawdust had to be added repeatedly to the available quantities of flour. It came about that whole detachments "deserted" with all their equipment from the base camps to the front line, because there they were entitled to one or two ounces more food. An examination along one section of the Italian front established that the average weight of individual soldiers was no more than fifty kilograms. Hardly a soldier possessed any longer a complete set of clothing. Some had a uniform but no underwear, others had underwear but no uniform; and all of them were in rags.

∞

9. Germany's Food Supply

The present world war is being waged with weapons which were unknown to any earlier age. Economic weapons have been added to military means of annihilation. In the forefront stands a scheme from which our opponents hoped great things

V.9 From Paul Eltzbacher, *Germany's Food: Can It Last?* (London: University of London Press, 1915), 1–3, 6–10.

even before the war, and which is now, after a succession of fearful defeats, doubly important to them. It is the famous starvation scheme. Our flourishing economic life has brought us into the closest connection with every country, and it is apparently only this connection which has enabled us to feed the ever-increasing population within our narrow borders; now our enemies desire to seal us hermetically from the outside world and to tie the veins of our economic life. Our army and fleet having shown themselves a match for half the world, our nation is to be conquered by hunger.

Germany and Austria are for the most part surrounded by hostile countries, the only neutral frontiers being those of Holland, Denmark, Switzerland, Italy, and Roumania. By means of a so-called command of the sea and by influencing our neutral neighbours it is hoped to cut off Germany and Austria from the rest of the world and so force them to their knees. Our enemies suppose that Germany and Austria cannot exist for any length of time without their enormous foreign trade, which in 1913 amounted to 21 milliards of marks (£1,050,000,000) for Germany and to 5 milliards (£250,000,000) for Austria. While much is hoped from tying up the export trade, greater results are expected from hindering the importation of all that we need for manufacture and daily life—wool, cotton, petroleum, copper, and the like, but, above all, food for man and beast. It is believed that we should find it difficult to hold out for any length of time without our exports—and quite impossible without our imports. This plan of campaign was originated by England, who, in her ruthless desire for power, has never hesitated to countenance the use of any weapon, and in her colonial wars has quite forgotten how to fight decently. The concentration camps of the Boer War afford the latest proof that the English gentleman is not ashamed to make war against women and children; now England desires to use this well-tried weapon on a large scale, and would like to make the whole of Germany one vast concentration camp. France, corrupted by her English alliance, has taken up the starvation idea with rapture, though it is little worthy of so chivalrous a nation. . . .

The English fleet takes care not to attack ours, but strives to impede our trade in every way. Though it is contrary to all modern idea of right, England has stubbornly refused to accede to the demands of the other Powers that she should respect the defencelessness of enemy private property at sea, and now her fleet's most enlightened task consists in crippling German merchant shipping. Even neutral shipping which could contribute to our support is hindered in every way. . . .

England's special object is to crush our foreign trade, and she hopes to attain that object the more thoroughly the longer the war lasts. Trusting to her insular seclusion, and because she carries on the war by means of a paid mercenary army, she has little to fear from a long war. With her cold business sense, she brought about and began the war, and apparently considers she has more to gain than to lose from a protracted one. . . .

While Germany, in common with Austria, prepares to meet, for years if necessary, the starvation scheme of her opponents by building up an economic state cut off from the rest of the world, a new problem presents itself to the political economist and the statesman—that of the political economy of the isolated German nation.

Not so very long ago it was thought that two new branches of learning should be placed beside political economy—world economics and special economics. World economics investigates the relations of various national political economies to each other rather than the political economy of a single nation; special economics, on the other hand, deals with the separate economies which make up every national economy, the agricultural, the industrial, and the commercial. World and special economics became so much the fashion that national political economy seemed almost in the background.

Now a situation has arisen in which we must remind ourselves that between world and special economics stands the political economy of our nation. Among the great acquisitions for which we have to thank the war, perhaps the greatest is that it has put new life into our national consciousness. Two dangers threatened us: love of everything foreign (or internationalism), and personal egotism (or individualism). In the most diverse paths of life, in art, literature, fashion, German characteristics seemed either to be forgotten in the general admiration of the foreigner, or to have lost all coherence in the strife of self-assertion. The war has changed all this. With our whole hearts we feel ourselves to be Germans. The cults of the foreigner and egotism have fallen from us as if they were unfitted to us. Each sees his highest aim in serving the Fatherland to the best of his ability, and it now seems absolutely natural that world connections as well as private interests should be placed in the background of our economic life, and that we should think only of the economic weal of the German people. Should circumstances compel Germany and Austria to become one isolated State, each one of us will adapt his thought and deeds to the necessity without further ado.

In an isolated State, economic thought experiences a complete transformation. So long as our national economic life was bound up with that of the rest of the world, the idea of production stood in the foreground; if we produced valuable goods no matter of how one-sided a nature, no one doubted the possibility of exchanging them abroad for all that we needed in our daily life. . . .

So long as our economic life was bound up with that of the rest of the world, great personal freedom in our economic demeanour was possible. Even those who had given up the principle of boundless *laisser faire* still feared any far-reaching restrictions of economic freedom; but in the difficult position which has arisen through the sudden isolation of German economic life that fear must disappear. Our economic life is subject to State regulation to an extent hitherto unheard of. The Federal Council has extensive powers to prohibit the export or fix the highest prices of objects of daily necessity, and they can also demand any restrictions of economic freedom which the situation may require. Patriotic feeling has, however, accepted this far-reaching State regulation as absolutely justified. Nowadays everyone is a Socialist, so to speak.

∽

10. A Bremen Family's Suffering

April 27, 1916

My beloved, darling Robert,

The days are so warm now that the children are scampering about as if it was the height of summer. I need to lengthen the summer clothes for our little ones. . . .

It is really a shame that you, my loving Robert, cannot watch the children develop. Don't be angry that I haven't answered every letter, but I have had so much sewing that there never was enough time. Tomorrow I am preparing you another package, and I'll include a spoon. . . .

When I was asked by [a worker for the Red Cross] whether we have had enough potatoes until now, . . . I responded: mornings, potatoes, afternoons and evenings potatoes.

Yes, she said she had more than enough coupons for bread, but she had eight people for Easter and only one-quarter pound of butter. To that I responded that when one has a succulent joint or something similarly tasty . . . , then one hardly needs butter. But we have never once had enough money to be able to buy bones for soup, and additional butter— . . . we weren't even able to consume during peacetime because of a lack of money.

Yes, she replied, the old shopkeepers are at fault. No, I retorted. The government did not fulfill its obligation. Suggestions were made by our side [presumably a reference to the local branch of the Social Democratic party]. My suggestion was for a city kitchen so that the rich wouldn't be able to get anything [better to eat] than the poor. We always had lectures about [the importance of] economizing; instead the rich lived better. . . .

Your Anna

May 22, 1916

My beloved, darling husband,

You mean, dear Robert, we should take some excursions. You should understand, though, that one has to have sturdy shoes for that, and all our money goes toward food. Eggs cost three marks per dozen; financial support [from the government for wives of soldiers] remains unchanged. Meat is so expensive!

V.10   From Anna Pöhland, *Die Pöhlands im Krieg* (Bonn: Pahl-Rugenstein, 1982), 105–106, 113.

We are drinking more milk, however, at times three liters. We get two liters daily from our milkman. Frau H. can only get half a liter. . . . When will things improve? . . .

Anna

11. No Meat in Berlin

Speech of Emanuel Wurm

Gentlemen, the question on the agenda, though of Socialist origin, has also been endorsed by the other parties. It is a common question of all the city aldermen to the Municipal Council. It reads: What measures does the Municipal Council intend to adopt for procuring and regulating the supply of meat for the Berlin population?

Only a few weeks ago we had to call attention from this very platform to the unsatisfactory supply of provisions for Berlin and especially for the poorer classes. At that time it was the lack of potatoes and the failure to take measures to insure the necessary amount of potatoes for the market. At present the only alteration to be recorded is that of a scarcity of fat; butter and meat have supervened on a scarcity of potatoes. You all know to what tumults, rushes, and collisions people are exposed in order to procure those few provisions accessible to them. For hours they have to wait in front of the stores only in the end to face the well-known "Sold out!" It scarcely needs mentioning that these hardships fall chiefly upon the working population. How can willing and capable women, employed on war work, find time to stand before the shops and actually beg the necessary food for their families? At the same time these faulty arrangements entail a waste of productive power and a danger to health in the weather we had last week. And yet the proper authorities who alone can afford effective relief fail to take the necessary steps.

When today we put this question of relief measures to the Municipal Council, we do so in the first place because we demand of this body, as the official government of Berlin, that it definitely inform the responsible imperial and state departments that this mismanagement cannot be any longer tolerated. . . .

The ridiculous anxiety as to what foreigners may think and say—anxiety which causes the suppression of every unpleasant utterance—is merely a shield against criticism. [*"Quite right!"*] If the safety of the Reich is really dependent on what foreigners know about us it would be in a precarious state, for a glance into the foreign press will convince one that it is often better informed about German affairs than we Germans.

V.11   From Ralph Haswell Lutz, ed., *Fall of the German Empire, 1914–1918*, 2 vols. (Stanford: Stanford University Press, 1932), 2:106–109. Copyright © 1940 by the Board of the Trustees of the Leland Stanford Junior University, renewed 1960. All rights reserved. Used with the permission of Stanford University Press. www.sup.org.

The renowned German organization is more and more being revealed as a mere dodge to protect the farmers against the towns. . . . The root of the evil lies in the fact that in our whole arrangement we have no uniform regulation for the entire Reich and that consequently the individual districts have to compete with each other in their attempts to supply the necessary provisions. . . .

We approve, further, the adoption of the recommendation of the Municipal Congress that there should be, after the autumn of this year, a strict regulation of the distribution and price of potatoes, so that Germany's supply for the ensuing year may be amply secured. . . .

The arrangements for supplying butter, too, are very paltry. The butter card is a barrier card; it limits upward but not downward. You know the lamentable situation. Well-to-do people order butter by telephone and it is being kept for them, whereas the poor people have to wait for hours to get a small pat or else none at all. . . . Recently the papers stated officially that Berlin had received 125 grams of butter a head, . . . consequently there should be no shortage of butter. The fact is that the Central Depot has never delivered this quantity allocated to the city. . . . This is an intolerable situation and the executive must really take energetic steps to bring relief. It seems to us that Berlin is being treated as a stepchild. . . . The supply brought by post must be subjected to control. . . . In addition to scarcity of potatoes and butter, Berlin has now to face a scarcity of meat. . . . According to a contract with a Pomeranian company, 2,000 pigs should be delivered in Berlin every week. . . . The recent weekly deliveries of that company have been 500, 1,000, and 1,500, respectively. . . . For some weeks Berlin has had a system of delivering fat cows, and the number of meat cards has been increased to 500,000. But the old pressure of crowds at the meat shops continues, . . . although the number of selling depots has been increased to 500. Even this number is insufficient. . . .

A second source of meat supply is the Cattle Syndicate. . . . This combine includes no representatives of urban interests. . . . It is in close touch with the farmers, and does not send forward supplies even in fulfillment of contracts. This is another cause of the evil plight of Berlin. The city should have weekly deliveries from the syndicate of 2,125 full-grown horned cattle, 2,185 calves, 4,500 sheep, and 14,000 pigs. But in the first three weeks of April there was a shortage of 2,831 cattle and 8,278 sheep, and a surplus of 3,889 calves; and instead of 42,348 pigs, only 2,000 were delivered—a shortage of 40,000! If contracts are to be fulfilled in this manner, the city, of course, is powerless. [*"Quite right!"*]. . . .

Now it has been argued that it would be an agricultural crime to slaughter lean beasts, and therefore they are being kept on the pastures to be fattened. . . . That would be quite right if people were living in times of peace and had enough to eat. But now Berlin must demand that cattle should be brought to market even though they be not quite fat. . . . In conclusion, we must demand an organization that would be truly a central department, to be headed by a man who will be fairer to the cities than has been the case hitherto. We need a central organization, an imperial department which has the right to attach and confiscate provisions and to deliver them to the municipal unions. Such a department has been advocated by my comrades for some time. . . . There has been enough talk. . . . Consumers must no longer be sacrificed for experimental purposes. . . . There is no sense in issuing meat cards, unless the system is being extended uniformly throughout the Reich. . . . Such a regulation must take place, for the present situation is unbearable. . . .

Speech of Berndt, Councillor

Gentlemen, the council fully shares the anxieties of the previous speaker. . . . The regulation of the meat distribution is based upon the Federal Order of March 27 last, two regulations of which must here be emphasized: (1) the procuring of meat, and (2) its distribution. The first task is assigned to the Cattle Trade Association, the second to the Municipal Council. This order, therefore, has wrought a complete change in the state of affairs. What formerly was done by free trades is now assigned to the city. . . . As regards the distribution of meat, the Municipal Council was obliged to employ the services of an existing organization, the Berlin Cattle Commissioners, whom it is paying a commission of one per cent. . . . The reason for this arrangement is that the council has no available staffs of suitable persons for taking up the new duties. . . . The difficulties besetting the supply of meat are almost insurmountable. . . . The council has done everything possible to overcome them. . . . In the last three or four weeks we have done everything within human capacity, but of what use are any measures whatsoever if no meat can be obtained? This is the crux of the question; but it is just at this point that the council is powerless. The supplies contracted for are not delivered. From one combine, instead of 16,000 pigs we got only 96. [*"Hear, hear!"*]

What is the cause of this defective supply? In my opinion it is not due to lack of cattle, for conditions are so much better in other cities and other federal states. The trouble is due entirely to defective organization, the poor functioning of the existing Cattle Trade Associations, and the insufficient regulation of financing. . . . The introduction of a meat-card system for Greater Berlin at present is impracticable. . . . In view of the scarcity of the present supplies in Berlin the daily ration can be only 50 grams, and to fix such a slender ration by a formal document would be inimical to the interest of the Fatherland because of the effect of the bad impression that such a measure would have abroad. . . . However, as soon as it is possible to fix the daily ration at 500 grams the council will not hesitate to introduce the meat-card system.

12. Workers' Diets

The following study of the diet of labouring class families in Glasgow was made as part of an investigation upon the etiology of rickets at present being carried

V.12   From M. Ferguson, "The Family Budgets and Dietaries of Forty Labouring Class Families in Glasgow in Wartime," *Proceedings of the Royal Society of Edinburgh*, 37 (1916–17), 117, 126–127, 130–131.

out in the Physiological Department of the University of Glasgow. But the information gathered by Miss Lindsay in her study of the diet of the same class in 1911–1912 makes possible a very interesting comparison between the conditions of living then and under the present war conditions, and the fact that these studies extended over three periods—(1) Summer of 1915, (2) Winter of 1915, (3) Spring of 1916—enables some idea of the progressive effects of war conditions to be obtained.

Forty families have been studied. . . .

This table [p. 190] is very interesting as showing the fluctuation of the values of the main articles of diet. The tendency of prices is upward, with a slight fall in one or two of the commonest articles in Autumn 1915.

At pre-war prices oatmeal was the most economical source of both energy and protein; peas following for protein, and wheat flour for energy.

A year later (June 1915) beans were our cheapest source of protein, and rice of energy. Next came peas for protein, and flour as a source of energy.

In November 1915 oatmeal had almost recovered its position, being the most economical source of energy, and taking the second place as a source of protein. Beans were still the cheapest protein obtainable, and rice followed oatmeal as the cheapest source of energy.

In June 1916 (1) lentils and (2) oatmeal were the cheapest sources of protein, and (1) oatmeal and (2) flour the cheapest sources of energy.

Sugar and potatoes have undergone the greatest changes in value. At pre-war prices sugar was the most economical source of energy, following oatmeal and flour. Being restricted in import, sugar has been more subject to the causes which brought about the rise in prices than many other foodstuffs. Potatoes being mostly home grown did not rise immediately on the outbreak of war; indeed for a short time in the Autumn of 1915 they were selling at 5d. a stone, and formed the cheapest food at the time. An early frost in the Autumn of 1915, however, wasted part of the crop, and potatoes have become very dear. For a short period in June 1916 they were selling at 2s. 6d. a stone, a prohibitive price for the working-class housekeeper.

Animal foods are expensive at all times. At pre-war prices protein could be obtained from flour, lentils, peas, and oatmeal at about one-sixth of its cost when got from beef and mutton.

In June 1916, although meat had not risen in price to the same extent as the vegetable foodstuffs, it was still five times as dear as a source of protein, and over seven times as expensive as a source of energy. . . .

Change in Cost of Living

These investigations enable some answer to be given to the question of whether real wages have risen or fallen since the outbreak of war.

Food Values Obtainable for 1d., according to Retail Prices in Glasgow at various Periods (calculated from Cooper & Co.'s Glasgow Price List)

	Immediately pre-War			June 1915			November 1915			June 1916		
	Price per lb. in Pence	Protein in Grams	Calories	Price per lb. in Pence	Protein in Grams	Calories	Price per lb. in Pence	Protein in Grams	Calories	Price per lb. in Pence	Protein in Grams	Calories
Beef (stewing)	9	9.6	132	12	7.2	98.75	12	7.2	98.75	13	6.6	91
Suet	10.5	1.9	337	10.5	1.9	337	10.5	1.9	337	11.5	1.7	308
corned	12	10	107	17	7	76	17	7	76	18	6.6	71
Mutton (cheaper parts)	8	6.8	132	12	4.5	88	12	4.5	88	12	4.5	88
Bacon	10.5	3.9	256	13.25	3.1	203	14.25	2.7	189	15	2.7	179
Cheese (Canadian)	8.5	15.5	241	12	11	171	10.5	12	195	13.5	9.8	152
Margarine	5.5	1	659	6	.9	587	6	.9	587	7	.8	504
Herring (fresh)	4	12.7	92	4	12.7	92	4	12.7	92	6	8.5	62
(smoked)	4	22.7	187	4	22.7	187	4	22.7	187	—	—	—
Sugar	2	—	930	3.5	—	—	3.75	—	—	5	—	372
Potatoes	.57	14.3	542	.57	14.3	542	.43	19.1	723	1.17	7.1	271
Oatmeal	1.23	59	1512	2.47	25.4	753	2.14	34	869	2.29	21.7	814
Wheat flour	1.43	36.26	1155	2.14	24.2	770	2.07	25	798	2.29	22.7	722
Bread	1.5	27.9	810	2	20.9	607	2	20.9	607	2.125	19.7	572
Lentils	2.5	47.2	648	3.5	33.7	463	7.5	16	216	3.5	33.7	463
Peas	2	56.8	827	3	37.9	552	4	28.4	414	5	22.7	331
Beans	2.5	41.8	640	2.5	41.8	640	3	34.8	533	3.5	24.1	457
Barley	2	19.3	825	2.5	15.4	660	3	12.9	550	3.5	11	471
Rice (Rangoon)	2	18.1	815	2	18.1	815	2	18.1	815	2.5	14.5	652

The percentage of unemployment has fallen from 3 per cent. in 1911 to 0.5 per cent. in June 1916. Thus under pre-war conditions unemployment represented a loss of 2.5 per cent. more of the weekly wage than in June 1916.

The weighted cost of food, calculated from the relative values purchased per penny in the family budgets studied at the two periods, has risen about 50 per cent. since 1911–12. In the families studied about two-thirds of income was spent on food, so that a rise of $^2/_3 \times 50$ per cent. $= 33^1/_3$ per cent. of income would be necessary to compensate for the advance in the price of food. Adding to this the 6 per cent. rise from other expenditure, and subtracting 2.5 per cent., the difference in the loss of wages due to unemployment at the two periods, a rise in wages of 36.8 per cent. would be required to keep the standard of well-being constant.

In the recently published interim report of the Committee appointed by the Board of Trade to investigate the principal causes which have led to the increase of prices of commodities since the beginning of the war, the rise in the weighted cost of food is estimated at 65 per cent., which is equivalent to a rise of 45 per cent. in the cost of living among the working classes. These figures are calculated from June 1914 to September 1916.

According to figures supplied by the Board of Trade Department of Labour Statistics to the above Committee, the weighted cost of food has risen by 6 per cent. since June, when the last group of the present dietary studies was carried out. This is equivalent to a further advance of 4 per cent. in the cost of living, or an increase of 41 per cent. since the outbreak of war, according to the present calculations. The difference between this figure and that estimated by the Board of Trade Committee may be due to the following causes: —

1. That the character and quantity of the commodities purchased by the house-keeper has altered somewhat in the direction of economy. The use of less meat in some families, the substitution of cheap for the dear cuts of meat in others, and the increased consumption of margarine are instances of this.
2. That the "weighting" from which the Board of Trade figures are calculated does not exactly correspond with the proportionate use made of the various commodities by the labouring classes in Glasgow. As above stated, an average of 40 per cent. of the total energy in the food of the forty families studied came from bread, which had only advanced from 3d. to 4¼d. for the 2 lb. loaf (or 42 per cent.) by June 1916.

Conclusions

If the results of these studies can be applied to the labouring classes in industrial centres generally, they show to June 1916:—

1. That on an average the food supply was not less adequate than in pre-war times, although there was a tendency to a decreased consumption of protein in meat and an increased consumption of fat.

2. That the cost of energy in food had risen about 50 per cent.
3. That the total cost of living had probably increased by 37 per cent.
4. That the increase in the cost of living, resulting in a diminished supply of the necessaries of life, is being chiefly felt by the families of labouring men with a fixed wage, say from 20s. to 30s. weekly. Among the men who were irregularly employed before the war, or are now doing Government work, or are otherwise having a good deal of overtime work, the surplus of income over the necessary expenditure has materially increased.

In conclusion, I should like to express my indebtedness to the housemothers for their kindly consent and co-operation, without which the studies could not have been made.

❧

13. Practicing Strict Economy

At the present juncture it is obvious that we have all got to practise strict economy at every conceivable point. Not only is this advisable; it is absolutely necessary. And economy, like charity, begins at home.

It is more than merely economy in food which we have to consider. We must try to combine at least five methods of saving:

1. Economy in Fuel.
2. Economy in Labour.
3. Economy in Time.
4. Economy in Health.
5. Economy in Food.

The first and the last are, to most people, those of chief importance.

Economy in fuel is a matter to be studied at every turn. Wood and coal are both likely to be greatly enhanced in price as time goes on; gas will rise coincidentally; oil is not, to most people, an acceptable substitute for the above. In days when we each and all are desirous to "do our bit" towards the national good, when many of us are perforce working at a rate and to an amount which we never attempted before, and when such a number of women are obliged to fit in bread-winning with housework, the care of labour and time are vitally important. Unfortunately, as every woman who can cook is aware, it takes a vast amount of time and trouble to "make-up" small tasty dishes, and to do so cheaply. Economy, plus palatability, means so much grating, chopping, mincing, pounding, frying, whisking, etc., etc., that the person who achieves some little culinary triumph is often much too tired even to wish to taste it. And she has, therefore, carried out her economy more or

V.13   From Mae Byron, *Mae Byron's How-To-Save Cookery* (London: Hodder & Stoughton, 1915), 1–5.

less at the expense of her health. Economy in health is a much more vital point than usually strikes one in connection with cooking. Most of us are feeling the wear and tear of hard and anxious times; few women are quite as "fit" as they were before the war. Worries react upon the digestion, and it is no use setting food before people which will disagree with them. In almost every household there is somebody who can't digest certain viands—whether farinaceous foods, sweet dishes, cheese, pulse foods, uncooked vegetables, root vegetables, pork, etc., etc., etc.—and although it is impossible to cater for that one person separately, it is no use concocting meals of which he or she cannot partake.

It is extremely difficult to reconcile these five methods of thrift in matters of cookery for a household.

Cold dishes in general save fuel, and to a great extent time and labour (even though they entail a certain amount of preliminary cooking), but they are not so wholesome or digestible as hot ones.

Hot dishes, especially those which use up odds and ends, are more palatable and digestible than others, and one can save in food and money by them; but they entail more expenditure in labour, time, and fuel. . . .

To begin with the actual material. It is increasingly difficult to say how one best may live cheaply in the matter of food. (1) Fish is at almost a prohibitive price; for this reason I have only dealt with the cheapest fish, and tinned fish such as salmon and sardines. (2) Eggs are dearer and dearer; therefore, so far as possible, I have omitted all dishes requiring more than one egg, and have regarded eggs according to their definite dietetic value—not to be squandered lightly. I recommend the use of egg-powder and custard-powder for puddings and cakes. (3) Cheese is abnormally expensive; so, instead of treating it as a little extra luxury, I have strictly considered it as a very valuable article of food. (4) Meat is rising sky-high in price; it was therefore necessary only to include the cheaper cuts, and methods of utilising cold meat where a joint might once-in-a-way be bought. All dishes of veal and lamb have been entirely omitted. Dripping and "stock" are such indispensable articles to the cook, that she may think the above omissions increase her difficulties. But dripping can be bought, as it is wanted, by the pound; so can bones, for breaking up and boiling down towards stock and gravy. And this is a much cheaper way of procuring them than when they are purchased as part of a joint, and at the same high price as solid meat. (5) Bacon and ham, which are already beyond most people's purses, are barely mentioned in this book . . . (6) Vegetables are none too cheap for the town-dweller; the more fortunate countrywoman can here secure many opportunities for thrift. In any case, however, they are less expensive than the more highly concentrated forms of nutriment—meat, cheese, eggs, etc. . . . (7) Sugar is dear; but as an article of food it is so invaluable, combined with farinaceous or fruitarian diet, that a large amount of space has been given to simple family puddings and wholesome cakes. (8) Flour is "up"; but the advantages of home-made bread are beyond question, and probably the greatest saving of all, from a health point of view, can be effected here.

In conclusion, a number of topical hints and suggestions have been inserted, for the help of the harassed housewife, to whom, with most sincere sympathy, I commend this little book.

Women

The first three selections address the issue of women's wartime role in Britain. Marie Seers documents in the banking sector what modern sociologists have dubbed the "glass ceiling" limiting the advancement of qualified women into management positions, but offers a measured verdict on women's overall progress. The second article approaches the question from the perspective of a pacifist, Helena Swanwick, who, after graduating from Girton College, Cambridge, with a degree in Economics, had worked tirelessly for women's political and economic rights. She had edited *Common Cause*, the journal of the National Union of Women's Suffrage Societies, and was an accomplished writer. Here she seeks to take stock of the war's impact on women of all social classes, but within an overall gendered framework. The famous poem, "Women at Munition Making," by Mary Gabrielle Collins, succinctly reminds readers of the special dilemma faced by these women workers: did their productive role to build weapons of death conflict with their reproductive role to bring new life into the world?

The following four documents probe related issues in wartime Germany. Helene Lange was a teacher and advocate of women's education (in 1890 she had founded the country's largest women's professional association, for female teachers). Lange believed in sexual differentiation and argued that women would emancipate themselves not by conforming to male standards, but by refining their natural maternal role as guardians of stable families. Women's compulsory war service, then, should ideally complement men's recruitment into uniform. Magda Trott, affiliated with the National Liberal party, warns against the assumption that women might seamlessly substitute for absent men, a view reinforced by the attitudes of many male German officials. In October 1916 the Army's High Command sought a more thoroughgoing mobilization of the nation's economic and human resources, which meant that the question of female labor had to be confronted directly. Source #19, a letter from the Chief of the General Staff to the Chancellor, Bethmann Hollweg, illustrates the persistence of patriarchal social attitudes, even where these conflicted with the dictates of modern war. Even as the situation deteriorated, the next extract, a March 1917 memorandum by an influential bureaucrat from the Ministry of the Interior, indicates how officials continued to cling to such concerns.

One wonders what these men would have made of Russian women like Maria Botchkareva. Of humble origins, she had been put to work at the age of eight. Seduced in her early teens and forced into prostitution, Botchkareva found an escape of sorts by disguising her appearance and joining the colors. She was decorated for bravery under fire, and in the selection below, relates some of her experiences in uniform. The final selection is a sad reminder about the war's youngest victims. Absent fathers, working mothers, and declining nutrition were staples of olympian bureaucratic discussions of the social order, but the psychological and physical toll on children was pervasive and heart-rending.

14. Women at Work

The war has brought many social changes, none perhaps more striking than that which has drawn the married women of the better classes into the ranks of the workers. For the present this change may be an economic necessity, which nevertheless has serious disadvantages in the dislocation of home life for which it is responsible, but it is quite unlikely that after the war is over all these women, who for the first time have achieved financial independence and have tasted the sweets of liberty, will be willing to return to the old order of things. And if they are willing, the return to domestic duties for many will be an impossibility, for in some cases there will be disabled soldier-husbands to be partly supported; many women will belong to that sad company, the war widows; and even where there is no compelling necessity the more adventurous will be found reluctant to return altogether to the narrow walls of home. As a direct result of the war, too, it is quite clear that thousands of unmarried women will be unable to find husbands and will perforce remain wage-earners. Woman's demand for a wider field for her activities perhaps marks a stage in the evolution of the race. The pages of the past bear witness to her enterprise, and perhaps something of the spirit of the queens who reigned in the East, of St Hilda, who in the seventh century ruled a community of both monks and nuns in the abbey of Whitby, or of the women-professors of the Middle Ages, animates her still.

The public has accepted the new conditions with equanimity, just as it has accepted other changes of an equally radical kind. And, on the whole, the public has had no reason to complain. It has indeed had cause for congratulation in that there existed this reserve of industrial power which could be pressed into the service of the State, for that the banks do national service cannot be disputed. They alone are responsible for the control of the credit system which at the present time supports the entire social fabric of the community. It is the function of a bank to deal in credit, to withhold it or grant it, as occasion demands, just as it is the function of lesser institutions either to sell their goods or to hold them in stock. Unlike the goods, credit is not a tangible commodity, but it is none the less real on that account. Cheques, bills of exchange, and various kinds of securities all represent credit, for they are promises to pay a certain specified sum of money, and the

V.14   From Marie W. Seers, "Women in Banking," in Gilbert Stone, ed., *Women War Workers* (London: G.G. Harrap, 1917), 90–92, 98–99, 107.

actual money concerned in the transaction does not change hands. If this credit system were to collapse the whole structure of commerce would be shattered. Its intricate machinery is the product of the development of the agency of exchange which has replaced the barter of the ancients. The business of a bank is not so much to produce capital as to economize it and direct its flow in the right direction, and to do this successfully requires ripe knowledge and experience. . . .

The fact that, on the whole, the salaries of women in banks are on a lower scale than those of the men may be due to the low standard of efficiency which is all the majority of them can offer as compared with that of the men. Time, however, will remedy this defect. It remains to be seen whether time will be equally kind as regards their salaries. The old contention that a man must be paid at a higher rate than a woman doing the same work because he has a wife and family to support is economically unsound, and leads to the underselling of men's labour because it has to compete with the cheaper and equally efficient labour of women. . . .

Will women ever be bank managers? The view held by many people is summed up in the concluding remark of a banker of many years' standing who had been discussing this question. "After all," he said, "when one wants any real work done one goes to a man!" Yet the speaker's views on the possibilities of women as bank clerks had on his own admission undergone radical changes during the last two years, and were, he asserted, capable of still further modification. As a matter of fact, however, there are one or two women bank managers already in existence. There is, for instance, a tiny branch of one of the great joint stock banks in a little Welsh town where the manager is a woman. This looks at first sight as though the vexed question had already been settled. But this is not the case. There is all the difference in the world between the responsibilities of the manager of a small branch of a bank and those of the manager of a large one. And it is not merely a difference in the quantity of the work for which he is responsible, although the large branch may have some thousands of accounts while the small one has only a hundred or so. . . .

The past two years have witnessed many changes of a wholly unexpected nature. As far as women are concerned not all the changes have been for the better, but since they were inevitable, and brought about by sharp necessity which knows no law, the public did well to accept them in a philosophical spirit. Necessity, not choice, made Woman take the place she holds to-day in the ranks of the industrial army. Presently she will be weighed in the balance, and it may confidently be affirmed that she will not be found wanting.

☙

15. A New Role for Women?

How has the war affected women? How will it affect them? Women, as half the human race, are compelled to take their share of evil and good with men, the

V.15   From Helena Swanwick, *The War in its Effect Upon Women* (n.p., 1916), 3–11, 13, 23–25.

other half. The destruction of property, the increase of taxation, the rise of prices, the devastation of beautiful things in nature and art—these are felt by men as well as by women. Some losses doubtless appeal to one or the other sex with peculiar poignancy, but it would be difficult to say whose sufferings are the greater, though there can be no doubt at all that men get an exhilaration out of war which is denied to most women. When they see pictures of soldiers encamped in the ruins of what was once a home, amidst the dead bodies of gentle milch cows, most women would be thinking too insistently of the babies who must die for need of milk to entertain the exhilaration which no doubt may be felt at "the good work of our guns." When they read of miles upon miles of kindly earth made barren, the hearts of men may be wrung to think of wasted toil, but to women the thought suggests a simile full of an even deeper pathos; they will think of the millions of young lives destroyed, each one having cost the travail and care of a mother, and of the millions of young bodies made barren by the premature death of those who should have been their mates. The millions of widowed maidens in the coming generation will have to turn their thoughts away from one particular joy and fulfilment of life. While men in war give what is, at the present stage of the world's development, the peculiar service of men, let them not forget that in rendering that very service they are depriving a corresponding number of women of the opportunity of rendering what must, at all stages of the world's development, be the peculiar service of women. After the war, men will go on doing what has been regarded as men's work; women, deprived of their own, will also have to do much of what has been regarded as men's work. These things are going to affect women profoundly, and one hopes that the reconstruction of society is going to be met by the whole people—men and women—with a sympathetic understanding of each other's circumstances. When what are known as men's questions are discussed, it is generally assumed that the settlement of them depends upon men only; when what are known as women's questions are discussed, there is never any suggestion that they can be settled by women independently of men. Of course they cannot. But, then, neither can "men's questions" be rightly settled so. In fact, life would be far more truly envisaged if we dropped the silly phrases "men's and women's questions"; for, indeed, there are no such matters, and all human questions affect all humanity.

Now, for the right consideration of human questions, it is necessary for humans to understand each other. This catastrophic war will do one good thing if it opens our eyes to real live women as they are, as we know them in workaday life, but as the politician and the journalist seem not to have known them. When war broke out, a Labour newspaper, in the midst of the news of men's activities, found space to say that women would feel the pinch, because their supply of attar of roses would be curtailed. It struck some women like a blow in the face. When a great naval engagement took place, the front page of a progressive daily was taken up with portraits of the officers and men who had won distinction, and the back page with portraits of simpering mannequins in extravagantly fashionable hats; not frank advertisement, mind you, but exploitation of women under the guise of news supposed to be peculiarly interesting to the feeble-minded creatures. When a snapshot was published of the first women ticket collectors in England, the legend underneath the picture ran "Superwomen"! It took the life and death of Edith Cavell to open the eyes of the Prime Minister to the fact that there were thousands of women giving life and service to their country. "A year ago we did not know it," he said, in the House of Commons. Is that indeed so? Surely in our private capacities as ordinary citizens, we knew not only of the women whose portraits are in the picture papers (mostly pretty ladies of the music hall or of society), but also of the toiling millions upon whose courage and ability and endurance and goodness of heart the great human family rests. Only the politicians did not know, because their thoughts were too much engrossed with faction fights to think humanly; only the journalists would not write of them, because there was more money in writing the columns which are demanded by the advertisers of feminine luxuries. Anyone who has conducted a woman's paper knows the steady commercial pressure for that sort of "copy."

The other kind of women are, through the war, becoming good "copy." But women have not suddenly become patriotic, or capable, or self-sacrificing; the great masses of women have always shown these qualities in their humble daily life. Now that their services are asked for in unfamiliar directions, attention is being attracted to them, and many more people are realising that, with extended training and opportunity, women's capacity for beneficent work would be extended. . . .

The problem of the readjustment of men's and women's work after the war is going to be so difficult and so great that we want none of this frivolous sentimentality in dealing with it. We want facts. We want a sober judgment. We want an alert mind, which will meet the problems with no dead obstructive prejudices, but with the single intention to make the very best use of the men and women who will emerge from this ghastly catastrophe. To condemn any section of the people to inaction, to restrict or cramp their powers of production and of healing, is going to cripple the nation and be the most unpatriotic course conceivable.

The Need for Production

It is often forgotten that for full prosperity a country needs to be producing as much wealth as possible, consistently with the health, freedom, and happiness of its people. To arrive at this desired result, it is quite clear that as many people as possible should be employed productively, and it is one of the unhappy results of our economic anarchy that employers have found it profitable to have a large reserve class of unemployed and that wage-earners have been driven to try and diminish their own numbers and to restrict their own output. To keep women out of the "labour market" (by artificial restrictions, such as the refusal to work with them, or the refusal to allow them to be trained, or the refusal to adapt conditions to their health requirements) is in truth antisocial. But it is easy to see how such antisocial restrictions have been forced upon the workers, and it is futile to blame them. A way must be found out of industrial war before we can hope that industry will be carried on thriftily. Men and women must take counsel together and let the experience of the war teach them how to solve economic problems by co-operation rather than conflict. Women have been increasingly conscious of the satisfaction to be got from economic independence, of the sweetness of earned bread, of the dreary depression of subjection. They have felt the bitterness of being "kept out"; they are feeling the exhilaration of being "brought in." They are ripe for instruction and organisation in working for the good of the whole. The desperate need of war blows away many obstructions, and we see now that the good of the country requires the hearty work of all, and anything which discourages or diminishes that work damages our chances of success in the war. We may hope that, with the aid of awakened women, we shall at last see that it damages our chance of success in peace also. Reactionary or repressive laws and regulations; the sweating and over-driving of the workers; the starvation and subjection of the mothers; the limitation of the child's right to education; the monstrous growth of luxury; the denial of the right use of the land, for the nourishment and refreshment of the whole people; the neglect to provide decent houses; all these lower vitality and limit output. But beyond any other cause for the limitation of output is the horrible waste caused by unemployment and the lack of incentive to the whole people to do their best.

> Work without hope draws nectar in a sieve,
> And hope without an object cannot live.

Under a profiteering system the worker has no hope. What is needed is a hopeful and trustful policy, constructive and vital, not coercive and timid.

Readjustment of Employment

Most people were astonished in 1914 at the rapidity with which industry and social conditions adapted themselves to the state of war, and there are those who argue that, because the fears of very widespread and continued misery at the outbreak of the war were not justified, we need not have any anxiety about any widespread and continued misery at the establishment of peace. Certainly depression or panic are worse than useless, and a serene and cheerful heart will help to carry the nation beyond difficulties. But comfortable people must beware of seeming to bear the sorrows of others with cheerfulness, and a lack of preparation for easily foreseen contingencies will not be forgiven by those who suffer from carelessness or procrastination. We know quite well what some, at least, of our problems are going to be, and the fool's paradise would lead straight to revolution.

It would be wise to remember that the dislocation of industry at the outbreak of the war was easily met; first, because the people thrown out by the cessation of one sort of work were easily absorbed by the increase of another sort; second, because there was ample capital and credit in hand; third, because the State was prepared to shoulder many risks and to guarantee stability; fourth, because there was an untapped reservoir of women's labour to take the place of men's. The problems after the war will be different, greater, and more lasting; much will depend upon whether the people see to it that a progressive and intelligent Government shall be in power to deal with vital issues with courage and in a living and constructive spirit, unhampered by precedent and unafraid of vested interests, or whether they will tolerate an unintelligent and timid Government which meets difficulties with inertia and the consequent unrest with coercion. Capital will have been destroyed, literally blown to pieces on a vast scale; yet there will be great need of the production of the necessaries of life. Unless the Government will boldly take the risks of the operations of peace on a scale as vast as the operations of war, at any rate for a time, there will be huge waste of life, of health, and of labour out of employment, and therefore degenerating, as all unused force does degenerate, with consequent misery and disorder. The return of millions of men to civil life and work will tax the goodwill and organising capacity of the whole nation. The change from war production to peace production will possibly be even greater. The readjustments required must necessarily be slow and difficult, and unless there can be co-operation between employers and employed, and between all sections of employed, there will be friction to the raw and many disastrous mistakes.

Because it will obviously be impossible for all to find work quickly (not to speak of the right kind of work), there is almost certain to be an outcry for the restriction of work in various directions, and one of the first cries (if we may judge from the past) will be to women: "Back to the Home!" This cry will be raised whether the women have a home or not. . . . We must understand the unimpeachable right of the man who has lost his work and risked his life for his country, to find decent employment, decent wages and conditions, on his return to civil life. We must also understand the enlargement and enhancement of life which women feel when they are able to live by their own productive work, and we must realise that to deprive women of the right to live by their work is to send them back to a moral imprisonment (to say nothing of physical and intellectual starvation), of which they have become now for the first time fully conscious. And we must realise the exceeding danger that conscienceless employers may regard women's labour as preferable, owing to its cheapness and its docility, and that women, if unsympathetically treated by their male relatives and fellow workers, may be tempted to continue to be cheap and docile in the hands of those who have no desire except that of exploiting them and the community. The kind of man who likes "to keep women in their place" may find he has made slaves who will be used by his enemies against him. Men need have no fear of free women; it is the slaves and the parasites who are a deadly danger.

The demand for equal wage for equal work has been hotly pressed by men since the war began, and it is all to the good so far as it goes. But most men are still far from realising the solidarity of their interests with those of women in all departments of life, and are still too placidly accepting the fact that women are sweated over work which is not the same as that of men. They don't realise yet that starved womanhood means starved manhood, and they don't enough appreciate the rousing and infectious character of a generous attitude on the part of men, who, in fighting the women's battles unselfishly and from a love of right, would stimulate the women to corresponding generosity. There are no comrades more staunch and loyal than women, where men have engaged their truth and courage. But men must treat them as comrades; they must no longer think only of how they can "eliminate female labour"; they must take the women into their trade unions and other organisations, and they must understand that the complexities of a woman's life are not of her invention or choosing, but are due to her function as mother of men.

The sexual side of a woman's life gravely affects the economic side, and we can never afford to overlook this. As mothers and home-makers women are doing work of the highest national importance and economic value, but this value is one which returns to the nation as a whole and only in small and very uncertain part to the women themselves. The fact that a woman is a wife and mother diminishes her value in the "labour market," and even the fact that she is liable to become a wife and mother has done so in the past. Unless men are prepared to socialise the responsibilities of parenthood, one does not see how women's labour is ever to be organized for the welfare of the whole, nor does one see how women are to perform their priceless functions of motherhood as well as possible if they are to be penalised for them in the future as they have been in the past. . . .

It does not at all follow that the best homes will be made by all women doing all the manual work of their own homes themselves. The mere waste of physical effort by the doing of work individually which might be done co-operatively is only one side of the waste. The work of motherhood is often very seriously crippled by the need for exhausting and unremitting toil on the part of the mother, and if the need to earn a wage in money is added the whole of the woman's work suffers. Organisation and rational development are urgent in the life of the working housewife. . . .

It has been dinned into the ears of women for ages past that "a woman's place is the home," and that her first duty is a private and individual one. Now, suddenly, women are told that they must come out of the home and that their country has first claim upon them, as upon men. Appeal is made even to mothers with husbands at the front to leave their children and go out to work.

Equal Wage for Equal Work

While the women were responding to these appeals as best they could, hampered by conflicting duties and insufficient training, they were met by another perplexing problem. Whereas a few women had of late years made persistent claim to equal pay for equal work and had been generally met with the reply that this was a ridiculous demand—unjust in view of women's smaller responsibilities, injurious to the women themselves, since it would drive them altogether out of the market— and whereas the great mass of women had, from custom and ignorance and docility, acquiesced in this lower status, they were suddenly assured that they must ask the same wage as the men they were displacing, otherwise the men would suffer when they returned to industry. . . .

[W]hen people talk of a "living wage" they must define who and how many are supposed to live upon this wage. Is it to be the single person, man or woman? That would be comparatively simple. Is it to be the person, man or woman, plus his or her "dependents"? That is very complex, because the number of dependents varies, not only between different people for the same period, but between different periods for the same people. Thus, on the whole, men have more dependents than women, and this has led to a general opinion that men ought to have higher wages than women. But a great many women have dependents, and some have as many as men. It frequently happens, also, that the women with most dependents (such as widows) are less capable of earning just at the time when the dependents are thrown upon them, or that (as in the case of unmarried women) the dependents are such as will never become independent (such as the old, the cripples, the wastrels). . . .

Important as the economic side of the question is, we must not forget, however, that there are other factors of ever-growing importance to be found in the change in the position of women and of their thoughts and ideals of motherhood. Even if motherhood were endowed by the State, and the individual parents relieved of personal anxiety about the upkeep of the children, we should have to take these thoughts and ideals into consideration. Those who deplore a falling birthrate never seem to see any other remedy than for the already married women to have larger families. But a much better remedy would be that more women should be married. Before the war there were about two-and-a-half millions of marriageable bachelors. If it had been made possible for these young men to marry and have two or three children, it would have been better than that the mothers of four or five children should be required to have two or three more, regardless of whether they want them. The preponderance of women over men is a bad thing in itself, and the largely artificial restriction of marriage accentuates the evil.

Married women have changed their outlook during the past century, and the birthrate must be treated as the product of a partnership in which the mother is nominated by nature as the predominant partner. If motherhood is woman's supreme function, it is important that it should be denied to as few as possible, and to women should belong its supreme direction. The racial instinct of women is of tremendous importance to the welfare of the race, and it is encouraging to note how scientific knowledge is coming to reinforce much of what is instinctive in the mother. She feels the value of temperance, soberness, and chastity; she feels the need to rest and recuperate; she feels the outrage of unwilling mother-hood. In addition to this, the modern woman feels urgently the need to be a complete person, to develop herself, to be a comrade to her husband and chil-dren and friends, and to take part in the wider world outside the home. She can-not live this complete life if she is to spend all her best years in incessant child-bearing, from which she will emerge stupefied and worn out. She looks round on the world and sees many women pining for children and many others overdone with them, and she sees little girls turned into little mothers before their time, docked of their education and their play, because their mothers require help with their intolerable burden. A modern woman expressed a woman's thoughts with mordant wit when she wrote of human beings as "the only animal alive that lives upon its young."

Enfranchisement and Emancipation

The course and conduct of the war, throwing upon women greater and greater responsibilities, bringing home to them how intimately their own lives and all they hold dear and sacred are affected by the government of the country, will tend greatly to strengthen and enlarge their claim for a share in the government. The growth of what was known as "militancy," in the last few years of the British suf-frage movement, was the disastrous result of the long denial of justice, the acrid fruit of government which had become coercion, because it was no longer by con-sent. Now that, for two years past, the women of Great Britain have made common cause with their men in this time of stress, the heat of the internal conflict has died down, and one hears on all sides that prominent anti-suffragists have become ardent suffragists, while others have declared their resolve at any rate never again to *oppose* the enfranchisement of women. The battle of argument was won long ago, but we are not, as a people, much given to theory; custom has a very strong hold over us. The shock of war has loosened that hold, and now almost every one who used to oppose, when asked whether women should be given votes, would reply: "Why not? They have earned them!" I cannot admit that representation is a thing that people should be called upon to "earn," nor that, if essential contribu-tion to the nation is to count as "earning," the women have not earned the vote for just as long as the men. . . .

What the war has put in a fresh light, so that even the dullest can see, is that if the State may claim women's lives and those of their sons and husbands and lovers, if it may absorb all private and individual life, as at present, then indeed the condi-tion of those who have no voice in the State is a condition of slavery, and English-men don't feel quite happy at the thought that their women are still slaves, while their Government is saying they are waging a war of liberation. Many women had long ago become acutely aware of their ignominious position, but the jolt of the war has made many more aware of it.

16. Women at Munition Making

Their hands should minister unto the flame of life,
Their fingers guide
    The rosy teat, swelling with milk,
    To the eager mouth of the suckling babe
    Or smooth with tenderness,
    Softly and soothingly,
    The heated brow of the ailing child.
    Or stray among the curls
    Of the boy or girl, thrilling to mother love.
But now,
    Their hands, their fingers
    Are coarsened in munition factories.
    Their thoughts, which should fly
    Like bees among the sweetest mind flowers,
    Gaining nourishment for the thoughts to be,
    Are bruised against the law,
"Kill, kill."
    They must take part in defacing and destroying the natural body
    Which, certainly during this dispensation
    Is the shrine of the spirit.
O God!
    Throughout the ages we have seen,
    Again and again
    Men by Thee created
    Cancelling each other.
    And we have marvelled at the seeming annihilation
Of Thy work.
    But this goes further,
    Taints the fountain head,
    Mounts like a poison to the Creator's very heart.
O God!
    Must It anew be sacrificed on earth?

V.16   From Mary Gabrielle Collins, *Branches unto the Sea* (London: Erskine Macdonald, 1916), 24.

17. Women's National Service in Germany

The national service of men reaches its ultimate destiny only in times of war, while the national service of women is essentially destined for constant duties throughout times of peace. The efforts of women in war are basically the same as their efforts in peace. These efforts consist of nursing and all sorts of organized welfare work. Thus we see that women need no special preparation for war. Peace offers them duties of service in all areas of social work. Through the introduction of a female service duty with preparation and training, we would gain forces for voluntary social service who would be truly qualified.

Female national service consists of voluntary management of social services, of boards of guardians, of care of the poor, of orphans, of youth services, etc. This civic duty should be delegated to women in the same way as it is delegated to men. Women should only be excused from carrying out these duties for the same reasons that apply also to men. With the exception of women with small children, or domestic conditions that allow them no free time for voluntary activities, this also applies to gainfully employed housewives.

Nursing the wounded is a particular service duty for women in wartime. This should be done as far as possible by professional nurses. However, volunteers must be used as aides in military hospitals. These volunteers must serve as part of their official female service duty.

The educational basis for all forms of female service duty is the capacity to manage a simple household. This must therefore be a prerequisite for further training, or it must form the content of the female service or training period.

Physical training must also be a major part of the female service year, since it has proved to be a considerable advantage in men's training.

Based upon these different prerequisites, it is clear that a different type of education is required for girls who will graduate from elementary schools and those who will graduate from secondary schools. These different types of education are analogous to different types of service duties for men.

(a) Girls who have graduated from elementary schools ought to receive one year of free education between their 17th and 20th years. This year should offer them a thorough grounding in home economics, with heavy emphasis on the national economic responsibilities of housewives: health-care, infant care, and a knowledge of civic affairs. Only with such an arrangement would the service year achieve its goal completely.

(b) A general introduction of such a service duty is not feasible for private and for national economic reasons at this time. However, a beginning in this

V.17   From Helena Lange, "Speech before the Congress of the Union of German Women Teachers," 1915. Reprinted in Susan Groag Bell and Karen M. Offen, eds., *Women, the Family, and Freedom*, 2 vols. (Stanford: Stanford University Press, 1983), 2:262–263. Copyright © 1983 by the Board of the Trustees of the Leland Stanford Junior University. All rights reserved. Used with the permission of Stanford University Press. www.sup.org.

direction could be attempted as follows: (1) a general extension of one-half year of the education of girls, devoted entirely to the practice of household manage-ment; (2) introduction of academic institutions modeled on Danish high schools, which offer older girls with an elementary education the opportunity to have a year's free service-education in the format suggested under (a) above; (3) an increase in the establishment of agricultural schools for household management.

Like voluntary soldiers who are doing their year of service, girls who have gradu-ated from secondary schools must pay the costs of their own training. Before enter-ing the service duty they must present proof of the household management training they have received either at home or in a designated institution of house-hold management. Their service training time—between the ages of 17 and 20—will be taken up with training for some social service. This could be a specialized training for infant care, care of the poor, nursing, etc.

By developing the women's schools we can prepare for compulsory introduction of the female service duty for this class of women.

✍

18. Keep Your Eyes Open

With the outbreak of war men were drawn away from the management of numer-ous organizations and, gradually, the lack of experienced personnel made itself felt. Women working in offices were therefore urged not to waste the opportunities offered them by the war, and to continue their education so that they would be prepared to take on the position once held by a male colleague, should the occa-sion arise.

Such occasions have indeed arisen much sooner than anticipated. The demand for educated women has risen phenomenally during the six months since the war began. Women have been employed in banks, in large commercial businesses, in urban offices—everywhere, in fact, where up till now only men had been employed. They are to be tested in order to see whether they can perform with equal success.

All those who were certain that women would be completely successful substi-tutes for men were painfully disappointed to discover that many women who had worked for years in a firm and were invited to step up to a higher level, now that the men were absent, suddenly handed in their resignations. An enquiry revealed that, especially in recent days, these notices were coming with great frequency and, strange as it may seem, applied mostly to women who had been working in the

V.18   From Magda Trott, "Women's Work: A Substitute for Men's Work," 1915. Reprinted in Susan Groag Bell and Karen M. Offen, eds., *Women, the Family, and Freedom*, 2 vols. (Stanford: Stanford University Press, 1983), 2:277–279. Copyright © 1983 by the Board of the Trustees of the Leland Stanford Junior University. All rights reserved. Used with the permission of Stanford University Press. www.sup.org.

same company from four to seven years and had now been offered a better and even better-paid job. They said "no" and since there was no possibility for them to remain in their old jobs, they resigned.

The enemies of women's employment were delighted. Here was their proof that women are incapable of holding down responsible positions. Female workers were quite successful as clerks, stenographers, and typists, in fact, in all those positions that require no independent activity—but as soon as more serious duties were demanded of them, they failed.

Naturally, we enquired of these women why they had given up so quickly, and then the truth of the matter became plain. All women were quite ready, if with some trepidation, to accept the new positions, particularly since the boss made it clear that one of the gentlemen would carefully explain the new assignments to them. Certainly the work was almost entirely new to the young ladies since till now they had only been concerned with their stenography, their books, and so forth. However, they entered their new duties with enthusiasm.

But even on the first day it was noticeable that not everything would proceed as had been supposed. Male colleagues looked askance at the "intruder" who dared to usurp the position and bread of a colleague now fighting for the Fatherland, and who would, it was fervently hoped, return in good health. Moreover, the lady who came as a substitute received exactly half of the salary of the gentleman colleague who had previously occupied the same position. A dangerous implication, since if the lady made good, the boss might continue to draw on female personnel; the saving on salaries would clearly be substantial. It became essential to use all means to show the boss that female help was no substitute for men's work, and a united male front was organized.

It was hardly surprising that all the lady's questions were answered quite vaguely. If she asked again or even a third time, irritated remarks were passed concerning her inadequacy in comprehension, and very soon the male teacher lost patience. Naturally, most of his colleagues supported him and the lady found it difficult, if not impossible, to receive any instruction and was finally forced to resign.

This is what happened in most known cases. We must, however, also admit that occasionally the fault does lie with the lady, who simply did not have sufficient preparation to fill a difficult position. There may be male colleagues who would gladly share information with women; however, these women are unable to understand, because they have too little business experience. In order to prevent this sort of thing, we would counsel all women who are seeking a position in which they hope to advance, to educate themselves as much as possible. All those women who were forced to leave their jobs of long standing might not have been obliged to do so, had they been more concerned in previous years with understanding the overall nature of the business in which they were employed. Their colleagues would surely and generously have answered their questions and given them valuable advice, which would have offered them an overview and thereby avoided the total ignorance with which they entered these advanced positions when they were offered. At least they would have had an inkling and saved themselves the questions that betrayed their great ignorance to their colleagues. They might even have found their way through all the confusion and succeeded in the new position.

Therefore, once again: all you women who want to advance yourselves and create an independent existence, use this time of war as a learning experience and keep your eyes open.

∞

19. We will Need the Woman as Spouse and Mother

It is also my opinion that women's work should not be overestimated. Almost all intellectual work, heavy physical labour, as well as all real manufacturing work will still fall on men—in addition to the entire waging of the war. It would be good if clear, official expression were given to these facts and if a stop were put to women's agitation for parity in all professions, and thereby, of course, for political emancipation. I completely agree with Your Excellency that compulsory labour for women would be an inappropriate measure. After the war, we will need the woman as spouse and mother. I thus strongly support those measures, enacted through law, perogative, material aid, etc., aimed at that effect. In spite of the strong opposition to such measures, it is here that vigorous action needs to be taken, in order to extinguish the influence of this female rivalry, which disrupts the family. Your Excellency would please gather from the above that I am not only concerned with the war, but that I am also aware that, for the development of our people *after* the war, healthy social conditions, i.e. in the first place the protection of the family, are necessary.

If I *nevertheless* urge that the requirement to work be extended to all women who are either unemployed or working in trivial positions, now and for the duration of the war, I do so because, in my opinion, women can be employed in many areas to a still greater degree than previously and men can thereby be freed for other work. . . . In particular, I want to stress again that I consider it especially wrong to keep secondary schools and universities, which have been almost completely emptied of men by conscription, open only for women. It is valueless, because the scholarly gain is minimal; furthermore, because precisely that rivalry with the family that needs to be combated would be promoted; and finally, because it would represent the coarsest injustice if the young man, who is giving everything for his Fatherland, is forced behind the woman.

V.19   From Ute Daniel, *The War from Within: German Working-Class Women in the First World War*, trans. Margaret Ries (Oxford: Berg, 1997), 68–69. Reprinted with permission of Berg Publishers, an imprint of Bloomsbury Publishing plc.

20. Something Disturbing about Female Labour

It cannot be denied that there is something disturbing about this entire development [of female labour in the war]. When one looks at women these days, how they are working in all of these difficult positions, the women in armaments factories, on the coach box, cleaning the streets, one has to look closely in order to tell whether one is looking at a woman or a man. Through the employment of women in male occupations, the entire female organism and the entire female sensibility is being pushed down other paths, and that ultimately expresses itself on the outside. We must, with all seriousness, take care to reverse this development. It will not always be easy. Women have found a very rewarding occupation in the various companies; they have, incidentally, often taken a great liking to this, and there will consequently be difficulties in removing them from these occupations. And yet this must be strived for in the interest of our common good, [and] simultaneously in the interest of the male worker as well. We must therefore proceed, on the one hand, with all advisable caution, but on the other, also with all the necessary energy.

21. A Woman in the Service of the Tsar

The news from the front was exciting. Great battles were raging. Our soldiers were retreating in some places and advancing in others. I wished for wings to fly to their succor. My heart yearned and ached.

"Do you know what war is?" I asked myself. "It's no woman's job. You must make sure before starting out, Marusia, that you won't disgrace yourself. Are you strong enough in spirit to face all the trials and dangers of this colossal war? Are you strong enough in body to shed blood and endure the privations of war? Are you firm enough at heart to withstand the temptations that will come to you, living among men? Search your soul for an answer of truth and courage."

And I found strength enough in me to answer "yes" to all these questions. I suppressed the hidden longing for Yasha in the depths of my being, and made the fateful decision. I would go to war and fight till death, or, if God preserved me, till the coming of peace. I would defend my country and help those unfortunates on the field of slaughter who had already made their sacrifices for the country.

V.20 From Ute Daniel, *The War from Within: German Working-Class Women in the First World War*, trans. Margaret Ries (Oxford: Berg, 1997), 101. Reprinted with permission of Berg Publishers, an imprint of Bloomsbury Publishing plc.
V.21 From Maria Botchkareva, *Yashka: My Life as Peasant, Officer, and Exile* (New York: Frederick Stokes, 1919), 72–81.

It was November, 1914. With my heart steeled in the decision I had made, I resolutely approached the headquarters of the Twenty-Fifth Reserve Battalion, stationed in Tomsk. Upon entering, a clerk asked me what I wanted.

"To see the Commander," I replied.

"What for?" he inquired.

"I want to enlist," I said.

The man looked at me for a moment and burst out laughing. He called to the other clerks. "Here is a *baba* [woman] who wants to enlist!" he announced jokingly, pointing at me. There followed a general uproar. "Ha! ha! ha!" they chorused, forgetting their work for the moment. When the merriment subsided a little I repeated my request to see the Commander, and his adjutant came out. He must have been told that a woman had come to enlist, for he addressed me gaily:

"What is your wish?"

"I want to enlist in the army, your Excellency," I answered.

"To enlist, eh? But you are a baba," he laughed. "The regulations do not permit us to enlist women. It is against the law."

I insisted that I wanted to fight, and begged to see the Commander. The adjutant reported me to the Commander, who asked to have me shown in.

With the adjutant laughing behind me, I blushed and became confused when brought before the Commander. He rebuked the adjutant and inquired what he could do for me. I repeated that I wanted to enlist and fight for the country.

"It is very noble of you to have such a desire. But women are not allowed in the army," he said. "They are too weak. What could you, for instance, do in the front line? Women are not made for war."

"Your Excellency," I insisted, "God has given me strength, and I can defend my country as well as a man. I have asked myself before coming here whether I could endure the life of a soldier and found that I could. Can't you place me in your regiment?"

"*Golubushka* [little dove]," the Commander declared gently, "how can I help you? It is against the law. I have no authority to enlist a woman even if I wanted to. You can go to the rear, enlist as a Red Cross nurse or in some other auxiliary of the service."

I rejected his proposal. I had heard so many rumors about the women in the rear that I had come to despise them. I therefore reiterated my determination to go to the front as a regular soldier. The Commander was deeply impressed by my obstinacy, and wanted to help me. He suggested that I send a telegram to the Tsar, telling him of my desire to defend the country, of my moral purpose, and pray that he grant me the special right to enlist.

The Commander promised to draw up the telegram himself, with a recommendation of his own, and have it sent from his office. He warned me, however, to consider the matter again, to think of the hardships I would have to bear, of the soldiers' attitude toward me, and the universal ridicule that I would provoke. I did not change my mind, though. The telegram was sent at my expense, costing eight rubles, which I obtained from my mother.

When I disclosed to my folks the nature of my visit to the Commander of the Twenty-Fifth Battalion they burst into tears. My poor mother cried that her Maria must have gone insane, that it was an unheard-of, impossible thing. Who ever knew of a baba going to war? She would allow herself to be buried alive before letting me enlist. My father sustained her. I was their only hope now, they said. They would be forced to starve and go begging, without my help. And the house was filled with sobs and wails, the two younger sisters and some neighbors joining in.

My heart was rent in twain. It was a cruel, painful choice that I was called upon to make, a choice between my mother and my country. It cost me so much to steel myself for that new life, and now, when I was seemingly near the goal, my long-suffering mother called upon me to give up this ideal that possessed me, for her sake. I was tormented and agonized by doubt. I realized that I must make a decision quickly and, with a supreme effort and the help of God, I resolved that the call of my country took precedence over the call of my mother.

Some time later a soldier came to the house.

"Is Maria Botchkareva here?" he questioned.

He came from headquarters with the news that a telegram had arrived from the Tsar, authorizing the Commander to enlist me as a soldier, and that the Commander wanted to see me.

My mother did not expect such an answer. She grew frantic. She cursed the Tsar with all her might, although she had always revered him as the Little Father. "What kind of Tsar is he?" she cried, "if he takes women to war? He must have lost his senses. Who ever heard of a Tsar calling women to arms? Hasn't he enough men? Goodness knows, there are myriads of them in Mother-Russia."

She seized the Tsar's portrait on the wall, before which she had crossed herself every morning, and tore it to bits, stamping them on the floor, with imprecations and anathema on her lips. Never again would she pray for him, she declared. "No, never!"

The soldier's message had an opposite effect on me, and I was thrown into high spirits. Dressing in my holiday costume, I went to see the Commander. Everybody at headquarters seemed to know of the Tsar's telegram, smiles greeting me everywhere. The Commander congratulated me and read its text in a solemn voice, explaining that it was an extraordinary honor which the August Emperor had conferred on me, and that I make myself worthy of it. I was so happy, so joyous, so transported. It was the most blissful moment of my life.

The Commander called his orderly in and instructed him to obtain a full soldier's outfit for me. I received two complete undergarments made of coarse linen, two pairs of foot-rags, a laundry bag, a pair of boots, one pair of trousers, a belt, a regulation blouse, a pair of epaulets, a cap with the insignia on it, two cartridge pockets and a rifle. My hair was clipped off.

There was an outburst of laughter when I appeared in full military attire, as a regular soldier of the Fourth Company, Fifth Regiment. I was confused and somewhat bewildered, hardly being able to recognize myself. The news of a woman recruit had preceded me at the barracks, and my arrival there precipitated a riot of fun. I was surrounded on all sides by green recruits who stared at me incredulously, but some were not satisfied with mere staring, so rare a novelty was I to them. They wanted to make sure that their eyes were not deceived, so they proceeded to pinch me, jostle me and brush against me.

"Get out, she ain't no baba," remarked one of them.

"Sure, she is," said another, pinching me.

"She'll run like the devil at the first German shot," joked a third, provoking an uproar.

"We'll make it so hot for her that she'll run before even getting to the front," threatened a fourth.

Here the Commander of my company interfered, and the boys dispersed. I was granted permission to take my things home before settling permanently at the barracks, and asked to be shown how to salute. On the way home I saluted every uniform in the same manner. Opening the door of the house, I stopped on the threshold. My mother did not recognize me.

"Maria Leontievna Botchkareva here?" I asked sharply, in military fashion. Mother took me for some messenger from headquarters, and answered, "No."

I threw myself on her neck. "Holy Mother, save me!" she exclaimed. There were cries and tears which brought my father and little sister to the scene. My mother became hysterical. For the first time I saw my father weep, and again I was urged to come back to my senses and give up this crazy notion to serve in the army. The proprietress of the house and old Nastasia Leontievna were called in to help dissuade me from my purpose.

"Think what the men will do to a lone woman in their midst," they argued. "Why, they'll make a prostitute of you. They will kill you secretly, and nobody will ever find a trace of you. Only the other day they found the body of a woman along the railroad track, thrown out of a troop-train. You always have been such a level-headed girl. What has come over you? And what will become of your parents? They are old and weak, and you are their only hope. They often said that when Marusia came back they would end their lives in peace. Now you are but shortening their days, dragging them to their graves in sorrow."

For a short space of time I vacillated again. The fierce struggle in my bosom between the two elements was resurrected. But I stuck by my decision, remaining deaf to all pleas. Then my mother grew angry and, crying out at the top of her voice, she shouted:

"You are no longer my daughter! You have forfeited your mother's love."

With a heavy heart I left the house for the barracks. The Commander of the Company did not expect me, and I had to explain to him why I could not pass that night at home. He assigned me to a place in the general bunk, ordering the men not to molest me. On my right and on my left were soldiers, and that first night in the company of men will ever stand out in my memory. I did not close my eyes once during the night.

The men were, naturally, unaccustomed to such a phenomenon as myself and took me for a loose-moralled woman who had made her way into the ranks for the sake of carrying on her illicit trade. I was, therefore, compelled constantly to fight off intrusions from all sides. As soon as I made an effort to shut my eyes I would discover the arm of my neighbor on the left around my neck, and would restore it to its owner with a crash. Watchful of his movements, I offered an opportunity for my neighbor on the right to get too near to me, and I would savagely kick him in the side. All night long my nerves were taut and my fists busy. Toward dawn I was so exhausted that I nearly fell asleep, when I discovered a hand on my chest, and before the man realized my intention, I banged him in the face. I continued to rain blows till the bell rang at five o'clock, the rising-hour.

Ten minutes were given us to dress and wash, tardiness being punished by a rebuke. At the end of the ten minutes the ranks formed and every soldier's hands, ears and foot-rags were inspected. I was in such haste to be on time that I put my trousers on inside out, provoking a veritable storm of hilarity and paroxysms of laughter.

The day began with a prayer for the Tsar and country, following which every one of us received the daily allowance of two-and-a-half pounds of bread and a few cubes of sugar from our respective squad commanders. There were four squads to a company. Our breakfast consisted of bread and tea and lasted half an hour.

At the mess I had an opportunity to get acquainted with some of the more sympathetic soldiers. There were ten volunteers in my company, and they were all students. After eating, there was roll-call. When the officer reached my name he read: "Botchkareva," to which I answered, "Aye." We were then taken out for instruction, since the entire regiment had been formed only three days previous. The first rule that the training officer tried to impress upon us was to pay attention, watch his movements and actions. Not all the recruits could do it easily. I prayed to God to enlighten me in the study of a soldier's duties.

It was slow work to establish proper relations with the men. The first few days I was such a nuisance to the Company Commander that he wished me to ask for dismissal. He hinted as much on a couple of occasions, but I continued to mind my own business and never reported the annoyances I endured from the men. Gradually I won their respect and confidence. The small group of volunteers always defended me. As the Russian soldiers call each other by nick-names, one of the first questions put to me by my friends was what I would like to be called.

"Call me Yashka," I said, and that name stuck to me ever after, saving my life on more than one occasion. There is so much in a name, and "Yashka" was the sort of a name that appealed to the soldiers and always worked in my favor. In time it became the pet name of the regiment, but not before I had been tested by many additional trials and found to be a comrade, and not a woman, by the men.

I was an apt student and learned almost to anticipate the orders of the instructor. When the day's labors would be completed and the soldiers gathered into knots to while away an hour or two in games or story-telling, I was always sought after to participate. I came to like the soldiers, who were good-natured boys, and to enjoy their sports. The group which Yashka joined would usually prove the most popular in the barrack, and it was sufficient to secure my cooperation in some enterprise to make it a success.

There wasn't much time for relaxation, though, as we went through an intensive training course of only three months before we were sent to the front. Once a week, every Sunday, I would leave the barracks and spend the day at home, my mother having reconciled herself to my soldiering. On holidays I would be visited by friends or relatives. On one such occasion my sister and her husband called. I had been detailed for guard duty in the barrack that day. While on such duty a soldier is forbidden to sit down or to engage in conversation. I was entertaining my visitors when the Company Commander passed.

"Do you know the rules, Botchkareva?" he asked.

"Yes, your Excellency," I answered.

"What are they?"

"A soldier on guard duty is not allowed to sit down or engage in conversation," I replied. He ordered me to stand for two hours at attention, at the completion of my guard duty, which took twenty-four hours. Standing at attention, in full military equipment, for two hours is a severe task, as one has to remain absolutely motionless under the eyes of a guard, and yet it was a common punishment.

During my training I was punished in this manner three times. The second time it was really not my fault. One night I recognized my squad commander in a soldier who annoyed me, and I dealt him as hard a blow as I would have given to any other man. In the morning he placed me at attention for two hours, claiming that he had accidentally brushed against me.

At first there was some difficulty in arranging for my bathing. The bath-house was used by the men, and so I was allowed one day to visit a public bath-house. I found it a splendid opportunity for some fun. I came into the women's room, fully dressed, and there was a tremendous outbreak as soon as I appeared. I was taken for a man. However, the fun did not last long. In an instant I was under a bombardment from every corner, and only narrowly escaped serious injury by crying out that I was a woman.

In the last month of our training we engaged in almost continuous rifle practice. I applied myself zealously to the acquisition of skill in handling a rifle and won a mention of excellence for good marksmanship. This considerably enhanced my standing with the soldiers and strengthened our relations of camaraderie.

22. Bitter Wounds

Most war orphans were infants when their fathers were killed, and the impact of the war on them can only be inferred. Central institutions in the child's life were shattered by the war. The family was disrupted not only by the prolonged absence of the father and older brothers, but also by the chronic worry and illness of the mother. Not infrequently, the mother too was forced to leave the children temporarily while she sought employment. Schools were also disrupted when male teachers went into the army. Together with this social dislocation was the ever-worsening health problem.

One surprise was that the infant mortality rate did not increase during the war. Possibly, since the overall birth rate dropped, more resources were devoted to the smaller number of infants. Or perhaps the very extremity of living conditions encouraged adults to be especially careful of babies. The war did, however kill slightly older children in significant numbers. [see table]

Children's death rate (1913 = 100)

		1914	1915	1916	1917	1918
Boys	5–10	106.4	142.9	129.3	150.3	189.2
	10–15	107	121.7	128.5	154.2	215
Girls	5–10	101.4	142.2	133	143.8	207.3
	10–15	104.1	128.3	131	152.9	239.2

Not only did girls generally have a higher death rate than boys of comparable ages, but the increase in the death rate was higher for girls than for boys. Why? Without further evidence, one can only guess. It may be that boys and girls endured the same hardships, but that girls proved more vulnerable. Or, it may be that boys and girls did not endure the same hardships, that in the distribution of scarce resources, little girls received less.

Children's physical deterioration during the war was obvious. They were underweight by as much as 8 to 12 percent. They did not grow normally; average height by age declined by 3 to 4 percent. Rickets, a disease associated with malnutrition, was common, and polio increased among teenagers. Ordinary childhood diseases did not increase significantly, but stomach disorders, such as vomiting and cramps, were common, and there was an increase in tuberculosis. Nervous disorders were frequent; for example, an "enormous increase" in bed-wetting was reported among school children. . . .

Before the age of 10 or 11, boys and girls showed little difference in their perceptions. Their drawings were of genderless stick-figures, their poems and essays tended not to distinguish between war and non-war. Poems to

V.22   From Robert Weldon Whalen, *Bitter Wounds: German Victims of the Great War, 1914–1939* (Ithaca, NY: Cornell University Press, 1984), 77–80. Copyright © 1984 by Cornell University. Reprinted with permission of Cornell University Press.

"O Hindenburg, O Hindenburg," quickly drifted into the more familiar rhythmic pattern of "O Tannenbaum, O Tannenbaum." To one 11-year old girl, the most important part of a victory celebration was that it involved a school holiday.

After the age of 10 or 11, however, a marked break appeared in the perceptions of the girls and boys. Boys demonstrated a passion for, and an amazing mastery of, military minutiae. Their drawings emphasized violent action, with abundant gore. Their identification with their soldier-fathers and brothers was intense. Of course, boys played at being soldiers, but they also collected maps, military photos, and pictures of war heroes, such as Baron von Richthofen. . . .

Girls seemed to experience the war in a totally different way. Their poems, drawings, and essays in the Breslau collection are melancholy and introspective. They concentrate on death and suffering. The war's "ruthless attack on the love-relationship of the family filled their souls. . . . Again and again, appears the same theme: death of the soldier and the grief of his loved ones, but in always new, extraordinarily diverse manifestations . . . many poems concern the soldier's grave—a theme which frequently appears in the girls' sketches." While sons tried to be heroic like their fathers and brothers, daughters mirrored the worry, grief, and passivity of their mothers.

VI

Whose Nation?

How did countries hold out under the unprecedented strains of the Great War? The answer lies, to a significant extent, in the ways that they sought to define who they were, a process that almost inevitably involved drawing contrasts with their opponents, establishing who they were not. These efforts at national self-definition often aimed at fostering a sense of unity by accentuating the particular population's collective sacrifice. Notions of common experience and shared commitment could be drawn from varied sources: from standards of respectable behavior that conformed to group expectations, from the exercise of religious faith, which provided a ready-made language of moral probity and willing sacrifice, or from conceptions of ethnic or racial homogeneity that reinforced the idea of a nation united in struggle. Surely, it seemed to contemporaries, if a nation was committed to victory, with everyone "on the same track," and if it deserved victory, because its pious populace merited God's favor, that nation must triumph in the end.

But over four years, that deceptively simple formula would prove both complex and elusive. Just whose nation was to be invoked would prove a highly contentious issue. After all, fear of internal strife had haunted many European politicians and military planners as they contemplated the prospect of major conflict. The persistent labor unrest of the prewar years, the growth of social democratic or labor parties, the fervent articulation of syndicalism and anarchism—all hinted at the potentially disruptive forces percolating in each of the combatant nations. In addition, leaders worried that national, ethnic, and religious minorities would prove untrustworthy in a time of crisis.

Hoping to emphasize cohesiveness, Europe's elites made strident appeals to patriotism and invoked the ideals of religion and national unity. A century before

Empires, Soldiers, and Citizens: A World War I Sourcebook, Second Edition.
Edited by Marilyn Shevin-Coetzee and Frans Coetzee.
© 2013 John Wiley & Sons, Ltd. except sources 1 to 19. Published 2013 by John Wiley & Sons, Ltd.

the Great War, nationalism was primarily associated with progressive political loyalties; as such, those in charge had sought to contain and repress it. By 1914, however, European leaders realized that nationalist sentiments, with their unifying power, could serve as an important new weapon in the war. But nationalism's appeal had limited breadth and depth, and there was no guarantee that it would sustain the governments that chose to emphasize it. As one example, a majority of Italians advocated that nation's neutrality in 1914, despite fiery pro-war rhetoric from the Right. When the conservative government finally committed Italy's troops to combat in 1915, it did so without support from either the Italian parliament or the majority of its citizens.

Nevertheless, ultranationalist organizations had become a pervasive presence in all the major European nations on the eve of the war. Their shrill clamor for increased military spending and their support from a patriotic citizenry mobilized against internal and external foes only aggravated the bellicose tenor of the period. Still, they could not attract and retain a broad, committed following, and they often alienated potential members by disparaging government policy.

Governments implemented a variety of measures meant both to ensure the support of its native-born citizens and restrict potential threats to states' security from enemy aliens or "outsiders." Laws constraining the movement of foreign nationals, including their incarceration in makeshift prison camps, sprung up, for example, in England. Print and visual propaganda in the form of posters, broadsheets and circulars, warning of spies, and other duplicitous individuals, flourished in all combatant countries. Many intentionally enraged passions against an enemy, imaginary or real, fabricating facts and, in so doing, serving to reinforce a sense of national unity. One of the more infamous and fictitious pieces of black propaganda was floated by British propagandists from Wellington House, the so-called "Corpse Conversion Factory Story" of 1917. Printed in numerous Allied newspapers, the story warned that Germans were using a factory in the Belgian city of Liège to distill human cadavers into oils. Only after the war did it become known that the British had transposed two separate photographs and captions, one of a train transporting dead soldiers from the front for burial, the other depicting horse cadavers being brought by train to fertilizer factories. The German government failed, despite its own best propaganda efforts, to quell these accusations. Of course, Germany, too, was a practitioner of deception and manipulation. Its propagandists stirred up racial fears among its populace by fabricating accounts of British and French colonial troops, who were accused of, among other things, slitting German soldiers' throats and keeping their ears and other body parts as souvenirs, drinking their blood, and cannibalizing innocent men. In both the British and German cases, propaganda helped to demonize and dehumanize the "enemy."

Religious passions contributed to the tension, too. Churchmen who might have been expected to press for international cooperation in the Christian spirit of brotherhood instead delivered incendiary sermons extolling Christ's sacrifice and the necessity of bloodshed to do His work against the nation's enemies. Some British clergy denounced the Germans as heathens from whom all of civilized Christendom needed saving; others equated German militarism with the devil incarnate. Prelates such as Belgium's Cardinal Mercier became articulate critics of the German campaigns, especially Germany's destruction of the library of Louvain and other atrocities reportedly committed against the Belgian population.

All combatants waged their war of scripture with equal vehemence. Respected German theologians issued the *Appeal to Evangelical Churches Abroad* in September 1914, claiming that Germany had to defend itself from the Russian barbarians, not the other way around. The British response, *To the Christian Scholars of Europe and America*, backed by the Archbishop of Canterbury, pointed to Louvain as proof of Germany's un-Christian mentality. Similar images of the Germans emerged from the sermons of French priests. Neither Protestant nor Catholic clergy could resist this sort of exaggeration. Only Pope Benedict XV steadfastly refused to bless one side's military campaigns at the expense of the other, even if his strict neutrality infuriated some. Already before 1914, the German Right had argued that war possessed a purifying and redemptive quality; therefore, most European nations viewed combat as a struggle against evil and as a striving for ultimate salvation.

Not surprisingly, clergy who served in the field and who witnessed the carnage emerged with sobered outlook and moderated rhetoric. The soldiers, for their part, had various reactions to the horror. Some drew closer to religion; others questioned the very existence of God. Superstition abounded; some soldiers carried trinkets and charms—shark's teeth, horseshoes, rabbit's feet, and dolls—into battle for protection.

Appealing to religious prescriptions offered one way to cultivate a united front. Fear of internal disintegration through espionage prompted some European nations to take extraordinary measures against their ethnic and religious minorities as well. In several cases, legislation such as Great Britain's Defence of the Realm Act (DORA), passed soon after the outbreak of hostilities and later revised, regulated the movement and actions of aliens living in the United Kingdom. Germans and Austro-Hungarians were required by the law to register their names, often at the nearest police station; some German-born naturalized citizens so dreaded being accused of spying for Germany and drawing reprisals from fellow Englishmen that they Anglicized their names. Even the ruling English monarchy, with its German ancestry (House of Saxe-Coburg), officially changed its name to the House of Windsor in July 1917.

Canada enacted legislation that forced citizens of "enemy nationality" to register with the government and report to local authorities regularly. Anyone whom the government accused of non-compliance with these regulations or was suspected of being security threats was interned throughout the country in special camps. Between 1914 and 1920 over 8,500 Canadians called these camps their home. Australia also held "enemy aliens," including women and children, in camps located in more remote regions of the country

The Austro-Hungarian monarchy, comprising a multitude of ethnic and religious minorities, stood to lose the most from internal dissension. Germans and Magyars represented approximately 43 percent of the total population (in 1910); other significant groups were Czechs and Slovaks (16 percent), Poles (10 percent), Ukrainians (8 percent),

Croats and Serbs (8.5 percent), Romanians (6 percent), Slovenes (2 percent), and Italians (1.5 percent). Initially the citizens of the Dual Monarchy obeyed mobilization orders, but the army's poor showing in the early campaigns left many shaken. Some minority soldiers defected in entire battalions. Others, interned in Russian and Serbian camps following capture, agreed to serve as soldiers for the enemy and took up arms to free their fellow ethnic and religious minorities from the Austro-Hungarian yoke. Indeed, the disparity between the composition of the rank and file and the officer corps, whereby a German-speaking minority dominated influential positions, paralleled the internal problems plaguing the empire.

In Germany, too, religious and ethnic minorities became suspects. Before 1914 Germany's extreme right-wing parties and extra-parliamentary associations demanded that the government tighten the laws against alleged spies. Early in the conflict, wild rumors abounded in Germany and other countries of spies on the loose, some hiding in coffins, others riding in trains disguised. Thus patriotic fervor and appeals to unity heightened ethnic tensions. The German government forever suspected the intentions of Poles and Alsatians even before the war and closely scrutinized their activities.

German Jews supported their nation's entry into the war and 85,000 Jewish men served in the armed forces. Ten thousand of them died in the war. Rabbis such as Göppingen's Dr. Aron Tänzer and Berlin's Leo Baeck ministered to their comrades in uniform at the front. Yet antisemitism still flourished, especially among the extreme Right, as associations such as the Pan-German League excoriated Jews as disloyal citizens and profiteers. In October 1916, the German High Command and the Prussian war minister issued the *Judenzählung*, or Jewish Census, to all German commanding officers. The order demanded statistical information on the numbers and activities of Jewish soldiers, officers, and administrative personnel serving under these officers' command, presumably to document whether the Jewish population had come forward for service in adequate numbers, and perhaps to expose draft evaders. Austro-Hungarian antisemites also charged the Dual Monarchy's Jewish population with shirking their duty at the front and engaging in profiteering. Three hundred thousand Austro-Hungarian Jews, however, served in the army, 25,000 of them as officers.

French and Russian Jews also rallied around their nations' flags. Some 46,000 of France's and Algeria's Jews were mobilized, one-third of them as volunteers, and 6,500 perished in battle. In the early days of the conflict, even notorious antisemites such as Maurice Barrès accepted Jews into the *union sacrée*. As the war dragged on, however, antisemitism would again creep into French society. In Russia, where Jews made up 4 percent of the population, they represented over 5 percent of the soldiers in the Russian army. While some Jews expressed patriotic sentiment and joined the ranks to defend the Russian motherland, most were forced into the army by a law that imposed stiff penalties for noncompliance or desertion.

In Britain, Parliament had shown signs of xenophobia and antisemitism even before 1914, with the reemergence of protectionism, condemnation of cosmopolitan finance, and immigration restriction in 1905 (the Aliens Act). The war would only aggravate such sentiments. Moreover, the paranoid elements of the British Right often linked antisemitism and Germanophobia. Journalists and respectable members of the medical profession railed against resident aliens and German-born naturalized citizens and accused them of spying for the kaiser. One right-wing newspaper even charged England's Jews with using German money to buy prostitutes, who in turn spread venereal disease and thereby undermined the nation's war-making powers.

Legal persecution of religious minorities was bad enough; physical violence, as in the decimation of the Armenians at the hands of the Turks, represented xenophobia at its most virulent. In the spring of 1915, the Turkish government secretly ordered the deportation of the Armenian population within its borders. The horrific results are treated later in this chapter, but the episode stands as among the most tragic in a conflict with no shortage of human suffering.

Aside from suppressing religious minorities and launching programs of what is now called "ethnic cleansing," the Entente and Allies alike stoked certain groups' desires for independence in an effort to destabilize vulnerable enemy regions. In Germany one notorious figure on the extreme Right urged a "holy war" against the British and French colonialists. In a plan spearheaded by Sir Roger Casement, German extremists and Irish nationalists sought unsuccessfully to overthrow British authority in Ireland in April 1916. Despite the failure of the so-called Easter Uprising, the nationalists controlled sections of Dublin for five days before British troops restored order. The German occupying government in Belgium also cultivated Flemish nationalism, in part because it resembled Germanic culture. More generally, however, the government hoped to divide Belgium by earning Flemish gratitude over the devaluation of rival Walloon, Francophilic influence. Likewise, Germany and its Turkish ally sought to disrupt the British war effort in India and the Middle East by stirring up anti-British sentiment. For their part, the British devised subversive plots of their own, especially in the Middle East, where T. E. Lawrence and General Edmund Allenby cooperated with Arab nationalists to dislodge the Turks from the region.

Racial hatred heated up during the first total war. Even before 1914, dire warnings had proliferated about the "yellow peril," and European leaders widely interpreted Russia's defeat at the hands of the Japanese in 1905 as a blow to European "superiority" over Asiatic peoples. During the war itself, France's and Britain's use of black colonial troops and manual laborers excited particular comment. The radical Right in Germany condemned this violation of the supposed customary conduct of war and accused France of promoting racial mixing and catalyzing the degeneration of pure Aryanism. When the United States joined the fray with contingents of African-American soldiers, western Europe feared for its racial purity. Those fears remained despite the persistence of racism and segregation in the American ranks.

Ultimately, for all the confident invocations of common purpose, they appear to have been balanced, if not outweighed, by widespread concern for the fragility of the social order and anxiety over the apparently tenuous nature of national unity. The dangers of national collapse, and the limited influence of nationalist appeals to alleviate or neutralize those strains, would grow ever more obvious as the war dragged on. By its end, every nation had been tested, and several would be found wanting.

Duty, Sacrifice and Morality

The documents in this section illustrate, using British examples, just how difficult it was to establish a durable domestic consensus on how the population
should behave during wartime. First, we have a classic exhortation toward duty,
unity, and sacrifice from the war's early days, though the British minister who
delivered this speech, David Lloyd George, imbued the familiar themes with a
fiery eloquence drawn from his own experience of Welsh nonconformity. A
year or so later, however, revivalist enthusiasm had waned, and the wartime
moral order appeared to have been endangered, if not undermined, by
unscrupulous profiteers who put individual self-interest above the concerns of
the nation. Such suspicions were increasingly aired in parliamentary debate: Sir
Henry Dalziel, the MP for Kirkcaldy, emphasized the seemingly unethical leaps
in food prices and company profits, while Andrew Bonar Law, the dour and
scrupulous future prime minister, somewhat sheepishly admitted from personal
experience to just how handsomely shareholders had been rewarded for their
investments. As victory proved elusive, domestic debate took on a sharper tone,
one example of which was the civilian susceptibility to hatred noted in the third
selection. Originally published anonymously in October 1916 in the liberal journal, *The Nation*, it was written by R.H. Tawney, later a distinguished economic
historian and an influential socialist intellectual. He had served in France for
two years until being wounded and invalided home.

The final selections serve as a reminder that the truth is often stranger
than fiction. In May and June 1918 the nation was enthralled by one of the
most remarkable trials in its long legal history. The defendant, Pemberton
Billing, was an eccentric and rabidly right-wing member of Parliament who
had made a public crusade of revealing corruption in high places. In the
spring of 1918, as the publisher of journals largely devoted to that task, *The
Imperialist* and *The Vigilante*, Billing went beyond accusations of profiteering
to explicitly link allegations of treason and transgressions of conventional
sexual morality to explain why the war had not yet been won. Charging that
German agents had compiled a "Black Book" listing 47,000 English men and
women whose sexual perversion and other moral failings left them vulnerable to blackmail (the claims published in *The Imperialist*), and coupling this
to a notice implying that the dancer Maud Allan, star of the production of
Oscar Wilde's *Salome*, was a lesbian (printed in *The Vigilante*), Billing was
sued for libel by Allan. The final extract is taken from a verbatim record of
the trial itself. Billing conducted his own very idiosyncratic defense, and,
thanks to the opportunity afforded by the weak handling of the case by the
presiding judge, Justice Darling, turned the proceedings into a circus. Billing
was acquitted, though the verdict is of less interest than the ways in which
respectable masculine behavior, "unnatural vice," and antialienism were
drawn together, confirming the importance of gender roles to fears about
the durability of the political and social order under duress.

1. The New Patriotism

The Sacrifice

I envy you young people your opportunity. They have put up the age limit for the Army, but I am sorry to say I have marched a good many years even beyond that. It is a great opportunity, an opportunity that only comes once in many centuries to the children of men. For most generations sacrifice comes in drab and weariness of spirit. It comes to you to-day, and it comes to-day to us all, in the form of the glow and thrill of a great movement for liberty, that impels millions throughout Europe to the same noble end. [*Applause.*] It is a great war for the emancipation of Europe from the thraldom of a military caste which has thrown its shadows upon two generations of men, and is now plunging the world into a welter of bloodshed and death. Some have already given their lives. There are some who have given more than their own lives; they have given the lives of those who are dear to them. I honour their courage, and may God be their comfort and their strength. But their reward is at hand; those who have fallen have died consecrated deaths. They have taken their part in the making of a new Europe—a new world.

I can see signs of its coming in the glare of the battlefield.

The "New Patriotism"

The people will gain more by this struggle in all lands than they comprehend at the present moment. [*Hear, hear.*] It is true they will be free of the greatest menace to their freedom. That is not all. There is something infinitely greater and more enduring which is emerging already out of this great conflict—a new patriotism, richer, nobler, and more exalted than the old [*Applause.*]. I see amongst all classes, high and low, shedding themselves of selfishness, a new recognition that the honour of the country does not depend merely on the maintenance of its glory in the stricken field, but also in protecting its homes from distress. [*Hear, hear.*] It is bringing a new outlook for all classes. The great flood of luxury and sloth which had submerged the land is receding, and a new Britain is appearing. We can see for the first time the fundamental things that matter in life, and that have obscured our vision by the tropical growth of prosperity. [*Hear, hear.*]

"The Vision"

May I tell you in a simple parable what I think this war is doing for us? I know a valley in North Wales, between the mountains and the sea. It is a beautiful valley, snug, comfortable, sheltered by the mountains from all the bitter blasts.

VI.1   From Lloyd George, *The Great War: Speech Delivered at the Queen's Hall, London, on September 19, 1914* (Toronto: Hodder & Stoughton, 1914), 15–16.

But it is very enervating, and I remember how the boys were in the habit of climbing the hill above the village to have a glimpse of the great mountains in the distance, and to be stimulated and freshened by the breezes which came from the hilltops, and by the great spectacle of their grandeur. We have been living in a sheltered valley for generations. We have been too comfortable and too indulgent, many perhaps, too selfish, and the stern hand of fate has scoured us to an elevation where we can see the great everlasting things that matter for a nation—the great peaks we had forgotten, of Honour, Duty, Patriotism, and clad in glittering white, the great pinnacle of Sacrifice pointing like a rugged finger to Heaven. We shall descend into the valleys again; but as long as the men and women of this generation last, they will carry in their hearts the image of those great mountain peaks whose foundations are not shaken, though Europe rock and sway in the convulsions of a great war. [*Enthusiastic and continued applause.*]

∽

2. War Profits

Sir H. Dalziel: I think there is a good deal of *disappointment* outside this House that the President of the Board has not used with greater success the great powers with which he is equipped for dealing with the prices of necessary foods. The House is, of course, familiar with the fact that there has been a substantial rise since the period previous to the War, and that the value of the sovereign to-day, roughly, is about fourteen shillings. The workers outside recognise that fact very materially. It is a reality to them. They are aware that any number of explanations and excuses are put forward on behalf of the Government as to why it is so, but they do not choose to inquire too closely into these explanations. They have the outstanding fact that so far as they are concerned their wages have been reduced to the extent of 6s. in the £. I wish to draw the attention of the President of the Board of Trade to the feeling which exists in regard to that matter and to ask him whether he cannot do something, and do it quickly, more than he has already done, in order that we may have a more reasonable state of things. The figures which have been published authoritatively have not been disputed. To remind the House of their extent I would like to read an official statement I have had this morning from one of the experts in the provision trade. In June, 1914, tea was 9d.; in June, 1915, 1s. Flour per sack, June, 1914, 24s. 6d. to 27s.; now 48s. to 53s. Butter, 115s. per cwt. last year; 145s. to-day. Irish butter, 110s. per cwt. last year; now 135s. Cheese (Canadian), 60s. per cwt. last year; 98s. per cwt. now. Bacon (Danish or Irish), 70s. last year; 95s. this year. Beef (Scotch), 7d. last year; 11d. this year. Beef

VI.2   From *Hansard's Parliamentary Debates*, vol. 72 (June 10, 1915), cols. 391–394; vol. 95 (July 3, 1917), cols 982–985. © Crown Copyright material reproduced with the permission of The Controller HMSO.

(Argentine), $5\frac{1}{2}$d. last year; $9\frac{1}{2}$d. this year. Sugar, 16s. per cwt. last year; 28s. per cwt. now. [British currency at the time was based upon the pound sterling which comprised twenty shillings (s), each shilling then divided into twelve pennies, abbreviated d; "cwt" is an abbreviation for 112 lb, one-twentieth of a ton.]

These are very striking facts, and the unfortunate aspect of them is that it is the very poorest people who have to suffer in the greatest degree. Many excuses have been given, but we cannot shut our eyes to the fact that there has been going on a great deal of gambling in the food of the people. There has been speculation for a rise in price and no adequate steps have been taken to stop it. There is the notorious case of the profits made by Spillers and Baker [flour manufacturers], of Cardiff, whose profit went up from £89,000 the year before the War, to £367,665. That is a remarkable profit to make, and it is a profit made practically entirely owing to the War. It is a curious comment on the view that these people take of the righteousness of making money out of the country's distress, that they actually engaged to pay for columns in nearly all the London papers in order to show how it was done. The chairman was careful to explain that most of it was made by stock and speculations for the future, and, as one of my hon. Friends says, by depressing the small trader. It ought not to be possible in time of war for any firm to so speculate in the food of the people as to make such an enormous profit. If they do make it we should see to it that they pay their proper share of the expenses of the country. The Government have very wisely taken steps to stop this speculation in other branches of business. For the financial interests of the City they made it a rule and a necessity that people could not deal in stocks and script which they did not possess, and the result has been to check gambling to a very large extent. I wish we could do the same thing in regard to other important necessities of life. . . .

Another question which affects the increased cost of living is the price of coal. The right hon. Gentleman very wisely appointed a Committee to deal with this matter, and though I think he appointed it much too late, certainly they have produced a very interesting report. In effect their report is that the coal proprietors and merchants are entitled to an increased profit of 3s. a ton, as the result of the War, but they are getting from 9s. to 11s. per ton increased profit. The question arises, who is getting this increased profit, and cannot something be done in the interest of the consumer? My own view is that this question of coal should have been dealt with in a much more drastic and effective fashion at the beginning of the War. I think we ought to have stopped the export of coal right away, except to our Allies abroad and those who are in sympathy with us. The hon. Member for Mansfield (Sir A. Markham) mentioned yesterday that the price of coal to the Italian Government was 17s. before the War, and that at present it is as high as 33s. or 34s. I think some explanation is required of this extraordinary increase in price. It is not the miners who are getting the money. . . .

Mr. Bonar Law: I have said more than once that in my opinion the Government ought not to have allowed shipowners to make the profits which they did make, and since my hon. Friend has dwelt upon it I shall give some indication of what these profits are. It was really very wrong of the Government to have allowed such profits to have been made. That is my view, but I said at the time I expressed that view before that I did not attribute the blame to the shipowners. They have done precisely as other traders have done, and the fault, if fault there be, was the fault of the Government which allowed such profits to be made. I wish the Committee to understand the real ground on which this change that we are now proposing is necessary. When this Government was formed my right hon. Friend the Prime Minister in this House, and after consulting me because as Chancellor of the Exchequer I would be affected by it, made this declaration as to the policy of the Government: "I think my right hon. Friend has already indicated to the House what we propose to do with regard to the shipping. It was never so vital to the life of the nation as it is at the present moment, during the War. It is the jugular vein, which, if severed, would destroy the life of the nation, and the Government felt that the time had come for taking ever more complete control of all the ships of this country. . . . so that during the War shipping will be nationalised in the real sense of the term." Then comes the other point. It is really very important, and it is not merely an appeal to prejudice: "The prodigious profits which were made out of freights were contributing in no small measure to the high cost of commodities"— That is true, though it is not the main cause—"I always found not only that, but that they were making it difficult for us in our task with labour Whenever I met organised labour"—I have had the same experience—"where I would persuade them to give up privileges, I always had hurled at me phrases about the undue and extravagant profits of shipowners."—That is not merely prejudice. The fact that the Government does not allow profits of such an undue character to be made is itself an argument when you appeal to other classes to make sacrifices for the carrying on of the War. These are real facts. . . .

I am going to give the Committee the effects these excess profits have. I say it advisedly, that if we have allowed profits of this kind and on this scale to go on, the more it became known among all classes of the community the more useless it would have been to make claims upon anybody to make sacrifices in carrying on the War. My hon. Friend who has just sat down asked me to tell the truth. That is not an unusual habit of mine, I hope. I am going to do it now. I rather dislike giving my own experiences in shipping, and I will tell the Committee one reason why I dislike it—I am really ashamed of it! It is utterly disgraceful that, in a time of war, any class of the community, while others are suffering every kind of privation, should be able to make profits such as I am now going to point out. I do not say it is the fault of the shipowners—I think it was the fault of the Government—but it is absolutely disgraceful that it should have been allowed. My hon. Friend suggested— it was a curious thing, and I was surprised he made the suggestion—that perhaps my experience was due to some special favour on the part of the shipowners with whom I have invested some of the money I have. I do not think that is true in any case, but, at all events, it would be curious, for this reason: that I invested in fifteen different shipping companies under the management of seven different owners. I admit they are all tramp steamers, and it may be possible that they did better than liners. I am not sure, but I have no experience of liners. I have no reason to doubt from the fact that these companies were managed by seven different owners that this is a fair representation of the profits of the owners of tramp steamers during the War. Now I am going to give the Committee the figures. I gave them in percentages the other day, but I do not think the Committee quite realise what they meant. The sum of money I had invested in shipping, spread over these fifteen different shipping companies, was £8,100. Five per cent, interest on that, which in ordinary times, I should have been glad to get, would be £405. For the year 1915, instead of £405, I received £3,624, and for the year 1916 I received £3,847.

∽

3. You are More Prone to Hatred

Of the first material reality of war, from which everything else takes its colour, the endless and loathsome physical exhaustion, you say little, for it would spoil the piquancy, the *verve*, of the picture. Of your soldiers' internal life, the constant collision of contradictory moral standards, the liability of the soul to be crushed by mechanical monotony, the difficulty of keeping hold of sources of refreshment, the sensation of taking a profitless part in a game played by monkeys and organized by lunatics, you realize, I think, nothing. Are you so superficial as to imagine that men do not feel emotions of which they rarely speak? Or do you suppose that, as a cultured civilian once explained to me, these feelings are confined to "gentlemen," and are not shared by "common soldiers"? And behind the picture of war given in your papers there sometimes seems to lurk something worse than, yet allied to, its untruthfulness, a horrible suggestion that war is somehow, after all, ennobling; that, if not the proper occupation of man, it is at least one in which he finds a fullness of self-expression impossible in peace; that when clothed in khaki and carrying rifles, these lads are more truly "men" than they were when working in offices or factories. Perhaps I do you an injustice. But that intimation does seem to me to peep through some of your respectable paragraphs. . . .

And you are more prone than you were to give way to hatred. Hatred of the enemy is not common, I think, among soldiers who have fought with them. It is incompatible with the proper discharge of our duty. For to kill in hatred is murder, and we are not murderers but executioners. I know, indeed, how much harder it is for you not to hate than it is for us. You cannot appease the anguish of your losses by feeling, as we feel, that any day your own turn may come. And it is right that there should be a solemn detestation of the sins of Germany, provided that we are not thereby caused to forget our own.

But it is not among those who have suffered most cruelly or where comprehension of the tragedy is most profound that I find the hatred which appals. For in suffering, as in knowledge, there is something that transcends personal emotion

VI.3   From R.H. Tawney, "Reflections of a Soldier," *The Nation*, October 21, 1916.

and unites the soul to the suffering and wisdom of God. I find it rather among those who, having no outlet in suffering or in action, seem to discover in hatred the sensation of activity which they have missed elsewhere. They are to be pitied, for they also are seeking a union with their kind, though by a path on which it cannot be found. Nevertheless, the contagion of their spirit is deadly. You do not help yourselves, or your country, or your soldiers, by hating, but only by loving and striving to be more lovable.

✍

4. A Scandalous Trial

a) "The First 47,000," from The Imperialist *(January 26, 1918)*

There have been many reasons why England is prevented from putting her full strength into the War. Hope of profit cannot be the only reason for our betrayal. All nations have their Harlots on the Wall, but . . . it is in the citadel that the true danger lies. Corruption and blackmail, being the work of menials, is cheaper than bribery. Moreover, fear of exposure entraps and makes slaves of men whom money could never buy. Within the past few days, the most extraordinary facts have been placed before me which coordinate my past information.

There exists in the *Cabinet noir* of a certain German prince a book compiled by the Secret Service from the reports of German agents who have infested this country for the past twenty years, agents so vile and spreading debauchery of such a lasciviousness as only German minds could conceive and only German bodies execute.

The officer who discovered this book while on special service briefly outlined for me its stupefying contents which all decent men thought had perished in Sodom and Lesbia. The blasphemous compilers even speak of the Groves and High Places mentioned in the Bible. The most insidious arguments are outlined for the use of the German agent in his revolting work. . . .

It is a most catholic [wide-ranging] miscellany. The names of Privy Councillors, youths of the chorus, wives of Cabinet Ministers, dancing girls, even Cabinet Ministers themselves, while diplomats, poets, bankers, editors, newspaper proprietors, and members of His Majesty's Household follow each other with no order of precedence. . . .

Wives of men in supreme position were entangled. In lesbian ecstasy the most sacred secrets of State were betrayed. The sexual peculiarities of members of the Peerage were used as a leverage to open fruitful fields for espionage. In the glossary of this book is a list of expressions used by the soul-sick victims of this nauseating disease so skillfully spread by Potsdam. . . .

VI.4   From Michael Kettle, *Salome's Last Veil* (London: Granada, 1977), 7–9, 18–19, 98, 143–144, 146, 224, 229.

As I have already said in these columns, it is a terrible thought to contemplate that the British Empire should fall as fell the great Empire of Rome, and the victor now, as then, should be the Hun. The story of the contents of this book has opened my eyes, and the matter must not rest. . . .

b) *"The Cult of the Clitoris," from* The Vigilante (*February 16, 1918*)

To be a member of Maud Allan's private performance in Oscar Wilde's *Salome* one has to apply to a Miss Valetta, of 9 Duke Street, Adelphi, W.C. If Scotland Yard were to seize the list of these members I have no doubt they would secure the names of several thousand of the first 47,000. . . .

c) *Verbatim Record of Trial*

JUDGE: Now tell us where you saw it and how you came to see it.

SPENCER: Among other books of German intelligence, which Prince William of Wied had, was a report or co-ordinated reports of German agents, appended to which was a list of names of people who might be approached, and the method in which they could be approached, for the purpose of obtaining information. . . .

COUNSEL: What necessity was there for heading this statement "The Cult of the Clitoris"?

SPENCER: In order to show that a cult exists in this country who would gather together to witness a lewd performance for amusement during war time on the Sabbath . . . "The Cult of the Clitoris" meant a cult that would gather together to see a representation of a diseased mad little girl.

COUNSEL: Just think what you are saying.

SPENCER: I have.

COUNSEL: The clitoris is part of the female organ?

SPENSER: A superficial part.

COUNSEL: In which the sexual sensations are produced?

SPENSER: It is what remains of the male organ in the female.

COUNSEL: Do you mean to tell my Lord and the Jury that when you wrote those words, "The Cult of the Clitoris," you meant anything more than this, the cult of those sensations by improper means?

SPENCER: I meant superficial sensations which did nothing to help the race.

COUNSEL: By improper methods, methods other than ordinary connections between man and woman?

SPENCER: Than the usual connection between man and woman. An exaggerated clitoris might even drive a woman to an elephant. . . .

BILLING: You stated in your cross-examination that Miss Maud Allan was administering to the cult? . . . Will you tell the Court exactly what you meant by that?

SPENCER: I meant that any performance of a play which has been described by competent critics as an essay in lust, madness and sadism, and is given and attracts people to it at from five guineas to ten guineas a seat, must bring people who have more money than brains; must bring people who are seeking unusual excitement, exotic excitement; and to gather these people together in a room, under the auspices of a naturalized alien, would open these people to possible German blackmail, and that their names, or anything that transpires, might find their way into German hands, and these people would be blackmailed by the Germans; and it was to prevent this that the article was written. . . .

BILLING: Gentlemen of the Jury, I am in your hands. It is nothing to do with his Lordship; it is nothing to do with the learned Gentlemen behind me. It is a matter between you and me. It is a case when, if we are to catch a glimpse, we have caught a glimpse, of the mysterious influences which are sterilizing our Empire . . . I expect there are people in this country today who think I am mad. I am mad . . . I am obsessed with one subject, and that is, bringing our Empire out of this war a little cleaner than it was when it went in. That is my obsession; and I plead guilty to it. . . . I do not profess to know anything about "evidence" . . . but what I do know is the plain point of view of what is decent and what is not . . .Such a play, about which we have heard ad nauseam in this Court for four or five days, is one that is calculated to deprave, one that is calculated to do more harm, not only to young men and young women, but to all who see it, by undermining them, even more than a German Army itself.

⌀

Religion

In France, the legacy of church–state relations complicated the efforts of politicians, military leaders, and publicists to provide moral justification for the war and to promote a sense of shared commitment by defining participation as a sacred duty. Since its establishment in 1870, the Third Republic had witnessed a strong strain of anticlericalism. For example, the government had attempted to reduce the role of the Catholic church in public education and to substitute instruction in republican citizenship for religious teaching. During the war, the Church sought to reclaim lost influence, but it was unclear whether deepened republican patriotism and renewed religious faith were compatible. Some writers evoked an eternal France, whose enduring qualities pre-dated the republican experiment, and they often emphasized that the French, despite their superficial differences, actually stood united by a higher commitment to the nation and its righteous cause. Ironically, the author of the similarly-themed first selection below, the prominent journalist and novelist Maurice Barrès, was actually a notorious antisemite and a hostile critic of republicanism. The second extract, a letter home by British clergyman Oswald Creighton, is written in a more reflective and introspective vein. Notice his lack of hatred for the enemy and his conviction that the omnipresence of death itself was no more distressing than the pervasive ignorance of true spiritual habits. Creighton died in 1918, aged thirty-five, during an aerial bombardment. Donald Hankey, observing his mostly working-class troops, recognized that they had already in peacetime been inclined to reject formal institutional religious observance, but that they retained their commitment to a more generalized Christian ethos of neighborliness and respectability. The horrors of the trenches, the prospect of imminent death, and daily injunctions to kill had not hardened the men to reject any sense of spirituality. But the Belgian socialist, Hendrik de Man, from whose memoirs of service in the trenches the fourth piece in this section is drawn, was not so sure. He suggests that the idealism and humility central to spiritual observance are not likely to lead to success in warfare.

How inclusive was the initial consensus on the role faith could play in helping people to make the sacrifices required by this colossal war? Was there room for the traditional pariahs, the Jews? Jewish clergy did serve in the field with the major armies to minister to Jewish soldiers, even if on occasion the absence of a rabbi meant that a Christian cleric had to substitute (as in the account by Barrès). Leo Baeck, a rabbi from Berlin and one of twentieth-century Judaism's leading figures, served in a religious capacity on the Western Front. He was deeply committed to the welfare of Germany's Jewish community, but, of course, his humane patriotism and honorable wartime service did not prevent his deportation to Theresienstadt in 1943 (though he was fortunate enough to survive and resume his career after the war in Britain and the United States). Here he relates his experiences near the beginning of the war as a field chaplain during the Jewish high holidays in the autumn of 1914. Although Baeck had encountered prejudice and discrimination that he hoped the reality of Jewish military service would dissipate, the situation in Russia, where half the world's Jewish population resided in 1914, was even more severe. Antisemitism was pervasive, nurtured by discriminatory laws and promoted by pogroms. The Russian government had forced six million Jews to live within designated geographic regions—Russian Poland and parts of western and southwestern Russia—known as the Pale. Restrictions on movement were compounded by special taxes, educational quotas, and constraints on ownership of property. When war broke out, popular distrust of Russia's Jewish community led to accusations that those in war zones were spying for, or otherwise collaborating with, German forces. Deportation, deprivation, and discrimination were the result. The speech reprinted below was delivered in August 1915 in the Russian parliament (*Duma*) by deputy Friedman, demanding an end to Jewish oppression in a war fought in the name of the entire nation.

5. The Sacred Union in France

The soul of France had been asleep; it had rested upon a pillow of vipers. The horrors of civil war seemed to threaten its very existence—but the bells rang out the tocsin, and the sleeper awaked to a paean of love. Catholics, Protestants, Israelites, Socialists, Traditionalists, all suddenly forgot their grievances. The blades of hate were miraculously turned aside, an eternal quarrel was silenced beneath a blazing sky. Each said to himself: "I will feel nothing, I will think nothing which may jeopardize the salvation of my country." The priest, in remembering the schoolmaster, and the schoolmaster remembering the priest, exclaimed: "Possibly I was mistaken each time that I mistrusted him who misunderstood"; and each Frenchman who saw the son of his adversary jump into a train on his way to the front wished the young soldier god-speed while greeting his parents.

It is a *sursum corda* [a lifting of hearts]; it is the harvest of a nation's soul. It is even more, it is a mobilization of the secret forces that spring from within.

From the dark shadows of our churches, the wax tapers burned—and the crowd pressed forward to kneel beneath their light. The Protestant chapel resounded with exhortations, the ancient synagogue with psalms of sorrow, and he who passed by these holy places, he who entered not, stood without and whispered a benediction. Houses of prayer, houses of refuge, we beseech you to aid the soldiers of France! The Socialists met, questioned the facts, and debated the arguments. They recognized that justice stood within the camp of the Allies and with one accord they vowed that they would serve France in the name of that socialistic Republic in which they believed.

No more criticism, no more suspicion! Each dwelt with sympathy upon the resources of the neighbor he had once depised. . . .

In the village of Taintrux, near Saint-Dié, in the Vosges, on August 29, 1914 (on a Saturday, the holy day of the Jews), the ambulance belonging to the 14th Corps took fire from the German shells. The stretcher-bearers, in the midst of flames and explosives, carried out the one hundred and fifty wounded men who were there. One of these, who was about to die, asked for a crucifix. He begged Mr. Abraham Bloch, the Jewish chaplain, whom he mistook for the Catholic chaplain, to give it to him. Mr. Bloch lost no time; he looked for it, found it, and carried to this dying man the symbol of the Christian faith. Only a few feet beyond he himself was struck down by an *obus* [shell or grenade]. He passed away in the arms of the Catholic chaplain, Father Jamin, a Jesuit, whose recital has made this scene public. . . .

Step by step we are uplifted; herein fraternity finds its most perfect expression; the venerable rabbi presenting to a dying soldier the immortal reminder of Christ on the cross is, indeed, a picture which can never perish. . . .

VI.5   From Maurice Barrès, *The Faith of France* (Boston: Houghton Mifflin, 1918), 2–3, 88–89, 195–196.

[A]ll of our spiritual groups in fighting for France persistently believe that they are defending a principle, a soul of which they are the custodians, and which can be of value to the whole human race. . . .

Our various spiritual families indulge in dreams that are universal and possible to all, dreams which they defend while defending France. This catholicity, this preoccupation as regards the whole of humanity, is the stamp of our national spirit; it is a deep and noble note which lends harmony to every diversity of expression.

⁓

6. A British Clergyman at the Front

France, early 1917

On Tuesday (27th) I was up at the batteries for a burial. The trench mortar working party was out and a shell fell among them, killing two men and wounding six. . . . The whole battery turned out, and we escorted the bodies to the grave. I talked a little about the meaning of death. But I never quite know if it helps people to realise the meaning of life and its persistence. There are few people who definitely wish to deny it. But men generally take up such an extreme agnostic position with regard to it, largely as an escape from the sloppy sentimentalism of hymns and Christmas cards, that they stand by the grave of their friends and merely shrug their shoulders. I think it is rather a splendid attitude. As Gibbon, I believe, said, the Turks fought with the fanaticism born of an overwhelming conviction of the joys of Paradise, and the Christians fought equally courageously though they had no such certainty. I suppose the finest character springs from those who see nothing beyond the present. And yet the future seems so increasingly clear and certain to me. Death is absolutely nothing to me now, except rather a violent shock, which one's peaceful and timid nature shrinks from. The gloomy articles in *The Nation*, for instance, which see nothing but the horror of Europe soaked in blood, and all the flower of youth being cut off, say very little to me. The horror of war is the light it throws on all the evil, ignorance, materialism, bigotry, and sectional interests in human nature. Surely death is not the horror of war, but the causes which contribute to war. The Cross is beautiful—the forces which lead up to it are damnable. It really does not in the least matter how many people are killed, who wins, whether we starve or anything else of a transitory nature, provided that in the process human nature is transformed in some way or another. I am not nearly so much depressed by death, or even by the thought of the success of the U-boat campaign or a revolution in Ireland, as by the absolute stone walls of ignorance, prejudice and apathy one finds oneself face to face with everywhere. . . .

VI.6   From Laurence Housman, ed., *War Letters of Fallen Englishmen* (London: Victor Gollancz, 1930), 77–79.

Curiously enough, another incident happened immediately after the funeral. I was in the mess, taking down particulars, when we heard the sound of machine-gun fire. We rushed out and found an aeroplane battle on. Some Boche planes had come right over the town and were swooping down on our observer. No anti-aircraft guns were firing at them. The Hun planes are tremendously fast. A plane just above us caught fire and dropped a flaming mass to the ground just behind the convent. Instinctively we all rushed round. I thought possibly one might be able to do something. There lay a smouldering mass of wreckage. They dragged it away, and there lay two charred, black, smouldering lumps, which a few minutes before had been active, fearless men. It was not a pleasant sight to one's refined and delicate feelings. I felt rather staggered, and it loomed before me all day and night. But after all what did it signify?—the utter futility of violence and force. Ignorance again.

The Colonel wanted a canteen started, and that same day I found a place for one behind the guns. It was the house belonging to a doctor, an eye specialist, sumptuously built, heated with hot water, with a nice garden at the back. We soon got the canteen going there. The men patronise it all the time. It is really extraordinary thepart played by the stomach in life. It simply rules the world, and affects all our outlook on life. We are paralysed, absorbed, hypnotised by it. The chief topic of conversation is rations with the men, and food and wine with the officers. Men pour into my canteens and buy everything up. For four Sundays I have been up to Arras to hold evening service. Twice I arranged it at the canteen. The men filed out when it began, and were back again for cocoa when it was over. (I have just stopped writing this to eat a piece of cake.) I felt rather furious last time. What is the use of feeding men if they deliberately set themselves against any attempt to teach or help them see the truth? I preached at all services one Sunday on "Man shall not live by bread alone," and said that while that was the first truth laid down by Christ, it was the last that man could understand. We have no need to worry about the U-boat campaign, but we must worry over the absolute famine of words proceeding from the mouth of God. What is Government doing now, but hurling invective and living in suppressed strife? How can there be a united nation without the passion for truth above all else? We are hypnotised by an unscrupulous press. We are always being taught to hate the Germans, and to refuse to think or speak of peace. We are told about our glorious cause till it simply stinks in the nostrils of the average man. We all know we have got to fight as long as we wear the uniform, and have thereby committed ourselves to slaughter as many Germans as possible. But I, for one, and I tell the men exactly the same, utterly refuse to hate the Kaiser or any of them or to believe that I am fighting for a glorious cause, or anything that the papers tell me. But if man learns to live a little more on the words coming out of God's, and not Northcliffe's, ecclesiastics', politicians', or any one else's mouths—the war does not really matter.

7. The Religion of the Inarticulate

I have said that the life of the barrack-room is dull and rather petty. In point of fact, it bears somewhat the same relation to ordinary working-class life as salt-water baths do to the sea. We used to read that Brill's Baths were "salt as the sea but safer." Well, barrack life is narrow and rather sordid, like the life of all workingmen, and it lacks the spice of risk. There is no risk of losing your job and starving. Your bread-and-margarine are safe whatever happens. As a result the more heroic qualities are not called into action. The virtues of the barrack-room are unselfishness in small things, and its vices are meanness and selfish-ness in small things. A few of the men were frankly bestial, obsessed by two ideas—beer and women. But for the most part they were good fellows. They were intensely loyal to their comrades, very ready to share whatever they had with a chum, extraordinarily generous and chivalrous if anyone was in trouble, and that quite apart from his desserts [sic]. At any rate, it was easy to see that they believed whole-heartedly in unselfishness and in charity to the unfortunate, even if they did not always live up to their beliefs. It was the same sort of quality, too, that they admired in other people. They liked an officer who was free with his money, took trouble to understand them if they were in difficulties, and considered their welfare. They were extremely quick to see through anyone who pretended to be better than he was. This they disliked more than anything else. The man they admired most was the man who, though obviously a gentleman, did not trade on it. That, surely, is the trait which in the Gospel is called humility. They certainly did believe in unselfishness, generosity, charity, and humility. But it was doubtful whether they ever connected these qualities with the profession and practice of Christianity.

It was when we had got out to Flanders, and were on the eve of our first visit to the trenches, that I heard the first definite attempt to discuss religion, and then it was only two or three who took part. The remainder just listened. It was bedtime, and we were all lying close together on the floor of a hut. We were to go into the trenches for the first time the next day. I think that everyone was feeling a little awed. Unfortunately we had just been to an open-air service, where the chaplain had made desperate efforts to frighten us. The result was just what might have been expected. We were all rather indignant. We might be a little bit frightened inside; but we were not going to admit it. Above all, we were not going to turn religious at the last minute because we were afraid. So one man began to scoff at the Old Testament, David and Bathsheba, Jonah and the whale, and so forth. Another capped him by laughing at the feeding of the five thousand. A third said that in his opinion anyone who pretended to be a Christian in the Army must be a humbug. The sergeant-major was fatuously apologetic and shocked, and applied the closure by putting out the light and ordering silence.

VI.7   From Donald Hankey, *Student in Arms*, 104–111.

It was not much, but enough to convince me that the soldier, and in this case the soldier means the workingman, does not in the least connect the things that he really believes in with Christianity. He thinks that Christianity consists in believing the Bible and setting up to be better than your neighbors. By believing the Bible he means believing that Jonah was swallowed by the whale. By setting up to be better than your neighbors he means not drinking, not swearing, and preferably not smoking, being close-fisted with your money, avoiding the companionship of doubtful characters, and refusing to acknowledge that such have any claim upon you.

This is surely nothing short of tragedy. Here were men who believed absolutely in the Christian virtues of unselfishness, generosity, charity, and humility, without ever connecting them in their minds with Christ; and at the same time what they did associate with Christianity was just on a par with the formalism and smug self-righteousness which Christ spent His whole life in trying to destroy.

The chaplains as a rule failed to realize this. They saw the inarticulateness, and assumed a lack of any religion. They remonstrated with their hearers for not saying their prayers, and not coming to Communion, and not being afraid to die without making their peace with God. They did not grasp that the men really had deep-seated beliefs in goodness, and that the only reason why they did not pray and go to Communion was that they never connected the goodness in which they believed with the God in Whom the chaplains said they ought to believe. If they had connected Christianity with unselfishness and the rest, they would have been prepared to look at Christ as their Master and their Saviour. As a matter of fact, I believe that in a vague way lots of men do regard Christ as on their side. They have a dim sort of idea that He is misrepresented by Christianity, and that when it comes to the test He will not judge them so hardly as the chaplains do. They have heard that He was the Friend of sinners, and severe on those who set up to be religious. But however that may be, I am certain that if the chaplain wants to be understood and to win their sympathy he must begin by showing them that Christianity is the explanation and the justification and the triumph of all that they do now really believe in. He must start by making their religion articulate in a way which they will recognize. He must make them see that his creeds and prayers and worship are the symbols of all that they admire most, and most want to be.

In doing this perhaps he will find a stronger faith his own. It is certainly arguable that we educated Christians are in our way almost as inarticulate as the uneducated whom we always want to instruct. If we apply this test of actions and objects of admiration to our own beliefs, we shall often find that our professed creeds have very little bearing on them. In the hour of danger and wounds and death many a man has realized with a shock that the articles of his creed about which he was most contentious mattered very, very little, and that he had somewhat over-looked the articles that proved to be vital. If the workingman's religion is often wholly inarticulate, the real religion of the educated man is often quite wrongly articulated.

8. Spiritual Consciousness

I have been asked many a time by clergymen, especially in America, whether I thought that the war had deepened the spiritual consciousness of most of the soldiers and made them more religious. I would myself call this question the supreme test of the psychological influence of the war on combatants, provided that religion be taken in such a broad sense that it becomes almost synonymous with idealism. But then the problem becomes so vast that I dare not answer by yea or nay. There are so many contradictory influences involved, and their relative importance varies so much according to the individuals or groups concerned, that I confess myself unable to discern what the ultimate balance will be. I would however dissuade people from overestimating the favourable effect of constant danger to life on the spiritual attitude of soldiers.

It is a popular notion, in Europe at any rate, that people whose occupation constantly confronts them with a danger that makes them seem like toys in the hands of a supernatural and eternal power, thereby become particularly religious. Sailors and deep-sea fishermen are the classical instances. It is often inferred that this must especially apply to combatant soldiers. I doubt very much, however, whether it is not merely superstition that in these cases is commonly assumed to be religion. From my experience with Flemish and French deep-sea fishermen, I would say that their attachment to the symbols of ancestral cult, their idolatry of innumerable saints, and the omnipotence of their local clergy are less in favour of their religious turn of mind than the general level of their morality is against it. I fail to see why the case of the soldiers should be different.

On the whole, I am inclined to believe that whilst the spiritual life of a minority who were truly religious from the outset may have been deepened by their experience of war, the great majority have not had enough native idealism to counteract the brutalising influence of the circumstances they have to live in. This majority have reacted to the hardships and the uncertainty of life by seeking solace in an essentially materialistic fatalism, accompanied by an inordinate desire for coarse physical enjoyment whenever the slightest opportunity occurred. When going on short leave from the front, for instance, the general disposition of mind was to "have a good time" at any cost; and so-called pleasures, which under ordinary circumstances would have disgusted a man by their vulgarity or immorality, were then excused with the argument that perhaps it was the "last chance, anyway." . . .

Anybody with some experience of the front will understand that the natural reaction to months and years of danger, hardships, sexual continence, and privation of practically any sort of entertainment, is anything but an inducement to spiritual self-communing. I am afraid that the exceptions to this rule are few. In spite of the pains I took not to miss the intellectual and spiritual benefit of

VI.8 From Hendrik de Man, *The Remaking of a Mind: A Soldier's Thoughts on War and Reconstruction* (New York: Scribner, 1919), 206–211.

my experiences, I would not even unreservedly claim the favor of this exception on my own behalf. Life at the front has made me superstitious to the extent that even now I find it hard not to ascribe my good luck to some "mascot" or other talisman in which I confess to have believed. I have often caught myself, just before passing a peculiarly dangerous spot, in the act of straightening my deportment, fingering the buttons of my uniform to make sure that they were all right, and reflecting whether I had shaved recently enough to meet death as a smart soldier; but at such moments I gave no thought to my conscience. I remember how, being on leave in Paris once after a particularly severe spell at the front, I felt tempted by the programme of a classical concert that was to be given that afternoon by a renowned symphonic orchestra. I thought it would do me good, for I had not heard any music but soldiers' songs and ragtime improvisations for more than two years. So I went there and listened for a couple of hours to Bach, Beethoven, and Mozart. I could have wept for delight in feeling like a human being again. It was as though I had suddenly been relieved of the armour which had become identified with myself for two long years. But after it was over it seemed to me that all my strength had been taken away from me together with my armour, and that it would hurt me beyond expression to put it on again. I never felt so womanish and altogether so miserable in my life. Then I realised that it did not do a trench mortar officer a bit of good to cultivate "soft spots" by worshipping musical beauty. All he had to do was to win the war by killing "Boches." The less he was a human being, the better he would be suited for his job—and there was no other job worth doing until the war was won. So I concluded that next time, rather than concert-going, I would spend my money on a good dinner with a big bottle of wine, to make up for four months of poor meals and gather strength for another four months (perhaps—"touch wood!") to come.

I am perfectly aware that this will seem supremely silly to many people. But then perhaps they do not care for good music as much as I do—or else they have never fired a trench mortar. Under these circumstances it has cost me some very hard fighting with myself not to lose my religion, or shall I say my idealism if the former term seems inappropriate to describe the spiritual attitude of a man haughty enough to think his religion too big for the size of any church or chapel. I doubt indeed whether the war has not made me lose some of the human modesty that is the fundamental attitude of mind required by any Church. I can still feel modest when I look up to a starlit sky, or for that matter, when I lie down in the grass and stare at the flowers and the insects— but I find it very hard to bow my head to any living human being or to any of their works. This kind of modesty has been *shelled* out of me. I am quite prepared to admit that this is probably a moral loss; but then this is no boast, but a confession. I merely think it necessary to make it, because I know that the same thing has happened to many men of a similar turn of mind who have been through the same experience.

9. A German Rabbi in the Field

Noyon, October 15, 1914

On the 28th day of September I moved from Allemant to Chauncy in order to celebrate Yom Kippur, the Day of Atonement.[1] Thanks to the commanding officer, a specific section of the Church of Notre Dame was set aside for it, since all other large rooms in the city were reserved for the military hospital and soldiers' barracks, while every free space was occupied by heavy goods' vehicles. I delivered my sermon twice, on Tuesday, the 29th of September at 5:30 p.m. and on Wednesday at 9:00 a.m. At the behest of those gathered I also offered a Neeila Service [closing service on Yom Kippur] with a sermon at 4:30 p.m.

All three services were attended in the same way by approximately 35–40 men from Chauncy, soldiers of varying ranks and doctors. The middle part of the church at our disposal, away from the altar and the other sacraments, lit by candles, made for an impressive sight. I presented the prayers and the sermon . . . from the lower pulpit; the seats for those gathered were placed in front of it. To my delight there were several members of our community among the small group. . . . I and all of the others were deeply stirred by the lines of Avinu Malkeinu [Our Father, Our King] repeated aloud. . . . I would also like to mention that before the concluding service the curé of the church, who is familiar with Germans, asked me [to be allowed] to attend the service, and requested a prayer-book in commemoration.

I stayed a week in Chauncy in order to visit the numerous field hospitals there as well as in its environs. Chauncy . . . is a central dispensary for the wounded. The way to the neighborhoods was facilitated for me by a wagon placed at my disposal for several days. These visits to the military hospitals prove to be an essential part of my duties. "A little piece of home" is brought to the wounded and their spirits are raised; they feel, as I have often noted, comforted that a chaplain attends to them [as he does] to those of other faiths. Next to this, the wounded are able to receive mail regularly. On some days I have quite voluminous amounts of mail to distribute.

In many cases I unfortunately have also had to send news about the death of a member. I have presided over the burial, at which the dead are mostly interned in a mass grave, along with the Protestant and Catholic clergymen. . . . I have always informed the relatives about the place and time of burial and other particulars about the deceased.

From Chauncy I embarked upon a longer journey, which would take me to the individual divisions. In order to get closer to the troops, it became apparent to me that I would have to join the individual divisions and brigades. I dedicated the

VI.9   From Eugen Tannenbaum, *Kriegsbriefe Deutscher und Österreichischer Juden* (Berlin: Neuer Verlag, 1915), 82–88. Translated from the German by Marilyn Shevin-Coetzee.
[1]On Yom Kippur, the holiest and most solemn day in the Jewish calendar, Jews fast for twenty-four hours, praying for forgiveness from God for all their transgressions and broken promises.

entire past week to this task and spent time with two divisions every three days. I held two small field services in the open and where Jewish soldiers are distributed only sporadically among a unit, I seek them out. Besides that I inquired about Jewish wounded in field hospitals and canteens. [Searching for them] in all places was often difficult and tiresome. Some villages in which I quartered at night were almost entirely destroyed by grenades, and the few houses that still had a roof and a few windows were understandably always reserved for the unit beforehand. But all of these problems were eased by the consideration of the unit leader, especially the General and the other high-ranking officers. . . .

I still have not been able to ascertain how my colleagues, who were called up as field clergymen, manage their duties. I have been able so far to meet only one. At the suggestion of the commandant, this fellow has taken a permanent position at headquarters. . . . Despite all the troubles, it is by all means necessary to visit all sections of the army. Only in so doing is it possible that perhaps not everyone, but at least many, will . . . [know] . . . that a rabbi is available to them. It is very important that Jewish soldiers are aware of this, but equally so that individuals of other religions know as well. This is of immense importance for the recognition of Judaism and . . . every acknowledgment of the Jews is first and foremost dependent upon the recognition of Judaism. It is also important for the position of the Jewish soldier that his religion is visible among the others.

♋

10. Russian Jews Demand End to Discrimination

In spite of their oppressed condition, in spite of their status of outlawry, the Jews have risen to the exalted mood of the nation and in the course of the last year have participated in the war in a noteworthy manner. They fell short of the others in no respect. They mobilized their entire enrollment, but, indeed, with this difference, that they have also sent their only sons into the war. The newspapers at the beginning of the war had a remarkable number of Jewish volunteers to record. Gentlemen, those were volunteers who were entitled through their educational qualifications to the rank of officers. They knew that they would not receive this rank; and nevertheless they entered the war.

The Jewish youth, which, as a result of the restrictions as to admission to the high schools of the country, had been forced to study abroad, returned home when war was declared, or entered the armies of the allied nations. A large number of Jewish students fell at the defense of Liege and also at other points on the western front.

The Zionist youths, when they were confronted with the dilemma of accepting Turkish sovereignty or being compelled to emigrate from Palestine, preferred to go to Alexandria and there to join the English army.

VI.10   From *The Jews in the Eastern War Zone* (New York: American Jewish Committee, 1916), 111–117.

The Jews built hospitals, contributed money, and participated in the war in every respect just as did the other citizens. Many Jews received marks of distinction for their conduct at the front.

Before me lies the letter of a Jew who returned from the United States of America:

"I risked my life," he writes, "and if, nevertheless, I came as far as Archangel, it was only because I loved my fatherland more than my life or that American freedom which I was permitted to enjoy. I became a soldier, and lost my left arm almost to the shoulder. I was brought into the governmental district of Courland. Scarcely had I reached Riga when I met at the station my mother and my relatives, who had just arrived there, and who on that same day were compelled to leave their hearth and home at the order of the military authorities. Tell the gentlemen who sit on the benches of the Right that I do not mourn my lost arm, but that I do mourn deeply the self-respect that was not denied to me in alien lands but is now lost to me."

Such was the sentiment of the Jews that found expression in numerous appeals and manifestations in the press, and finally also in this House. Surely these sentiments should have been taken into account. One should have a right to assume that the Government would adopt measures for the amelioration of the fate of the Jews who found themselves in the very center of the war-like occurrences. Likewise, one should have taken into account the sentiments of hundreds of thousands of Jews who shed their blood on the field of battle.

Instead of that, however, we see that from the beginning of the war the measures of reprisals against the Jewish populace were not only not weakened but, on the contrary, made much stronger. Banished were Jewish men and women whose husbands, children, and brothers, were shedding their blood for the fatherland. . . .

In a long war lucky events alternate with unlucky ones, and in any case it is naturally useful to have scapegoats in reserve. For this purpose there exists the old firm; the Jew. Scarcely has the enemy reached our frontiers when the rumor is spread that Jewish gold is flowing over to the Germans, and that, too, in airplanes, in coffins, and—in the entrails of geese!

Scarcely had the enemy pressed further, than there appeared again beyond dispute the eternal Jew "on the white horse," perhaps the same one who once rode on the white horse through the city in order to provoke a pogrom. The Jews have set up telephones, have destroyed the telegraph lines. The legend grew, and with the eager support of the powers of Government and the agitation in official circles, assumed ever greater proportions. A series of unprecedented, unheard-of, cruel measures was adopted against the Jews. These measures, which were carried out before the eyes of the entire population, suggested to the people and to the army the recognition of the fact that the Jews were treated as enemies by the Government, and that the Jewish population was outside the law.

In the first place these measures consisted of the complete transplanting of the Jewish population from many districts, to the very last man. These compulsory migrations took place in the Kingdom of Poland and in many other territories. All told, about a half million persons have been doomed to a state of beggary and vagabondage. Anyone who has seen with his own eyes how these expulsions take place, will never forget them as long as he lives. The exiling took place within twenty-four hours, sometimes within two days. Women, old men, and children, and sometimes invalids, were banished. Even the feebleminded were taken from the lunatic asylums and the Jews were forced to take these with them. . . .

I saw also the refugees of the Government of Kovno. Persons who only yesterday were still accounted wealthy were beggars the next day. Among the refugees I met Jewish women and girls, who had worked together with Russian women, had sewed garments with them and collected contributions with them, and who were now forced to encamp on the railway embankment. I saw families of reservists. I saw among the exiles wounded soldiers wearing the Cross of St. George. It is said that Jewish soldiers in marching through the Polish cities were forced to witness the expulsion of their wives and children. The Jews were loaded in freight cars like cattle. The bills of lading were worded as follows: "Four hundred and fifty Jews, en route to ———."

There were cases in which the Governors refused outright to take in the Jews at all. I myself was in Vilna at the very time when a whole trainload of Jews was stalled for four days in Novo-Wilejsk station. Those were Jews who had been sent from the Government of Kovno to the Government of Poltawa, but the Governor there would not receive them and sent them back to Kovno, whence they were again reshipped to Poltawa. Imagine, at a time when every railway car is needed for the transportation of munitions, when from all sides are heard complaints about the lack of means of transportation, the Government permits itself to do such a thing! At one station there stood 110 freight cars containing Jewish exiles.

Another measure which likewise is unprecedented in the entire history of the civilized world, is the introduction of the so-called system of "Hostages," and, indeed, hostages were taken not from the enemy, but from the country's own subjects, its own citizens. Hostages were taken in Radom, Kieltse, Lomscha, Kovno, Riga, Lublin, etc. The hostages were held under the most rigorous régime, and at present there are still under arrest in Poltava Jewish hostages from the Governments of Kieltse and Radom.

Some time ago, in commenting upon the procedure against the Jews, the leader of the Opposition, even before the outbreak of the war, used the expression that we were approaching the times of Ferdinand and Isabella. I now assert that we have already surpassed that era. No Jewish blood was shed in defense of Spain, but ours flowed the moment the Jews helped defend the Fatherland.

Yes, we are beyond the pale of the laws, we are oppressed, we have a hard life, but we know the source of that evil; it comes from those benches (pointing to the boxes of the Ministers). We are being oppressed by the Russian Government, not by the Russian people. Why, then, is it surprising if we wish to unite our destinies, not with that of the Russian Government, but with that of the Russian people? . . .

We likewise hope that the time is not distant when we can be citizens of the Russian State with full equality of privileges with the free Russian people.

Before the face of the entire country, before the entire civilized world, I declare that the calumnies against the Jews are the most repulsive lies and chimeras of persons who will have to be responsible for their crimes. [*Applause on Left.*]

It depends upon you, gentlemen of the Imperial Duma, to speak the word of encouragement, to perform the action that can deliver the Jewish people from the terrible plight in which it is at present, and that can lead them back into the ranks of the Russian citizens who are defending their Fatherland. [*Cries of "Right."*]

I do not know if the Imperial Duma will so act, but if it does so act it will be fulfilling an obligation of honor and an act of wise statesmanship that is necessary for the profit and for the greatness of the Fatherland. [*Applause on Left.*]

✎

Race and Ethnicity

Race and ethnicity could underpin definitions of "otherness," and thus be more likely to represent points of division and exclusion rather than of unity and inclusion. Nowhere was this more prevalent than in the Austro-Hungarian empire, a fragile patchwork of competing and sometimes antagonistic nationalities. It often seemed as if the empire was waging two battles simultaneously: one against its foes on the battlefields, the other against internal nationalist movements. The Hungarian Magyars, who governed from Budapest, proved the most resistant to calls for autonomy (or even independence) from Czechs, Slovaks, Serbs, Croats, and Ukranians, among others, but their hegemony over the eastern half of the empire could only be retained through military victory. Defeat would spell disintegration. The complex situation is untangled below by a recent Hungarian historian.

Another multi-ethnic empire for which military defeat would be fatal was the Ottoman (or Turkish). Its leaders were especially concerned that the large Armenian minority within its borders would align with Russia and constitute a dangerous fifth column. Scattered partisan actions aggravated matters, and to forestall that possibility, the Turkish government undertook what has been described as a stark episode of ethnic cleansing or a defining instance of genocide. In 1915 it ordered the removal of roughly 1.75 million Armenian civilians (including women and children), some of whom were shot and many more of whom died during the deportation toward Syria and Mesopotamia from abuse or neglect. Most historians agree that at least 800,000 Armenians perished. The American counsel in Harput (in east-central Turkey) was well-placed to observe the process by which the Armenian population was reduced, and he filed this devastating eyewitness report to his superiors in the State Department in 1917.

The third selection, by a British academic serving in the political intelligence department of the Foreign Office was written privately, rather than under official auspices. Its author, Edwyn Bevan, was an eminent scholar of religion and philosophy in the ancient world, and he turns his attention here to a consideration of racial issues in the conflict. The disruption of established patterns of authority and racial subjugation that the war entailed, he believes, both poses a threat and offers an opportunity. Postwar racial conflict might be mitigated by the positive role that

genuine Christianity might play. The next extract, dealing with questions of nationality and allegiance, reflects a debate revolving more around notions of vigilance
than of reconciliation. Britain, which had prided itself upon its acceptance of political and other refugees (though in practice the numbers admitted rarely matched the
self-congratulatory image), faced a particular dilemma with regard to German-born
immigrants who had subsequently been naturalized as British citizens, as well as
those who had simply settled there as aliens. In this June 1916 parliamentary
debate, William Joynson-Hicks (whom we already encountered with regard to
Zeppelins and aerial defense) urged the government to take stringent measures
to restrict aliens within the country, to combat the threat of domestic subversion
and espionage, and to ensure that England "shall be for the English." Dismissing
such arguments as unduly alarmist, Home Secretary Herbert Samuel offered a
measured response on behalf of the government.

11. Ethnic Minorities in the Austro-Hungarian Empire

After the outbreak of the war, and even more so after the defeats suffered from the
Serb and Russian armies, the Serb and Ukrainian minorities living in the Monarchy were greatly oppressed. The greatest part of the Hungarian territories inhabited by Serbs and Ukrainians also belonged to the military zone, which was under
the management of the supreme command. The Hungarian government, exercis-
ing its special powers, also took some harsh measures.

In November 1912, a secret codicil marked "Cs–1" had been added to the
service regulation of the gendarmerie. This codicil summed up the duties of the
gendarmerie concerning the prevention of espionage. Article 11 ordained that
"persons under acute suspicion of espionage should be detained on the day of
mobilization." "Suspicion of espionage" was used in such a wide sense that it
could be applied to almost any person belonging to the nationalities living near
the border.

The arrests started on July 25. In a few days, they reached such enormous proportions that on August 2 the minister of the interior modified Article 11 of the
secret regulation by a circular: only those persons were to be arrested who "really
had a harmful influence on our preparations for the mobilization," while those
under suspicion were to be reported to the police of the municipal authorities, but
were not to be detained. Mass arrests went on, however, on various other pretexts.
Thus e.g. people suspected of being members of the Narodna Odbrana[2] were
arrested without any other reason. Many of them were not set free even later.
Internment also attained mass proportions.

VI.11   From Josef Galantai, *Hungary and the First World War* (Budapest: Akademiai Kiado, 1989),
95–102. Reprinted with permission of Akademiai Kiado, Hungary.

The measures taken against the Serb population of the southern regions were in some cases just local atrocities, mostly, however, they were based on central directives. On the day after the rupture of diplomatic relations with Serbia, the prime minister instructed the lord lieutenants: "I call your attention with particular emphasis to the attitude to be taken towards the non-Hungarian population . . . We must show them our strength." In his letter of September 5 to the government commissioner of the territories inhabited by Serbs, Tisza advised moderation in connection with local excesses, demanding at the same time "relentless severity against the criminals," and actions to be taken "without much ado."

The emergency measures were in force in Croatia too, where they were mostly used against the Serb population. The authorities turned first of all against the Serb Sokol associations functioning in Croatia. Even before the outbreak of the war, on July 14, the Minister of Defence Krobatin had informed Tisza that in Croatia-Slavonia "the Serb Sokol associations and popes were the main agitators of the Great Serb revolutionary movement." When the war broke out, the members and leaders of the Sokol were arrested. Not even the immunity of MPs was respected. Krobatin had already mentioned in his letter that "some of the MPs are positively agitators and promoters of revolutionary propaganda." Now several Croatian Serb MPs were arrested on various pretexts. E.g. Srdjan Budisavljević, a member of the Zagreb provincial diet and as its delegate, a Hungarian MP, was detained on the pretext that he was the president of the Krajiska district center of the Sokol associations. Later Tisza intervened for him because "he is being calumniated for a trifle," he wrote.

Before the war, the Hungarian government had not been very interested in the domestic situation in Bosnia and Herzegovina. Now, however, Tisza attached great importance to the fact that the Serb population of Hungary and Croatia was closely attached to the Bosnian Serb population. One of the basic principles of Tisza's policy was that the annexation of Serbia and the union of the Serb population living in the Monarchy were out of the question. Therefore not only the links of the Serbs of Hungary, Croatia and Bosnia with Serbia demanded a counter-action, but also their aspirations at unity within the Monarchy. At the beginning of the war Tisza wanted the expected gains of the Monarchy to be distributed according to the dualist principle. He even included in his plans Bosnia and Herzegovina, which were treated as separate provinces. If Austria gained some Polish regions, Bosnia and Herzegovina could become Hungarian crown provinces. This idea was one of the reasons why the Hungarian government paid special attention to Bosnia during the war.

Even in the state of emergency, the Serbs of Hungary, Croatia, and Bosnia found ways to express their sympathy with the war waged by Serbia. The

[2]The National Defense Association sought to create a Greater Serbia at the expense of both Austria and Turkey.

minister of the interior, as we have seen, made mention of this fact at the cabinet meeting held in late August 1914. Another proof was furnished by the documents captured later, at the occupation of Serbia, especially by the Belgrade archives of the Narodna Odbrana. These show that many of the Austro-Hungarian soldiers of Serb nationality captured by the Serbian troops asked to be admitted to the Serbian army. 21 Hungarian Serb soldiers figured in the lists. Many young men who had not been enlisted yet fled to Serbia . . . and joined the Serbian army as volunteers. . . .

The measures taken against the Serb civil population also gave rise to some disagreements between the Hungarian government and the commanders of the common army units stationed in southern Hungary. As we have already seen, the Austrian emergency law invested the military authorities with far-reaching rights against the civil population, while the Hungarian one extended the rights of the government agencies, but did not invest the military authorities with governmental rights. The commanding officers of the common units stationed in Hungary, especially in the territories qualified as "military zones," often behaved as if they were in Austria, i.e. according to the Austrian emergency measures. This provoked protests from the Hungarian authorities. Already in late August Tisza sent a telegram to Burián, in Vienna, saying: "Excesses committed by military commanders disregarding government and authorities are increasing . . . Please do everything possible by all means to stop this madness . . . I shall be obliged to see His Majesty and make this a matter of principle." In these frictions the government was trying to preserve its sovereignty; at the same time it was obvious, however, that the military proceedings were more serious even than the special civil proceedings permitted by the emergency law.

A characteristic example of such a friction took place at Zombor. In early September 1914 soldiers and civilians demanded in a chauvinistic demonstration the removal of Cyrillic notices from shops. One Serb shopkeeper refused to do so, and, fleeing the insults of the mob, ran into his house and shot at the demonstrators. The civil authorities arrested him. The joint military command of Zombor demanded his extradition, threatening the public prosecutor and the police commissioner with arrest. At this, the latter gave in. Tisza heard about the matter from the mayor's report, and wanted to ask for a severe inquiry against the Zombor military command. They, however, had acted quickly: the shopkeeper had been sentenced to death by court martial and the sentence had been carried out straight away. In addition, the court martial designated twelve hostages among the Serb intellectuals and landowners of Zombor, saying that "if the population revolted against the military proceedings and hampered the functioning of the militia with its treacherous behaviour, the hostages will be arrested and immediately executed by the military authorities." On September 15 Tisza addressed a lengthy memorandum concerning this and other similar matters to the commander in chief, Archduke Frederick himself. He wrote that in the question of competence "the situation had really become intolerable" between the military authorities and the Hungarian government agencies. He was therefore asking for vigorous action. A few days later Tisza thanked the archduke for the quick action. . . .

With the Slovaks and Croats, if only for military reasons, the government tried to avoid any actions that could give rise to agitation. At the beginning of the war they counted on the Croatian regiments and Slovak soldiers as reliable troops.

In the first weeks of the war the Hungarian prime minister was trying to restrain the chauvinistic tone of the Hungarian papers of Upper Hungary. In late August he gave a satisfactory answer to the complaints lodged by Slovak politician Matus Dula, and on September 10 he spoke in support of allowing the banned daily *Slovenský Dennik* to appear again. But in this area as well, the liberal tone was to change soon.

Following the autumn defeats of the Monarchy a Czechoslovak movement began to take shape among the emigrés. The Hungarian government showed concern not so much for Masaryk's camp as for the movement of the Slovak emigrés in Russia. It was even more disquieting for the government that as a result of the defeats the idea of Czechoslovak unity within the Monarchy was gaining ground among the Slovaks. The Hungarian government had already considered this problem a year before the war. At that time it had received several indications that this trend was gaining strength among the Slovak population. In his report of June 26, 1913, addressed to the prime minister and marked "Confidential! Into his own hands!", the lord lieutenant of Trencsén county had also warned that this movement was supported from Bohemia by economic means: "The small banks and savings banks fed by Czech money . . . give credit to the people even at a time when money is lacking all over the world." In November 1913 the government drew up a 23-page memorandum for domestic use entitled "The Problems Concerning the Slovak Nationality Living in Hungary." The summary characterized all Slovak trends. . . . "The Slovak national movement has hardly any favor which is not backed by Bohemian-Moravian agitation, culture, and money. Movements founded purely upon the racial strength of the Slovaks themselves can hardly be encountered today, which is certainly the result of long years of steady work done by the Czechs . . . Owing to the strong Czech influence the idea of the racial separatism of the Slovaks is being completely relegated to the background."

Following the military defeats suffered by the Monarchy, the Czechoslovak tendency grew stronger among the Slovaks. Now Tisza was urging the authorities and the local forces to act with more determination. In February 1915 he intervened over the minister of justice, because he considered the steps taken too lenient. However, he could not prevent the Slovak national movement from gaining ground. The editorial in the July 31, 1915 issue of *Národnie Noviny*, the paper of the Slovak National Party . . . , raised, cautiously but explicitly, the issue of dismissing the idea of the Hungarian national state. The Hungarian government attached great importance to this . . . : "The Slovaks constitute, at present, an element faithful to the dynasty and the state," but the ideas of a Czechoslovak union had "spread among the Slovaks too," and the war conditions were highly suitable for the government to take "the necessary preventive measures." . . .

In Croatia, in the first few months of the war the government was occupied with the reprisals and preventive measures taken against the Serbs. Quite soon, however, difficulties arose in connection with the Croats as well. Among the Croats, the Great Croat tendency was gaining more and more ground. The ban of Croatia, Baron Ivan Sherlecz, who adjusted himself to the policy of the Hungarian government, was constantly signalling this fact from late 1914 on. The Hungarian prime minister also gave account of the size of the movement. "Quite a lot of Croatians," he wrote, . . . "have trialist Great Croat delusions." [Trialists advocated adding a third Slavic component to the Dual Monarchy.]

The idea of a South Slav union led by the Croats within the Monarchy, which would at the same time entail the transformation of the Dual Monarchy into a trialist one, was not a new idea. It was after the outbreak of the war, however, that it became widespread in Croatia. At first the strengthening of this trend did not affect the military efficiency of Croatia, on the contrary, precisely because of this "austrophil" and at the same time Croat nationalist tendency, the morale of the Croatian regiments was among the best. The commander of the Zagreb Army Corps for this reason even supported the movement. This led to serious disagreements between the Ban of Croatia [the viceroy], who followed the policy of the Hungarian government, and the Zagreb military commander. In February 1915 this infuriated Tisza so much that he wrote . . . : "I shall be obliged to ask for the removal of the Zagreb military commander and for his successor to be categorically forbidden any contact with the opposition."

There were other factors, too, which favoured the strengthening of the Great Croat movement after the outbreak of the war. Before the war, the provincial government of the ban relied on the Croatian-Serb coalition, forcing Frank's Croatian Party of Rights into opposition. Owing to the highly restricted franchise and the electoral system, the Croatian-Serb coalition got the majority in the provincial diet. However, this governmental basis had become highly unstable already during the Balkan wars, since the Serb wing of the coalition could not be relied on. Károly Khuen-Héderváry, whom Tisza regarded as a specialist in Croatian affairs, wrote to the prime minister on August 7, 1913 regarding Croatia, the Balkan events had "dispelled many an illusion. The traditional disagreement between Croats and Serbs is being revived." After the beginning of the war against Serbia, and especially after the atrocities committed against the Serb population, the government could no more rely on the Croatian Serb politicians who had, until then, supported the provincial regime. But the Croats, who supported the ban, were only in majority in coalition with the Serbs. Because of this the former basis of the regime was upset. Frank's opposition party with its trialist aspirations came increasingly to the foreground and became ever stronger. On the other hand, the Hungarian government, i.e. the ban, no longer had a reliable political basis in Croatia. In these

circumstances the ban tried to gain some support by making minor concessions. Thus in the summer of 1915, he supported the Croatian idea that on the
occasion of the large-scale manifestation of homage planned for September 2, a
separate Croatian delegation should be sent to Vienna. Tisza, however, for fear
that this might favour the Great Croat tendency, insisted on sending a joint
delegation. He succeeded in having his way, and rebuked the ban, who was one
of his men of confidence, in a fulminatory letter: "It will come to no good if
you try at every moment to assert here the worries of a few Croatians about
your attitudes instead of settling them of your own authority, by persuasion
and reassurance if possible, or, if not, with determination. You yourself must
have the leading and directing role, and not let yourself be pushed." In his later
letters, too, he often reproached the ban for similar cases of indulgence and
urged him to adopt a harsher attitude.

The increasing severity of the Hungarian government's Croatian policy was
also due to a certain extent to fear of the influence of the Croatian emigrés.
The Croatian movement which demanded separation from Austria-Hungary
found its first supporters among the Croats living in the United States. Already
on July 4, 1914, the Pittsburgh Croatian paper *Hrvatski Glasnik* had outlined, in
connection with the assassination of Archduke Francis Ferdinand, a program
based on the idea of the death of the Monarchy and the creation of an independent Croatian kingdom. Later, the center of the movement shifted to Italy,
where the leading role was played by the members of the Croatian diet who
had left the country, Fran Supilo and Hinko Hinković, and the former mayor
of Spalato (Split), Ante Trumbić. The Hungarian authorities made extensive
investigations of Supilo in order to isolate him from those inside the country.
Reprisal against the Croatian emigrés was one of the main reasons for the
enactment of the law "On the Financial Responsibility of Traitors to the
Country" (Article XVIII of the Act of 1915).

∞

12. The Fate of Turkey's Armenians

On Saturday afternoon, June 26th, we were all startled by the announcement that
the Turkish Government had ordered the deportation of every Armenian, man,
woman and child (there were not many men left), in Mamouret-ul-Aziz, Harput
and the adjacent villages. This announcement was made by the town crier,
Mahmoud Chavoosh, who went around the streets, accompanied by a small boy
beating a drum, and called out the terrible proclamation in a stentorian voice. The
orders were that all those living in one part of Mamouret-ul-Aziz were to leave on
Thursday, July 1st, the rest of the Armenians in Mamouret-Ul-Aziz were to leave

VI.12   From February 9, 1918 report by American consul Leslie Davis (Harput, Turkey), 13–16, 19,
34–35.

on Saturday, July 3rd, those in Harput were to go on Monday, July 5th, and those in the neighboring villages of Huseinik, Kessrik, and Yegheki a few days later.

The alleged destination of the Armenians was Ourfa, which was about a week's journey from Harput by wagon. I never believed, however, that this meant the city of Ourfa or that they would be allowed to remain in that city, even if they reached there, as I wrote in my report of June 30, 1915, to the Embassy . . . I suggested in that report that if any survived the journey they might be sent to some part of the Mesopotamian plain beyond Ourfa and this is what actually happened. Knowing by experience the difficulties and hardships of the journey, which was by no means easy for a small party traveling by wagon with every convenience and able to carry plenty of food, I predicted that few of these people would ever reach Ourfa, which was all too true a prediction. Much of the way was over the desert where little food or water could be obtained. It was summer and there is no protection from the sun on the hot Mesopotamian plain. For these women and children to make the journey on foot, as most of them would have to do, would require a month, and, as they could not carry food enough with them for more than a few days and would often have to go for several days without finding water, it was certain that most of them would perish on the way. . . .

The scenes of that week were heartrending. The people were preparing to leave their homes and to abandon their houses, their lands, their property of all kinds. They were trying to dispose of their furniture and household effects, their provisions and even much of their clothing, as they would be able to carry but little with them. They were selling their possessions for whatever they could get. The streets were full of Turkish women, as well as men, who were seeking bargains on this occasion, buying organs, sewing machines, furniture, rugs, and other articles of value for almost nothing. I know one woman who sold a two thousand dollar organ to a Turkish neighbor for about five dollars. Sewing machines which had cost twenty-five dollars were sold for fifty cents. Valuable rugs were sold for less than a dollar. Many articles were given away, as their owners were unable to sell them and were obliged to leave them behind. The scene reminded me of vultures swooping down on their prey. It was a veritable Turkish holiday and all the Turks went out in their gala attire to feast and to make merry over the misfortunes of others. . . .

Although the difficulties of the journey were known to some extent, no one fully realized at that time what "deportation" really meant. The Government had said that the men in prison would be released and allowed to go with their families. It had also promised to provide donkeys and ox-carts for all who wished them, although, as a matter of fact, there were not enough animals in the Vilayet for five per cent of the people who were deported, and had given every assurance that they would be conducted safely to their destinations. Some were simple enough to believe this and to think that they would be allowed to settle down in some other place where they would begin life over again. They went away smiling and full of hope. Most of the Armenians, however, were in real fear and they had good reasons to be. Rumors had come of what had happened to the men who had been sent away from prison, although nothing definite was then known about their fate.

The most definite report received had been brought by some women who had come from Itchme a week or two before that time saying that all the men of that village had been taken up in the mountains by gendarmes and killed. The women saw the gendarmes washing the blood off their hands and weapons after their return to the village and, upon asking what had become of the men, were told by the gendarmes that they had been killed. The report of these women proved to be absolutely true. . . .

There were parties of exiles arriving from time to time throughout the summer of 1915, some of them numbering several thousand. The first one, who arrived in July, camped in a large open field on the outskirts of the town, where they were exposed to the burning sun. All of them were in rags and many of them were almost naked. They were emaciated, sick, diseased, filthy, covered with dirt and vermin, resembling animals far more than human beings. They had been driven along for many weeks like herds of cattle, with little to eat, and most of them had nothing except the rags on their backs. When the scant rations which the Government furnished were brought for distribution the guards were obliged to beat them back with clubs, so ravenous were they. There were few men among them, most of the men having been killed by the Kurds before their arrival at Harput. May of the women and children also had been killed and very many others had died on the way from sickness and exhaustion. Of those who had started, only a small portion were still alive and they were rapidly dying. . . .

The parties that came remained for a few days and were then pushed on without any apparent destination. Each time they left there were many who stayed behind because they were too sick or too feeble to continue with the others. The most horrible scene I have ever witnessed, one not surpassed by any in Dante's "Inferno", was the group of those who remained at the first large camp after the majority of the exiles had gone. The first time I saw this group was in the dusk of the evening. There were several hundred of the dead and dying scattered about the camp, the most of whom were under a clump of trees at one end of it. One or two gendarmes were on guard, but they made no objection to my walking among them. Right in the road, stretched flat on his back, lay the body of a middle-aged man who had apparently just died or been killed. A number of dead bodies of women and children lay here and there, while all around were the sick and the dying. Old men sat there mumbling incoherently. Women with matted hair and sunken eyes sat staring like maniacs. One, whose face has haunted my memory ever since, was so emaciated and the skin was drawn so tightly over her features that her head appeared to be only a lifeless skull. Others were in the spasms of death. Children with bloated bellies were on the ground wallowing in filth. Some were in convulsions. All in the camp were beyond help. Within a few feet of them was a long trench and each day those who were dead, or thought to be dead, were gathered up by the gendarmes and dumped into it. The exiles themselves were compelled to dig this trench as long as any of them were able to work. Hundred of Armenians were buried in this field in the summer of 1915. Today there is hardly a trace of the camp left, but whenever I have ridden past it I have always

thought of the hellish scenes that took place there during the "deportation" of the
Armenians.

∽

13. War and the "Colour Bar"

The war which we are witnessing marks an epoch, not only in the history of England or of Europe, but in the history of mankind. If there were any spectator who,
through the unnumbered ages, had followed the course of the creature called Man
upon this planet, he would have seen naked cave-men, thousands of years ago,
drive each other in pursuit and flight over the hill-sides with stones and clubs; he
would have seen, later on, the mail-clad armies of Assyria and Rome move over
wide regions, sacking and slaying; and in recent time he would have seen the still
larger armies of Europeans fight with weapons that mowed men down at long
range. But he would never have seen a war which engaged so large a part of the
men upon earth, which affected, directly or indirectly, the whole world, as this war
does. And the reason is that this war has come at the end of an epoch wherein a
certain process, which our supposed spectator would be able to follow, has gone
forward at a rate such as he would not have observed at any earlier time. That
process is the formation in the human family of ever-larger groups with common
purposes, common interests and tasks. What made the process possible was a
development by spasmodic steps forward, over the course of the centuries, in the
means of communication. Intercourse of man with man among the cave-men had
to depend upon speech and gesture; the great States of antiquity had writing, and
the speed of horses for traffic, and wind-wafted ships; but in the last few generations the process has made a leap forward, with steam, electricity, petrol. The
whole world has been bound together as never before. It has got, as it were, a single
nervous system. The agitation in one part is communicated almost directly to
other parts far away. . . . A war of the great nations, supervening upon such a state
of the world, inevitably means a more widespread convulsion than any former war.
Larger masses of men come into action, and can be handled organically: a battle
has a front extending two hundred miles, and may require weeks to be fought out.
Men of all races, in all continents, feel in their private lives the disturbance in the
vast system of international business.

Now, before the war had come, this process of the drawing of the world
together, this diminishing of distances, equivalent, in some of its effects, to a
shrinkage of the surface of the globe, had brought up great problems for the new
generation: and that because the human species thus drawn into closer contiguity
was not all of one kind. The contact, as men then were, between alien races, was
not altogether happy and comfortable. Masses of men were brought together
before either side was ready for the encounter. What is called "the Colour

VI.13 From Edwyn Bevan, *Brothers All: The War and the Race Question, Papers for Wartime* © 4
(Oxford: Oxford University Press, 1914), 3–16. Reprinted with permission of Oxford University Press.

Question" had become acute in certain regions. Already, before the discovery of steam-power, advance in the art of navigation had made it possible for the white men of Europe to go to the lands inhabited by brown and black men in sufficient numbers to win a predominant position in far-off countries, and one may believe that even then the dark man was conscious that the intruder belonged to a widely different breed from himself. But the introduction of steam accentuated the difference; for as the journey became shorter, and the communication of the white man with his home became easier, he retained his European character and European interests with less adaptation to the new environment than his predecessors had done. It is said that the Englishmen in India before the Mutiny had a human relation with the people of the land such as the official of to-day, less high-handed indeed but more distant, is seldom able to establish. The new conditions at the same time made it easier for the peoples of Asia to go to countries occupied by Europeans, so that the contact of races took place, not only where the white man was the stranger, but where the brown or yellow man was the latest comer. Contact in either sphere brought its special variety of friction. We had not only unrest in India and anti-foreign feeling in China, but the thorny Indian question in South Africa and Canada, and the agitation against the yellow man in the United States.

The Co-operation of the East

And now we have suddenly ceased to talk of these questions. Instead, we find brown men and yellow men and black men joined with ourselves in one colossal struggle, pouring out their treasure, pouring out their blood, for the common cause—Japanese and English and Russians carrying on war as allies on the shores of the Pacific, Hindus and Mohammedans from India coming to fight in European armies on the old historic battlefields of Europe, side by side with Mohammedans from Algiers and black men from Senegal. We had often spoken of the wonderful drawing together of the world in our days, but we never knew that it was to be represented in such strange and splendid and terrible bodily guise.

To our enemies the disregard of the "colour bar" in the combination against them is a matter for reproach. We know already that they charge us with disloyalty to the cause of European culture, and we must be prepared to hear the charge flung against us with still greater passion when the war is over, and echoed in German books for generations to come. It has not yet appeared that they consider the employment of Indian and African troops a disloyalty: in the book, so often referred to, by General Bernhardi, the employment of "coloured" troops by France and England is spoken of as something to be expected, with no note of blame; it is our alliance with Japan that arouses their indignation. The difference is, no doubt, that Indian and African troops seem to be used merely as instruments for the purposes of the European Powers, whereas the European has entered into alliance with Japan as with an independent Power of equal standing; that is the abominable thing!

The distinction here indicated may show an imperfect apprehension of the facts on the German side. The idea involved in the distinction, however, may help us to see the real significance of what is before our eyes. As a matter of fact, there is nothing very new or strange in the employment by a civilized Power of alien troops, as a weapon. It does not involve the admission of the aliens to any footing of equality. There is no question of co-operation in the real sense. They are used, just as horses are, as the instruments of a purpose not their own. The French had already used black troops against the Germans in the war of forty-four years ago. If we were merely using Indian troops in the same way, without any will of their own, there would be nothing so very remarkable in it. The mere fact, taken by itself, that Indians are fighting side by side with British soldiers is not the point. In India they fought side by side with the British for one hundred and fifty years. What gives the moment its significance is that the presence of these Indian troops does not represent solely the purpose of England. It represents in some degree the will of India. However the complex of feelings which we describe as "loyalty" in India is to be analysed—and a true analysis would probably differ largely in the cases, say, of a Rajput prince, a Parsi merchant, and a Bengali journalist—behind the Indian troops there is the general voluntary adherence of the leading classes in India, the fighting chiefs and the educated community, to the cause for which England stands. We may speak truly of co-operation in the case of India, as in the case of Japan.

It is the promptitude, the eagerness and the unanimity of this voluntary adherence which has seemed to England almost too good to be true. Some one present when Mr. Charles Roberts read to the House of Commons the message from India has reported that he had never before known the House so moved. After all, whatever the shortcomings of the British rule in India, there has been a great mass of good intention concerned in it; and we had been told so often that it was absurd to expect any recognition of good intentions from the mass of the Indian people. When, at the test, the recognition comes in such generous volume, we are almost taken aback, perhaps a little ashamed of what may seem a want of generosity in our own previous attitude; we are conscious of a new glow of friendliness not unmixed with compunction. The atmosphere is changed in temperature, and some of the barriers which seemed so dead-hard in the old days show a tendency to melt. Indian students moving about in London feel that the eyes which rest upon them are kindly and welcoming, and no longer hostile or suspicious. Almost in a moment the atmosphere has been changed, and that alone is a great thing. One cannot say what may come of it; but things that seemed impossible before seem so no longer in the new day.

It was such a change in our temper as this that Christianity might have brought about, if it had been effectual. It is somewhat humiliating to think that it has been brought about, not by Christianity, but by participation in a war. The reason, one supposes, is that the British public generally has risen to the level represented by, "Love those who love you," but not yet to the Christian level of loving in advance. It could not show any warmth of goodwill to the oriental stranger while he was still a dark mystery and his goodwill problematic; the war has given occasion for him to prove his goodwill, and we hold him out the hand.

However true it may be that war is the outcome of sin, and productive of sin, we must recognize here too how good things are in strange wise brought out of evil by the divine art running through history. It looks as if the human family would really have made a step towards the ideal of brotherhood by waging war together, as if the cynic had some truth on his side, who said: "There is no bond like a common enmity." Each people will soon feel of all other peoples but one that they are brothers in arms; we cannot imagine ourselves without a kindliness for many years to come towards French and Russians and Belgians. No doubt the fact that one has to make an exception in a brotherhood so conditioned—"to all other peoples but one"— shows it imperfect from the Christian point of view, shows something fatally defective in its basis. Yet here meanwhile is the new glow of friendliness, and we cannot do otherwise than recognize it as a good. It seems obvious wisdom to take it for all it is worth, and to work from it to something more. The "colour bar," against which Christianity had beaten itself, largely in vain, has been weakened by another force. The other force has to that extent made the task of Christianity in the future easier. There is no reason why Christians should not be thankful for that.

Should the "Colour Bar" be Maintained?

But one must remember that the German people as represented, not only by its military caste, but by its thinkers and spiritual leaders—the persons, for instance, who signed the *Appeal to Evangelical Christians Abroad*—points to this very disregard of the "colour bar" as an evil. It is probable that there are many amongst ourselves who sympathize with that view. Just at the present moment, while applause of India fills the press and the Japanese are being so obviously useful to us on the Pacific, such persons may not give utterance to their feelings, or their utterance may be drowned. But that many Englishmen shared all the colour prejudice of the Germans last July is certain, and it would be miraculous if in these few weeks all that inveterate prejudice had ceased to exist. When the applause dies down, the voices of these men will be heard again. We cannot afford to overlook their objection.

So far as the mere fact of a difference in complexion, taken by itself, is urged as a barrier which we should not try to transcend, the prejudice appears in a form so crude that it would perhaps be vain to argue with it. The antipathy of men of different complexions to each other, we are sometimes told, is something deep-lying and essential in human nature. . . .

Where the objection to our close association with Indians and Japanese takes a more reasonable form it might perhaps be stated as follows: "It is not the difference in complexion in itself" (so the objector might say) "that matters; it is the fact that in the present state of the world a brown complexion and a yellow complexion go with a religion and culture and social tradition different from the tradition of Christendom. The white races represent a higher culture—or at any rate a culture that ought to be kept uncontaminated by alien elements. For this reason it is important that the material power of the white races, taken as a whole, should not be diminished as against the power of the non-European peoples. If the white races fight amongst themselves, their power as a whole is not necessarily decreased; it may be merely shifted from one European nation to another. If, on the other hand, Asiatic peoples are allowed to take part in the struggle, Europe parts with some of its power to non-Europeans. "The power of Europeans in the world," the objector might continue, "is not entirely due to superior material force. It is largely a matter of prestige, of suggestion; the imagination of the other races must be held captive. In all conflicts, *morale* is a prime factor. It would be fatal for the predominance of Europeans if non-Europeans in large numbers lost the sense of the white man's superiority. If they face a European enemy and take part in his defeat, awe of the white man, as such, is gone."

The Great Opportunity

One surely cannot deny that this reasoning has something in it. It is true that we Christians believe the culture of Europe—permeated, however imperfectly so far, with Christianity—to have in it something of special value for the world. It is true that the position of Europeans as rulers, outside Europe, has in the past been secured largely by their impressing the imagination of the peoples they governed. It is further true that if this prestige, this control by suggestion, were taken away, and no better relation substituted for it, the result might be worse than the present state of things—a lapse of the East into chaos.

"*And no better relation substituted for it*"—that is the great issue of the present crisis. We have been forced by events into a position where safety is to be found only by going forward. We are being called to new things; the fatal thing is to stand still. While we are rightly glad and proud at the cordial advance of India, while the air is full of congratulation and applause, quiet reflection may recognize that the entry of India upon the scene has its dangers. It is big with possibilities of evil. For one thing, it means inevitably a disturbance of the situation in India. Yes, but it is big too with possibilities of good, because that disturbance of the situation may open the way to something much better. It would be a mistake to suppose that in the loyalty of India at the present moment we had attained everything; we have really attained little, except an immense opportunity. It depends how we use it. We shall be less able after the war than before to take our stand in India on some supposed superiority of the white man, as such. We have given way on that ground. And to any one who would tell us that our sacrifice of the white man's prestige is rash and foolish, we can answer that in any case, even apart from the war, circumstances were forcing us from that ground. As European education spread in India, as India awoke more and more to the modern world, that ground would have become increasingly untenable. Sooner or later, if India remained a member of the British Empire, it would be because India chose the association voluntarily, intelligently, with head held high. By admitting India to cooperation in a European war, we have accelerated the disappearance of the old imaginative awe. But the war has given us an opportunity we could never have forecast of substituting for the old relation a new relation built on the consciousness of great dangers faced and great things done together, feelings of mutual friendship and respect and trust. In the kindled atmosphere of the present moment, when hearts are warm and quickly stirred, things may take a new shape which time will so solidify that the attachment of the British and Indian peoples to each other in the future will be stronger than any bond which conquests of the old style could fashion. It all depends, as has been said, how we use the opportunity.

The cry that a Christian Power which in any circumstances enters into cooperation and alliance with a non-Christian Power against Christians commits an act of treachery seems to spring from a deeper loyalty to Christianity. But, to be honest, is the motive behind the declamatory protest after all not just the old bad feeling of race prejudice, the pride of the white colour, which is the very antithesis of real Christianity? What is really the source of the cry is the refusal to acknowledge that the whole human race is all potentially one in Christ. It departs from the fundamental principles of Christianity—the principle of truth and the principle of charity. It departs from the principle of truth, because it goes by names and appearances and labels, instead of by realities. The nations of Europe have become Christian only to a very imperfect degree. When the action of a so-called Christian State is determined by the very anti-Christian principles of national egoism and "will to power" it is untrue to regard it as a Christian State, even if one can point to a nucleus of real Christianity among its people. Supposing we wished to present a false appearance to the non-Christian world, to cover up the truth for fear of scandal, it would be in vain. The sooner the non-Christian world realizes that Christendom is not yet Christian, the better for the prospects of Christianity. And whilst one has to admit a great mass of paganism, still unleavened, in Christendom, one ought to recognize in all that is morally sound in the non-Christian civilizations something germane to Christianity, something due to the same Spirit who is fully manifested in Christ.

Even apart from the direct action of Christianity upon these races in recent times, that would be true. But we know, as a matter of fact, that just as in England and France and Germany there has been a nucleus of real Christianity for many centuries, influencing in various degrees the national life as a whole, so there is now in India and China and Japan a nucleus of real Christianity, whose influence is already making itself felt far outside the limits of the organized Church. In the case of the individual, it is a part of Christian charity to recognize, even when the Christian name is not assumed, the fruit of the Christian spirit: in the same way, to label the Asiatic peoples of today in that absolute way as non-Christians, to shut them out from cooperation in the work of establishing righteousness in the world, where they are prepared to act on righteous principles, is not only a disloyalty to truth but a breach of Christian charity. And that is not the way to win Asia for the Universal Church.

Of one thing we may be sure: neither Europe nor Asia will be left by the war the same as before. It is too soon to affirm that they will be made better by it. A harvest of good will not come automatically out of this convulsion. Its outcome, for good or evil, will be determined largely by the action of England, by the action of the Christian Church, at this crucial time. It may be that neither England, nor the Christian Church, will ever be given such an opportunity again.

☙

14. German Subversion in London

Mr. Joynson-Hicks: Now let me give the facts: In August or September, 1915, a young Czech friend of my own, a young man about whom I made the most careful and adequate inquiries, about whom I have consulted one of the most eminent Czech members of the Austrian Parliament, who is now over here, and upon whose head a penalty has been put by the Austrian Government—it is well known that Czechs are fighting for Russia when they can, and that they are only too anxious to fight for us against the tyranny of Austria—and I find that reports with regard to this restaurant made by this young man were taken down to the police day after day in September of last year, more than seven months before the right hon. Gentleman spoke in the May of this year.

It is rather interesting that we should see what goes on in London in the heart of the Empire seven months before the police swoop down on this place, and I will read some of the reports. On the 9th of September, the day after a Zeppelin raid, my young friend reported: "V. had for dinner on the menu Zeppelin Soup"—that was actually on the menu:—

> They told me they knew beforehand about last night's raid and were waiting for it at V., as this place was out of the danger zone. There was general rejoicing in the restaurant. One said "it was the happiest day of his life." Another one had a complete list of all the places where damage was done. He knew every house and mentioned the factories, warehouses and offices by their names. I seldom saw such a crowd of happy people. They were mocking the English, who, as they said, fled in panic at the Zeppelin raids.

Sir George Makgill, secretary of the British Empire Union, took that report down to Scotland Yard on the following day. On the 11th of September this young man went again. He called again in the evening at 8.45. He says:

They are expecting the Zeppelins this night as they have information of their arrival. About 11 p.m. there are still about fifteen customers there. Voigt is called to the telephone. He comes back from the telephone cabin, exclaiming, "They are here. In an hour they will be in London." The others shout, "Long live Germany!" and are mad with joy.

VI.14   From *Hansard's Parliamentary Debates*, June 29, 1916, cols. 1055–1069, 1079–1080. © Crown Copyright material reproduced with the permission of The Controller HMSO.

They came here that night. They were on the East Coast. I am not dealing with unknown raids or raids that were kept secret. This was made public. They were on the East Coast about that time. Fortunately they did not come to London. On the 12th of September he was there again. He met some Hungarians. They were more anti-English than the Germans. One of them, an old man, perhaps fifty-five years of age, said to someone who disapproved of their German sentiments, "Just wait! When the Germans come to London I will denounce you, and you will be one of the first to be shot as a traitor." That was reported to the police.

I will not weary the Committee with all these reports, but I will give a concluding episode. I have seen the young man and talked to him again and again. On the 21st of September he was there again, and the young son in our Army was back on furlough, and he was speaking in this restaurant, and he said—fortunately we know now these things to be right—that there was great unrest amongst the English troops, and that there were complaints by the soldiers, and that they are all sick of this War. Then he makes remarks about the Canadians, which I will not read. One of the Germans said, "It is a shame that you have to be side by side with niggers and Indians. It is a disgrace to Britain." My young friend could not stand this any longer, as he was a loyal friend of the Allies, and he said something about German atrocities. They asked him what he meant, and he replied, "Read Lord Bryce's Report." This German said, "Lord Bryce's report! Lord Bryce is a blank, blank liar! Wait until the Germans come to London, and then you will see that we do not commit atrocities." The proprietor called out, "People like you will be hanged for this. We will take good care. You dare to insult the German Army! You are a Czech; get out of this!" After some more language my young friend got outside. I should like to know whether the son is still in our Army. It may perhaps be said that those are very excited statements of my young friend. I do not think they are. At all events those statements were sent to Scotland Yard, and seven months afterwards their general accuracy was admitted in the Home Secretary's statement that he had discovered a public-house kept by a naturalized German which might become a most dangerous centre, and that he had interned practically the whole lot of them. Suppose that the case of that naturalised German had been considered by one of these remissions committees. Suppose that his position had been considered, or that Scotland Yard had been keeping an eye on these naturalised Germans who keep German restaurants, which are naturally German centres.

There are—my right hon. Friend has had a list of them—a dozen German restaurants in London to-day which are just as much German as if they were in Berlin itself where alien enemies congregate, naturalised or unnaturalised, where, if you are not a Scotland Yard detective looking British all over, wearing British boots, and if you are a man who can pass himself off as a German, you can go and hear most instructive statements. Here is a bill of fare for one of those German restaurants in London for the day before yesterday. It is written in German. I am not a good German scholar, and I do not understand everything here, but there are such things as gries suppe, wiener rostbraten, rindfleisch, wirsing kohl, kartoffeln, gurken salat, and pfankuchen. If you go into that German restaurant you will see notices on the wall in German, you will see that the waiters are German, and if you ask for an English bill of fare you will not get it. It does not exist. It is a German restaurant and might be in Berlin. There are a dozen of them in London to-day in the very heart of the Empire while we are fighting for our lives. In order that this might be confirmed I asked a great personal friend of my own to go to this restaurant yesterday. Two ladies went to lunch, and into this German restaurant for lunch yesterday an English soldier in uniform was brought in by German friends. There is no question about that. I will tell the right hon. Gentleman who the ladies were. It was in Kleinschmarger's Restaurant. We do not want our soldiers to be taken into lunch by people speaking German. I do not say that it was a trap or that they were spies; I only say that we do not want the existence of Germans in the shops where our soldiers are brought in. We ought to be protected from it. There is only one remedy—sweep the whole lot of them away and then it will not exist. Night after night in these restaurants you will find German women of bad character congregating. One knows for what purpose—to worm things out of English soldiers. All the gossip of the German camps goes there. Men who come out go where they will get German food and meet fellow Germans, and all the gossip and news of the camp flies from mouth to mouth in these same restaurants. Another instance was brought to my notice only last week. In Manchester a man was arrested, whose name was William Sauter; he was not a naturalised German at all; he was a German pure and simple, for he had served fourteen and a half years in the German army as lieutenant, and when the police raided his lodgings they found a German ordnance map of France and letters from Germans hostile to this country. The magistrate very rightly sentenced him to six months' imprisonment, and directed that he was to be interned as soon as he came out. If the police had received orders to intern all Germans, that man would not have been at large. . . .

I have only given a few examples, and it must not be supposed for a moment that I know all the cases; but if we have these samples you may be perfectly certain that there are other cases. But the most important point is that these men are really the outposts of German trade after the War is over. I should like to see all the alien enemies of military age and alien women repatriated. We have now some 40,000 or 50,000 interned, and at the end of the War these men will come out. In the meantime their businesses have been carried on by their wives or by managers, as far as they possibly can, as going concerns; they will be more bitter than ever against this country when they do come out, and they will go on with their businesses as the outposts of German trade. I want to call attention to a very wise observation made by the French Minister of Commerce when he said that:

> Germany is preparing for a trade war against us. She is getting ready to swamp the world's markets with damned goods the moment the War is ended. The Allies must beware against employing Germans in any capacity in commerce and industry.

I believe I am right in saying that while Russia has sequestrated a very large number of German establishments, France at once sequestrated every German business entirely. They know how to deal with this subject, and we might take a lesson from our Allies in this respect. At the end of the War these interned Germans will come out, and what reason is there for this feeling of kindness and tenderness to the German enemies in our midst. There is a very strong idea throughout the country—I do not want to make accusations, of course, against any member of the Government—that the Government do not really appreciate the determination of the people to stop this German menace in our midst, and, after the War is over, to see that England shall be for the English. We do not want these Germans; we do not want to be friends with men and women who are the relations of those who have so cruelly treated our men at Ruhleben and other camps in Germany. We do not want to encourage relations with men and women, cousins and uncles, and so forth, of the men who have treated Belgium and France as we know the Germans have treated those countries. We want to get rid of them. We want to see that the existing power with regard to internment is carried out much more stringently, and above all, that the power of repatriation shall be exercised in the case of every German man and German woman, where it can possibly be done without cruelty. We want to see them sent back to their own country, where they will receive a warmer welcome than they get here. . . .

Mr. H. Samuel: The next instance I will give is from a newspaper with a vast circulation—one of the largest in the country. It printed a letter not long ago from a correspondent stating that "Germans are being encouraged to leave the Isle of Man to work in hotels," and this imaginative person, like a true artist, in order that his work should be as complete as possible, gave all the details of the employment these men would get, and the terms of payment. They were to receive 15s. a week, and everything found, the only restriction being that they were to be indoors by 7 p.m. I have looked through the records, and find that in the last six months during which I have been at the Home Office, not a single waiter has been released from the internment camps, and no one has contemplated for a moment the release of any men for that purpose. At a meeting of the hop trade recently, a member of that business declared that the taxi-cab driver who had driven him to the gathering was, he had discovered, an alien enemy, an Austrian, and his statement was received with every sign of disapproval by his audience. That seemed to me very odd, because, as a matter of fact, all licences were withdrawn from alien enemy taxi-cab drivers at the beginning of the War. But the police, having received a letter the same day to the same effect, they made inquiries, and they found that the taxi-cab driver in question was a natural-born British subject of British parents, but that he had an impediment in his speech and a broad Yorkshire accent. The following statements were made in Scotland by a councillor and a justice of the peace:

Our War Office seems to be under German influence.

An Hon. Member: He was made a J.P.

Mr. Samuel: Not on account of this.

> There are in Edinburgh German pork butchers, barbers, hotel-keepers, caterers, etc., dominating Edinburgh, and I am in possession of information which if known would stagger the country. I know for a fact that on the Saturday night previous to the raid on Edinburgh a considerable number of Germans left this city and went to country towns and returned again on the Monday after the raid was over. I have absolute proof that telegraph wires were cut and telephone wires were cut also.

This gentleman, having been challenged by the military authority under the Defence of the Realm Act to produce his evidence, signed the following statement:

> I regret that I have made these statements as they are not statements of facts.

⚮

War of Ideas

In the various combatant nations, intellectuals came forward to explain that their particular nation's cause was just. The governments involved were only too happy to have the weight of learning and prestige thrown behind their efforts to stimulate war enthusiasm. *The Times* (of London) published the famous letter that follows in September 1914, signed by fifty-two British men of letters. The signatories included such illustrious literary figures as J.M. Barrie (author of *Peter Pan*), Arnold Bennett, G.K. Chesterton, Sir Arthur Conan Doyle, John Galsworthy, Thomas Hardy, Rudyard Kipling, and H.G. Wells. The nearly universal condemnation of Germany's violation of Belgian neutrality and the widespread allegations of the German army's brutal behavior there prompted German academics to respond to restore their nation's honor. Among the ninety-three professors and scientists who signed this strenuously argued appeal were the Nobel Prize-winning chemist, Fritz Haber, the physicist Walter Nernst, and the economist Gustav von Schmoller. The next round in this war of words came in December 1914 with the British Government's appointment of a committee, chaired by Lord Bryce, to investigate and verify instances of German atrocities in Belgium. The fact that Bryce was widely known and highly respected in America (he had served as ambassador to that country) and any report of his would play well to the American public, did not go unnoticed. The Bryce Committee reviewed some 1,200 depositions, mainly by Belgian civilians, supplemented by captured German soldiers' diaries, but did not interrogate witnesses under oath. As a result, its eventual published report was not above criticism, but its discussion of the broader outlines, reprinted as the third extract, gives a reasonable idea of the dimensions of the issue. The more profound question of how the murder of more than 6,000 Belgian civilians could have occurred was taken up by the Belgian sociologist and eventual diplomat, Fernand van Langehove. Influenced by theories on the psychology of collective behavior (by Maurice Halbwachs, among others), he diagnosed the mass hysteria which gripped German units and predisposed them to see enemies in every church steeple or behind every bush.

Effective government use of information could make a difference in the war effort, but many people came to distrust much of that information in the belief that official pronouncements were often disingenuous. Materials laced with exaggerations or outright lies were labeled with the relatively new term *propaganda*, though, of course, the real challenge was to distinguish truth from falsification and invention. It was generally assumed that the Allies had been more effective in disseminating propaganda, and the following selection is taken from one of the first scholarly studies of the topic. George Bruntz, a high school social sciences teacher in Los Gatos, California, published this account, based upon the research he undertook for his 1936 doctoral dissertation at Stanford University.

15. Britain's Destiny and Duty

The undersigned writers, comprising amongst them men and women of the most divergent political and social views, some of them having been for years ardent champions of good will towards Germany, and many of them extreme advocates of peace, are nevertheless agreed that Great Britain could not without dishonour have refused to take part in the present war.

No one can read the full diplomatic correspondence published in the White Paper without seeing that the British representatives were throughout labouring wholeheartedly to preserve the peace of Europe, and that their conciliatory efforts were cordially received by both France and Russia.

With these efforts failed, Great Britain had still no direct quarrel with any Power. She was eventually compelled to take up arms because, together with France, Germany, and Austria, she had solemnly pledged herself to maintain the neutrality of Belgium. As soon as danger to that neutrality arose she questioned both France and Germany as to their intentions. France immediately renewed her pledge not to violate Belgian neutrality; Germany refused to answer, and soon made all answer needless by her actions. Without even the pretense of a grievance against Belgium, she made war on the weak and unoffending country she had undertaken to protect, and has since carried out her invasion with a calculated and ingenious ferocity which has raised questions other and no less grave than that of the wilful disregard of treaties.

VI.15   From *The Times*, September 18, 1914.

When Belgium in her dire need appealed to Great Britain to carry out her pledge, this country's course was clear. She had either to break faith, letting the sanctity of treaties and the rights of small nations count for nothing before the naked force, or she had to fight. She did not hesitate, and we trust she will not lay down arms till Belgium's integrity is restored and her wrongs redressed.

The treaty with Belgium made our duty clear, but many of us feel that, even if Belgium had not been involved, it would have been impossible for Great Britain to stand aside while France was dragged into war and destroyed. To permit the ruin of France would be a crime against liberty and civilization. Even those of us who question the wisdom of a policy of Continental Ententes or Alliances refuse to see France struck down by a foul blow dealt in violation of a treaty.

We observe that various German apologists, official and semi-official, admit that their country has been false to its pledged word, and dwell almost with pride on the "frightfulness" of the examples by which it has sought to spread terror in Belgium, but they excuse all these proceedings by a strange and novel plea. German culture and civilization are so superior to those of other nations that all steps taken to assert them are more than justified; and the destiny of Germany to be the dominating force in Europe and the world is so manifest that ordinary rules of morality do not hold in her case, but actions are good or bad simply as they help or hinder the accomplishment of that destiny.

These views, inculcated upon the present generation of Germans by many celebrated historians and teachers, seem to us both dangerous and insane. Many of us have dear friends in Germany, many of us regard German culture with the highest respect and gratitude; but we cannot admit that any nation has the right by brute force to impose its culture upon other nations, nor that the iron military bureaucracy of Prussia represents a higher form of human society than the free constitutions of Western Europe.

Whatever the world-destiny of Germany may be, we in Great Britain are ourselves conscious of a destiny and a duty. The destiny and duty, alike for us and for all the English-speaking race, call upon us to uphold the rule of common justice of small nations, and to maintain the free and law abiding ideals of Western Europe against the rule of "Blood and Iron" and the domination of the whole Continent by a military caste.

For these reasons and others the undersigned feel bound to support the cause of the Allies with all their strength, with a full conviction of its righteousness, and with a deep sense of its vital import to the future of the world.

16. Manifesto of German University Professors

To the Civilized World!

As representatives of German Science and Art, we hereby protest to the civilized world, against the lies and calumnies with which our enemies are endeavouring to stain the honour of Germany in her hard struggle for existence—in a struggle which has been forced upon her.

The iron mouth of events has proved the untruth of the fictitious German defeats, consequently misrepresentation and calumny are all the more eagerly at work. As heralds of truth we raise our voices against these.

It is not true that Germany is guilty of having caused this war. Neither the people, the Government, nor the "Kaiser" wanted war. Germany did her utmost to prevent it; for this assertion the world has documentary proof. Often enough during the 26 years of his reign has Wilhelm II shown himself to be the upholder of peace, and often enough has this fact been acknowledged by our opponents. Nay, even the "Kaiser," whom they now dare to call an Attila, has been ridiculed by them for years, because of his steadfast endeavours to maintain universal peace. Not till a numerical superiority which had been lying in wait on the frontiers, assailed us, did the whole nation rise to a man.

It is not true that we trespassed in neutral Belgium. It has been proved that France and England had resolved on such a trespass, and it has likewise been proved that Belgium had agreed to their doing so. It would have been suicide on our part not to have been beforehand.

It is not true that the life and property of a single Belgian citizen was injured by our soldiers without the bitterest self-defense having made it necessary; for again, and again, notwithstanding repeated threats, the citizens lay in ambush, shooting at the troops out of the houses, mutilating the wounded, and murdering in cold blood the medical men while they were doing their Samaritan work. There can be no baser abuse than the suppression of these crimes with the view of letting the Germans appear to be criminals, only for having justly punished these assassins for their wicked deeds.

It is not true that our troops treated Louvain brutally. Furious inhabitants having treacherously fallen upon them in their quarters, our troops with aching hearts, were obliged to fire a part of the town, as a punishment. The greatest part of Louvain has been preserved. The famous Town Hall stands quite intact; for at great self-sacrifice our soldiers saved it from destruction by the flames. Every German would of course greatly regret, if in the course of this terrible war any works of art should already have been destroyed or be destroyed at some future time, but inasmuch as in our love for art we cannot be surpassed by any other nation, in the same degree we must decidedly refuse to buy a German defeat at the cost of saving a work of art.

It is not true that our warfare pays no respect to international laws. It knows no undisciplined cruelty. But in the east, the earth is saturated with the blood of women and children unmercifully butchered by the wild Russian troops, and in the west, dumdum bullets mutilate the breasts of our soldiers. Those who have allied themselves with Russians and Serbians, and present such a shameful scene to the world as that of inciting Mongolians and Negroes against the white race, have no right whatever to call themselves upholders of civilization.

It is not true that the combat against our so-called militarism is not a combat against our civilization, as our enemies hypocritically pretend it is. Were it not for German militarism, German civilization would long since have been extirpated. For its protection it arose in a land which for centuries had been plagued by bands of robbers, as no other land had been. The German army and the German people are one, and to-day, this consciousness fraternizes 70 millions of Germans, all ranks, positions and parties being one.

We cannot wrest the poisonous weapon—the lie—out of the hands of our enemies. All we can do is to proclaim to all the world, that our enemies are giving false witness against us. You, who know us, who with us have protected the most holy possessions of man, we call to you:

Have faith in us! Believe, that we shall carry on this war to the end as a civilized nation, to whom the legacy of a Goethe, a Beethoven, and a Kant, is just as sacred as its own hearths and homes.

For this we pledge you our names and our honour.

⚭

17. Alleged German Outrages

We may now sum up and endeavour to explain the character and significance of the wrongful acts done by the German army in Belgium.

If a line is drawn on a map from the Belgian frontier to Liège and continued to Charleroi, and a second line drawn from Liège to Malines, a sort of figure resembling an irregular Y will be formed. It is along this Y that most of the systematic (as opposed to isolated) outrages were committed. If the period from August 4th to August 30th is taken it will be found to cover most of these organised outrages. Termonde and Alost extend, it is true, beyond the Y lines, and they belong to the month of September. Murder, rape, arson, and pillage began from the moment when the German army crossed the frontier. For the first fortnight of the war the towns and villages near Liège were the chief sufferers. From the 19th of August to the end of the month, outrages spread in the directions of Charleroi and Malines and reach their period of greatest intensity. There is a certain significance in the fact

VI.17   From *Report of the Committee on Alleged German Outrages* (London: HMSO, 1915), 39–44.
© Crown Copyright material reproduced with the permission of The Controller HMSO.

that the outrages round Liege coincide with the unexpected resistance of the Belgian army in that district, and that the slaughter which reigned from the 19th August to the end of the month is contemporaneous with the period when the German army's need for a quick passage through Belgium at all costs was deemed imperative.

Here let a distinction be drawn between two classes of outrages.

Individual acts of brutality—ill-treatment of civilians, rape, plunder, and the like—were very widely committed. These are more numerous and more shocking than would be expected in warfare between civilised Powers, but they differ rather in extent than in kind from what has happened in previous though not recent wars.

In all wars many shocking and outrageous acts must be expected, for in every large army there must be a proportion of men of criminal instincts whose worst passions are unloosed by the immunity which the conditions of warfare afford. Drunkenness, moreover, may turn even a soldier who has no criminal habits into a brute, who may commit outrages at which he would himself be shocked in his sober moments, and there is evidence that intoxication was extremely prevalent among the German army, both in Belgium and in France, for plenty of wine was to be found in the villages and country houses which were pillaged. Many of the worst outrages appear to have been perpetrated by men under the influence of drink. Unfortunately little seems to have been done to repress this source of danger.

In the present war, however—and this is the gravest charge against the German army—the evidence shows that the killing of non-combatants was carried out to an extent for which no previous war between nations claiming to be civilised (for such cases as the atrocities perpetrated by the Turks on the Bulgarian Christians in 1876, and on the Armenian Christians in 1895 and 1896, do not belong to that category) furnishes any precedent. That this killing was done as part of a deliberate plan is clear from the facts hereinbefore set forth regarding Louvain, Aerschot, Dinant, and other towns. The killing was done under orders in each place. It began at a certain fixed date, and stopped (with some few exceptions) at another fixed date. Some of the officers who carried out the work did it reluctantly, and said they were obeying directions from their chiefs. The same remarks apply to the destruction of property. House burning was part of the programme; and villages, even large parts of a city, were given to the flames as part of the terrorising policy.

Citizens of neutral states who visited Belgium in December and January report that the German authorities do not deny that non-combatants were systematically killed in large numbers during the first weeks of the invasion, and this, so far as we know, has never been officially denied. If it were denied, the flight and continued voluntary exile of thousands of Belgian refugees would go far to contradict a denial, for there is no historical parallel in modern times for the flight of a large part of a nation before an invader.

The German Government have, however, sought to justify their severities on the grounds of military necessity, and have excused them as retaliation for cases in which civilians fired on German troops. There may have been cases in which such firing occurred, but no proof has ever been given, or, to our knowledge, attempted to be given, of such cases, nor of the stories of shocking outrages perpetrated by Belgian men and women on German soldiers.

The inherent improbability of the German contention is shown by the fact that after the first few days of the invasion every possible precaution had been taken by the Belgian authorities, by way of placards and hand-bills, to warn the civilian population not to intervene in hostilities. Throughout Belgium steps had been taken to secure the handing over of all firearms in the possession of civilians before the German army arrived.

These steps were sometimes taken by the police and sometimes by the military authorities.

The invaders appear to have proceeded upon the theory that any chance shot coming from an unexpected place was fired by civilians. One favourite form of this allegation was that priests had fired from the church tower. In many instances the soldiers of the allied armies used church towers and private houses as cover for their operations. At Aerschot, where the Belgian soldiers were stationed in the church tower and fired upon the Germans as they advanced, it was at once alleged by the Germans when they entered the town, and with difficulty disproved, that the firing had come from civilians. Thus one elementary error creeps at once into the German argument, for they were likely to confound, and did in some instances certainly confound, legitimate military operations with the hostile intervention of civilians.

Troops belonging to the same army often fire by mistake upon each other. That the German army was no exception to this rule is proved not only by many Belgian witnesses but by the most irrefragable kind of evidence, the admission of German soldiers themselves recorded in their war diaries. Thus Otto Clepp, 2nd Company of the Reserve, says, under date 22nd of August: "3 a.m. Two infantry regiments shot at each other—9 dead and 50 wounded—fault not yet ascertained." In this connection the diaries of Kurt Hoffmann, and a soldier of the 112th Regiment (diary No. 14) will repay study. In such cases the obvious interest of the soldier is to conceal his mistake, and a convenient method of doing so is to raise the cry of "*francs-tireurs*." [*francs-tireurs*: literally, free-shooters, civilian irregular soldiers]

Doubtless the German soldiers often believed that the civilian population, naturally hostile, had in fact attacked them. This attitude of mind may have been fostered by the German authorities themselves before the troops passed the frontier, and thereafter stories of alleged atrocities committed by Belgians upon Germans such as the myth referred to in one of the diaries relating to Liege, were circulated amongst the troops and roused their anger.

The diary of Barthel when still in Germany on the 10th of August shows that he believed that the Oberburgomaster of Liège had murdered a surgeon general. The fact is that no violence was inflicted on the inhabitants at Liege until the 19th, and no one who studies these pages can have any doubt that Liège would immediately have been given over to murder and destruction if any such incident had occurred.

Letters written to their homes which have been found on the bodies of dead Germans, bear witness, in a way that now sounds pathetic, to the kindness with which they were received by the civil population. Their evident surprise at this reception was due to the stories which had been dinned into their ears of soldiers with their eyes gouged out, treacherous murders, and poisoned food, stories which they have been encouraged by the higher military authorities in order to impress the mind of the troops as well as for the sake of justifying the measures which they took to terrify the civil population. If there is any truth in such stories, no attempt has been made to establish it. For instance, the Chancellor of the German Empire, in a communication made to the press on September 2 and printed in the "*Norddeutsche Allgemeine Zeitung,*" of September 21, said as follows: "Belgian girls gouged out the eyes of the German wounded. Officials of Belgian cities have invited our officers to dinner and shot and killed them across the table. Contrary to all international law, the whole civilian population of Belgium was called out, and after having at first shown friendliness, carried on in the rear of our troops terrible warfare with concealed weapons. Belgian women cut the throats of soldiers whom they had quartered in their homes while they were sleeping."

No evidence whatever seems to have been adduced to prove these tales, and though there may be cases in which individual Belgians fired on the Germans, the statement that "the whole civilian population of Belgium was called out" is utterly opposed to the fact.

An invading army may be entitled to shoot at sight a civilian caught red-handed, or anyone who though not caught red-handed is proved guilty on enquiry. But this was not the practice followed by the German troops. They do not seem to have made any enquiry. They seized the civilians of the village indiscriminately and killed them, or such as they selected from among them, without the least regard to guilt or innocence. The mere cry "Civilisten haben geschossen" [the civilians shot at us] was enough to hand over a whole village or district and even outlying places to ruthless slaughter.

We gladly record the instances where the evidence shows that humanity had not wholly disappeared from some members of the German army, and that they realised that the responsible heads of that organisation were employing them, not in war but in butchery; "I am merely executing orders, and I should be shot if I did not execute them," said an officer to a witness at Louvain. At Brussels another officer says: "I have not done one hundredth part of what we have been ordered to do by the High German military authorities."

As we have already observed, it would be unjust to charge upon the German army generally acts of cruelty which, whether due to drunkenness or not, were done by men of brutal instincts and unbridled passions. Such crimes were sometimes punished by the officers. They were in some cases offset by acts of humanity and kindliness. But when an army is directed or permitted to kill non-combatants on a large scale, the ferocity of the worst natures springs into fuller life, and both lust and the thirst of blood become more widespread and more formidable. Had less licence been allowed to the soldiers, and had they not been set to work to slaughter civilians, there would have been fewer of those painful cases in which a depraved and morbid cruelty appears.

Two classes of murders in particular require special mention, because one of them is almost new, and the other altogether unprecedented. The former is the seizure of peaceful citizens as so-called hostages to be kept as a pledge for the conduct of the civil population, or as a means to secure some military advantage, or to compel the payment of a contribution, the hostages being shot if the condition imposed by the arbitrary will of the invader is not fulfilled. Such hostage taking, with the penalty of death attached, has now and then happened, the most notable case being the shooting of the Archbishop of Paris and some of his clergy by the Communards of Paris in 1871, but it is opposed both to the rules of war and to every principle of justice and humanity. The latter kind of murder is the killing of the innocent inhabitants of a village because shots have been fired, or are alleged to have been fired, on the troops by someone in the village. For this practice no previous example and no justification have been or can be pleaded. Soldiers suppressing an insurrection may have sometimes slain civilians mingled with insurgents, and Napoleon's forces in Spain are said to have now and then killed promiscuously when trying to clear guerillas out of a village. But in Belgium large bodies of men, sometimes including the burgomaster and the priest, were seized, marched by officers to a spot chosen for the purpose, and there shot in cold blood, without any attempt at trial or even inquiry, under the pretence of inflicting punishment upon the village, though these unhappy victims were not even charged with having themselves committed any wrongful act, and though, in some cases at least, the village authorities had done all in their power to prevent any molestation of the invading force. Such acts are no part of war, for innocence is entitled to respect even in war. They are mere murders, just as the drowning of the innocent passengers and crews on a merchant ship is murder and not an act of war.

That these acts should have been perpetrated on the peaceful population of an unoffending country which was not at war with its invaders but merely defending its own neutrality, guaranteed by the invading Power, may excite amazement and even incredulity. It was with amazement and almost with incredulity that the Committee first read the depositions relating to such acts. But when the evidence regarding Liège was followed by that regarding Aerschot, Louvain, Andenne, Dinant, and the other towns and villages, the cumulative effect of such a mass of concurrent testimony became irresistible, and we were driven to the conclusion that the things described had really happened.

The question then arose how they could have happened. Not from mere military licence, for the discipline of the German army is proverbially stringent, and its obedience implicit. Not from any special ferocity of the troops, for whoever has travelled among the German peasantry knows that they are as kindly and good-natured as any people in Europe, and those who can recall the war of 1870 will remember that no charges resembling those proved by those depositions were then established. The excesses recently committed in Belgium were, moreover, too widespread and too uniform in their character to be mere sporadic outbursts of passion or rapacity.

The explanation seems to be that these excesses were committed—in some cases ordered, in others allowed—on a system and in pursuance of a set purpose. That purpose was to strike terror into the civil population and dishearten the Belgian troops, so as to crush down resistance and extinguish the very spirit of self-defence. The pretext that civilians had fired upon the invading troops was used to justify not merely the shooting of individual *francs-tireurs*, but the murder of large numbers of innocent civilians, an act absolutely forbidden by the rules of civilised warfare.

✎

18. Explaining German Atrocities

The German army which invaded Belgium supplied, in fact, the whole of the conditions which, in accordance with established laws, bring about the greatest number of distortions in the relation of observed facts.

In every army mobilization brutally tears the soldier away from his accustomed mode of life, and plunges him into a chaos of tumultuous and extraordinary events. Exposed to the surprises of the enemy, submitted to shocks of combats, his mind suffers the most violent excitements; it is in a manner overthrown, and only a weakened perception controls the facts.

These circumstances are general and common to all wars. There are in addition others which are characteristic of the German army of invasion in Belgium. This army did not expect, in penetrating into Belgian territory, to meet there an armed resistance. Moreover, the Belgian staff had deliberately adopted a stratagem consisting of harassing the invader without truce. Some isolated detachments, mobile and elusive, were dispatched far outside the lines; dispersed about the country, their mission was to retard the advance of the enemy by opposing him with guerilla warfare, to disturb his columns, and to menace his communications.

Again, the preconceived ideas which dominated the mind of the German soldier, and which resulted from his environment, oriented in a particular way the distortion which facts received at his hands. The memory of the French *francs-tireurs* of 1870 had remained deep-rooted in Germany; the army was still entirely impregnated with it; it had extracted therefrom a lesson and a doctrine for military operations in an enemy country. Trained during peace time according to these principles, the soldiers were necessarily dominated by the apprehension of *francs-tireurs*. Their imaginations anticipated the attacks.

Moreover, outside military education a whole popular literature had contributed to keep up the memory of the last campaign. Certain novels devoted to the war of the future had even applied it in advance to the future conquest of Belgium. Thus the soldier unconsciously transposed into reality these subjective impressions

VI.18   From Fernand van Langenhove, *The Growth of a Legend: A Study Based Upon the German Accounts of Franc Tireurs and "Atrocities" in Belgium* (New York: G.P. Putnam's Sons, 1916), 299–303.

which haunted his mind, wherein were already united all the constitutive elements of legend.

Other predispositions acted in a similar manner upon the main body of the German army of invasion. The first rumours of treacherous attacks were not long in getting disseminated in Germany. A double official confirmation had given them a vast celebrity and concentrated upon them general attention. The foolish tales circulated everywhere and were the subject of all conversations.

The German residents expelled from Belgium at the declaration of war had, on their part, reported stories of horrors. They had told of monstrous crimes committed by a furious population upon defenceless foreigners. The press had published this delirium of refugees, but had said nothing of the exasperation which gave rise to it. Thus was awakened in Germany a violent hatred against the Belgians, and an ardent desire for revenge. The armies which spread themselves over Belgium had been mobilized in this atmosphere of feverish excitement. At the moment of crossing the frontier, they were deeply intoxicated by it. All their thoughts were contaminated and inclined by a natural bent towards an attitude hostile to the Belgians.

The psychology of the German soldier at the beginning of the invasion thus produced a collection of conditions which inevitably engendered some legendary elaborations. Further, this was not confined to the imagination of each individual, but on the contrary convergent predispositions common to the mass oriented them in a definite sense.

The birth in the German army of the tales of the popular fury in Belgium was then inevitable; it appeared there as, in a sense, a necessary phenomenon, dictated by laws.

But it is not alone the considerations derived from this determinism which demonstrate the legendary character of these tales. Some precise observations afford a direct proof by allowing one to reconstruct with clearness the principal phases of their genesis.

These observations show the tendency of the mind to connect every chance circumstance with the idea of the danger upon which it concentrates attention; they show the confusions and the erroneous interpretations which result; they show this fixed tendency acting on the nervous system, and provoking in the soldier an immediate reflex identical in all cases; they show the influence which the all-powerful suggestion of the *franc-tireur* exercises, and the common orientation which this impresses upon the imagined explanations of incidents with unknown causes; they show, finally, the progressive constitution of a legendary amplification, by the addition of successive elements.

19. Propaganda

A study of the leaflets, books, and pamphlets issued by the Allies against the enemy reveals that the propaganda material went through five fairly well-defined stages. Each of these stages had a definite aim, and all led up to the final aim: the destruction of the German Empire. Although it is impossible to state exactly when one stage left off and the other began, the five types of propaganda material are quite clearly distinguishable in the following order: (1) propaganda of enlightenment; (2) propaganda of despair; (3) propaganda of hope; (4) particularistic propaganda; and (5) revolutionary propaganda. . . .

Propaganda of Enlightenment

In time of war no nation gives out information regarding the military or political situation which would be detrimental to the fighting power of the country or disheartening or depressing to its population. France, by the law of August 5, 1914, forbade the publication of any news of a military or diplomatic nature that might have the effect of weakening the morale of the people. Only such military or diplomatic news could be printed as came from the War Department. In England the Defence of the Realm Act regulated the printing and distribution of pamphlets and leaflets. This act made it an offense for any person by word of mouth or by writing or by means of any printed book, pamphlet, or document to spread reports or make statements "calculated to cause disaffection to His Majesty or prejudice His Majesty's relations with foreign powers." . . .

The press of Germany was no less restricted than that of the Allies. The German General Staff set up the "*Kriegspresseamt*," which supplied the press with war news. In all of the warring nations, therefore, there were restrictions on the type of news that could be printed, and war news emanated from official sources only.

This restriction meant that facts of a military nature were withheld from the public. If the Germans failed to tell their people of their military defeats, the English failed to report all of the ships lost in the submarine campaign. If the Germans neglected to inform their people of the actual size of the American forces coming to the aid of France, the French failed to report the full facts of the military situation before the coming of the Americans. In other words, none of the warring nations allowed facts that would weaken the people's will to fight to be published. . . .

The first task of the Allied propagandists was, therefore, to impart to the German people those facts which their military leaders kept from them. A "Trench

VI.19 From George Bruntz, *Allied Propaganda and the Collapse of the German Empire in 1918* (Stanford: Stanford University Press, 1938), 85–89, 102–104, 106–107, 109. Copyright © 1938 by the Board of Trustees of the Leland Stanford Junior University, renewed 1966. All rights reserved. Used with the permission of Stanford University Press. www.sup.org.

Newspaper" was published by the British and distributed to the German troops. This was a single-page "newspaper" which told of the victories of the Allies; it also illustrated the advances of the British from month to month by means of maps. The French issued the *Truppen Nachrichtenblatt,* which, though it was only a small leaflet, contained such pointed statements as these: "Foch Leading New Attack," "Entente Armies Press Forward on Another Wide Front," "Turkish Army in Palestine Destroyed," "No Further Opposition to English Expected," "20,000 Prisoners Taken."

Charts and diagrams showing plainly the number of prisoners taken and the number of dead and wounded on each side were sent to the German trenches. . . .

Propaganda of Despair

The second phase of the propaganda campaign aimed to bring despair to the Germans. The leaflets stressed the horrors of war and announced the intention of the Entente to fight to the bitter end. One leaflet was addressed "To you in the fields of death!" The German troops were told that wherever they marched there was death. "Look about you! All that you can see is the work of death!" The Allies then asked "Why are you here with the dead? Why are you marching over the dead?" And at the end of the leaflet the propagandists told the German soldier, "You will lie where your comrades are lying—in the field of death." . . .

A great deal of propaganda of despair had in it a touch of sentimentalism. It called attention to the suffering of the wives and children of the soldiers. . . .

Cartoons were also used to bring home to the German soldiers the situation at home. The French, for example, published a drawing in *Die Feldpost* in December 1915 which showed the kitchen of a German family. The table was bare, and two emaciated children were staring pitifully at the empty table. The father, nothing but skin and bones, remarks to his spouse, who still has a little life in her, "My insides are rumbling with hunger." Whereupon the wife replies, "Then don't go on the street or you will be arrested for disturbing the peace." . . .

Another method of promulgating the propaganda of despair was to paint a picture of the rewards of the crippled soldiers after the war. Stories were circulated that veterans of the war of 1870 died of hunger in the parks of Berlin while begging from the rich who scorned their pleas for help. One leaflet shows a picture of a poor crippled soldier standing at the entrance of a large restaurant or hotel. Fat men and buxom women, dressed in the richest evening clothes, are coming out of the place with a look of contentment and happiness on their faces. Not one of them notices the war-exhausted, hungry cripple. The inference was that such a reward awaited the soldiers who were wounded while fighting for the Fatherland. . . .

Propaganda of Hope

It was not enough to bring to the attention of the German troops the fact that they were fighting a losing battle, that they were the slaves of the military and Junker classes. They had to be given something better to strive for. The soldiers were told that they were being mistreated, and forced to fight for the wealthy aristocrats of Germany. But where would they be treated better? They were told that they were certain to meet death if they continued to fight for their militarists. But what else could they do? They were reminded that the war was taking away their best, that it was destructive of their economic life and ruinous to the common people. But if they made peace, what assurance had they that the Allied peace conditions would not be equally as destructive to their economic life as the war? Here, then, was the task for the propaganda of hope.

One way by which the German soldier could hope to save his life, and perhaps return to his family unmaimed, was by surrendering to the Allies. Propaganda purporting to come from the German prisoners already in the Allied camps was used most extensively. These leaflets contained letters supposedly from prisoners in France or England which told of the good food, the comfortable quarters, and the fine treatment that they were receiving at the hands of their captors.

One of these letters from "a German prisoner" to his comrades still in the trenches said:

> Comrades!
>
> From the war prisons we are sending you a few words and hope that they will meet with a little success and bring the end of this war a little nearer.
>
> *First.* Do not believe those who tell you that you will be treated cruelly in prison. On the contrary we can assure you that we get more to eat in one day than you get from your murderous leaders in three.
>
> *Second.* Warm clothing and shoes and kind treatment from the English officers such as a German soldier can hardly imagine.
>
> *Third.* For whom are you taking your hide to market? For whom are your wives and children suffering? For the Hohenzollerns and Junkers. . . . Don't you hear them laugh? . . .

Still other letters lament the fact that their German comrades at the front continue to fight for the Hohenzollerns whose "thirst for blood is not yet quenched." They appeal to the men to think of their wives and children at home. "For you do not know why you are fighting," says one appeal, "while the French are fighting to recover their fatherland and for the rights of humanity. Come over! Break the bonds that hold you down, and see for yourselves how a free man is treated in a free land."

VII

Dissent, Mutiny and Revolution

The war decisively altered the relationship between state and society, public and private spheres, and authority and compliance. Given the unprecedented demands of total war, European leaders felt justified in using government regulation and intervention to impose on, to an unprecedented degree, their citizens' rights and liberties. The simultaneous challenges of cultivating national unity and curtailing dissent, of ensuring an adequate flow of men and material to the front and of laborers into the workplace, and of preserving standards of living while minimizing industrial conflict all contributed to the state's pervasive intrusion into society. These wartime exigencies aggravated existing social tensions and brought many of the combatant nations to a crisis by the war's latter stages.

Misguided assumptions that the war would be brief and that it would have a minimal impact on citizens' daily life were responsible in part for the growing gap between popular expectations and the reality of increasing state authority. Initially, governments were hesitant to create special administrative agencies for smoothing the transition from peacetime to wartime, and in some cases individual initiatives were as important to the establishment of such agencies as official state directives. Throughout Europe, governments lacked relevant models of how to mobilize for total war, and had to innovate as they went along, mixing private enterprise and bureaucratic regulation. In Germany, for example, much of the initial pressure for a rationalization of war production came from the industrialist Walter Rathenau. He pressed the German government to establish a War Raw Materials Section, known as the *Kriegsrohstoffabteilung* (KRA), to oversee the distribution of raw materials to crucial war-related industries and to prevent shortages of them. In Italy public opposition to the war and economic disorganization led the government to

Empires, Soldiers, and Citizens: A World War I Sourcebook, Second Edition.
Edited by Marilyn Shevin-Coetzee and Frans Coetzee.

impose military discipline in the factories and to allow the country's industrialists considerable leeway in matters of production. Meanwhile, in Russia, critical munitions shortages, a disorganized transportation network, and competing and overburdened administrative agencies forced the government to adopt a policy of industrial mobilization by the spring of 1915.

The British government, however, aware that war would interrupt the natural flow of the economy, took only a handful of immediate measures, among them the control of the nation's railway network, to ensure the distribution of food and manpower, and thus to avoid economic chaos. Britain made the first step toward a total war economy in August 1914 with the passage of the Defence of the Realm Act (DORA), which initially protected the public safety but subsequently covered food policy and other areas. Until 1915–1916, in short, the British pursued "business as usual." With rising food prices in 1915, the implementation of conscription in 1916, and the concomitant departure of men from the labor force, the government under David Lloyd George was forced to review its voluntarist policies.

Reluctant to erect additional bureaucratic structures, the French government relied largely on prevailing market forces as well as on the cooperation of French businessmen. Once industrial mobilization was officially instituted in September 1914, the French pursued a policy of "organized economy" under which capitalist ideals (profit, private production) were combined with elements of collectivist organization.

Whether economic mobilization was prompted by individual or by state initiative, the ways in which it was implemented directly affected both domestic and military morale. The change most visibly affected the shop floor. All European governments imposed special measures to ensure the uninterrupted flow of industrial goods. In establishing the Industrial Mobilization (MI), the Italian government sought to prevent dissension within Italy's workforce by making strikes illegal, reducing workers' job mobility, and enforcing strict factory discipline, even among women and children. To dissuade workers from going against the grain, the Italian military also maintained a physical presence on the factory floor.

While Italian labor relations were particularly harsh, restrictions also squeezed the German workforce. With the support of most of its Socialist representatives, the German parliament approved the passage of the *Hilfsdienstgesetz*, or Auxiliary Service Law, in early December 1916. The law may be seen as a compromise between the interest of Germany's industrialists, who feared declining profits and potential ammunition shortages, and those of the trade unions. The law satisfied the demands of the industrialists by providing for industrial conscription for all males between the ages of seventeen and sixty and by restricting workers' right to change employment (other than for higher wages). So as to forestall industrial unrest and general war weariness, the law strengthened the hand of Germany's trade unions by legitimizing them as arbitrators of the working classes.

In Britain, in an effort to maximize labor power and to hold down industrial wages, the government negotiated the so-called Treasury Agreement (which lacked legal sanction) with a number of Britain's trade union leaders in March 1915. Under this agreement workers in war industries agreed not to strike and to submit all industrial disputes to arbitration; in return, the government would safeguard wage standards. Not long after the agreement, the government sought to legalize it with the passage of the Munitions of War Bill.

Relations among government, factory owners, and industrial employees generally deteriorated as the war progressed and as skyrocketing food prices and rents cut into real wages. Throughout Europe, workers flouted laws barring them from striking, and by 1917 strike activity peaked. Although British workers did not want for food as their counterparts on the Continent did, their wages could not keep pace with higher food prices and rents, and they deplored the widespread profiteering, especially in the coal-mining and shipbuilding industries. In July 1915, 200,000 coal miners in South Wales went on strike. Instead of jailing them, the government, fearful of provoking further industrial unrest, granted them wage concessions. In other work stoppages the government responded in a less conciliatory fashion, banishing some of the strike leaders to various parts of the country, but by 1917, after an increase in the number of strikes, Parliament had conceded to workers the right to occupational choice. The trade unions, rather than being subdued by government legislation, benefited in the short run. Union membership spurted from 4 million in 1914 to 6 million by the armistice and 8.3 million in 1920.

In Germany the Allied blockade brought a scarcity of foodstuffs, high food prices, longer working hours, poor working conditions, and a restlessness with the length of the war. German workers responded with strikes, sporadically in 1915 and more intensively in 1917 and 1918. Although industrial wages in fact increased, they were offset by inflation; indeed, the cost of living was reportedly 200 percent higher than in 1914. The Ruhr and Upper Silesian districts (with their concentration of heavy industry and coal) were flashpoints of strike activity in the summer of 1917. More than 50,000 workers took industrial action during each month of 1917, and approximately 100,000 struck during 1918. As in Britain, Germany's trade unions, whose membership had fallen initially, increased in 1917–1918.

In Italy the women who had entered the labor force in large numbers in 1916 led the initial labor unrest. Dissatisfied with their treatment on the factory floor and with the strict control imposed by a military presence, women struck for better conditions. By 1917 they were joined by their male counterparts, despite men's vulnerability to prosecution for striking under Italy's laws. Perhaps the most vociferous strike action occurred in Turin in August 1917, when workers erected barricades in their districts and staved off the Italian army for three days.

French industries too saw a jump in strike activity during 1917. Most of the labor unrest in 1916–1917 stemmed from disputes over wages, which could not keep pace with rapidly rising food prices. As in Italy, French women workers in war industries composed a high proportion of the militant strikers. They complained about insufficient wages, overwork, and rude foremen. If the 1917 strikes concerned economic benefits, those in 1918 took a political turn, advocating an immediate peaceful settlement to the war. France's trade union, the *Confédération général du travail* (CGT), grew during the war from 355,000 members in 1913 to a record 600,000 by 1918, following patterns in Germany and England.

By far the most intensive strike activity occurred in Russia. Labor unrest had been a part of the Russian worker's daily existence before 1914. In the last two prewar years, nearly 75 percent of the industrial workforce took part in strikes, and work stoppages continued for at least the first seven months of the war. In 1916 their intensity and frequency increased substantially as a result of higher food prices (which had doubled since 1913), a rise in factory accident rates and illness (especially among children and women), greater demands on workers (including longer working hours), and the presence of government factory inspectors who acted as informants to deter unrest among workers. As Russian workers' real wages steadily declined and as food prices climbed, some laborers, even in higher-paying metalworking jobs, were forced to spend a minimum of 75 percent of their income on food and clothing. The strike movement that had been gaining momentum throughout 1916 exploded in January and February 1917 and continued until the autumn of 1917, encompassing the overthrow of the tsarist regime and the subsequent Provisional Government.

As the war ground on, growing unrest in the workplace was a symptom of broader-based dissent on the home front and the battle front. Early in the war, active, vocal dissent was confined to a relatively small number of individuals and organizations. Some French syndicalists spoke out against the war in the periodical *La Vie Ouvrièr*, and Charles Merrheim was one of the first figures openly to oppose France's entry into the war. Marx, of course, had argued earlier that workers in different countries owed their ultimate allegiance not to their respective national governments but to the idea of international proletarian solidarity. Many nationalists had feared that when war did break out, the constituent member parties of the Second International would reject entry into the conflict as participation in a war that would promote the interests of capitalism and hinder those of working people. In fact, most of Europe's socialist parties had supported their respective nations' decision to enter the war, believing that doing so was a defensive response.

Nonetheless, the elevation of transnational class solidarities over national and patriotic loyalties was one strand feeding into pacifist opposition to the conflict. So, too, was a genuine horror at the human and financial cost of war, as well as the influence of moral inhibitions against the taking of human lives. Organizations such as Britain's Union of Democratic Control, which advocated a negotiated peace and open, democratic conduct of foreign policy, were small in numbers but rich in talent. Prominent opponents of the war included Bertrand Russell, the famous philosopher, and Ramsay MacDonald, chairman of the Labour party and a future prime minister.

The debate surrounding conscientious objection to military service in Britain provides perhaps the clearest illustration of the moral dilemmas posed by the war. That nation had entered the conflict with a long-standing, deeply entrenched tradition of hostility to standing armies, and so for the first two years of war Britain relied on volunteers. By 1916, however, the notion that compelling men to serve by means of a draft was an unwarranted intrusion by the state on individual liberty had fallen victim to the army's continuing need for soldiers, and conscription was introduced. Now legal sanctions reinforced moral pressure to "join up," yet some 15,000 men refused to do so. Individuals who would not accept conscription were then afforded the opportunity to plead their case before a tribunal of civilian and military representatives. Men citing religious scruples might be exempted (Quakers, for example, almost always were), but the tribunals were highly suspicious of, and frequently insulting toward, objectors who lacked clear denominational ties or who appealed to their freedom of conscience. Tribunals often asked objectors whether they would not take up arms to protect a sister's chastity; if they admitted that in some circumstances they might resort to force, their objections were denied. Perhaps a third of conscientious objectors were imprisoned for their failure to serve, but many more found themselves the targets of virulent abuse. In York, for example, a town with a prominent Quaker community, advocates of conscription complained bitterly that "this crowd of physical and mental degenerates are left behind to produce, in conjunction with the unparticular women who would be satisfied to mate with weaklings like these, a race that would, like their sires, sell our land to the unspeakable Hun, and all for a purely imaginary conscience."

These sorts of ravings had originally inclined some socialists to be skeptical of the appeals to patriotic unity, but initially most accepted the idea of participation as a legitimate defensive measure. By 1917 several ideological rifts were undermining that original position. Only the Italian Socialist party (*Partito socialista italiano*, or PSI) initially opposed the war, but it later was forced into adopting a neutral position. In 1917 Germany's Social Democratic party (SPD) split into three factions: the Majority Socialists (those who supported the war and who remained within the original SPD organization), the Independent Social Democratic party (*Unabhängige Sozialdemokratische Partei Deutschlands*), and the Spartacists, the latter two of which were smaller groups opposed to the war's continuation and contained the more radical left-wing elements of the former SPD. In France, too, dissenting voices were heard within the *Section française de l'International ouvrière* (SFIO) by the autumn of 1916. A minority of Socialists on the extreme Left under the leadership of Fernand Loriot eventually formed the nucleus of the French Communist party (*Parti communiste français*, or PCF) in the 1920s. Thus, although a majority of Europe's trade unionists and socialists supported their countries' initial involvement in the war, by 1917 even the most diehard patriot had come to cherish a relatively swift, peaceful settlement.

Impatience with victory, dissatisfaction with incompetent or inefficient military authority, and an unwillingness to be sacrificed for the sake of a few hundred meters of land led to mutiny in the French army in the spring of 1917, while inaction and a suicidal final mission prompted rebellion in the German navy in the autumn of 1918. Eager to reverse the debacle at the Somme, and convinced that the Allies must seize the offensive against the German forces before they were shifted from the Eastern to the Western Front following the Russian Revolution, French general Robert Nivelle, one of the victors of Verdun, ordered French soldiers into battle once again in April 1917. His ill-conceived plan, about which the Germans had knowledge, resulted in the massacre of 40,000 Frenchmen on the first day of the offensive at Chemin des Dames. Nivelle's dismissal did nothing to relieve the overwhelming feeling among the *poilus* (French soldiers) that they had been sacrificial lambs. Recent research has demonstrated that the troops asserted their rights as citizen-soldiers serving within a republican tradition to protest exploitation by the High Command. Tens of thousands of rank-and-file troops openly refused to participate in further fruitless offensives (though they did not refuse to bear arms in a defensive role). General Philippe Pétain, who replaced the detested Nivelle, conceded in May to the demand that the French army adopt a more defensive posture that would not squander more lives. Some mutineers were incarcerated and brought to trial for their disobedience; although hundreds of the most serious offenders were condemned to death by French courts, the sentences were imposed on less than 10 percent of those involved.

The mutiny in November 1918 at the German port of Kiel on the Baltic Sea differed in immediate impact from its French counterpart. The rebellion ignited revolutionary action throughout Germany. On the other hand, the sailors' decision openly to defy their superiors' orders to set sail out of Kiel to attack the British navy also constituted a rebellion against military authority. Worried that the impending armistice would require the German navy to surrender to the British fleet, high-ranking naval officials had sought a final encounter with their bitter rivals. But the attack would not occur. Years of dissatisfaction with shipboard working conditions, poor relations with their officers, refusal to be sacrificed for the sake of naval pride, and frustration over Kaiser Wilhelm II's reluctance to abdicate his throne and submit to constitutional reform prompted the sailors' mutinous action.

Popular defiance of military and civilian authorities exploded in revolutions in three of the combatant countries: Russia, Austria-Hungary, and Germany. In Russia the stark consequences of military defeat had already been apparent a decade earlier, when Russia's dismal performance in a war against Japan had prompted revolution in 1905. In that case, the tsar had retained power only through substantial concessions, most notably the creation of constitutional government and a parliamentary legislature, the Duma. The Bolshevik leader V. I. Lenin believed that "Nicky" would never repeat the blunder of involving Russia in a disastrous war, and he despaired of ever seeing revolution achieved during his lifetime. But the strain of total war aggravated a number of persistent sources of discontent: the peculiar concentration of Russian heavy industry and the harsh discipline prevailing in that sector; the indebtedness and minimal living standards of the peasants, who, despite formal emancipation in 1861, had never developed into the conservative class of owner-occupiers characteristic of Napoleon III's France; and the dissatisfaction of the intelligentsia, who perceived Nicholas and his bureaucrats as unwilling to accept representative government as a legitimate legislative partner and unable to administer the war effort effectively (witness the excessive influence of the mad monk Rasputin).

In the spring of 1917, these pressures grew too great to contain. Strikes, food riots, and political demonstrations signaled a challenge to the tsar's authority, and, because the military was tied up at the front (and its ultimate loyalty no longer unquestioned), the full repressive arsenal of the state could not be mobilized to preserve domestic order. With no victory in sight and with mounting casualties and lengthening bread lines, Nicholas II abdicated in March 1917 (February by the old Russian calendar). A Provisional Government emerged, with responsibility to over-see the war effort until elections could be held, a constitution written, and a more representative political system introduced.

What resulted, however, was a system of dual power, whereby the constitutionalist Provisional Government found itself forced to share authority with the rapidly emerging representative councils (the so-called soviets) elected by military units, factories, and the like. Ultimately, dual power proved unworkable, for the various soviet workers' and soldiers' councils (especially the most prominent, in Petrograd) disagreed fundamentally with the Provisional Government over the war's future course. The soviets insisted on an eventual peace settlement without annexations and on a relaxation of discipline and working hours in the factories, while the Provisional Government (headed by Aleksandr Kerensky and others) was committed to victory with territorial gains and insisted that increased production, longer hours, and more stringent discipline were the only means to secure the expulsion of German soldiers from Russian soil. During the summer of 1917, a major Russian military offensive failed (with further horrendous losses), as did an attempted right-wing coup led by General Lavr Kornilov. With the revolution seemingly in danger and with victory as elusive as ever under the Provisional Government, the Bolshevik platform of peace, land, and bread attracted growing support and illustrated Kerensky's vulnerability. Finally, in November 1917 (October in the older calendar), the Bolsheviks ended the system of dual power, dissolving the Provisional Government and substituting authority in the name of the soviets, although, as Lenin had indicated, a dictatorship of the proletariat would be justified to preserve a socialist revolution in its vulnerable early stages.

The unfolding of events in Russia and the growing momentum of strikes and food riots placed Europe's governments on the defensive. In Austria-Hungary and Germany, however, impending defeat, food shortages, mounting casualties, war weariness, and the slow response by their monarchs toward reform aggravated already explosive domestic situations. Another significant factor in the Dual Monarchy's collapse was the nationality problem. In the autumn of 1918, Czech nationalists controlled Bohemia, while Serbs, Croats, and Slovenes created a Yugoslav council. Distressed by the attempts at secession from the empire, Emperor Charles, who succeeded Franz Joseph on his death in November 1916, proclaimed in October self-government for all nationalities within Austria—but not within Hungary. Military defeat at the hands of the Italian army, however, eliminated what shreds of authority he still possessed; by the end of the month, republics had been proclaimed in the major components of the now defunct Hapsburg dynasty—Austria, Czechoslovakia, Hungary, and Yugoslavia.

In Germany the revolution of 1918 did not lead to the dictatorship of the masses as in Russia or to the establishment of individual nations as in Austria-Hungary. The Kiel naval mutiny inspired unrest throughout other parts of Germany. In early November sailors' councils assumed control of Wilhelmshaven, Germany's largest naval base, and sailors and soldiers in Hamburg demanded control of food distribution and of the dissemination of communications. From northern Germany revolutionary activities spread to the Rhineland and then to Bavaria, where, in its capital of Munich, left-wing socialist Kurt Eisner and his supporters seized power and announced the formation of the Bavarian Republic. Convinced that the events in Bavaria foreshadowed the dissolution of the German empire, Prince Max of Baden, who assumed the position of chancellor in September 1918, announced the resignation of his government and the intention of both Kaiser Wilhelm II and the crown prince to relinquish their rights to the throne. The leader of the Majority Socialist party, Friedrich Ebert, became the new chancellor, and on November 9 Wilhelm II fled to Holland, leaving Ebert to quell further revolutionary unrest, to deal with the provisions of the armistice of November 11, and to form the new Weimar Republic in January 1919.

Industrial unrest, political dissent, and revolution suggested that the restrictions placed by the various European states on their citizens' civil and moral liberties were permeable. They did as much to generate new energies as to stifle them, and they promoted both constructive and destructive tendencies.

The Cost of Conscience

The war threw into bold relief not just the dictates of individual conscience, but the prospect that the costs incurred in seeking victory might prove too great. The issue was central to discussion in Britain over conscientious objection, as illustrated by the first extract, a classic liberal defense of individual freedom from *The Nation*. It also informed discussions of electoral reform, for by mid-1917 it was clear that an extension of the right to vote was essential because many working-class soldiers were excluded from the franchise (property and residential qualifications made it hard for some workers to qualify to vote). No politician would argue that men prepared to lay down their lives could remain disenfranchised, but a significant number of Conservative MPs favored depriving conscientious objectors, who had not shown the same willingness, of the right to vote after the war. Ronald McNeill (an Ulster MP) expresses this view, only to be countered from his own benches by Lord Hugh Cecil, a talented son of former Prime Minister Lord Salisbury and a staunch advocate of spiritual concerns. Whether pacifists could be deprived of certain civic rights was a volatile enough issue, but could opposition to war in wartime be construed as a political crime, as treason? Hélène Brion had the distinction in 1918 of being the only female pacifist prosecuted for treason by the French government. A Parisian nursery school teacher who had been active in the feminist and socialist movements, Brion was dismissed from her teaching position and prosecuted for breaching state-imposed censorship. She was convicted but given a suspended (three-year) sentence. Her statement in her own defense at the trial is the final document in this section.

1. Is War Incompatible with Right?

With what ideals did we go into this war, and with what realities are we ending it? High principles of international justice, national right, humanity, even in warfare, were on our lips eighteen months ago. Nor were they on our lips alone. Those do their countrymen deep injustice who do not recognize that the cause of Belgium animated tens of thousands of those young men who marched the roads to the tune of "Tipperary" in those golden September days. Beyond the case of Belgium there was a sincere feeling—indeed, we should call it a true perception—that this country stood for the solidarity of human interests, and for the distinctive ideals of Western democracy. This truth—the fundamental truth about the war—has never been shaken by criticism, but has, on the contrary, been fortified by the further revelation of German methods. But there was another kind of sceptical or pessimistic criticism not so easy to meet. "You go to war," it said, "to maintain certain sacred rights. But war is in practice incompatible with right—not only an unjust, as you would admit, but even and equally a just, war. War is an impartial tyrant that forces upon all who yield to it essentially the same system of disregard of primary human obligations. It is not only the laws, as the Romans admitted, which are silent amid arms; but morals, conscience, religion, humanity. You may make up your mind over and over again that it shall not be so. But the facts will be too strong for you. You give yourself over to the drill-sergeant. Even worse, you give yourself over to that thing of terror, the non-combatant. You abandon your political or personal freedom. These things are alien from war, where one must command and all the rest obey. In a word, fighting for liberty, democracy, and right, you inevitably hand yourself over to the control of a spirit which knows liberty, democracy, and right only to hate them and trample them under foot."

The great internal or domestic question of the war has been and will be whether this pessimistic criticism would justify itself. That there would have to be many restrictions on personal liberty was, of course, recognized by the most optimistic; but they would have argued that the crisis was of the gravest, and that restrictions honestly held necessary to preserve the existence of the nation, could not fairly come under the ban. But there have been departures which cannot be justified by this criterion. Of these the treatment of the Conscientious Objector to military service is perhaps the most flagrant. We say nothing for the moment of the general case for or against conscription. But accepting conscription, the Government, like everyone else, was aware that there was a small but perfectly sincere and resolute body of men who would refuse conformity. In the case of the larger section of this body, the Society of Friends, the reasons are familiar to all, and have been familiar for two centuries and more—so familiar that even Hegel, the philosophic sponsor of the Prussian

VII.1   From *The Nation*, May 20, 1916.

State, suggests that for Quakers and Anabaptists it would be reasonable to find a substitute for military service. It was also matter of current knowledge that besides Quakers there were a few others who, some as Christians, others as Socialists, hold the taking of human life a thing absolutely unlawful, and refuse to take part in it directly or indirectly. Parliament saw the danger of a clash between law and conscience, and saw also that it could be averted. The number to be considered was so small that it could have no sensible effect on our military efficiency. All that was necessary was to have some assurance that the conscientious objection was genuine and not a mere cloak for slackness or for convenience. Unfortunately, the intention of Parliament was haltingly and inadequately expressed, and the tribunals which it set up were, in many cases, unequal to the task of doing justice to opinions which they, like most of us, hold to be in fact mistaken. The result is that in numerous cases, after a most unedifying exhibition of dialectics as to the meaning of some exceedingly plain passages in the Gospels, or as to the probable action of the objector in various imaginary contingencies, his appeal is either refused altogether or he is passed for non-combatant service, which, as a rule, he regards morally on one plane with the actual fighting. Of these men, a number are proving their sincerity, and therefore *ipso facto*, the error of the tribunal, by maintaining their refusal to serve, against the full pressure of military authority. Some have been sent to hard labor, and others—most sinister of all—to France. As to the fate of these men, the question is urgent and critical. The Government makes some vague disclaimers as to the death penalty, but Government disclaimers are valueless. We are launched upon what is, in effect, a religious persecution, and if no adequate protest is made, we may at any moment hear that, for the first time, we suppose, for two centuries under English law, a man has gone deliberately to his death for his religious faith. The peculiar vice of this persecution is that every step it takes proves, out of its own mouth, the sincerity of its victims and the inequity and inconsistency of its own methods. For the principle, accepted by Parliament, upon which the whole scheme of compulsion rests is that the true Conscientious Objector shall be free. Every man persecuted is being threatened, punished, imprisoned, and in danger of death because he has been held not to be a sincere objector, and every threat or act of persecution that he steadily confronts proves the contention to be false, proves the tribunal that refused him exemption to be wrong, proves that he is precisely not that which he is punished for being. . . .The war is not being helped by the diversion of the efforts of various good soldiers from their proper business of fighting the Germans to the futile task of forcibly converting a good citizen into a reluctant non-combatant camp follower. It is a question, not merely of saving innocent lives, but of maintaining our good name and ensuring the hopes and ideals with which we went into the war, and for which, in all good faith, scores of thousands of the best of our sons and brothers have given their blood.

2. Britain's Parliament Debates Conscientious Objection

Mr. R. McNeill: . . . If these conscientious objectors choose to say, "You cannot make us do what your law and your morals may allow to us, and we would rather suffer death or dishonour than take the life of man, and we are entitled to do so." But why? They are entitled to do so because their action in that case affects no one, injures no one but themselves. Substantially speaking they will be justified in abstaining from taking life under those circumstances, because it is their own concern. But in the case of the conscientious objectors, which we are considering, it is exactly the opposite. The action they take does not injure themselves; in so far as one can see the immediate effect of it is to benefit themselves. They benefit themselves, but they injure everybody else. They benefit themselves by escaping from the burden, or escaping from the obligation, and they injure other people, because the inhabitants are bearing their common burden, and anyone who stands away necessarily imposes a greater burden upon those who are left. They injure the whole community in which they live; they even endanger the State of which they form a part, or, if they do not endanger it, the only reason is because they are not numerous enough to be a serious danger. They are comparatively few. . . .

Let me ask the Committee for a moment to consider—that being, in my opinion, the aspect of their conduct and their conscience—what it means in the eyes of their fellow countrymen. We have at the present time a combination of the most democratic and ethical-minded peoples on the earth, all in complete agreement upon a matter which is a moral purpose, in complete agreement that unless these peoples withstand Germany and fight Germany to defeat her, the only alternative to that is the loss of all the highest ideals of humanity and of civilisation. That has been expressed time after time by the most representative minds in all the nations of the West. Then against that universal conviction of all these combined peoples we have a small handful of men setting up a little circumscribed, ignorant, uninstructed, dogmatism of their own, many of these men being, so far as we can judge from what we have heard in the House and what we read in the papers, almost half crazy, and, so far as I can remember, not one of them a man who has had any past record established to claim to be accepted as either a leader of thought or a guide of conduct in this country. . . .

Then the question comes: Are they to be allowed to exercise the franchise after the War is over? In other words, are they, when this peril is over and when the Army returns and peace is restored, to enjoy all the rights and privileges of the State which they would not lift a hand to preserve? When the ship was in danger these men would not soil their hands by taking a turn at the pumps. Are these men to be allowed not only to have enjoyed immunity from the work we are engaged in, but also to be allowed to share both the honours and the promotions with the men who have brought the ship into port? To do so would [be] an outrage upon all the enlightened conscience of the nation as a whole. . . .

VII.2   From *Hansard's Parliamentary Debates*, June 26, 1917. © Crown Copyright material reproduced with the permission of The Controller HMSO.

Lord H. Cecil: . . . Unfortunately, I think both from a lower and a higher point of view my hon. Friend's argument is defective. First of all, I think he very much underrated the force of the consideration that what he is really proposing is to impose a retrospective penalty upon persons who have done nothing worse than avail themselves of an exemption which Parliament themselves afforded them. Personally, I think Parliament did right; but whether Parliament did right or wrong, it is at any rate bound in honour by what it did. To go to people first of all and say, "If you allege a conscientious objection, and the tribunals we have appointed find you are sincere, you shall be exempted," and then to turn round on them after they have done what Parliament has offered and allowed them to do, and say "You have done this thing, you are the basest of mankind, and unfit for the franchise"—to do that without warning them beforehand would seem to me to transgress all the principles of legislation and national justice. My hon. Friend, in an extraordinarily interesting speech, tried to lay down—if I may say so, a very courageous enterprise—a basis on which the State ought to deal with questions of opinion, and he certainly laid down a basis which would have justified the persecution of the Christians in the first days of Christianity, and still more clearly of the Protestants of Holland. . . .

Nothing is more foolish than to underrate the virtue of persecutors. They are very sincere people. They thought, and quite correctly, that the institution which was to them much more valuable than life itself was threatened by those they persecuted. They thought, and often quite correctly, that the persons they were persecuting were a small minority, ignorant and defiled by many faults and infirmities. The error they fell into is much more obvious than the one often imputed to arrogance. The error they fell into was in assuming that human beings have the right to impose opinions upon one another. I am following my hon. Friend on that ground, although I do not think it is necessary to traverse it for the purpose of this discussion. I am quite satisfied that the State can only act wisely in respect to opinions by not going into the reasonableness of any opinion whatever, but allowing liberty of opinion, because in the end it is in the interest of truth that liberty of opinion should be allowed. I am quite as certain as my hon. Friend that the conscientious objectors are wrong, but I am also quite certain that, shall we say, Presbyterians are wrong. It is a question of opinion. . . .

Captain Gwynn: . . . I agree with the Noble Lord in his opposition to this Amendment, but I do not know that I could give exactly the same reasons. Substantially, however, I think they are the same. I agree with him that these are people who are not a blight upon the community; they may very probably prove to be, in my opinion, the very salt of the community. I am speaking now as one who has seen war. I think that everybody who has seen war has one governing desire, and that is to see war abolished from the world. I am not at all sure that these people, whom we propose to reject as the outcasts of the State, may not be the best people to help in the fight to make an end of war. There is one thing that nobody can deny them—I am speaking now, as the Noble Lord spoke, of the real conscientious objector, let us put the other people aside—and that is courage, the most difficult form of courage in the world, the courage of the individual against the crowd. That is a courage which every State would do well to protect and guard. That is the courage which, above all others, makes for freedom. It is for that that I desire to see these men electors, and that I vote for giving them votes—just exactly as I would give votes to the soldiers—because they are the people who have shown not merely physical courage, but because they have made civic responsibility their plea. They have shown a spirit of initiative. These people, in refusing to act, must have taken action which must have been extremely difficult to take, and when we are told that the good of the nation is to be somehow impaired by allowing these men a voice in our national councils, I ask myself, What is "the good of the nation"? Are you going to advance the real interests of this country, or of any country, by stamping out such people from among your full citizens? Progress, as far as I can understand, comes not with the crowd, but with individuals. Freedom in the last resort is won by individuals working against the crowd, and these are the people who make for freedom. It is in the interests of freedom during a war that is fought, at all events professedly, for freedom that I resist this attempt to limit what is the exercise of their legal freedom, and what is, I think with the Noble Lord, the exercise of higher morals.

3. Pacifism—A Political Crime?

I appear before this court charged with a political crime; yet I am denied all political rights.

Because I am a woman, I am classified *de plano* [without standing] by my country's laws, far inferior to all the men of France and the colonies. In spite of the intelligence that has been officially recognized only recently, in spite of the certificates and diplomas that were granted me long ago, before the law I am not the equal of an illiterate black from Guadeloupe or the Ivory Coast. For *he* can participate, by means of the ballot, in directing the affairs of our common country, while *I* cannot. I am outside the law.

The law should be logical and ignore my existence when it comes to punishments, just as it is ignored when it comes to rights. I protest against its lack of logic.

I protest against the application of laws that I have neither wished for nor discussed.

This law that I challenge reproaches me for having held opinions of a nature to undermine popular morale. I protest even more strongly and I deny it! My discreet and nuanced propaganda has always been a constant appeal to reason, to the

VII.3 From Hèlene Brion, "L'Affaire Hèlen Brion au 1. Conseil de Guerre," 1918, reprinted in Bell and Offen, *Women, the Family, and Freedom*, 2:273–275. Copyright©1983 by the Board of the Trustees of the Leland Stanford Junior University. All rights reserved. Used with the permission of Stanford University Press. www.sup.org.

power of reflection, to the good sense that belongs to every human being, however small the portion.

Moreover, I recall, for form's sake, that my propaganda has never been directed against the national defense and has never called for peace at any price: on the contrary, I have always maintained that there was but one duty, one duty with two parts: for those at the front, to hold fast; for those at the rear, to be thoughtful.

I have exercised this educational action especially in a feminist manner, for I am first and foremost a *feminist*. All those who know me can attest to it. And it is because of my feminism that I am an enemy of war.

The accusation suggests that I preach pacifism under the pretext of feminism. This accusation distorts my propaganda for its own benefit! I affirm that the contrary is true, and it is easy for me to prove it. I affirm that I have been a militant feminist for many years, well before the war; that since the war began I have simply continued; and that I have never reflected on the horrors of the present without noting that things might have been different if women had had a say in matters concerning social issues. . . .

I am an enemy of war because I am a feminist. War represents the triumph of brute strength, while feminism can only triumph through moral strength and intellectual values. Between the two there is total contradiction.

I do not believe that in primitive society the strength or value of woman was inferior to that of men, but it is certain that in present-day society the possibility of war has established a totally artificial scale of values that works to women's detriment.

Woman has been deprived of the sacred and inalienable right given to every individual to defend himself when attacked. By definition (and often by education) she has been made a weak, docile, insignificant creature who needs to be protected and directed throughout her life.

Far from being able to defend her young, as is the case among the rest of creation, she is [even] denied the right to defend herself. In material terms she is denied physical education, sports, the exercise of what is called the noble profession of arms. In political terms she is denied the right to vote—what Gambetta called "the keystone of every other right"—by means of which she could influence her own destiny and have at least the resource to try to do something to prevent these dreadful conflicts in which she and her children find themselves embroiled, like a poor unconscious and powerless machine. . . .

You other men, who alone govern the world! you are trying to do too much and too well. Leave well enough alone.

You want to spare our children the horrors of a future war; a praiseworthy sentiment! I declare that as of now your goal has been attained and that as soon as the atrocious battle that is taking place less than a hundred miles from us has been brought to a halt, you will be able to speak of peace. In 1870 two European nations fought—only two, and for scarcely six months; the result was so appalling that throughout all of Europe, terrified and exhausted, it took more than forty years before anyone dared or was able to begin again. Figure that as of now we have fought, not six months, but for forty-four long months of unbelievable and dreadful combat, where not merely two nations are at odds, but more than twenty—the elite of the so-called civilized world—that almost the entire white race is involved in the melee, that the yellow and black races have been drawn into the wake. And you say, pardon me, that as of now your goal has been achieved!—for the exhaustion of the world is such that more than a hundred years of peace would be instantaneously assured if the war were to end this evening!

The tranquility of our children and grandchildren is assured. Think about assuring them happiness in the present and health in the future! Think about some means of providing them bread when they need it, and sugar, and chocolate to drink! Calculate the repercussions that their present deprivation will have on this happiness that you pretend to offer them by continuing to fight and making them live in this atmosphere, which is unhealthy from every possible point of view.

You want to offer freedom to enslaved people, you want—whether they like it or not—to call to freedom people who do not seem ready to understand it as you do, and you do not seem to notice that in this combat you carry on for liberty, all people lose more and more what little they possess, from the material freedom of eating what they please and traveling wherever they wish, to the intellectual liberties of writing, of meeting, even of thinking and especially the possibility of thinking straight—all that is disappearing bit by bit because it is incompatible with a state of war.

Take care! The world is descending a slope that will be difficult to remount.

I have constantly said this, have written about it incessantly since the beginning of the war: if you do not call women to your rescue, you will not be able to ascend the slope, and the new world that you pretend to install will be as unjust and as chaotic as the one that existed before the war!

〰

Authority Challenged

Labor unrest in Britain was especially pronounced in Scotland, and work stoppages in the Clydeside shipbuilding region (around Glasgow), for example, were notorious. Other issues that prompted working-class organization included rent strikes to protest the escalating cost of housing, and it was within this movement that James Maxton, a future Labour MP, gained organizational and political experience. His memoirs, from which the first selection is drawn, provide insight into the formation of a political identity that embraced the Labour Party and repudiated the old Liberal Party as the advocate for progressive change. People like Maxton, and the strikes they supported, worried the British government, which appointed an official commission to study the growing scale of industrial action in 1916–1917. Its findings are reviewed in the second source, a review article in the prestigious *Economic Journal* by Edwin Cannan, a professor at the London School of Economics. Perhaps the authorities' greatest fear was that the dissatisfaction so evident in workshops and factories would spread to the armies and that the soldiers themselves would down tools. In France, there was no doubt that, in the face of repetitious and fruitless attacks, resignation in the trenches was turning to frustration. The spring of 1917, in the wake of Russia's February Revolution which toppled the tsarist regime, was the critical period when discontent escalated into mutiny. These entries from a French soldier's diary describe the temporary disruption of normal command authority in many army units.

Military officers were apt to blame outside "agitators" for outbreaks of mutiny, an explanation that conveniently if erroneously absolved them of primary responsibility for the breakdown of order. There were, of course, calls from some more radical socialists for workers and soldiers to recognize their universal brotherhood and end their own exploitation by refusing to serve any longer. The Second International had served as a forum for pan-European socialist cooperation and proletarian unity, but had collapsed in the face of patriotic sentiment in 1914. The socialists who attempted to revive the spirit of the International issued an appeal in December 1916 while meeting in neutral Switzerland. Reprinted as the fourth source in this section, it rejected as half-hearted or illusory the recent overtures to Germany and American President Wilson to promote a negotiated peace. Even if, with the exception of Russia, the major parties of the left still lent support to the war effort, it was no longer unconditional. Germany's SPD, for example, began to reevaluate its earlier commitment to a *Burgfrieden* (atmosphere of absolute civic unity), and that new attitude is evident in Hugo Haase's warning to his fellow deputies in the German parliament, the *Reichstag*, that the government could not expect workers to sacrifice on behalf of a state that continued to treat them with contempt. Similar frustration was emerging among the ordinary ranks in the military, especially the fleet, which had lain nearly idle at anchor for long stretches. In the sixth document, seaman Richard Stumpf (whom we have encountered before), reflects on the third anniversary of the war in August 1917 and the growing war-weariness of his mates.

The bonds of imperial authority were subject to challenge as well. Within the British empire, two of the more egregious violations of the spirit of liberty and universal rights by which the Allies might justify their conduct of the war were India and Ireland. Annie Besant, a feminist and secularist who married a clergyman inclined toward neither attitude, worked on behalf of self-government, or Home Rule, for Ireland, and then, when the parallels seemed too compelling to ignore, for India as well. Reprinted below is her 1917 presidential address to the Indian National Congress (founded in 1885, it was the preeminent institution in the struggle for Indian independence). In Ireland the situation was equally complex. When war broke out, Britain itself had been badly divided over home rule for Ireland, but many Irish political leaders (notably John Redmond, leader of the Irish Nationalist party) wasted little time in pledging

Ireland's loyalty. British troops need not be diverted from the Western Front to secure Ireland, they promised. Moreover, some 200,000 Irishmen volunteered for service against Germany. Yet republican elements within Ireland, who scorned any limited measures of Home Rule that might emerge after the war and sought nothing short of full independence, believed that Britain's absorption against Germany marked their opportunity to cast off the yoke of British rule. Their response was a 2,000-man armed uprising in Dublin on Easter Monday in April 1916. The final source is the proclamation they issued of a republic. British forces defeated the rebels within a week, but their harsh overall response made many initially skeptical Irish citizens more sympathetic to the ideal of complete independence from British rule.

4. Working-Class Resistance in Britain

As I sit down to write my recollections of the War years I remind myself that nearly twenty-one years have elapsed since the outbreak of war, and my memory of how I felt and thought at that time is somewhat cloudy. I was twenty-nine years of age and had been a Socialist for about ten years. I was an assistant teacher in a Glasgow Elementary School, Chairman of the Scottish Independent Labour Party [ILP], with a certain reputation as a propagandist and agitator.

When the war broke out I was in the middle of my summer holiday. I found it very difficult to believe that there would be war. I can recall that the incident which jolted the minds of British Socialists into a full realisation of the disturbed state of Europe was the assassination of Jean Jaurès in a Paris café. . . .

The following day I had to go north to Perthshire. A socialist comrade of mine, Robert Nichol, . . . had taken a holiday job as a clerk at a fruit farm to assist the work of picking the raspberry crop. The actual picking was done by a large body of men and women, recruited mainly from the slums of Dundee, Edinburgh and Glasgow. Their wages were the most disgraceful that I have ever had first-hand experience of. Nichol had persuaded them to come out on strike, and wired me to come and give him a hand with the job. I went, and we managed to secure concessions from the employers on all the three matters in dispute. A meeting arranged to be addressed by us . . . on the question of the strike became a huge gathering. . . . The war possibilities were now getting into the minds of the people, and I imagine that the huge meeting was due rather to the war feeling in the air than to the issues of the strike. One or two anti-war utterances by Nichol and myself let us know that our attitude was not fully shared by our hearers. Our strike, however, came to an abrupt end. The war was declared, and the male portion of our army of strikers vanished in twenty-four hours to line up at the recruiting offices to fight

VII.4   From James Maxton, "War Resistance by Working-class Struggle," in Julian Bell, ed., *We Did Not Fight, 1914–1918: Experiences of War Resisters* (London: Cobden–Sanderson, 1935), 213–222.

for the country which was only giving them the meanest level of existence. Nichol and I were already beginning to learn something of war psychology.

From that time onward the life of a member of the I.L.P. was one of stress and struggle while the war lasted. We were "white-livered curs," bloody pro-Germans, friends of the Kaiser, traitors to our country. A large proportion of our members, particularly elected persons, left us or withdrew from all activities. We had to hold conferences throughout the country with our own members explaining our attitude and encouraging them to stand up to it. At a very early date all of us who were recognised speakers or representative men were asked to take part in joint recruiting campaigns. Refusal to do this roused much public hostility, and when many Labour men in the country agreed to go on recruiting campaigns it made the position of those who refused all the worse. . . .

During this period . . . a Clyde Workers' Committee, consisting of men in the various engineering and shipbuilding works on the Clyde, was organising and directing working-class struggle, not primarily against the war but about industrial and social grievances. . . . One of the first successes of the agitations on the Clyde was the agitation against the attempt of the house owners to raise the rents. This agitation resulted in the passing of the first Rent Restriction Act. Employers had to make wage concessions, but now in our agitational work we had to have regard to the Defence of the Realm Act and the Munitions Act, both of which provided heavy penalties for offences which had to be committed if Socialist or anti-war agitation were to be carried on at all. I remember a fellow teacher, Mr. J. B. Houston, being sentenced to a term of imprisonment with the option of a heavy fine for a sentence or two in a speech which were held to be prejudicial to recruiting. Some ships' joiners in one of the Clyde shipyards were imprisoned for making a demand about wages which was held to impede the production of munitions.

The Clyde Workers' Committee . . . carried on very active agitational work and produced a weekly newspaper which was widely read. One week-end I went to London to attend a meeting of the No-Conscription Fellowship. When I returned to Glasgow on the Sunday morning it was to learn that the active men in the Clyde Workers' Committee had been seized from their homes during the previous night and been carted away somewhere out of Glasgow, no one knew where. I was due to speak that afternoon on Glasgow Green against conscription. I went there, but a large portion of my speech dealt with the deportation of these men. A few days afterwards I also was arrested in the middle of the night, and after a period of some weeks in jail was tried and sentenced to twelve months imprisonment for a breach of the Defence of the Realm Act. . . .

When my time expired I came out and began to adjust myself to the new situation. I was unemployed and without resources. I had been dismissed from my teaching position and there was no chance of a man of my age, reputation and record getting back. Within a few days I was called before the Military Service Tribunal. I told them my grounds for refusing military service, and admitted that they were political and not religious. The Military Representative was good enough to say that he had no particular desire to have me in the army, for reasons which he did not intend to be flattering to myself, and I was given exemption on condition that I found some work of national importance, as it was called. Work was not difficult to get, but people with my attitude to the war had to find jobs which were not directly assisting the work of slaughter. It was impossible to do any work at all that did not help in some way, but I felt that staying in prison helped the progress of the war in so far as it precluded me from carrying on my work of Socialist agitation. I appreciated and understood the attitude of my friends who absolutely declined to do anything, and suffered continuous imprisonment over the whole war period, but it did not suit my philosophy, which demanded active carrying on of class struggle, nor did it suit my temperament to be cribbed, cabined and confined when the urge within me was to be out trying to influence my fellows to use the opportunities presented by war conditions for the purposes of social revolution.

I got a job in a small Clyde shipyard which was not engaged in making warships or troopships, but was engaged in the peaceful task of making barges to be used for the conveyance of cocoanuts and fruit on West African rivers. I had no doubt that the boats would in some way assist the progress of the war, but they would never kill anyone, and the hope of most of my workmates, who were not so anti-war as myself, was that they would be sunk on their way to Africa, so that they would get more to build. I am afraid I am not able to claim that I have been one of the great shipbuilders of the world, but I did get experience of all the unskilled and semi-skilled work around a shipyard, and got to know how ships were built. What was of more importance for my immediate purposes was that I got into close relationships with the manual workers and was able to participate in the struggles of that time as one of themselves.

By this time war weariness was setting in and it was much easier to make anti-war speeches. The workers as a whole had become more vocal, and although work was plentiful and wages higher, the constant grind had aroused a great irritability among them, and the Socialist agitator was listened to with greater appreciation than ever before in my experience. I carried on my usual agitational and propaganda work for the I.L.P., and whereas the early days of the war had seen our membership diminish, now we, in common with other Socialist organisations, found our membership going up. The speeches I made were much more revolutionary and provocative to the authorities than the one that had got me imprisoned, but by this time they did not feel so confident in proceeding with prosecutions. . . .

When the Russian revolution took place we were at first dumbfounded. It was what our Socialist teaching had told us should take place and must take place sooner or later, but it had come sooner than most of us had expected, and it had come in a place where we had not expected it; but when we recovered from our surprise the Revolution was hailed enthusiastically by all sections of the working class movement, and those of us who had held a revolutionary point of view set out forthwith with the idea of seeing similar revolutionary achievement in the various European countries. That did not happen. It came very near to happening in several of them, and in all of them working class consciousness became more strongly developed than ever before. For some years that attitude of mind remained, and then came reaction. Reaction which is still with us, but should this reaction lead the peoples into another world conflict, the experiences of the last struggle justify us in believing that the capitalist system would not survive it. The human race would suffer terribly, but the human race would survive, to build a different social order.

✑

5. Strikes in Britain

[N]ot quite three years after the beginning of the war a Commission was appointed by the Prime Minister to "inquire and report upon Industrial Unrest and to make recommendations to the Government at the earliest practicable date." . . .

With the aid of the Commissioners' reports it is not very difficult to see what the main causes of the unrest have been.

In the first place we may take the loss of individual liberty. Of course, many of the restrictions imposed by war measures, while irritating enough to the people in general, can scarcely be regarded as causes of "industrial" unrest, inasmuch as they are not directly connected with employment. Such are the liquor restrictions, and the fact is probably the explanation of the sharp divergence of opinion between the various panels of the Commission when they ask themselves whether the liquor restrictions have been a cause of industrial unrest. . . . The Commissioners in general adopt the view very naïvely expressed in the North-Western report, that "the matter should be sensibly dealt with, not from the high ideals of temperance reformers, whose schemes of betterment must be kept in their proper place till after the war, but from the human point of view of keeping the man who has to do war work in a good temper, which will enable him to make the necessary sacrifices in a contented spirit," beer being to many of the best citizens of the country "not only a beverage, but a sacred national institution."

Conscription appears at first sight not to be a distinctively industrial matter, any more than the liquor restrictions, but it becomes so in consequence of the necessary exceptions to its universality. The loss of liberty involved in every man of a certain age being compelled to serve was a popular loss among almost all classes, because the man of military age who was not willing to serve was disliked, but whether or not, it could not have been a cause of specifically industrial unrest. But when it was found that universality was impossible, and the loss of liberty took the form of tribunals deciding who was to go and who to stay, the situation was completely altered. Decisions that this man and that man, though of military age and

VII.5   From Edwin Canaan, "Industrial Unrest," *The Economic Journal* (December 1917), 454–459.

fitness, shall be allowed to stay at home in safety because they are indispensable to the industry in which they are employed are and must be industrial decisions, and, human nature being what it is, they are absolutely certain to become a cause of industrial unrest. Moreover, the Army itself, though its efforts are directed to the destruction of the enemy, is an industrial organisation, and offers great variety of occupation: the selection of men for the various occupations is entirely in the hands of the military authorities, and would be far from giving universal satisfaction, even if those authorities were perfectly wise. As things are, it is not surprising to hear from the Scotch Commissioners that "the whole system of the operation of the Military Acts is, in the opinion of the great bulk of the working classes, an exhibition of bungling incompetence and of exasperating dilatory methods," and that the opinion generally held of the unfair working of the Acts is "a great cause of unrest."

While willing to submit to the loss of liberty involved in universal military service, the working classes to a man were strenuously opposed to "industrial conscription." Now it is true that no man has been industrially conscribed in the sense of being directly compelled to take some particular employment, but a great deal of what may be called negative industrial conscription has been introduced by restricting men's freedom to abandon their employment, either by way of strike or in order to take other employment. As the West Midlands Commissioners say, "The Munitions of War Acts have revolutionised industry. In normal times the workman is free to leave his employment, whether to secure better wages or on personal grounds; now he can do neither unless his employer consents or the Munitions Tribunal grants a certificate. . . . In normal times wage changes are settled by collective bargaining; now they are settled by the State. In normal times the employer disciplines his own men; now discipline is enforced publicly in a criminal court. Lastly, the Trade Unions have fought, rightly or wrongly, and in the engineering trades have fought successfully, for the principle that certain men or certain unions alone were entitled to certain work. Now this has been swept away, and men and women of rival unions, or of no unions at all, work alongside skilled craftsmen. These changes are strongly resented as infringements of personal liberty, to which men are deeply attached." . . .

The eight panels of the Commission are unanimous in regarding the opinion of the working classes, that they have been exploited by the rise of food prices, as the universal and most important cause of industrial unrest.

The other great reason for the failure of the rise of money wages to placate the wage-earners has been the fitfulness of its distribution. . . . The war changes have not only altered the distribution of earnings between different industries, but have altered the distribution between different classes of workers inside each industry at haphazard, so that individuals working in the same shop have seen their relative positions reversed. . . .

The war caused changes which can be grouped under three heads:—

First, the introduction of semi-skilled and unskilled men and women into work previously regarded as skilled men's work.

Second, the largely increased output of existing processes giving a greater earning power for the same piece rate, and

Third, the introduction of many new processes easily learnt and yielding a high wage at the agreed piece rates. To this must be added the great speeding-up which the beginning of the war called out, and the fact that it was very wisely determined that piece rates existing before the war should not be reduced. The result has been as great a revolution in industry as any similar period has witnessed. The output has been vastly increased, old processes have been scrapped, and new and more efficient ones introduced. Our industries stand on a different plane from the pre-war period. Now the effect of increased production coupled with a fixed piece rate has been a great increase of the earning power of workers doing repetition work. The rates were fixed in peace time, when not only were conditions more leisurely, but orders were received in dozens and grosses where they are now received in thousands and tens of thousands. Hence the machine can now be worked for a longer productive period, the output is enormously increased, and the wages earned have reached a height hitherto undreamt of. In the engineering trade four pounds a week for [a] man or woman, who has entered the trade since the war, is not an unusual wage; whilst in many cases the wage reaches six, eight, and ten pounds a week or even more, all, be it understood, by workers with no previous experience. At the same time the tool-maker and the gauge-maker, both skilled men whose skill is the basis on which the machine operates, are still working on a pre-war rate, plus the bonuses and advances received since the war, but taking all these into account, are receiving considerably less than the piece-worker.

The result may be imagined. The skilled man with a life's experience behind him sees a girl or youth, whom perhaps he himself has taught, earning twice as much as he does. The injury to his self-respect is as great as that to his pocket. . . .

The discontent which exists takes the form of anger with the Government, not in the sense of the particular group of politicians who happen to form the Cabinet or the Ministry, but the whole machine. The Government is directly employing an astonishingly large proportion of the whole population, and a large proportion of the remainder are employed by firms which are mere puppets in the hands of the Government. We hear no more of grandmotherly legislation; dropping that, the State has become the Grand-employer, and the employees do not like it in that capacity. The Commissioners for the North-Eastern and the South-Western divisions, indeed, do not seem to have been much impressed by the feeling against the Government, but the other six panels have no doubt of its strength and importance. The machine is regarded as slow, stupid, and untrustworthy in all the six divisions. The two of them which have the most independent life of their own— Scotland and Lancashire—think it too remote, and demand more local autonomy; but in the London area, within easy call of Whitehall, there is but "a fading confidence in Government departments," and "a distinct opinion amongst both employers and workmen that the Government has intervened to a much greater extent than is desirable or useful in the relations between employers and employed"; in the West Midlands the distrust of Government "is both widespread and deep"; in the Yorkshire and East Midland division, not only the skilled engineering and electrical trades, but members of a dozen less skilled unions "all alike without a single exception expressed distrust in, and total indifference to, any promise the Government may make, while some referred to 'Russia,' and openly declared the one course open for Labour was a general 'down tools' policy to secure reforms that constitutional action was failing to effect"; and the South Wales Commissioners say: "An outstanding feature of our inquiry has been the unqualified hostility on the part of witnesses, both on the men's and the employers' side, to Government interference."

∞

6. The French Mutinies

April 4

Many men get drunk. Morale is low. They are fed up with the war. Certain corps court-martial some men for desertion, theft, insolence, etc.; after condemnation (with reprieve in the majority of cases) they are transferred to another corps. My company is infested with them. Special strictly disciplined companies are needed, prison sentences are useless. . . .

June 1

The spirit of the troops is turning sour. There is talk of mutiny and of troops refusing to go to the lines. The "bad hats" amongst them are more vociferous.

June 3

All the companies are in a state of turmoil; the men are receiving letters from friends informing them of the present spirit and urging them not to march; the ringleaders are becoming insolent; others are trying to influence their comrades. My company does not escape this plague: a squad, under the sway of its corporal, refuses to fall in, the men claiming they are ill. Just as we move to take them to the guardroom, they run off in the fields and insult the N.C.O.s [noncommissioned officers]. Some only return the following day.

I have five court-martialled, to get rid of the worst. Alas! that's just what many want—a motive to be court-martialled, so as to spend a year in prison; they are counting on some future amnesty and, during their stay in prison, they will be far from the Front. Once again, it will be the good who will go and get themselves killed and the scoundrels who will be protected.

VII.6   From Henri Desagneaux, *A French Soldier's War Diary* (Morley: Elmsfield Press, 1975), 38–40. Reprinted with permission of Editions Denoel.

In addition, a law has just increased the men's pay: first payment today. These men who are getting 20–30 francs rush to spend them on drink; drunkenness all along the line. Command becomes difficult.

June 5

I sit in judgment at the court-martial. What a procession of rogues! How stupid they seem in front of their judges. In their company they tried to be smart, insulted their superiors, tried to get their chums to desert; here they are now, sheepish, not daring to look up, full of repentance. . . .

The Army is becoming more and more a prey to this ill-feeling; those on leave on their return home from the front, are assailed by agitators who, going as far as uncoupling the trains, urge them not to return. I must go to Meaux to re-establish order.

June 7

On my arrival at Meaux at 9.30 I organize my troops at the station and in town.

One platoon for the town and hospital (where there's a load of brutes), two platoons at the station, one in reserve, in case of need.

At 3 p.m. the first train of those on leave arrives at the station from the front. As soon as the train enters, you would say a horde of savages, all the doors opening on both sides and the men flooding out on the platforms.

Shouts, insults, threats fly in all directions: death to the shirkers at home, murderers and pigs that they are; long live the Revolution, down with war, it's peace we want, etc. We empty the station to avoid conflict; the station staff don't dare show themselves. That's why I'm here. At La Ferté-sous-Jouarre a company of machine-gunners is on guard. At Chateau-Thierry, a company of light infantry: each division has its zone.

4 p.m., second train. The troops invade a garden. The owner kindly offers to let them pick flowers, provided they don't do any damage. There is one mad rush and everything is destroyed; they attack the house too, the windows are broken and the blinds torn down. They shout the same cries and insults: Death, long live the Revolution, down with war.

5 p.m., third train. As soon as it stops, the troops surge out menacingly. There is an empty train in the station: the men seize stones and break every window. During the journey, a man had fallen on the track and had had his foot cut off. The military superintendent of the station—a lieutenant aged 55—rushes up with four men and a stretcher to carry him away. Seeing his white band the troops call him a murderer and beat him black and blue. It all happened so quickly that the attack passed unnoticed and we found this officer lying unconscious on the platform after the departure of the train.

Often scenes such as these happen at the last moment, as the train is leaving, so that we can't intervene.

The trains are in a lamentable state; the doors are wrenched off and thrown on the track during the journey; all the windows are broken, and the seats slashed to ribbons.

That's the state of affairs. My men are well-disciplined and will be ready to act at the first signal. I have no fears in this respect. The situation however, is delicate, for how can I intervene, should the need arise, with 30 or 40 men, against a frenzied horde of a thousand individuals, the majority of them in a state of intoxication?

June 8

At La Ferté, same scenes. At Chateau-Thierry a deputy station-master is injured. A general who was on the platform was manhandled and had his képi snatched from his head. The guard intervened and a man was arrested. Immediately all the troops got off and uncoupled the train. They only consented to leave when their comrade had been freed. The station staff are so ill-treated that they go into hiding when these trains arrive and refuse to do their duties.

At Meaux my guard duty passes normally. My men, well turned-out, parade in the town and are a source of admiration to everyone. This is because at Meaux, there are only fatigue sections: bakers, drivers who have no idea of smart turn-out, good discipline.

The day passes with the usual cries of: down with war, death to the slackers, long live the Revolution and that's all, except for a drunk who got out a razor to show how he cut the Boches' heads off; we cart him off to prison.

June 12

The postal service informs me that letters seized are full of threats and plans for revolution. No-one hides the fact things are bad and everyone is fed up.

☙

7. A Socialist Appeal to Workers

The third year of war is now a reality. Two and a half years of uninterrupted slaughter, two and a half years of unprecedented destruction and devastation, are not enough. The beast unchained on August 1, 1914, after several years of systematic preparation on the part of all the capitalist governments, is not yet satiated. New streams of blood must still be shed. Still more refined and cruel methods must be devised to slaughter men. Still heavier sacrifices will be made until Europe is completely impoverished and exhausted.

Why? For what reason?

The causes of this self-destruction of peoples were indicated in the manifestoes of Zimmerwald and of Kienthal. They are: greediness, desire of the capitalist classes for conquest, their imperialist lust, and their criminal desire to augment profits in their own as well as in the conquered countries and to procure for themselves new sources of wealth.

This truth cannot be effaced either by diplomatic lies, by the prevarications of statesmen, or by the chauvinist phrases of ignoble ex-socialists. This truth has been evidenced and confirmed once more by the events of recent months.

Rumania, whose national glory and esteem were supposed to be increased—in reality she is nothing but a pawn on the chessboard of the great imperialist powers—lies broken on the ground. She underwent the fate of Belgium, Serbia, Montenegro, the fate which tomorrow awaits Greece and other yet neutral states. The miserable farce of the "liberation" of Poland, a country which was not worse off even under the Tsar's whip than under the regime of the Austro-German "liberator," proves how little the military victor thinks of anything but complete robbery and pillage. The deportation of Belgian and Polish proletarians for the purpose of putting them at forced labor far from their native lands, the transformation of all the belligerent states into national penitentiaries, the ghastly terror against all those who appeal to common sense and reason in order to terminate the horrible massacre, the prisons overflowing with the best and most courageous of the fighters of the laboring class—all these facts constitute so many reasons for indicting the ruling classes, so many proofs of their military lies and of the vile motives, greediness, and rapacity which underlie both this war and previous wars.

Today this war is passing through a crisis: "No victors, no vanquished—or rather all vanquished, all bleeding, all ruined, all exhausted." The statesmen of belligerent countries, caught in their own traps, dominated by the war, are now staging the comedy of peace. Just as in peacetime they play with the menace of war, so during the war they prostitute the idea of peace.

The Central Powers have offered to open peace negotiations with their adversaries. But how? By arming themselves to the teeth, by placing their last man under the yoke of organized manslaughter, by acclaiming their victories! Really, such negotiations are utter buffoonery, conducted for the purpose of hiding the truth from the peoples. No doubt these peace proposals will be rejected and thus the ferment of national hatred and of chauvinism will be revived.

The reply of the opposing Entente Powers is worthy of the proposition of the Central Powers. The guardians of the bloody Tsar feel at ease in the terrible bath of blood in their own country. The advocates of pogroms prepare for a general European pogrom. In order to extend their power to Constantinople, to the Straits, and to Prussian Poland, they are ready to sacrifice to the last man the youth of Europe, for they have never stopped even at the most disgraceful acts so long as their power could be maintained over the peoples oppressed by Russia.

The renegade Briand seeks by phrases of hatred and contempt to conceal from France the fact that in reality by continuing the war she is spilling her own blood and moving toward destruction and that she is doing this for the Allied Powers. The greatest demagogue of the century, Lloyd George, advances deliberately the false assertion that England is fighting for the complete liberation of the oppressed peoples. Does he, like his friend Briand, forget that England and France, through their diplomacy and war policy, are bound to Russia's war aims? Do they forget what aspirations England is pursuing in the Orient, in Mesopotamia, and in Asia Minor?

And what about the note of the President of the United States? It cannot lose the character, scarcely disguised, of a war note. Very well, if Wilson wishes peace, America should stop every individual, without any exception, from gaining billions on war deliveries and, with that, as proof, appear before the world as an apostle of peace.

Truly, even today the governments do not want peace, because the leaders of the war fear the inevitable settling of accounts which must follow, and others find war profits more attractive than the highest interests and human rights. There is only one power that can force them to conclude peace: the awakened force of the international proletariat, the firm will to turn one's weapons not against one's own brothers but against the internal enemy in every country.

Meanwhile this force is not yet very large. Even endless calamities and terrible blows have not yet opened the eyes of the peoples. However, something is stirring in every nation on earth. There is no country in which the energetic proletariat does not raise the banner of socialism signifying peace and liberty; there is not a state which does not ban these champions from society and persecute them, thus proving that they are feared as the only force in favor of a real and lasting peace.

This struggle of socialist minorities against their governments and against social patriotic hirelings must be continued without truce or delay. The duty toward one's own class, toward the future of mankind, must stand above everything else. To accomplish this task must be the unbreakable resolve of all workers in the belligerent states as well as in the neutral countries, the former by assembling all the forces in every country in order to oppose them to the dominant class, and the latter by supporting with all their moral and financial power the struggle of the minorities.

At an hour when the war has come to an impasse;

At an hour when the diplomats' hypocritical gestures of peace will lead only to still more atrocious massacres if the masses do not prove their will for peace at the price of the greatest sacrifices;

At an hour when the phantoms of want and famine have become realities —

Now it is imperative to act with faithfulness and complete devotion in the spirit of revolutionary international socialism in order to secure a prompt ending of war. It is necessary to fight for the Workers' International, the liberator of the peoples.

Hail the class struggle!

Hail peace!

Hail the Workers' International!

The Socialist International Committee in Berne

8. A Warning from the SPD

Gentlemen, the idea that actuated the Social-Democratic Party at the outbreak of war was that it is our duty to do everything for the protection of our own country. [*Applause from Social-Democrats.*] These endeavors are not thwarted by public criticism; on the contrary, they are strengthened by criticism of the right sort. The Social-Democratic Party has never thought of asking for any presents in return for its vote of August 4. . . . It is not considering and has never considered its vote as a trade transaction. But we cannot approve of the Government on the whole presenting nothing but the budget to a Reichstag gathering in the eighth month of a war that has upset the whole world. The sacrifices which our people are bearing are overwhelming. Our brothers in the field, facing death every moment, are doing their duty with an almost superhuman strength [*"Quite right!"—S.D.*], all of them equally; and under such circumstances the Government must no longer evade its task of seeing to it that the amount of political rights should be equal to the amount of the duties. [*Hearty assent from S.D.*] It is quite unbearable that all citizens, without difference of class, party, religion, and nationality, are not being granted full equality. [*Renewed assent by S.D.*]

Gentlemen, the workmen's organizations have supplied more than 20 army corps from amongst their members. [*"Hear, hear!"—S.D.*] On the battlefields and at home they have done great things, as the Government itself has acknowledged, and now is a session of the Reichstag to pass, without doing away with the exceptional regulations concerning the rights of coalition which are directed against them? What we ask for is equality in all respects [*"Quite right!"—S.D.*], not only as a reward for the immense sacrifices but also as the fulfilment of an undeniable claim. [*"Quite right!"—S.D.*] Gentlemen, it is always being put forward that our chief care must be not to lower the sentiment of our brothers in the front ranks who are doing wonders in bearing privations and sufferings; but those who want to act thus must first see to it that our brothers, when they come home, are not looked upon one day longer as citizens of lesser rights in empire, state, and parish. [*Hearty assent by S.D.*] Nothing will hurt the masses more deeply than consciousness of the fact that those who on account of the war are restricted in their earning power will on that account be marked as citizens of lesser rights. [*"Quite right!"—S.D.*] There is no more room within the German Empire for class suffrage.

If the Government will actively set its mind to it, it will, with the aid of our people, overcome all obstacles. The more openly and decisively it acts, the more easily it will reach its goal. . . .

We shall again put forward a motion to that end, and if the Government will maintain its reluctant and evasive position, the soldiers coming back from the war, together with those of their comrades who stayed at home, will claim their

VII.8   From Ralph Haswell Lutz, ed., *Fall of the German Empire, 1914–1918*, 2 vols. (Stanford: Stanford University Press, 1932), 2:201–205. Copyright © 1940 by the Board of the Trustees of the Leland Stanford Junior University, renewed 1960. All rights reserved. Used with the permission of Stanford University Press. www.sup.org.

rights impetuously. [*"Quite right!"—S.D.*] We must not close our eyes to the fact that after the blood and health of hundreds of thousands of men have been sacrificed for the protection of the Empire, the fight for equal rights and the democratization of organizations will be continued with more stress than ever. [*Assent by S.D.*]

With growing discontent we are watching the restrictions and even the destruction of the liberties already won, for instance, the rights of association and assemblage, as also those of the press. The present state of affairs is not based on the constitution of our Empire. The latter only allows the declaration of the state of war in case the public safety of one of the Federated States is threatened. But hardly anyone would venture to say that in the whole German Empire the public safety is in danger. Our people have waited in vain for the end of the state of siege in the interior of the Reich, as was promised at the outbreak of the war; but the restrictions on the contrary have been rather increased and have caused growing discontent, the importance of which the authoritative circles evidently do not grasp. [*"Quite right!"—S.D.*] In various districts even the closed meetings must be sanctioned and supervised by the police and the speakers are obliged to submit their manuscripts for approval to the Censor, before the meeting is allowed to be held.

How the censorship is being handled! The fate of political lectures and papers is laid in the hands of censors who have never before had anything to do with politics and accordingly have no understanding of the matter. The reasons for which newspapers have been prosecuted and prohibited indeed defy all description. . . .

Gentlemen, the reference to the so-called "party truce" frequently becomes a nuisance. The party truce, as it has been proclaimed, requires that, in the political struggle, attacks against parties or religions in a hateful personal form should be avoided; but it should not lead to a denial of principles or to the renunciation of a Weltanschauung. It would be a misfortune for our people if the party truce should lead us to the peace of a cemetery. [*"Quite right!"—S.D.*]

When *Vorwärts* was suppressed, the Censor expressly permitted that during the party truce every newspaper should be able to discuss all happenings of public life and of the world in the light of its Weltanschauung. Only under this reservation did *Vorwärts* declare that it would not touch on the theme "Class Struggle and Class Hatred" during the war. It gave assurance that it would abstain from every hateful polemic against any class, which, by the way, it had done even before its suppression.

Gentlemen, the question arises now whether the newspapers have actually been given full scope of expression. Nobody will be able to assert that. Week after week new regulations are being given out. Only yesterday meetings for women were forbidden [*"Hear, hear!"—S.D.*], an action which demands the same criticism. The Chancellor wants the German people to be a free people. The condition just described is not worthy of a free people and should be cleared away immediately. A free people deserve free speech. [*Hearty assent by S.D.*] This is especially requisite as soon as the war approaches its end. The German people should not allow themselves to be pushed aside when the fateful question of their future is being settled. [*Hearty assent by the S.D.*] They have the right to take part in discussions and preparations.

Gentlemen, in all countries dread of the war makes itself felt more every day. It is natural that the longing arises everywhere to put an end to the terrible butchery of the nations. To express this is not a sign of weakness and can least of all be looked upon as such by us. For our military successes are indisputable; our social life, stimulated by the war industry, has been revived in a surprising manner; our finances have proved themselves to be strong. It is just the strong who may first hold out the hand of peace. My party as representative of international socialism has always been the peace party, and it knows that this is the case for the Socialists of other countries as well. Our desire is for a lasting peace, such a one as does not include new difficulties and does not contain seeds of future quarrels. That can be obtained if the nations do not oppress each other [*Approval by S.D.*] and if the peoples see the advantage of the peaceful exchange of culture. The delusion that the German people can be annihilated has been destroyed. [*"Quite right!"—S.D.*] Our people are not to be annihilated any more than any other nation which defends its independence and self-reliance with all its strength. Until the bloody struggle has come to a close, we in Germany have the great task to fulfil that in any case the feeding of the people be made safe. Our people cannot be forced to their knees by hunger; that is our conviction. The food will have to be regulated without regard to special interests. Up to now much has been done amiss. We cannot save the Government this reproach. My "Fraktion" has already in the middle of August, and since then, continually drawn the attention of the Government to taking the necessary measures in conformity with this proposal. A timely embargo on wheat would have greatly increased our store of food. The high prices of bread-grains, . . . were not necessary. The timely slaughter and conserving of pigs would have saved great quantities of potatoes for human food. The unfortunate idea of establishing economical housekeeping by raising the price of potatoes deserves the strictest condemnation. [*Hearty assent by S.D.*]

The task of the Government is to make safe what food we have for the people, and to distribute it appropriately at moderate prices to the consumer. No interest should come before that of the consuming population. [*Approval by S.D.*] He who withholds food with the intention of profiteering should be dealt with severely and should be held in contempt by everybody. [*Applause by S.D.*] At a time when our best people are dying on the battlefields it is more than ever our duty to prevent the population which remains behind from becoming weak by underfeeding. It is more than ever our duty to see to it that a healthy, strong generation grows up. Besides other regulations, as for instance weekly assistance for women during confinement, it is necessary to procure food at moderate prices for the whole population, especially for the poorer classes. The increase of prices, which is not to be avoided anyhow, makes it a duty also to raise the money for this purpose. At the same time the law concerning the maintenance of military persons and their survivors will have to be amended. . . .

Gentlemen, never before has the Reichstag had its ordinary session in such difficult times as now. It has great tasks to accomplish. We shall strive to the end that effective and successful work may be rendered and that these tasks may be brought to a favorable solution. [*Lively applause by S.D.*]

⁊

9. Mutiny and Revolution in the German Fleet

Today's date is August 2. It is the third anniversary of the declaration of war on France and Russia. I tried to recapture the spirit of 1914 by recalling my impressions. The feverish excitement which then gripped our emotions has vanished completely. I still tremble whenever I think of the events of three years ago. Those who were the most enthusiastic supporters of the war are now to be found in the camp of the pessimists and defeatists. On August 2 we regarded such great events as the outbreak of a two-front war as unimportant in relation to the fateful question: what will England do? It seems almost incredible to remember that at the time we felt "that the war would be no fun without England."

However now the war is no fun even "with" England. All of us ought to beat our breasts and confess *mea culpa*. I am utterly convinced that England is no more responsible for the war than we. We provided England with the best rationale for its intervention by our injustice to Belgium.

All the statesmen who participated in igniting the powder keg are no longer in office. The Kaiser's well-intentioned servant, the honorable philosopher of Hohenfinnow,[1] resigned recently. He has been succeeded by a Bismarckian mind [Georg Michaelis], a man who is deadly earnest in [his intention to] obtain an early and honorable peace. In his most impressive speech he stated: "I do not know what will happen. But I cannot conceive of the misery resulting from an unexpected announcement that Germany does not have enough food to last until the next harvest!" These words from such an important source electrified all of Germany. He was Director of the War Wheat Control Administration. In my opinion, this is the only organization which has completely fulfilled its responsibilities without mismanagement. He is Germany's first bourgeois chancellor.

If I were called upon to render a medical diagnosis of the present state of feelings among the enlisted men, it would read something like this:

High state of excitement caused by a total lack of confidence in the officers. Persistence of the fixed notion that the war is conducted and prolonged solely in

VII.9   From Daniel Horn, *War, Mutiny and Revolution in the German Navy* (Brunswick, NJ: Rutgers University Press, 1967), 344–347, 420–427. Copyright © 1967 by Rutgers, the State University. Reprinted by permission of Rutgers University Press.

[1]Stumpf is referring to Chancellor Theobald von Bethmann-Hollweg (1909–1917).

the interests of the officers. Manifestations of bitter anger due to fact that the enlisted men are starving and suffering while the officers carouse and roll in money.

Is it therefore any wonder that the men should now inevitably turn to revolt as a means of improving their sordid lot? As far as I have been able to tell, the mutiny raged most strongly on the ships of the *Kaiser* class, especially on *Prinzregent Luitpold* and *König Albert*. Apparently the Captain bears most of the blame. He arrested a stoker for collecting subscriptions to *Vorwärts*.[2] The joint protests of two crews of stokers compelled the Captain to set him free again. The next morning the Captain was missing, his body was found later floating near the submarine nets. . . . No one knows what happened; whether it was murder, suicide, or an accident. At any rate, it constitutes a warning to all officers.

These unpleasant events were discussed at a commanders' meeting on the *Posen* on Friday morning. Afterward our Captain assembled the crew on deck and gave an explanation. Some very unfortunate things had occurred on *Prinzregent Luitpold*, he said. "Three days ago one of the watches was scheduled to go to the theater, but for some reason the production did not take place. Instead they were to see a film. As the showing began the projector failed to function properly. Since it was too late to start anything else, the next day's schedule was substituted. The men were marched to the drill field for military exercises. A large number of the crew refused to obey and left the field without permission. Later on, 350 of the men were found at Fort Schaar. They rested there, got hungry and returned to their ship. There is evidence that foreign agents were involved (outraged muttering from the men). At a time when thousands of your comrades lay down their lives for the Fatherland in Flanders and are about to drive the Russians out of Galicia, it is tragic that you should entertain such ideas. This is precisely what our enemies desire. Our internal dissension and hatreds will give them what they could not achieve in honorable battle. I feel sorry for these unfortunate, misguided people; they will suffer the full consequences of the law. Dismissed!". . .

How Did It Happen?

This question should not have been placed here, but at the beginning of my diary. By "it" I mean the mutiny or revolution, which is greeted with horror by most people, by many as the fulfillment of their ideals and by a small group as the reward for their work. Now the revolution has arrived! This morning I heard the first flutter of its wings. It came like lightning. Unexpectedly it descended with one fell swoop and now holds all of us in its grip.

Even though I was in the midst of things, I did not realize how quickly word spread this morning to "prepare to demonstrate on shore." The Division Officer, the First Officer and the Adjutant came down to our quarters and asked us in a crestfallen manner what it was that we wanted. We replied, "We have nothing against our officers. Nevertheless we shall parade in the streets to obtain our rights."

---

[2]The official newspaper of the Majority Socialist party.

However each one of us looked upon these "rights" as the fulfillment of his own wishes. Since things seemed to be getting interesting, I put on my parade uniform and went along. "I can't stop you," the First Officer commented with resignation.

Hardly any of the men stayed behind. At the Old Port Barracks a long line of marines armed with rifles stood assembled. At our approach they broke out in a loud shout of joy and gave three hurrahs. People streamed in from all sides. Within a matter of minutes a huge crowd of sailors had gathered on the parade grounds. Occasionally someone tried to address the crowd. At last we decided to march to the flagship in order to enlist its crew in our demonstration. The only interesting part of the entire story occurred at this point. A verbal duel ensued between the Captain of the ship and several spokesmen of the demonstrators. The crew of the *Baden*, which stood assembled on the top deck, would be the reward for the victor. Had the Captain been a reasonably accomplished speaker, our spokesmen would have been forced to depart without a single man. However both the deathly pale officer and the Sailors' Council handled themselves badly. Consequently roughly a third of the crew joined our ranks.

Later on I saw more. Since it was difficult to maintain order in the huge mob, loud calls for music rang out. The harbor band and several of us fetched our instruments and played the old military songs and marches. The mighty throng, more or less inspired [by the music] moved along the docks. At the Peterstrasse we were met by a forty-man patrol led by an officer. The men came over to our side with their weapons. It was very comical to watch the lieutenant when he realized suddenly that he was all alone. Because of the music we received large reinforcements from all directions. At first I thought that we would release the imprisoned sailors at the jail. But I soon realized that we lacked leadership and that the crowd was driven along by sheer mob instinct.

The great gate at the Marine Barracks was bolted. In an instant the gate was off its hinges. An elderly major blocked the way. He thrust a pistol against the first sailor who broke in. He was disarmed immediately, hands reached for his sword while others tried to tear off his epaulettes. My sympathy went out to this unfortunate man who courageously tried to do his duty, and disgust at such brutality rose in my throat. I felt like shaking his hand.

The seemingly endless procession moved along the sides of the great drill field and joined at the center. Hastily a speaker's platform was erected. Then all at once twenty men began to speak. It was an excellent opportunity to study the thoughtlessness of the mob in action. Even the most ridiculous demands were greeted with stormy applause. A demand to hang the Kaiser could easily have been pushed through. I must admit, however, that there were also repeated demands for order and discipline. This is somewhat encouraging. It indicates that the radical, irresponsible elements have not yet gained the upper hand. I hope it remains this way. Then I will not be sorry that I participated.

We next moved in the direction of the Torpedo Division. I was able to observe the gradual rise of bestiality [in the mob]. Every woman was greeted with coarse remarks and whistles. Incredibly red cloths waved in the air. In the place of a

banner someone carried a red bedsheet on a pole. It was certainly no great honor
to march behind this dirty rag. But because it was the first day of our new freedom
we gladly ignored these superficialities.

It was evident that we received little support from the townspeople in their windows. Surely the shortage of handkerchiefs alone could not have been responsible.
The townspeople understood quite well that the collapse of the fleet meant the
end of the growth of their city. In the future Wilhelmshaven will remain an
insignificant medium-sized town.

Relentlessly the procession moved across the drill field toward the Teichbrücke
and the torpedo boats. Everyone there applauded us but no one joined us
because—it was lunch time. When the mob began to grumble at this, a crew member yelled across to us: "Calm down, friends. We've put out the fires long ago, but
now we're having lunch." Lunch—everyone began to feel pangs of hunger. In nervous and planless haste we moved on.

An hour later we stood assembled in front of the Station Headquarters. A
statue of Admiral Coligzy [Coligny?], drawn dagger in hand, towered over us.
Breathless silence prevailed when a speaker arose from the crowd. He
announced that Admiral Krosigk had agreed to accept the demands of the Kiel
Sailors' Council. Rousing applause. "All political prisoners in the fortress are to
be released." The mob resisted: "We want all [prisoners] released, all! Down
with Kaiser Wilhelm." The speaker handled all these protests very effectively by
ignoring them.

Now a dockworker stepped up to speak. The man had a typical, classic criminal
face, I thought. Only from such a face could come the demand for the establishment of a "Soviet Republic." I felt sorry for the fellow even more so for the crowd
which applauded these stupidities.

When the first speaker rose again and suggested that we return to our posts
immediately, he was met with resounding laughter. But then everyone disappeared in the direction of the nearest kitchen. The revolution had triumphed
bloodlessly.

In order to stage a proper celebration, a great triumphal meeting was organized
the next day. Although the [rest of the] fleet had still not arrived and its attitude
was still questionable, we ignored these problems. Our representatives wrangled
throughout the night about which of them should be elected to the so-called
Council of Twenty-One. It was not a pretty scene. Naturally each of them wanted
to see his signature affixed to some proclamation, especially since no risk was
involved. Early the following morning a broadsheet listing all the gains we had
already made was distributed.

This time I scornfully refused to join the demonstration and went into town all by
myself. Things were even more hectic than on the previous days. This time most of
the demonstrators were civilians and shipyard workers, but I also noticed some officials and a sprinkling of deck officers without their swords. Red flags abounded and
they were in better condition than yesterday. In order to simplify the matter [of
identification] each of the flags indicated the organization it represented. The

procession lasted for twenty-eight minutes. A speaker in a flowing cloak and with gesticulating hands was already talking in the square. Could it be [Reichstag] Deputy Noske?[3] But no. In his first sentence I heard him say that the Reichstag deputies had accepted bribes from food speculators and the war profiteers. "I also know their names," shouted the speaker. "Yes, I know who they are. Deputy [Giesberts of the Centrist Party] is one of them." At that point I began to realize who had instigated the whole uproar. There was a long pause while the band played a few selections. In the meantime a Seaman First Class amused the gathering by reciting his family secrets and personal problems. Today a soldier's wife with her five children had been to see him. Her application for an increased allowance had been rejected. "All of you must be aware of whom I mean?" A voice from the rear, "The mayor!" "Yes, indeed, he is the one." (The same voice again) "Away with him! Away with him! Pfui, pfui!" echoed the voices of thousands in the audience. I was astonished at the patience of the crowd, for it allowed the loudmouth to repeat the story all over again. But when he attempted it for a third time, the band drowned him out ingloriously.

Thereupon a sailor stepped onto the platform and informed the "honorable party members, comrades and workers" that the principal objective [of the revolution] had thus far not been implemented and that the Kaiser and all the federal princes should herewith be deposed. "True, true!" they shouted to the sky with the same sort of fervor they had manifested over the misdeeds of the mayor. All those who accepted this demand were told to raise their right hands to signify their approval. About one half [of the people in the crowd] managed to raise their hands, the same hand which had once sworn loyalty and obedience to the head of state. Now I was overcome with disgust. I wandered around for a while longer and then departed.

While I was busy recording these impressions, a terrific noise interrupted my thoughts. Someone stuck his head through the door and bellowed: "All hands to receive rifles and ammunition!" I stopped the first man I met and asked. "What's going on? Why the rifles?" "Treason," he gasped, foaming with rage. "The loyalists are firing on us at Rüstringen!" Someone else shouted, "The Tenth Army Corps is marching against us. We shall shoot them down like dogs!" That I would like to see. The uproar was terrific. Everybody called for the Executive Officer and the armorer. Then the first men carrying rifles and bayonets came out. I said to myself, this means blood will be spilled; these people are absolutely insane. The streets were like a madhouse. Armed [men] ran through the gates from all directions: there were even a few women dragging cases of ammunition around. What madness! Is this the way it has to end? After five years of brutal fighting, shall we now turn our guns against our own countrymen? Since even the most reasonable and stable of the men I saw were in a state of semi-hysteria, only a miracle could prevent a disaster.

But the miracle occurred. With the same care of planning and direction that had gone into spreading the rumor, the "Soldiers' Council" now saw to it that order was restored. Men in cars and on bicycles spread the word that it had all been a

---

[3]Gustav Noske, who belonged to the right wing of the German Socialist party, was sent by the government in Berlin to quell the rebellion in the northern port city of Kiel.

"false alarm." Later on one of the representatives even admitted that this was merely a stratagem to obtain possession of the weapons. At any rate it was certainly not a proper way to behave. It was an unbelievably reckless playing with fire. By evening, however, everything was peaceful and quiet once more.

November 8, 1918

Within the past two days an unbelievable change has taken place within me. [I have been converted] from a monarchist into a devout republican. . . .

(I find that I can no longer devote even fifteen minutes to my work. Spectacular events occur in bewildering succession. This veritable witches' sabbath has completely upset my mental equilibrium. Never before has Wilhelmshaven looked like this! Thousands upon thousands of flaring rockets rise in the air, all the sirens howl, the searchlights gleam by the dozen, the ships' bells clang madly and the guns of the fort roar out their salute. This is really too much all at once.)

November 10, 1918

I think that the time has come for me to reorganize my thoughts. But since my mood keeps vacillating every hour between extreme exultation and deathlike despair, I find it extremely difficult to narrate my impressions and feelings in a sensible order. Although I wrote earlier that I have become a convinced republican, I came to regret my decision within a matter of hours.

November 10 may perhaps turn out to be the most significant day of this war. At least this is the way I felt on Sunday morning as I gazed down upon a mob of "a hundred thousand." For the first time I felt somewhat solemn. A springlike sun was shining and the happy and gay faces of the men indicated that they welcomed the arrival of the new era with open arms. Although the procession had already lasted two hours, a constant stream of new battalions of sailors and soldiers came streaming from the center of town. Amidst wild cheering Stoker First Class Kuhnt introduced himself as the first president of the Republic of Oldenburg. Low-flying aircraft dropped down bundles of handbills. To the thunderous applause of the mob, the huge Imperial war flag was lowered and the red flag of liberty, equality and fraternity rose up over the barracks. I could no longer resist and was swept along by the mass hysteria.

All my qualms of conscience evaporated when the Kaiser abdicated and my Bavaria proclaimed itself a Republic. I felt as if a heavy weight had suddenly been lifted from my heart, particularly when I learned that the revolutionary movement had spread to the French-Italian front. This automatically signified the conclusion of an armistice. The proletarians of all nations would embrace each other and the capitalists, of course, they would pay the price. . . . Was this not an exhilarating and an infectious prospect?

10. The Case for India

[T]he present movement in India will be very poorly understood if it be regarded only in connexion with the movement in the East. The awakening of Asia is part of a world-movement, which has been quickened into marvellous rapidity by the world-war. . . . In the East, the swift changes in Japan, the success of the Japanese Empire against Russia, the downfall of the Manchu dynasty in China and the establishment of a Chinese Republic, the efforts at improvement in Persia, hindered by the interference of Russia and Great Britain with their growing ambitions, and the creation of British and Russian "spheres of influence," depriving her of her just liberty, and now the Russian Revolution and the probable rise of a Russian Republic in Europe and Asia, have all entirely changed the conditions before existing in India. Across Asia, beyond the Himalayas, stretch free and self-ruling Nations. India no longer sees as her Asian neighbours the huge domains of a Tsar and a Chinese despot, and compares her condition under British rule with those of their subject populations. British rule profited by the comparison, at least until 1905, when the great period of repression set in. But in future, unless India wins Self-Government, she will look enviously at her Self-Governing neighbours, and the contrast will intensify her unrest.

But even if she gains Home Rule, as I believe she will, her position in the Empire will imperatively demand that she shall be strong as well as free. She becomes not only a vulnerable point in the Empire, as the Asian Nations evolve their own ambitions and rivalries, but also a possession to be battled for. Mr. Laing once said: "India is the milch-cow of England," a Kamadhenu, in fact, a cow of plenty; and if that view should arise in Asia, the ownership of the milch-cow would become a matter of dispute . . . Hence India must be capable of self-defence both by land and sea. There may be a struggle for the primacy of Asia, for supremacy in the Pacific, for the mastery of Australasia, to say nothing of the inevitable trade-struggles, in which Japan is already endangering Indian industry and Indian trade, while India is unable to protect herself.

In order to face these larger issues with equanimity, the Empire requires a contented, strong, self-dependent and armed India, able to hold her own and to aid the Dominions, especially Australia, with her small population and immense unoccupied and undefended area. India alone has the man-power which can effectively maintain the Empire in Asia, and it is a short-sighted, a criminally short-sighted, policy not to build up her strength as a Self-Governing State within the Commonwealth of Free Nations under the British Crown. The Englishmen in India talk loudly of their interests; what can this mere handful do to protect their interests against attack in the coming years? Only in a free and powerful India will they be safe. Those who read Japanese papers know how strongly, even during the War, they parade unchecked their pro-

VII.10   From Annie Besant, "The Case for India": The Presidential Address Delivered by Annie Besant at the Thirty-Second Indian National Congress Held at Calcutta, December 26, 1917, 12–14.

German sympathies, and how likely after the War is an alliance between these two ambitious and warlike Nations. Japan will come out of the War with her army and navy unweakened, and her trade immensely strengthened. Every consideration of sane statesmanship should lead Great Britain to trust India more than Japan, so that the British Empire in Asia may rest on the sure foundation of Indian loyalty, the loyalty of a free and contented people, rather than be dependent on the continued friendship of a possible future rival. For international friendships are governed by National interests, and are built on quicksands, not on rock. . . .

As the War went on, India slowly and unwillingly came to realize that the hatred of autocracy was confined to autocracy in the West, and that the degradation was only regarded as intolerable for men of white races; that freedom was lavishly promised to all except to India; that new powers were to be given to the Dominions, but not to India. India was markedly left out of the speeches of statesmen dealing with the future of the Empire, and at last there was plain talk of the White Empire, the Empire of the Five Nations, and the "coloured races" were lumped together as the wards of the White Empire, doomed to an indefinite minority. . . .

✑

11. Rebellion in Ireland

Poblacht na h-Eireann

The Provisional Government of the Irish republic to the people of Ireland

Irishmen and Irishwomen: In the name of God and of the dead generations from which she receives her old tradition of nationhood, Ireland, through us, summons her children to her flag and strikes for her freedom.

Having organized and trained her manhood through her secret revolutionary organization, the Irish Republican Brotherhood, and through her open military organizations, the Irish Volunteers, and the Irish Citizen Army, having patiently perfected her discipline, having resolutely waited for the right moment to reveal itself, she now seizes that moment, and, supported by her exiled children in America and by gallant allies in Europe, but relying in the first on her own strength, she strikes in full confidence of victory.

We declare the right of the people of Ireland to the ownership of Ireland, and to the unfettered control of Irish destinies, to be sovereign and indefeasible. The long usurpation of that right by a foreign people and government has not extinguished the right, nor can it ever be extinguished except by the destruction of the Irish people. In every generation the Irish people have asserted their right to national freedom and sovereignty; six times during the past three hundred years they have asserted it in arms. Standing on that fundamental right and again asserting it in arms in the face of the world, we hereby proclaim the Irish

VII.11   From *The Times*, May 1, 1916.

republic as a sovereign independent state, and we pledge our lives and the lives of our comrades-in-arms to the cause of its freedom, of its welfare, and of its exaltation among the nations.

The Irish republic is entitled to, and hereby claims, the allegiance of every Irishman and Irishwoman. The republic guarantees religious and civil liberty, equal rights and equal opportunities to all its citizens, and declares its resolve to pursue the happiness and prosperity of the whole nation and of all its parts, cherishing all the children of the nation equally, and oblivious of the differences carefully fostered by an alien government, which have divided a minority from the majority in the past.

Until our arms have brought the opportune moment for the establishment of a permanent national government, representative of the whole people of Ireland, and elected by the suffrages of all her men and women, the Provisional Government, hereby constituted, will administer the civil and military affairs of the republic in trust for the people. We place the cause of the Irish republic under the protection of the Most High God, whose blessing we invoke upon our arms, and we pray that no one who serves that cause will dishonour it by cowardice, inhumanity, or rapine. In this supreme hour the Irish nation must, by its valour and discipline, and by the readiness of its children to sacrifice themselves for the common good, prove itself worthy of the august destiny to which it is called.

Signed on behalf of the provisional government,

Thomas J. Clarke, Sean MacDiarmada, Thomas MacDonagh, P. H. Pearse, Eamonn Ceannt, James Connolly, Joseph Plunkett

Revolution in Russia

Although many European socialists initially supported the war, some remained adamantly opposed from the outset. In stark contrast to the German SPD's willingness to grant war credits stands the strong condemnation of such actions by the Russian Bolshevik leader V.I. Lenin. Lenin was the most uncompromising and influential theorist in Russian social democracy, an eminence that forced him to spend much of the war in exile. He returned to Russia only after the February Revolution in 1917. Surveillance, oppression, and exile were tactics that the Russian state had employed against its sharpest critics for some time, but could it withstand similar opposition from the more moderate parties? A defining moment came on 1 November 1916 when Paul Miliukov, the leader of the Constitutional Democrats (a moderate liberal party of professionals and academics) pilloried the government (and by extension the whole tasarist regime) in a devastating speech for its inept prosecution of the war. After each major point, he asked his audience whether those mistakes were the result of stupidity or treason. Either way, the answer pointed to a rapidly growing sense of mistrust or disgust that undercut the state's ability to survive. Even with the tsar's overthrow in St. Petersburg/Petrograd, however, a solution proved elusive, and the cumbersome division of authority between a constitutional government and direct soldiers' and workers' councils was enshrined in the notorious Order #1. Its substance and repercussions are outlined in the third selection, by General Anton Denikin, whose analysis of the Eastern Front we have already encountered. Some idea of what the revolution entailed at the front, as seen from the perspective of a soldier, is provided by the final extract, a continuation of the odyssey of Maria Botchkareva, a female soldier in the Russian ranks.

12. Lenin's View of the War

1. The European and World War has the sharp and definite character of a bourgeois, imperialist, and dynastic war. The struggle for markets and the looting of countries, the intention to deceive, disunite, and kill off the proletarians of all countries, by instigating the hired slaves of one nation against the hired slaves of the other for the benefit of the bourgeoisie—such is the only real meaning and purpose of the war.

2. The conduct of the leaders of the German Social Democratic party of the Second International (1889–1914)—who have voted the war budget and who repeat the bourgeois chauvinist phrases of the Prussian Junkers [arch-conservative Prussian landowners] and of the bourgeoisie—is a direct betrayal of socialism. In no case, even assuming an absolute weakness of that party and the necessity of submitting to the will of the bourgeois majority of the nation, can the conduct of the leaders of the German Social Democratic party be justified. In fact, this party leads at present a national liberal policy.

3. The conduct of the leaders of the Belgian and French Social Democratic parties, who have betrayed socialism by entering bourgeois cabinets, deserves the same condemnation.

4. The betrayal of socialism by the majority of the leaders of the Second International (1889–1914) means an ideological collapse of that International. The fundamental cause of this collapse is the actual predominance in it of petty-bourgeois opportunism, the bourgeois nature and danger of which has long been pointed out by the best representatives of the proletariat of all

VII.12   From Olga Hess Gankin and H.H. Fisher, eds., *The Bolsheviks and the World War: The Origin of the Third International* (Stanford: Stanford University Press, 1940), 140–143. Copyright © 1940 by the Board of the Trustees of the Leland Stanford Junior University, renewed 1968. All rights reserved. Used with the permission of Stanford University Press. www.sup.org.

countries. Opportunists have long been preparing the collapse of the Second International by renouncing the socialist revolution and substituting bourgeois reformism for it; by renouncing class struggle, with its transformation into civil war, which is necessary at certain moments; by preaching bourgeois chauvinism under the guise of patriotism and defense of the fatherland and by ignoring or renouncing the ABC truth of socialism, expressed long ago in the "Communist manifesto," that workers have no fatherland; by confining themselves in the struggle against militarism to a sentimental Philistine point of view instead of recognizing the necessity of a revolutionary war of the pro-letarians of all countries against the bourgeoisie of all countries; by turning the necessity to utilize bourgeois parliamentarism and bourgeois legality into a fetish and forgetting that illegal forms of organization and agitation are imperative during epochs of crises. One of the organs of international oppor-tunism, the *Socialist Monthly*, which has long taken the national-liberal stand, is right in celebrating its victory over European socialism.

5. Of the bourgeois and chauvinist sophisms by which the bourgeois parties and governments of the two chief rival nations of the continent, Germany and France, are especially fooling the masses, and which are being slavishly repeated by the socialist opportunists trailing behind the bourgeoisie (the open as well as the covert opportunists), the following should be especially noted and branded: when the German bourgeoisie refers to the defense of the fatherland, to the struggle against Tsarism, to the protection of the freedom of cultural and national development, they lie; for the Prussian Junkerdom, headed by Wilhelm II, and also the big bourgeoisie, have always pursued the policy of defending the Tsarist monarchy, and whatever the outcome of the war, they will not fail to direct their efforts toward supporting that monarchy; they lie, for, in fact, the Austrian bourgeoisie has undertaken a plunder march against Serbia, the German bourgeoisie oppresses the Danes, the Poles and the French (in Alsace-Lorraine) by waging an aggressive war against Belgium and France for the sake of robbing the richer and freer countries, by organizing the onslaught at the moment considered by them to be the most convenient for utilizing their latest improvements of military technique, and on the eve of the introduction of the so-called big military program by Russia. Similarly, when the French bour-geoisie refer to the defense of the fatherland, etc., they also lie; for in reality they defend countries which are backward in their capitalist technique and which develop more slowly, by hiring with their billions the Black Hundred gangs of Russian Tsarism to wage war for the purpose of plundering Austrian and German territories. Neither of the two belligerent groups of nations is behind the other in the cruelty and barbarism of waging war.

6. The task of Social Democracy in Russia consists in the first place in a merciless and ruthless struggle against the Great Russian and Tsarist-monar-chist chauvinism, and against the sophistic defense of this chauvinism by Rus-sian liberals, Constitutional Democrats, and others and by some of the *Narodniks* [populists]. From the point of view of the laboring class and the

toiling masses of all the peoples of Russia, the lesser evil would be the defeat of the Tsarist monarchy and its army which oppresses Poland, the Ukraine, and a number of other peoples of Russia and which inflames national hatred for the purpose of strengthening the oppression of other nationalities by the Great Russians and for the stabilization of the reaction and the barbarous government of the Tsarist monarchy.

7. The slogans of Social Democracy at the present time should be: First, a thorough propaganda (to be spread also in the army and the area of military activity) for a socialist revolution and for the necessity of turning the weapons not against brothers, hired slaves of other countries, but against the reaction of the bourgeois governments and parties of all countries—to carry on such propaganda in all languages it is absolutely necessary to organize illegal cells and groups in the armies of all nations—a merciless struggle against chauvinism and the "patriotism" of petty townsmen and against the bourgeoisie of all countries without exception. It is imperative to appeal to the revolutionary conscience of the working masses, which carry the heavy burden of the war and which are hostile to chauvinism and opportunism, against the leaders of the contemporary International, who have betrayed socialism. Second—as one of the immediate slogans—agitation in favor of German, Polish, Russian, and other republics, along with the transformation of all the separate states of Europe into a republican united states.

$$\infty$$

13. Stupidity or Treason?

What a difference, gentlemen, there is now, in the 27th month of the war! A difference which is especially striking to me, after several months spent abroad. We are now facing new difficulties, and these difficulties are not less complex and serious, not less profound, than those that confronted us in the spring of last year. The Government needed heroic measures to combat the general disorganization of the national economy.

We ourselves are the same as before; we, in this 27th month of the war, are the same as we were in the tenth and in the first month. And heretofore, we are striving for complete victory; as heretofore, we are prepared to make all the necessary sacrifices; and, as heretofore, we are anxious to preserve our national unity. But, I must say this candidly: there is a difference in the situation. We have lost faith in the ability of this Government to achieve victory . . . because, as far as this Government is concerned, neither the attempts at correction nor the attempts at improvement, which we have made here, have proved successful.

VII.13   From Frank Golder, ed., *Documents of Russian History, 1914–1917* (Gloucester, MA: Peter Smith, 1964), 154–155, 164–165.

All the Allied Powers have summoned to the support of the Government the best men of all parties, all the confidence, and all those organizing elements present in their countries, which are better organized than our own. What has our own Government accomplished? Our declaration has told that. When there was formed in the Fourth Duma a majority [Progressive Bloc], which the Duma lacked before, a majority ready to vote its confidence in a cabinet worthy of such confidence, then nearly all those men who might in some slight degree have expected confidence were forced, systematically, every one of them, to leave the cabinet. And, if we have formerly said that our Government had neither the knowledge nor the ability which were indispensable at the moment, we say now, gentlemen, that this present Government has sunk beneath the level on which it stood in the normal times of Russian life. . . . And now the gulf between us and that Government has grown wider and impassible. . . .

Today we see and understand that with this Government we cannot legislate, any more than we can, with this Government, lead Russia to victory. . . . Formerly, we tried to prove that it was impossible to start a fight against all the vital forces of the nation, that it was impossible to carry on warfare within the country when there was war at the front, that it was necessary to utilize the popular enthusiasm for the achievement of national tasks, and that otherwise there could be only killing oppression, which would merely increase the very peril they were trying to avert by such oppression. . . .

And, does it matter, gentlemen, as a practical question, whether we are, in the present case, dealing with stupidity or treason? When the Duma keeps everlastingly insisting that the rear must be organized for a successful struggle, the Government persists in claiming that organizing the country means organizing a revolution, and deliberately prefers chaos and disorganization. What is it, stupidity or treason? . . . Furthermore, gentlemen, when the authorities, in the midst of this general discontent and irritation, deliberately set to work stirring up popular outbreaks,—is that being done unconsciously or consciously? We cannot, therefore, find much fault with the people if they arrive at conclusions such as I have read here . . .

You must realize, also, why it is that we, too, have no other task left us today, than the task which I have already pointed out to you: to obtain the retirement of this Government. You ask, "How can we start a fight while the war is on?" But, gentlemen, it is only in wartime that they are a menace. They are a menace to the war, and it is precisely for this reason, in time of war and in the name of war, for the sake of that very thing which induced us to unite, that we are now fighting them.

14. Upheaval in Petrograd and in the Army

The first outbreak began on February 23rd, when crowds filled the streets, meetings were held, and the speakers called for a struggle against the hated power. This lasted till the 26th, when the popular movement assumed gigantic proportions and there were collisions with the police, in which machine-guns were brought into action. On the 26th an ukaze was received proroguing the Duma, and on the morning of the 27th the members of the Duma decided not to leave Petrograd. On the same morning the situation underwent a drastic change, because the rebels were joined by the Reserve battalions of the Litovski, Volynski, Preobrajenski, and Sapper Guards' Regiments. They were Reserve battalions, as the real Guards' Regiments were then on the South-Western Front. These battalions did not differ, either in discipline or spirit, from any other unit of the line. In several battalions the Commanding Officers were disconcerted, and could not make up their minds as to their own attitude. This wavering resulted, to a certain extent, in a loss of prestige and authority. The troops came out into the streets without their officers, mingled with the crowds, and were imbued with the crowds' psychology. Armed throngs, intoxicated with freedom, excited to the utmost, and incensed by street orators, filled the streets, smashed the barricades, and new crowds of waverers joined them. Police detachments were mercilessly slaughtered. Officers who chanced to be in the way of the crowds were disarmed and some of them killed. The armed mob seized the arsenal, the Fortress of Peter and Paul, and the Kresti Prison. . . .

ON THE FIRST OF MARCH THE SOVIET OF WORKMEN AND SOLDIERS' DELEGATES ISSUED AN ORDER OF THE DAY No. I., WHICH PRACTICALLY LED TO THE TRANSFER OF ACTUAL MILITARY POWER TO THE SOLDIERS' COMMITTEES, TO A SYSTEM OF ELECTIONS AND TO THE DISMISSAL OF COMMANDING OFFICERS BY THE MEN. THAT ORDER OF THE DAY GAINED WIDE AND PAINFUL NOTORIETY AND GAVE THE FIRST IMPETUS TO THE COLLAPSE OF THE ARMY.

ORDER No. I.

March 1st, 1917. To the Garrison of the Petrograd District, to all Guardsmen, soldiers of the line, of the Artillery, and of the Fleet, for immediate and strict observance, and to the workmen of Petrograd for information. The Soviet of Workmen and Soldiers' Delegates has decreed:

(1) That Committees be elected of representatives of the men in all companies, battalions, regiments, parks, batteries, squadrons and separate services of various military institutions, and on the ships of the fleet.

VII.14   From General Anton I. Denikin, *The Russian Turmoil* (London: Hutchinson, 1922), 40, 61–62.

(2) All military units not yet represented on the Soviet of Workmen's Delegates to elect one representative from each company. These representatives to provide themselves with written certificates and to report to the Duma at 10 a.m. on March 2nd.

(3) In all its political activities the military unit is subordinate to the Soviet, and to its Committees.

(4) The Orders of the Military Commission of the Duma are to be obeyed only when they are not in contradiction with the orders and decrees of the Soviet.

(5) All arms—rifles, machine-guns, armoured cars, etc.—are to be at the disposal and under the control of Company and Battalion Committees, and should never be handed over to the officers even should they claim them.

(6) On parade and on duty the soldiers must comply with strict military discipline; but off parade and off duty, in their political, social and private life, soldiers must suffer no restriction of the rights common to all citizens. In particular, saluting when off duty is abolished.

(7) Officers are no longer to be addressed as "Your Excellency," "Your Honour," etc. Instead, they should be addressed as "Mr. General," "Mr. Colonel," etc. Rudeness to soldiers on the part of all ranks, and in particular addressing them in the second person singular, is prohibited, and any infringement of this regulation and misunderstandings between officers and men are to be reported by the latter to the Company Commanders.

(Signed) The Petrograd Soviet.

15. Revolution at the Front

The first swallow to warn us of the approaching storm was a soldier from our Company who had returned from a leave of absence at Petrograd.

"Oh, my! If you but knew, boys, what is going on in the rear! Revolution! Everywhere they talk of overthrowing the Tsar. The capital is aflame with revolution."

These words spread like wildfire among the men. They gathered in knots and discussed the possibilities of the report. Would it mean peace? Would they get land and freedom? Or would it mean another huge offensive before the end of the war? The arguments, of course, took place in whispers, behind the backs of the officers. The consensus of opinion seemed to be that revolution meant preparation for a general attack against the Germans to win a victory before the conclusion of peace.

VII.15 From Maria Botchkareva, *Yashka: My Life as Peasant, Officer and Exile* (New York: Frederick Stokes, 1919), 139–145.

For several days the air was charged with electricity. Everybody felt that earth-quaking events were taking place and our hearts echoed the distant rumblings of the raging tempest. There was something reticent about the looks and manners of the officers, as if they kept important news to themselves.

Finally, the joyous news arrived. The Commander gathered the entire Regiment to read to us the glorious words in the first manifesto, together with the famous Order No. 1. The miracle had happened! Tsarism, which enslaved us and thrived on the blood and marrow of the toiler, had fallen. Freedom, Equality and Brotherhood! How sweet were these words to our ears! We were transported. There were tears of joy, embraces, dancing. It all seemed a dream, a wonderful dream. Who ever believed that the hated regime would be destroyed so easily and in our own time?

The Commander read to us the manifesto, which concluded with a fervent appeal to us to hold the line with greater vigilance than ever, now that we were free citizens, to defend our newly won liberty from the attacks of the Kaiser and his slaves. Would we defend our freedom? A multitude of throats shouted in a chorus, that passed over No Man's Land and reverberated in the German trenches, "Yes, we will!"

Would we swear allegiance to the Provisional Government, which wanted us to prepare to drive the Germans out of Free Russia before we returned home to divide the land?

"We swear!" thundered thousands of men, raising their right hands, and thoroughly alarming the enemy.

Then came Order No. 1, signed by the Petrograd Soviet of Workmen and Soldiers. Soldiers and officers were now equal, it declared. All the citizens of the Free Russia were equal henceforth. There would be no more discipline. The hated officers were enemies of the people and should no longer be obeyed and kept at their posts. The common soldier would now rule the army. Let the rank and file elect their best men and institute committees; let there be Company, Regimental, Corps and Army committees.

We were dazzled by this shower of brilliant phrases. The men went about as if intoxicated. For four days the festival continued unabated, so wild with the spirit of jubilation were the boys. The Germans could not at first understand the cause of our celebration. When they learned it they ceased firing.

There were meetings, meetings and meetings. Day and night the Regiment seemed to be in continuous session, listening to speeches that dwelt almost exclusively on the words of peace and freedom. The men were hungry for beautiful phrases and gloated over them.

All duty was abandoned in the first few days. While the great upheaval had affected me profoundly, and the first day or two I shared completely the ecstasy of the men, I awoke early to a sense of responsibility. I gathered from the manifestoes and speeches that what was demanded of us was to hold the line with much more energy than before. Wasn't this the concrete significance for us of the Revolution? To my questions the soldiers replied affirmatively, but had no power of will to tear themselves away from the magic circle of speech-making and visions. Still dazed, they appeared to me like lunatics at large. The front became a veritable insane asylum.

One day, in the first week of the revolution, I ordered a soldier to take up duty at the listening-post. He refused.

"I will take no orders from a *baba*," he snorted, "I can do as I please. We have freedom now."

I was painfully stunned. Why, this very same soldier would have gone through fire for me a week before. And now he was sneering at me. It seemed so incredible. It was overwhelming.

"Ha, ha," he railed. "You can go yourself."

Flushed with chagrin, I seized a rifle and answered:

"Can I? I will show you how a free citizen ought to guard his freedom!"

And I climbed over the top and made my way to the listening-post where I remained on duty for the full two hours.

I talked to the soldiers, appealing to their sense of honor and arguing that the revolution imposed greater responsibilities upon the man in the ranks. They agreed that the defense of the country was the most important task confronting us. But didn't the revolution bring them also freedom, with the injunction to create their own control of the army, and the abolition of discipline? The men were in a high state of enthusiasm, but obedience was contrary to their ideas of liberty. Seeing that I could not get my men to perform their duties, I went to the Commander of the Company and asked to be released from the army and sent home.

"I see no good in sticking here and doing nothing," I said. "If this is war, then I want to be out of it. I can't get my men to do anything."

"Have you gone insane, Yashka?" the Commander asked. "Why, if you, who are a peasant yourself, one of them, beloved by all the rank and file, can't remain, then what should we officers do? It is the obligation of the service that-we stay to the last, till the men awake. I am having my own troubles, Yashka," he confided, in a low voice. "I can't have my way, either. So you see, we are all in the same boat. We have got to stick it out."

It was abhorrent to my feelings, but I remained. Little by little things improved. The soldiers' committees began to function, but did not interfere with the purely military phases of our life. Those of the officers who had been disliked by the men, or who had had records typical of Tsaristic officials, disappeared with the revolution. Even Colonel Stubendorf, the Commander of the Regiment, was gone, retiring perhaps because of his German name. Our new Commander was Kudriavtzev, a popular officer.

Discipline was gradually reestablished. It was not the old discipline. Its basis was no longer dread of punishment. It was a discipline founded on the high sense of responsibility that was soon instilled into the gray mass of soldiery. True, there was no fighting between us and the enemy. There were even the beginnings of the fraternization plague that later destroyed the mighty Russian Army. But the soldiers responded to the appeals from the Provisional Government and the Soviet in the early weeks of the spring of 1917. They were ready to carry out unflinchingly any order from Petrograd.

Those were still the days of immense possibilities. The men worshipped the distant figures in the rear who had brought them the boon of liberty and equality. We knew almost nothing of the various parties and factions. Peace was the sole thought of the men. They were told that peace could not come without defeating or overthrowing the Kaiser. We, therefore, all expected the word for a general advance. Had that word been given at that time nothing in the world could have withstood our pressure. Nothing. The revolution had given birth to elemental forces in our hearts that defied and ever will defy description.

Then there began a pilgrimage of speakers. There were delegates from the army, there were members of the Duma, there were emissaries of the Petrograd Soviet. Almost every day there was a meeting, and almost every other day there were elections. We sent delegates to Corps Headquarters and delegates to Army Headquarters, delegates to a congress in Petrograd and delegates to consult with the Government. The speakers were almost all eloquent. They painted beautiful pictures of Russia's future, of universal brotherhood, of happiness and prosperity. The soldiers' eyes would light up with the glow of hope. More than once even I was caught by those enticing traps of eloquence. The rank and file were carried away to an enchanted land by the orators and rewarded them with tremendous ovations.

There were speakers of a different kind, too. These solemnly appealed for a realization of the immediate duty which the revolution imposed upon the shoulders of the army. Patriotism was their keynote. They called us to defend our country, to be ready at any moment for an attack to drive the Germans out and win the much-desired victory and peace. The soldiers responded to these calls to duty with equal enthusiasm. They were ready, they would swear. Was there any doubt that they were? No. The Russian soldier loved his Mother Country before. He loved her a hundred-fold now.

The first signs of spring arrived. The rivers had broken, the ice fields had thawed. It was muddy, but the earth was fragrant. The winds were laden with intoxicating odors. They were carrying across the vast fields and valleys of Mother-Russia tidings of a new era. There was spring in our souls. It seemed that our long-suffering people and country were being born for a new life, and one wanted to live, live, live.

But there, a few hundred feet away, were the Germans. They were not free. Their souls did not commune with God. Their hearts knew not the immense joy of this unusual spring. They were still slaves, and they would not let us alone in our freedom. They stretched themselves over the fair lands of our country and would not retire. They had to be removed before we could embark upon a life of peace. We were ready to remove them. We were awaiting the order to leap at their throats and show them what Free Russia could do. But why was the order postponed? Why wait? Why not strike while the iron was hot?

Yet the iron was allowed to cool. There was an ocean of talk in the rear; there was absolute inactivity at the front. And as hours grew into days and days into weeks there sprang forth out of this inactivity the first sprouts of fraternization.

"Come over here for a drink of tea!" a voice from our trenches would address itself across No Man's Land to the Germans. And voices from there would respond:

"Come over here for a drink of vodka!"

For several days they did not go beyond such mutual summons. Then one morning a soldier from our midst came out openly into No Man's Land, announcing that he wanted to talk things over. He stopped in the center of the field, where he was met by a German and engaged in an argument. From both sides soldiers flocked to the debaters.

"Why do you continue the war?" asked our men. "We have thrown over the Tsar and we want peace, but your Kaiser insists on war. Throw over your Kaiser and then both sides will go home."

"You don't know the truth," answered the German. "You are deceived. Why, our Kaiser offered peace to all the Allies last winter. But your Tsar refused to make peace. And now your Allies are forcing Russia to continue in the war. We are always ready for peace."

I was with the soldiers in No Man's Land and saw how the German argument impressed them. Some of the Germans had brought vodka along and gave it to our boys.

VIII

Legacies

How should societies memorialize the sacrifice of the fallen and honor the service of those who survived? Which elements from the war should they choose to recall, to inscribe in the public, collective memory, and which should be permitted to languish in oblivion? With these questions in mind, we can appreciate that contemporaries' search for answers was neither simple nor straightforward. The war's immediate legacy, after all, was multi-faceted. If it evoked painful images of death, destruction and suffering, it also inspired ideals of comradeship, patriotism and sacrifice.

While much of the grieving process was deeply private, commemoration was conducted in public. The First World War unleashed a new-found devotion to war memory with the erection of memorials and museums in Australia, Belgium, Canada, France, New Zealand, the UK, and the USA. Their purpose was to serve as permanent reminders to future generations that the war had promoted national unity and shared personal experiences. Tangible items such as personal diaries, letters, literature, photos and even battle gear—ephemera that would survive well after the last veterans passed—would ensure that a personal connection to the conflict would not simply fade away. Memorials and museums also provided a specific context, and a consecrated space, in which to enact rituals of remembrance such as the moments of silence on Armistice Day. By highlighting certain aspects of the war, these commemorative spaces and rituals shaped a particular understanding of the war, one that accorded with the concerns we have explored in Chapter VI. The cultural historian, George Mosse, commented that "those concerned with the image and the continuing appeal of the nation worked at constructing a myth which would draw the sting from death in war and emphasize the meaningfulness of the fighting and sacrifice," and in so doing would "make an inherently unpalatable past acceptable, important not just for the

Empires, Soldiers, and Citizens: A World War I Sourcebook, Second Edition.
Edited by Marilyn Shevin-Coetzee and Frans Coetzee.
© 2013 John Wiley & Sons, Ltd. except sources 1 to 11. Published 2013 by John Wiley & Sons, Ltd.

purpose of consolation but above all for the justification of the nation in whose name the war had been fought."

In contrast to this carefully cultivated image (some would say 'myth') of a popular and unimpeachably good war, an increasingly powerful contrasting view of the war as tragedy began to take hold. It emerged with particular force a decade or so after the fighting stopped, but the first outlines of this alternate perspective were already apparent during the war. France's Henri Barbusse was among the more celebrated wartime authors to challenge French censors and the government's sanitized version of war. A journalist and published author before the outbreak of the war, Barbusse wrote the novel *Under Fire* (*Le Feu*) from the trenches. Published in 1916, Barbusse's portrayal of the horrors of war was so compelling that his style has been compared subsequently to that of the great realist Emile Zola. The novel's antiwar message and its sympathy with the fate of all soldiers, including those of the enemy, reflected the author's socialist sympathies and underscored his conviction that wars waged for the sake of nationalism and imperialism were immoral and unjust.

Among those who followed the trail blazed by Barbusse were Roland Dorgelès, who fought as a corporal and published his version of trench warfare as *Wooden Crosses* in 1919, and the physician with a literary penchant, Georges Duhamel, who produced two novels, *The New Book of Martyrs* (1917) and *Civilisation 1914–1917* (1918), based on his four years as a medical officer in the French army. Romain Rolland remained true to his original pacifist outlook, choosing to stay in Switzerland for the duration of the conflict, where he assisted the Red Cross in ministering to prisoners of war. He wrote numerous journal articles decrying France's participation in the war, many of which are collected in *Above the Battle*.

The antiwar literary perspective took somewhat longer to emerge in Britain and Germany, but when it did, it rapidly became, at least in Britain, the most influential stance. Literary historian Paul Fussell has argued that this mode, emphasizing irony above all else (and thus the absurdity of the war), became the dominant form in modern British literature, and by extension, the decisive influence in modernist thought. The immediate question is just how representative the more famous British writers, such as Edmund Blunden, Rupert Brooke, Robert Graves, Wilfred Owen, and Siegfried Sassoon, who were predominantly middle-class, actually were. After all, the armed services themselves were overwhelmingly working-class.

Female authors left their recollections as well, as in Vera Brittain's haunting *Testament of Youth* and Helen Zenna Smith's provocative *Not So Quiet*, which convey the anguish of war for women and men alike. Written in 1933, *Testament of Youth* records Brittain's experiences as a volunteer nurse in London, Malta, and France. Brittain abandoned her dream of attending Somerville College, Oxford, to enlist in the nursing corps; although she considered herself a pacifist, socialist, and feminist, the diaries she kept revealed her elitist and even patriotic side. Nonetheless. *Testament of Youth* illustrates the reconstruction of gender relations in wartime Britain. Although less known than Brittain, Evadne Price, who wrote under the name Helen Zenna Smith, in *Not So Quiet* (1930) produced an intriguing novel recounting the wartime experiences of six English female field ambulance drivers. The French accorded the book, which they believed "promoted international peace," one of their most prestigious literary awards.

Surely the work above all that came to encapsulate the authentic war experience, and to distill its meaning for subsequent generations was Erich Maria Remarque's *All Quiet on the Western Front* (1928). In stark contrast to Ernst Jünger's ode to war, *Storm of Steel*, Remarque exposed the futility of war. He condemned the conflict not only for inflicting physical scars on Germany's youth but also for spawning a "Lost Generation" of young men, who were subsequently alienated from the corrupt political and social order for which they had fought. *All Quiet on the Western Front* was based in part on its author's limited war experience. In 1916, at the age of eighteen, Remarque was conscripted, subsequently wounded, and sent to recuperate in a military hospital, where he spent the remainder of the war. Despite his limited military duty, he clearly saw death all around him, a theme omnipresent in the novel. In its poignant conclusion, the narrator is killed on a day so uneventful (thereby rendering his death meaningless) that officially "nothing new" occurred on the Western Front.

Artists, too, found ways of portraying the modernity and anonymity of the conflict, as in the cubist influence on camouflage and the paintings of C.R.W. Nevinson, with their disconcerting angular forms. But, as historian Jay Winter has reminded us, many other writers or artists sought to make sense of the conflict, or come to terms with it, by employing more traditional forms and motifs. In France, for example, the *Images d'Epinal* (almost a form of comic strip) were a highly popular visual rendition of the war, and the images of knights and damsels testified to a persistent sentimentality that was not simply superseded by a more caustic resort to irony. In art and literature, as in other aspects of life, the war both exercised a modernizing influence and reinforced more traditional inclinations. Where the line between the two would be drawn, or whether a balance would be struck, depended on the differing contexts and the issues in question.

The war's impact was impossible to avoid. Its effects persisted long after the guns fell silent. Despite the widespread desire for a "return to normalcy," voiced in American President Warren Harding's famous (and mangled) phrase, efforts to resume life as though nothing had changed over the past four years were as illusory as those undertaken by the architects of the Restoration after the defeat of Napoleon a century before.

No issue received greater attention (or subsequent condemnation) than efforts to fashion a lasting peace settlement. Germany's military collapse occurred rapidly in late-1918 after four years of war fought almost exclusively on foreign soil. The collapse lent apparent credence to the utterly unjustified accusation that German soldiers had not lost the war but had been "stabbed in the back" by pacifist politicians and profit-hungry financiers who "lacked the stomach" to continue the conflict. Thus, even before a peace conference convened, politicians faced a difficult task in forging an agreement acceptable to all victors.

The peacemakers—or, more accurately, the victors, for Germany was only summoned to *accept* a treaty—met in Paris to settle the framework for postwar Europe. In attempting to do so, they were guided by their interpretation of the war's origins. In practice, that meant recognizing the rights of subject nationalities to self-determination (nationalist and ethnic rivalry having destabilized southeastern Europe and prompted the July crisis) and stripping the defeated Germany (presumed to have been the principal aggressor) of its colonial empire and much of its military capacity. The result was a redrawn map of Europe from which the collapsed Austro-Hungarian and Ottoman empires disappeared. A series of new states arose in eastern Europe that, the peacemakers anticipated, might also provide a buffer between democratic Europe and Soviet Russia. In retrospect, these new states were often divided by ethnic rivalries and proved too small to withstand German and Soviet expansion in the late 1930s.

The enormous cost of the war and the prospect of tangible rewards for cooperating in the war effort (in response to an appeal by governments seeking to preserve morale) encouraged the discussion of reparations, namely, financial restitution to be paid to the victors by the losers. While not a new concept—reparations had figured, for example, in the settlement of the Franco-Prussian war in 1871—they took on a particular importance in the Versailles treaty. The famous "War Guilt" clause 231 assigned Germany full responsibility for the war's outbreak and for the damages incurred in its conduct. Clause 231 unwittingly strengthened the hand of German extremists who contended that the Allies maintained a double standard in their care to recognize the rights of nationalities in so many cases but their eagerness to trample on those of the Germans. Assigning Germany the financial burden of the war proved both unrealistic (though the extent of that burden has often been exaggerated because the required payments were scaled back and then further reduced by the ravages of inflation) and unwise in saddling that nation's first democratic government, the Weimar Republic, with an economic and emotional albatross.

Just as the immediate impact of the war reached far beyond the battlefields, so too its legacy stretched beyond the Versailles settlement. Issues of religion, gender, the work ethic, the nature of authority, social conventions, and moral and civic responsibilities all collided on the battlefields and the home fronts. If the First World War initiated change with respect to international relations and geographic boundaries, it also reinforced or accelerated political and social trends already underway before August 1914. For example, states now bore even heavier social responsibilities, including the payment of veterans' pensions. The entry of women in the workplace, a crisis of masculinity, and social and religious discrimination all quickened as a result of the war.

In the end, Sir Edward Grey's prophecy on 4 August 1914 proved correct, for the lamps of European civilization as he had known it were not relit within his lifetime. The war proved to be a watershed in European affairs. Most nations' economies had suffered harsh blows from which they could not fully recover, as would be revealed in the prolonged fiscal crisis from 1929 onward. Liquidated investments, accumulated debts, and disrupted trade patterns all bore witness to the conflict's dislocating effects. But in a deeper philosophical sense, too, the war had changed something. Liberalism, which seemed so confident of progress over the course of the long nineteenth century, appeared powerless to deal with the postwar realities of the twentieth. Promoting the rational mediation of disputes had not forestalled the war (as again it would not in 1939) and the elevation of the responsible, sovereign individual as the basic unit of society withered in the face of the slaughter and a vast extension of state authority. After 1918, ideologies extolling group identities, collective action, and the liberating role of violence proved the more influential, most notably fascism and communism.

Finally, the entry of the United States into the conflict and its crucial financial role in the war and the postwar settlement reflected a shifting of gravity in political and economic affairs. Despite persistently strong isolationist sentiment at home, the United States was now inextricably linked to Europe. If one appreciates the importance of the war in hastening revolution in Russia, it becomes clear how the polarization of European superpowers in the aftermath of the Second World War owed so much to the impact of the First. In that sense, too, perhaps in a way Grey did not anticipate, Europe would never look the same again.

***

Shortly after the conclusion of the armistice in November 1918, an Imperial War Graves Commission assembled in London to discuss plans for the erection of war cemeteries in France to honor British and imperial soldiers. To reconcile its members' divergent opinions on this matter, the commission appointed the director of the British Museum, Sir Frederic Kenyon, to advise them on the aesthetic and religious concerns related to the construction of the cemeteries. Kenyon's recommendations follow, based on his observations of French cemeteries and discussions with military and religious officials as well as with relatives of the fallen soldiers. The report offers a unique insight into how the commission sought to commemorate the ideal of sacrifice in an appropriately spiritual way while not trespassing on sensitive social, racial, and religious convictions. The second source, a haunting poem by Rupert Brooke, was written shortly before the author, who served in the Mediterranean with the Royal Naval Division, fell victim, not to enemy bullets, but to a mosquito bite. He died in Greece of blood poisoning in April 1915.

In addition to cemeteries or heartfelt tributes to comrades, there was a wide variety of commemorative sites. In the third document, the Hungarian-born art critic Paul Konody, familiar to British audiences from his reviews in the *Observer* and the *Daily Mail*, also grapples with the issues of commemoration in a war of mass casualties: how to balance recognition of individual sacrifice with that of collective effort, and how to incorporate individuality but not eccentricity. While Konody was approached to advise the Canadians and address national concerns, localities, such as towns or counties, were also motivated to record their contributions. C.R. Grundy, editor of an illustrated magazine for collectors entitled *The Connoisseur*, published this influential guidance on how smaller institutions like local museums could best proceed to document the war effort before much of the necessary material was lost.

But to some, artifacts or written accounts still failed to evoke the true human dimensions of the conflict or to assuage the real emotional pain of the bereaved. For them, spiritualism offered the prospect of communicating with the fallen soldiers and restoring the link with family members that had been shattered in war. Ironically, one of the most ardent spiritualists was Arthur Conan Doyle, who endowed his enduring fictional detective, Sherlock Holmes, with an exacting rational bent and a deep skepticism of beliefs or occurrences not susceptible to scientific verification. But Doyle, who lost his son, brother, and brother-in-law to the conflict, found solace in spiritualism, lectured on the subject, and wrote for the benefit of those who sought "the touch of a vanished hand and the sound of a voice that is still." His interest in psychical phenomena and prominence in the spiritualist movement was matched by that of Oliver Lodge, a distinguished British physicist and principal of Birmingham University. Lodge's longstanding interest in the subject took on greater urgency after one of his sons, Raymond, was killed in action in September 1915. A year later, in a bestselling book titled *Raymond* for his fallen son, Lodge documented from a series of séances the sensational claim that Raymond had indeed contacted his family from the beyond. Although many witnesses reported paranormal activity (such as the ghosts of dead soldiers returning to warn their surviving comrades of dangers or other-worldly faces appearing in photographic images), Lodge's *Raymond* remained in many ways the wartime face of the spiritualist movement and, as such, attracted close attention from skeptics and critics. Prominent among them was Dr. Charles Mercier, a London physician who studied insanity, whose critical evaluation of Lodge's position is reprinted below.

Others devoted their energies to the survivors and sought ways to repair, or at least compensate for, the physical or emotional damage many veterans had suffered. John Galsworthy, the English novelist famous for his study of Edwardian social relations, *The Forsyte Saga*, worked as a hospital orderly in France and put his pen to use on behalf of the disabled in the sixth document. The next source provides a comparative survey of the treatment of disabled soldiers in other countries. Its author, Cecil W. Hutt, the deputy medical officer in the fashionable seaside resort of Brighton, thought that these measures might serve as examples for similar initiatives in Britain. J.B. Priestley, another prominent British novelist and playwright, served for two years before he was sent home after being wounded in 1916. He dwelled less on the immediate emotional toll of losing so many comrades, and more on what the absence of these men meant a decade or two later. "The lost generation" was his term for a country saddled with the unanticipated survival in power of second-rate minds because the cohort which should in the normal course of things have succeeded them had been bled white, "lost," in the conflict. Thus, the war's shadow would darken the lives of the survivors for years to come.

One way to commemorate that loss, and to publicize a collective commitment that such sacrifice would never be forgotten, was to establish a national day of mourning or remembrance. November 11, the day of the armistice on the Western Front, was the day selected in France and Britain (as well as the United States). The ninth extract, a 1922 appeal from the French Federal Union (the country's largest federation of veterans' societies) is intriguing for the inclusion of conventional republican rhetoric and also for the absence of evocations of French military power or glorious parades; rather, it is a call to arms in the service of peace. As such, it tells us a lot about the public mood in Western Europe during the interwar period and the likely constraints upon any bellicose politicians intent upon rearmament such as had occurred before 1914.

Indeed, around the world, too much had changed for things to go back to the way they had been. The French veterans' appeal makes no mention of the soldiers from West Africa who had fought with such tenacity for the tricolor, but the next excerpt from the reminiscences of a Senegalese veteran, Nar Diouf, makes clear that he would no longer see his relationship to colonial authority (or his fellow villagers) in the same way. Much the same attitudes are evident in South Africa, in the remaining text from the December 1918 petition to King George V excerpted in Chapter III. None of the dramatic developments this petition sought would be enacted in response, but the process of change had been set in motion.

1. War Cemeteries

Report

Your Royal Highness, My Lords and Gentlemen

I have the honour to lay before you the following report on the subject referred to me by the resolution of your Commission on 20th November, 1917.

In accordance with the instructions contained in that resolution, and in order to carry out the task entrusted to me, I visited France on two occasions. I was able to see a considerable number of cemeteries of various types; large base cemeteries . . . ; large independent cemeteries . . . ; cemeteries which form adjuncts to French communal cemeteries . . . ; cemeteries adjoining or amalgamated with French military cemeteries . . . ; small isolated cemeteries . . . ; and finally, an immense number of single burials, as over the whole area of the battles of the Somme. . . . I was able to visit cemeteries along all parts of the front . . . and thereby was able to form an idea of the variety of problems arising in connection with their arrangement, decoration and upkeep.

I have also had opportunities, both abroad and at home, of consulting representatives of the principal interests involved—the Army, the relatives of the fallen, the religious denominations, and the artists and others whose judgement may be of value in a work demanding imagination and taste and good feeling. . . . Among others, I have made a point of obtaining opinions from those who are qualified to

VIII.1   From Sir Frederic Kenyon, *War Graves: How the Cemeteries Abroad Will Be Designed* (London: HMSO, 1918), 3–14. © Crown Copyright material reproduced with the permission of The Controller HMSO.

speak for India and for the Dominions which have sent so many of their sons to lie in the graves which for generations to come will mark the line of our front in France and Flanders. My endeavour has been to arrive at a result which will, so far as may be, satisfy the feelings of relatives and comrades of those who lie in these cemeteries; which will represent the soldierly spirit and discipline in which they fought and fell; which will typify the Army to which they belonged; which will give expression to those deeper emotions, of regimental comradeship, of service to their Army, their King, their Country and their God, which underlay (perhaps often unconsciously) their sacrifice of themselves for the cause in which they fought, and which in ages to come will be a dignified memorial, worthy of the nation and of the men who gave their lives for it, in the lands of the Allies with whom and for whom they fought. . . .

And while dealing with this part of the subject, it may be as well to remind some who may read this report that of many who have fallen in this war there can be no identified grave. Many bodies are found but cannot be identified; many are never found at all; many are buried in graves which have subsequently been destroyed in the course of fighting. This is especially the case in areas such as that of Ypres, where the same ground has been contested for three consecutive years, and the whole countryside has been blasted and torn with shell fire. Therefore, whatever may be done in the way of placing individual monuments over the dead, in very many cases no such monument is possible. Yet these must not be neglected, and some memorial there must be to the lost, the unknown, but not forgotten dead.

Equality of Treatment

The Commission has already laid down one principle, which goes far towards determining the disposition of the cemeteries; the principle, namely, of equality of treatment. . . . As soon as the question was faced, it was felt that the provision of monuments could not be left to individual initiative. In a few cases, where money and good taste were not wanting, a satisfactory result would be obtained, in the sense that a fine individual monument could be erected. In the large majority of cases either no monument would be erected, or it would be poor in quality; and the total result would be one of inequality, haphazard and disorder. The cemetery would become a collection of individual memorials, a few good, but many bad, and with a total want of congruity and uniformity. The monuments of the more well-to-do would overshadow those of their poorer comrades; the whole sense of comradeship and of common service would be lost. The Commission, on the other hand, felt that where the sacrifice had been common, the memorial should be common also; and they desired that the cemeteries should be the symbol of a great Army and an united Empire.

It was therefore ordained that what was done for one should be done for all, and that all, whatever their military rank or position in civil life, should have equal treatment in their graves.

It is necessary to face the fact that this decision has given pain in some quarters, and pain which the Commissioners would have been glad to avoid. Not a few relatives have been looking forward to placing a memorial of their own choosing over the graves which mean so much to them; some have devoted much time and thought to making such a memorial beautiful and significant. Yet it is hoped that even these will realize that they are asked to join in an action of even higher significance. The sacrifice of the individual is a great idea and worthy of commemoration; but the community of sacrifice, the service of a common cause, the comradeship of arms which has brought together men of all ranks and grades—these are greater ideas, which should be commemorated in those cemeteries where they lie together, the representatives of their country in the lands in which they served. The place for the individual memorial is at home, where it will be constantly before the eyes of relatives and descendants, and will serve as an example and encouragement for the generations to come. A monument in France (and still more if further afield) can be seen but seldom; a monument in the parish church or churchyard is seen day by day and week by week, from generation to generation.

If any further argument is needed, I would say that the contrast now presented between the military and communal cemeteries, where they adjoin one another, provides it. The communal cemeteries are a jumbled mass of individual monuments of all sorts and sizes and of all variety of quality, packed much more closely than the monuments in an English churchyard; and the result is neither dignified nor inspiring. Side by side with these, the military cemeteries, whether French or English, with their orderly rows of crosses (the French ones bearing, in addition, a tricolour *cocarde*), have both dignity and inspiration. It is this impression which it is sought to perpetuate in the treatment now proposed for permanent adoption.

Headstones

The principle of equality and uniformity of treatment having been adopted, there are two main alternative methods by which it may be carried out: (1) either the individual graves will be undistinguished (except perhaps by an inconspicuous number), and the names of the dead will be commemorated on a single inscription, placed in some convenient position in the cemetery; or (2) each grave will have its own headstone, of uniform dimensions, on which the name of the dead will be carved, with his rank, regiment, and date of death.

In the first alternative, the cemetery would have the appearance of a small park or garden, composed of turf or flower beds divided by paths, planted with such shrubs or trees, and in no way recognizable as a cemetery, except by the presence of some central monument or monuments (of which more will be said later).

In the second alternative, the cemetery (besides such central monument or monuments) will be marked by rows of headstones of uniform height and width, though perhaps with some variety of pattern, as indicated below. The graves themselves might, in principle, be either separate mounds or a continuous flat surface. In practice I strongly recommend the latter, as being both easy to maintain and (especially where graves are so crowded as they necessarily are in these cemeteries) more satisfactory in effect, and also better adapted for decoration by flowers.

Of these two alternatives, my recommendation is definitely in favour of the second, for the following reasons:—

(a) The headstones clearly indicate the nature of the enclosure, that it is a cemetery and not a garden. Although it is not desired that our war cemeteries should be gloomy places, it is right that the fact that they are cemeteries, containing the bodies of hundreds of thousands of men who have given their lives for their country, should be evident at first sight, and should be constantly present to the minds of those who pass by or who visit them.

(b) The rows of headstones in their ordered ranks carry on the military idea, giving the appearance as of a battalion on parade, and suggesting the spirit of discipline and order which is the soul of an army. They will perpetuate the effect, which all who have seen them feel to be impressive, of the present rows of wooden crosses.

(c) The existence of individual headstones will go far to meet the wishes of relatives, who above all things are interested in the single grave. Many of them, as indicated above, will be disappointed that they are not allowed to erect their own monument over their own dead; but they will be much more disappointed if no monument except a mere indication number marks that grave at all. The individual headstone, marking the individual grave, will serve as centre and focus of the emotions of the relatives who visit it.

(d) Although opinion is not unanimous, it is my impression from all the interviews and conversations which I have had on the subject, that a large majority of those whose opinions are most entitled to consideration (including soldiers, relatives and artists) would be in favour of the use of headstones.

I recommend that the headstones should normally be 2 ft. 6 in. in height and 1 ft. 3 in. in width; not so large as to be cumbrous and oppressive, but large enough to convey the effect desired. Subject to this latter consideration, the smaller the dimensions the smaller will be the expense, and the less will be the difficulty of accommodation in the more crowded cemeteries. . . .

Regimental Patterns of Headstones

In order to secure a certain amount of variety in uniformity, and at the same time to gratify the regimental feeling which is so strong a characteristic of the British Army, it is proposed that each regiment, or other convenient unit, should have its own pattern of headstone, incorporating the regimental badge, which will be erected over the grave of every man of that regiment, wherever he may be buried. It is desirable that regimental feeling should be consulted as to the design of these headstones, and consequently (the approval of the Commission having been given to the principle) a circular has, I understand, been issued to units inviting suggestions or designs from men of artistic knowledge and experience. In the case of British regiments, the circular is being issued through the Colonels of regiments; in the case of other units, through such channels as are most in accordance with military practice. The designs, when received, will be submitted to a committee representing artistic taste and experience, and one will be selected to serve as the regimental pattern for each unit. . . .

Inscriptions on Headstones

The inscription carved on each headstone will give the rank, name, regiment and date of death of the man buried beneath it. There is some difference of opinion as to whether leave should be given to relatives to add anything further. It is clearly undesirable to allow free scope for the effusions of the mortuary mason, the sentimental versifier, or the crank; nor can space be given for a lengthy epitaph. On the other hand it would give satisfaction in many individual instances to be allowed to add an appropriate text or prayer or words of dedication. . . .

Central Monuments

The question of the central monument (I mean by this central in interest, not necessarily in position) in each cemetery which will strike the note, not only of the cemetery itself, but of the whole of this commemoration of the fallen, is one of great importance, and also of some difficulty. It is essential that it should be simple, durable, dignified and expressive of the higher feelings with which we regard our dead. In order to do this, it must have, or be capable of, religious associations, and while it must satisfy the religious emotions of as many as possible, it must give no reasonable ground of offence to any. The central sentiment of our commemoration of the dead is, I think, a grateful and undying remembrance of their sacrifice; and it is this sentiment which most persons will wish to see symbolised in the central monument. . . .

One suggestion was made at an early stage . . . which has been received with a considerable amount of approval. This was to the effect that the main memorial in every British cemetery should be "one great fair stone of fine proportions, 12 ft. in length, lying raised upon three steps, of which the first and third shall be twice the width of the second; and that each stone shall bear, in indelible lettering, some fine thought or words of sacred dedication." This stone would be, wherever circumstances permit, on the eastern side of each cemetery, and the graves will lie before it, facing east, as the Army faces now. It would have the character of permanence, as much as any work of man can hope for it. It would meet many forms of religious feeling. To some it would merely be a memorial stone, such as those of which we read in the Old Testament. To others it would be an altar, one of the most ancient and general of religious symbols, and would serve as the centre of religious services. As an altar, it would represent one side of the idea of sacrifice, the sacrifice which the Empire has made of its youth, in the great cause for which it sent them forth. And wherever this stone was found, it would be the mark, for all ages, of a British cemetery of the Great War.

The idea and symbolism of this great memorial altar stone go far to meet our requirements, but they do not go all the way. It lacks what many (probably a large majority) would desire, the definitely Christian character; and it does not represent the idea of self-sacrifice. For this the one essential symbol is the Cross; and I have no doubt that great distress would be felt if our cemeteries lacked this recognition of the fact that we are a Christian Empire; and this symbol of the self-sacrifice made by those who lie in them. The Jews are necessarily intermixed with their Christian comrades; but it is believed that their feelings will be satisfied by the inclusion of their religious symbol (the double triangle, or "Star of David") in the design of their headstones, and that they would not be offended by the presence of the Cross in the cemetery. For the great majority the Cross is the symbol of their faith, which they would wish to see in the cemeteries where their comrades or their kinsmen lie. One large and important class must be dealt with separately. It will be understood that where our Mohammedan, Hindu, and other non-Christian fellow subjects lie (and care has always been taken to bury them apart) their graves will be treated in accordance with their own religious beliefs and practices, and their own religious symbol will be placed over them. . . .

My recommendation, therefore, after much consideration and consultation with representatives of many points of view, definitely is that these two forms of monument should be combined; that in every cemetery there should be, on the east side, unless local conditions render it impracticable, a memorial stone . . . ; and elsewhere in the cemetery a cross. The cross should not be of the bare pattern, which would provoke comparison with the crucifixes habitually found in French cemeteries, but rather of the nature of the crosses found in many English country churchyards, or the Celtic crosses characteristic of northern Britain. The size, pattern, and position would be left to the artist who designs each cemetery. The cross and stone combined would be the universal mark of the British war cemetery. . . .

Other Buildings

Besides the cross and stone, some form of building will, for practical reasons, be required in all except the smallest cemeteries. In every cemetery a register of graves will have to be kept; in most some form of tool-house will be required. But beyond these needs, it will be convenient to have some shelter for visitors from the weather, some place where simple religious services may be held. . . . In general it may be worthwhile to emphasise the fact that the buildings, like the other features of the cemetery, should be as durable as possible, and should involve as little cost in upkeep as possible. Permanence should be the note of our cemeteries, but we desire both the lessons of the war and the expressions of our gratitude to those who gave their lives in it to be permanent. . . .

Summary of Preceding Recommendations

If the recommendations made in the preceding portion of this Report are carried out, the general appearance of a British cemetery will be that of an enclosure with plots of grass or flowers (or both) separated by paths of varying size, and set with orderly rows of headstones, uniform in height and width, but with slight difference of shape. Shrubs and trees will be arranged in various places, sometimes as clumps at the junctions of ways, sometimes as avenues along the sides of the principal paths, sometimes around the borders of the cemetery. The graves will, wherever possible, face towards the east, and at the eastern end of the cemetery will be a great altar-stone, raised upon broad steps, and bearing some brief and appropriate phrase or text. Either over the stone, or elsewhere in the cemetery, will be a small building, where visitors may gather for shelter or for worship, and where the register of the graves will be kept. And at some prominent spot will arise the Cross; as the symbol of the Christian faith and of the self-sacrifice of the men who now lie beneath its shadow. . . .

Different parts of it appeal differently to different persons, but there appears to be a general consensus of opinion that the scheme, carried out under good artistic guidance, will give a dignified and harmonious result, and that future generations will not be ashamed of what will be regarded as the characteristic British memorial of the Great War. It leaves ample scope for the display of artistic talent in adapting the scheme to the details of the ground in each particular instance, and the credit for satisfactory results will rest with the designer. All that is desired here is to ensure that all the designers shall work on a common plan. Each cemetery, it is hoped, will be beautiful, or at least satisfying, in itself; but their effect becomes cumulative if all, under whatever circumstances, have the same main features and express the same ideas, and so typify the common spirit of the nation, the common purpose of the Army, and the common sacrifice of the individual.

⚬⚬

2. The Dead

These hearts were woven of human joys and cares,
Washed marvellously with sorrow, swift to mirth.
The years had given them kindness. Dawn was theirs,
And sunset, and the colours of the earth.
These had seen movement, and heard music; known
Slumber and waking; loved; gone proudly friended;

VIII.2   From Rupert Brooke, *Collected Poems of Rupert Brooke* (London: J. Lane, 1918), 110.

Felt the quick stir of wonder; sat alone;
Touched flowers and furs and cheeks. All this is ended.
There are waters blown by changing winds to laughter
And lit by the rich skies, all day. And after,
Frost, with a gesture, stays the waves that dance
And wandering loveliness. He leaves a white
Unbroken glory, a gathered radiance,
A width, a shining peace, under the night.

✑

3. Canadian War Memorials

When the idea was conceived to provide Canada with a War Memorial to keep before the eyes of future generations a complete pictorial record of the Dominion's sacrifices and achievements in the great war, the organisers of the scheme were faced with considerable difficulties. Not the least of these was the extraordinary complexity of the material that had to be dealt with, if the record was to comprise every phase of a war that was fought not only on land on three continents, but on the sea, under the sea, in the air, and, more than on any previous occasion, on what has been aptly called the home front. The work in munition factories and dockyards, in training camp and hospital, in the lumber camps and on the land, in aviation works and in camouflage ateliers, on railway and on road, was as important as the fighting activity at the front. To do complete justice to all these phases was obviously an impossibility. The most that could be done was to select a few typical scenes of every kind of war work, which would show the progress from the earliest stages of preparation to the more exciting happenings in the trenches and on the battlefields.

The second consideration was of a purely aesthetic nature: how to maintain some kind of homogeneity in so comprehensive a scheme, whilst avoiding the deadly monotony of the dull array of battle pictures which line the endless walls of the Palace at Versailles, which is as depressing as the clash and confusion of the haphazard gatherings of the ordinary picture gallery. Conditions to-day are vastly different from those prevailing in the golden days of the Renaissance, when a master-painter could with a light heart undertake the fresco decoration of entire churches or monasteries.

He was the head of a bottega [workshop or studio], and had under him a small army of trained assistants who worked under his direction in his own manner. If he died before the work was completed, another master, trained in the same tradition, could take it up and carry it to a successful conclusion. . . .

VIII.3 From Paul G. Konody, *Art and War: Canadian War Memorials* (London: Colour, 1919), 14–15.

Today the bottega system has become obsolete. We live in an age of individualism, and nowhere is this more pronounced than in art. In painting, the present condition is nothing short of chaotic. Apart from the men who stand outside all groups, we have academic painters, realists, naturalists, plein-airists, impressionists, neo-realists, neo-impressionists, expressionists, cubists, vorticists, futurists, representative of every step leading from strictly representational to abstract art. To make the collection of memorial paintings truly representative of the artistic outlook during the momentous period of the great war, examples of all these conflicting tendencies had to be included. A completely homogeneous plan, like the great decorative enterprises of the Renaissance could not be thought of. The aim was bound to be diversity rather than uniformity, but diversity kept under control, with a definite end in view. This end was, that the principal pictures should maintain a certain unity of scale and decorative treatment which would make them suitable to take their place in a specially designed architectural setting, the smaller paintings and sketches being left to be arranged in groups in the various galleries provided for this purpose. A carefully organised decorative scheme was thus to be supplemented by a comprehensive pictorial record. A balance was to be maintained between the historical and the aesthetic aspects.

The importance of the proper housing of the collection cannot be overestimated. Such a series of pictures can never be housed adequately or exhibited appropriately in the manner of a general exhibition gallery. Europe is full of examples good and bad generally bad which might serve as precedents on conventional lines. Excuses may be made for them in many cases on the grounds of sentiment and tradition, but no one can deny that the majority, even those containing many of the world's masterpieces, are a weariness in themselves, and do but little assist the appeal of the pictures on the walls. But here there can be no excuse for such failure. These works have a message to deliver to the future. They are a memorial of sacrifice and heroism, expressive of a concentration of effort and production and denial which emanates from a complete and distinctive period.

✐

4. Local War Museums

We may fondly imagine that the war in which we are now engaged is so stupendous in its extent, and so decisive in its influence on the future destiny of the world, that no important episode connected with it will be forgotten, and that the names of those now fighting in the cause of justice and righteousness will always be held in honour. Yet unless we do differently to what we have done in the past this

---

VIII.4   From C. Reginald Grundy, *Local War Museums: A Suggestion* (London: W. Claude Johnson, 1917), 5–8.

will not be so. In fifty years' time the story of the war will be condensed into half a dozen pages of the orthodox school histories. Only the names of the more important and decisive battles will be remembered, and localities now hallowed to us by deeds of matchless heroism and the memories of those of our nearest and dearest who have fallen there will relapse once more into obscurity. The memorials erected to the fallen will be passed with as little attention as that now paid to the memorials of heroes fallen in earlier wars. A few names of celebrated commanders will linger in popular memory, but the names of the millions of the rank and file, who have served by land or sea, will be forgotten by everyone except their immediate descendants.

To prevent this happening, and to redeem the reproach leveled at us, too often with some justice, that we only remember our soldiers and sailors in our hours of need, we must devise a scheme that shall keep the events of the great war fresh in public memory and seize the imaginations of posterity, so that instead of leaving them merely bad records of names and events—none the less bald because inscribed on stately memorials—we must provide for them material that will enable them to visualize the experiences through which we have passed, and partake of our hopes, fears, disappointments and triumphs. One way of doing this would be by the establishment of a War Museum in every centre of population. It need not be a separate building, for portions of museums already existing could be used for the purpose. In these could be accumulated relics of the war—not merely articles of obvious military or naval interest, like those shown in the United Service Museum, but the little things, now part of our everyday life, which appear so insignificant as to be hardly worth the saving. I think that posterity will take a keen interest in our flag days, and samples of these little painted pieces of paper by which thousands of pounds have been raised for war charities should certainly be included; patriotic stamps, used for the same end, though not nearly so successful, should not be omitted; and examples of the street lamps with their sides rendered almost opaque with heavy coats of paint, so as to make them invisible to Zeppelin raiders, should be represented. Then there are the recruiting posters, by which we raised the largest volunteer army the world has ever seen; the War Loan posters, which helped to bring hundreds of millions of pounds to the national treasury; war workers' badges and armlets; the remnants of bombs dropped by Zeppelins, and Zeppelins themselves which have been brought down; as well as dozens of other little items, which will convey to posterity a more vivid idea of the life of our non-military population during the war, of their endurance, patriotism and charity, than any amount of written description.

But all these articles are merely subsidiary, a background intended to illustrate civilian life and work during the war, while the main display should form a permanent memorial to the sailors and soldiers who have offered their lives for their country's service. The memorial should be local rather than national in its scope, commemorating the patriotism of the men from the surrounding district, so that those who have come back from the Empire's far-flung battle line, in West or East, may feel that their heroism is appreciated by the fellow-citizens; and the kindred and friends of those who have not returned will have their sorrow assuaged by pride in the record of their deeds. Those purposes cannot be adequately effected by a general memorial in which the names of individuals are not recorded. Though John Smith's friends may know that he is one of twenty thousand unnamed men who died for their King and country, posterity will not know it, and it should be both our pride and duty to see that the name of every one who has risked his all for our sakes should be permanently inscribed on the Empire's roll of honour. . . .

But though these roles will afford a record of the men who served in the war, it will be but a bald record. . . . How are we to supply this deficiency and hand down to posterity such a vivid idea of the doings of John Smith and his companions that their imaginations may be lit up and their hearts thrilled at the picture of John Smith's bravery? . . .

[W]e are all at one in the consciousness that every direct relic of the war is of supreme interest. Yet here again we must be careful that nothing is overlooked, for articles which are so common to-day that we think they are hardly worth caring for may have disappeared in a few years' time. As all collectors know, the valuables of every generation are more or less plentiful because they are instinctively preserved; it is the trifles and things apparently of no account which altogether vanish, and this is the more to be regretted because these little things often throw a more intimate light on the period than the great ones. It is essential, then, that nothing should be overlooked. Illiterate letters from privates at the front giving an insight into their experiences, in fifty years' time may be rated as more interesting than official dispatches, while regimental newspapers will possess a far greater chance of immortality than more important and ambitious productions. Of course, uniforms, badges, accoutrements, and weapons of all kinds, both those of the enemy and our own, should appear in the collection, and with these should be included articles of attire, which cannot be strictly classified as portions of regimental uniforms, such as trench boots, waders, body shields, gas and ordinary helmets, or sheepskin coats. Interesting trophies from the battlefield should be given an important place; and war medals, instead of being hidden away with art exhibits, should here be awarded their proper position as records of bravery and self-sacrifice. They will be regarded with tenfold more interest because spectators have around them ample materials by which to realize the bravery of the action for which the decoration was awarded. . . .

It would be no small thing to accomplish this [to make each museum an epitome of local patriotism and heroism]; to bring home to the people of every locality, however obscure, that they and their ancestors have played their part in the making of Britain and her empire, and that their share in her greatness and the glory of her achievements ennobles them and gives them a cause of higher pride than the possession of either rank or riches can bestow.

5. Spiritualism

At the present time, this country, and doubtless other belligerent countries also in some degree, are suffering from an epidemic of spiritualism or mediumism, in the specious form of alleged communications with the dead. This terrible war has brought bereavement into tens of thousands of families in this country, and desolation into tens of thousands of homes. The sudden severance of the life of one who is near and dear produces in the survivors an irresistible longing for some hope, some encouragement to believe, that the separation is either not eternal or is not complete. To these bereaved and desolate souls the Church gives the comfort that the separation is not eternal, and Sir Oliver Lodge essays to give the comfort that it is not complete.

I refrain from inquiring into the grounds on which the claim of the Church is founded, and I refrain for two sufficient reasons: first that, whether well or ill founded, it has beyond all dispute brought consolation and comfort to innumerable sorrowing people; and second, because it does not profess to be founded upon reasoning from observed facts, and therefore is not susceptible of examination and testing by the canons of logic. The religious belief is founded upon Faith, upon the dicta of Authority, and these constitute a realm altogether distinct and apart from the induction of conclusions from facts of experience. Sir Oliver Lodge's efforts are of a different kind and have a different result. They have a different result in this respect: that they do not offer, or at least do not convey, a complete and restful assurance on which the mind can repose in tranquillity. They offer a quasi-assurance based upon observation and inferences from observation; upon observations that can be made only under conditions that are uncertain, fluctuating, capricious, and special; that have no value and no meaning until they are interpreted; that are open to several interpretations, of which those of Sir Oliver Lodge are diametrically opposed to the interpretations of other people; and even when interpreted by Sir Oliver Lodge himself in the most favourable sense for the purpose of carrying conviction of survival after death, yield nothing but trivialities. . . .

The business of mediumism was never so brisk as it is to-day. Mediums of every grade and quality are driving a roaring trade. It appears that there is actually an institution calling itself the British College of Psychic Science, which has, it appears, for one of its functions, the provision of mediums . . .

That what may be comprehensively called spiritualism or mediumism, that is to say, the consultation of mediums for the purpose of witnessing supernatural occurrences or receiving supernatural communications, is inordinately prevalent at the present time is certain; and for this state of things two factors are mainly responsible: the luxuriance of the crop is due first to the preparation of the ground, and second to the skilful sowing of the seed.

VIII.5   From Charles Arthur Mercier, *Spiritualism and Sir Oliver Lodge* (London: Watts, 1917), 4–5, 10–12.

How the ground is found ready prepared for the seed has already been indicated. It is prepared by the events of this terrible war. It is the experiences of
the war and the effects of the war that have profoundly affected the minds of
men and women, and have predisposed them to raise their eyes from the business, the pleasures, the trite occurrences of daily life, and to fix them once
more, as men and women in such times of stress and storm have always fixed
their eyes, upon the ultimate mysteries. It is in time of trouble, it is in all our
troubles and adversities whensoever they oppress us; it is all those that are in
danger, necessity, and tribulation; it is the fatherless children and widows, and
all that are desolate and oppressed; it is those who are any way afflicted or distressed in mind, body, or estate; it is the sighing of a contrite heart and the
desire of such as be sorrowful; these are the times, these the circumstances, in
which recourse is had to spiritualism, mediumism, and all the rest of it; these
are the people who frequent the offices of the mediums, whether sumptuous
Persian-carpeted and beflowered apartments in Bond Street [a fashionable
street in central London], or the dingy antimacassared [small cloths placed on
furniture to prevent stains] room over the suburban greengrocer's shop; and
these are the motives that prompt the seekers. In times like the present the
ground is but too well cultivated. It is dug, raked and drilled, it is ploughed
and harrowed, and it gapes for the seed to be sown. It is in these circumstances
that mediumism flourishes, and it is in ground thus prepared that Sir Oliver
Lodge sows his seed. It is not to be wondered at that in such conditions, in
such ground, the seed germinates and brings forth abundantly.

The second factor is the skilful sowing of the seed. In this Sir Oliver Lodge has
been extraordinarily successful. . . . The chief reason for his success undoubtedly
is that he is a man with an assured position in the world of Science. It is on this
account that he speaks with such unimpeached authority, and on this account that
his utterances on the question carry such weight and are accepted without hesitation. His position at the head of a University and his long and unblemished career
place his honesty above suspicion; and his achievements in the realm of science
seem to preclude the possibility that he can be mistaken in a matter of such importance, to which he has given so much attention, and on which he speaks with such
assured certainty.

∽

6. The Sacred Work

The Angel of Peace, watching the slow folding back of this darkness, will look
on an earth of cripples. The field of the world is strewn with half-living men.
That loveliness which is the creation of the aesthetic human spirit; that flowering

VIII.6   From John Galsworthy, "The Sacred Work" in *Another Sheaf* (New York: Scribner, 1919), 4–
13.

of directed energy which we know as civilisation; that manifold and mutual service which we call progress—all stand mutilated and faltering. As though, on a pilgrimage to the dreamed-of Mecca, water had failed, and by the wayside countless muffled forms sat waiting for rain; so will the long road of mankind look tomorrow.

In every township and village of our countries men stricken by the war will dwell for the next half-century. The figure of Youth must go one-footed, one-armed, blind of an eye, lesioned and stunned, in the home where it once danced. The half of a generation can never again step into the sunlight of full health and the priceless freedom of unharmed limbs.

So comes the sacred work.

Can there be limit to the effort of gratitude? Niggardliness and delay in restoring all of life that can be given back is sin against the human spirit, a smear on the face of honour. . . .

To lift up the man who has been stricken on the battlefield, restore him to the utmost of health and agility, give him an adequate pension, and re-equip him with an occupation suited to the forces left him—that is a process which does not cease till the sufferer fronts the future keen, hopeful, and secure. And such restoration is at least as much a matter of spirit as of body. Consider what it means to fall suddenly out of full vigour into the dark certainty that you can never have full strength again, though you live on twenty, forty, sixty years. The flag of your courage may well be down half-mast! Apathy—that creeping nerve disease—is soon your bedfellow and the companion of your walks. A curtain has fallen before your vision; your eyes no longer range. . . .

The flesh torn away, the lost sight, the broken ear-drum, the destroyed nerve, it is true, we cannot give back; but we shall so re-create and fortify the rest of him that he shall leave hospital ready for a new career. Then we shall teach him how to tread the road of it, so that he fits again into the national life, becomes once more a workman with pride in his work, a stake in the country, and the consciousness that, handicapped though he be, he runs the race level with his fellows, and is by that so much the better man than they. And beneath the feet of this new workman we shall put the firm plank of a pension." . . .

Of little use to man or nation would be the mere patching-up of bodies, so that, like a row of old gossips against a sunlit wall, our disabled might sit and weary out their days. If that were all we could do for them, gratitude is proven fraudulent, device bankrupt, and the future of our countries must drag with a lame foot.

To one who has watched, rather from outside, it seems that restoration worthy of that word will only come if the minds of all engaged in the sacred work are always fixed on this central truth: "Body and spirit are inextricably conjoined; to heal the one without the other is impossible." If a man's mind, courage and interest be enlisted in the cause of his own salvation, healing goes on apace, the sufferer is remade. If not, no mere surgical wonders, no careful nursing, will avail to make a man of him again. . . .

The sacred work is not departmental; it is one long organic process from the moment when a man is picked up from the field of battle to the moment when he is restored to the ranks of full civil life. Our eyes must not be fixed merely on this stressful present, but on the world as it will be ten years hence. I see that world gazing back, like a repentant drunkard at his own debauch, with a sort of horrified amazement and disgust. I see it impatient of any reminiscence of this hurricane; hastening desperately to recover what it enjoyed before life was wrecked and pillaged by these blasts of death. Hearts, which now swell with pity and gratitude when our maimed soldiers pass the streets, will, from sheer familiarity, and through natural shrinking from reminder, be dried to a stony indifference. "Let the dead past bury its dead" is a saying terribly true, and perhaps essential to the preservation of mankind. The world of ten years hence will shrug its shoulders if it sees maimed and *useless* men crawling the streets of its day, like winter flies on a windowpane.

It is for the sacred work to see that there shall be no winter flies. A niche of usefulness and self respect exists for every man, however handicapped; but that niche must be found for him. To carry the process of restoration to a point short of this is to leave the cathedral without spire. . . .

The great publics of our countries do not yet, I think, see that they too have their part in the sacred work. So far they only seem to feel: "Here's a wounded hero; let's take him to the movies, and give him tea!" Instead of choking him with cheap kindness each member of the public should seek to reinspire the disabled man with the feeling that he is no more out of the main stream of life than they are themselves; and each, according to his or her private chances, should help him to find that special niche which he can best, most cheerfully, and most usefully fill in the long future.

The more we drown the disabled in tea and lip gratitude the more we unsteel his soul, and the harder we make it for him to win through, when, in the years to come, the wells of our tea and gratitude have dried up. We can do a much more real and helpful thing. I fear that there will soon be no one of us who has not some personal friend disabled. Let us regard that man as if he were ourselves; let us treat him as one who demands a full place in the ranks of working life, and try to find it for him.

In such ways alone will come a new freemasonry to rebuild this ruined temple of our day. The ground is rubbled with stones—fallen, and still falling. Each must be replaced; freshly shaped, cemented, and mortised in, that the whole may once more stand firm and fair. In good time, to a clearer sky than we are fortunate enough to look on, our temple shall rise again. The birds shall not long build in its broken walls, nor lichens moss it. The winds shall not long play through these now jagged windows, nor the rain drift in, nor moonlight fill it with ghosts and shadows. To the glory of man we will stanchion, and raise and roof it anew.

Each comrade who for his Motherland has, for the moment, lost his future is a miniature of that shattered temple.

To restore him, and with him the future of our countries, that is the sacred work.

7. Training the Disabled

When the War produced war-cripples, owing to their previous experience of the problem of disabled men the Belgian Government were prompt in making suitable provision; within a few months of the beginning of the War a large school for disabled soldiers was started at Rouen.

In December 1914 a home for discharged soldiers was instituted at Havre which has gradually merged into a school for vocational re-education.

L'Hospital Anglo-Belge was opened later in December for about fifty men more or less convalescent, in some rooms in one of the military barracks. It has gradually grown and now comprises about 250 beds with two dependent establishments providing an additional 700 beds. Gradually into this hospital, all the aids of medical science were introduced, mechanotherapy, thermotherapy, radiology, electrotherapy, medical gymnastics and gymnastics. In addition artificial limbs were made and fitted at the hospital, enabling the stumps to be educated to their maximal mobility and function.

The accommodation for training these men in useful work . . . opened in August, 1915. . . . The land provided was part of a forest; a saw mill was erected, the trees scientifically thinned out, the timber not used for building the huts was sold. The smaller wood was made into pickets and stakes for the use of the Belgian Army. The cost of the buildings, 450,000 francs (£18,000), was repaid out of profits on the lumber; the cost of the equipment and plant for the workshops (£12,000) has been repaid out of the profits of the different workshops, which have sold their output at a cheap rate to the Belgian War Office thus effecting a double economy to the Government. A large farm forms part of the establishment; on it horses wounded in the War are cared for and made useful again.

There is at present accommodation for 800 patients; in addition attached to the Institute is a staff of 350 quasi-civilians unfit for military duty on account of age or on medical grounds; they serve as teachers, overseers, manual instructors or as workmen.

The fact that the entire population of Belgium is mobilized for military duty enables Captain Haccour, the director of the technical work, to requisition the services of the very best craftsmen in the different trades for the teaching staff who receive the ordinary pay of a soldier.

The cost per day to the Belgian Government for each man is just over 2 francs; the feeding and clothing cost 1 franc, 54 centimes, the daily pay is 43 centimes, the cost of lighting and heating is 8 centimes per man per day.

Forty-three different trades are taught including almost every imaginable occupation. The workshops provide for instruction in book-keeping, shorthand, type-writing, telegraphy, moulding in clay, wood carving, drawing and designing of all descriptions, wall paper designing and painting, the manufacture of motor vehicles, and electrical machinery of all descriptions, tinsmithing and plumbing,

VIII.7   From Cecil W. Hutt, *The Future of the Disabled Soldier* (London: John Bale, 1917), 15–18, 63–67.

tailoring, bootmaking, basket-making, poultry farming, and rabbit farming to which fur curing, dyeing and trimming are added.

The Institute makes all the tools used by the workmen besides a large number for the Army. All the printing and photographic work required is done on the premises in addition to much work for the Government. The men are paid in addition to their Army pay from 5 to 20 centimes an hour, according to the work they do; the surplus profits are now being funded for the benefit of the men.

The underlying principle of the whole establishment is constant work; no man is permitted to be idle. In part of the buildings is a small hospital for men who become ill or are temporarily suffering from their old wounds. Unless these men are absolutely helpless they are required to do some sort of work in bed, the hospital orderlies being efficient instructors of such work as net-making or light basket-work. . . .

Germany

Germany was fortunate in being able to utilize the organization already in existence for some ten years for dealing with cripples. In 1914, fifty-four institutions had already been established for cripples providing 221 workshops for training in all trades of every description, some fifty-one trades being taught. Full use is being made of these institutions; after treatment at hospital schools, the disabled man is transferred to the Orthopædic Institution nearest his home for continuation of his medical treatment and vocational training. The men are kept under military discipline, the institution being placed under the command of an officer detailed as military director.

Special institutions have been created for the one-armed at Berlin and Heidelberg. Employment is obtained through the local labour bureau for the province; in some bureaux special departments have been formed to deal with disabled men.

The State will find work for its own disabled employees; in Germany the State is relatively a larger employer than in England, many enterprises such as railways which are with us under private control are under the State in Germany. A proposal widely advocated is that the State when placing orders with private companies or firms shall impose the condition that a proportion of the labour employed should consist of disabled men.

Many municipalities have inserted a clause to this effect in the regulations relating to municipal contracts.

No effort is spared to impress upon the wounded soldier and the public the fact that even severely disabled men can be taught to work and earn their living. The measures utilized include continuous propaganda by the Press, both lay and medical, lectures illustrated by lantern slides, visits to institutions for cripples, the distribution of pamphlets to soldiers and the visiting of the wounded men in hospital to advise and persuade them to take up training where necessary.

The mass of expert opinion is opposed to the establishment of large colonies of disabled men, although in some instances colonies of forty to fifty families provided with workshops have been formed near towns. Wherever possible, it is considered that the man should return to his own home and resume his former work and employment and become an ordinary member of the community.

Stress is laid on the need for providing the disabled with skilled advice as to future employment. The general tenor of the advice given is that disabled men should when possible return to their pre-war occupations. . . .

In Prussia, local authorities are required to exercise caution in granting licences as pedlars to disabled men. . . .

At Mannheim, a Military Orthopædic Hospital (for non-amputation cases) was opened in April, 1915, with a school attached to provide instruction, both practical and theoretical, of an elementary nature during medical treatment. Stress is laid on the value of theoretical training to increase the patient's knowledge of his former occupation.

The subjects taught are:—

Theoretical.—Writing and arithmetic, shorthand and typing, English and French. Special lectures are given on building trades, metal work including electrical work, commercial subjects.

Practical.—Carpentering, bootmaking, locksmith's work, metal work including electrical work, wheelwright's work, bookbinding.

During the first seven months over 700 patients attended the various courses, about 300 at any one time receiving instruction. . . .

Munich has arranged for training in almost every branch of manual work. The men taught are still under medical care, the institution being both a convalescent home and school.

✍

8. The Lost Generation

"And the men who were boys when I was a boy will sit and drink with me": thus the poet. I hope he is luckier than I am. I belong to the wrong generation. Most of the men who were boys when I was a boy cannot sit and drink with me. Loos and Gallipoli and the Somme did for them. They went and saved something and never came back. What it was they saved I cannot exactly tell, but I do know that I have never seen anything since 1918 that was worth their sacrifice.

When people wonder what has been wrong with England these last twelve years it seems to me that they forget the War. It is all very simple. The men who would

VIII.8　From J.B. Priestley, "The Lost Generation" (Washington DC: Women's International League for Peace and Freedom, 1930). Reprinted by permission of United Agents on behalf of The Estate of J. B. Priestley.

be assuming leadership now in politics, the professions, the arts, business—if there had been no war—are dead.

Who can tell what genius was poured down that vast drain? We can guess, but those of us who remember those ardent and generous spirits, nearly always the first to go, can make a tragically shrewd guess. We flung away brilliant young manhood as if it were so much dirt, and now we are paying the price for it. There is still a flourishing pre-war generation and there is, of course, a flourishing, if not markedly vital, post-war generation. But in between there was a generation that belonged to the war itself, that grew to manhood in the trenches, and now is a remnant.

This is the generation to which I belong, for I celebrated my twenty-first birthday in 1915 in the front line. I have a few good friends and a great many acquaintances; but sometimes I feel like an old man, for I seem to know intimately more dead men than living ones. To think about an old playing field is to see a crowd of ghosts.

I know very well that a man may have been killed in battle and yet have been a poor creature. It is not sentimentalism that makes me declare emphatically that the most eager, promising and finest members of my generation were lost to us through the war. I know it for a fact. I knew them, was with them. We who are left—the lucky ones—are a miserable remnant; and sometimes I wonder if any of us are quite sane, even though we may never have appeared in police court and pleaded our war service.

I doubt if you can grow to manhood under such circumstances, if you can spend the most impressionable years of your life among shells and blood-stained barbed wire, and be quite normal. There are wounds of the soul as well as wounds of the body. In the life of a young man there is a period—let us say between the ages of nineteen and twenty-three—when, though he may be working hard at a university or learning a business, he can lead, what is on the whole, a carefree, cheerfully irresponsible existence.

It is the age at which young men sit up very late at night, smoking brand new pipes, drinking beer and gigantically settling the affairs of the universe. It is also the age at which, very idealistically, they first fall in love and take to writing sonnets, after illuminating experiences at college dances.

My generation missed all that. It spent that period watching its dearest friends being killed. And when, after the war, it came back blinking, bewildered, it had to grab a livelihood and do it when everybody else seemed to be greedy and grabbing. Can you wonder then that we seem at times a trifle hysterical? Perhaps we don't; perhaps we seem jolly, healthy-minded fellows, but then you are not there when two or three of us are gathered together.

Writing then as one of this remnant, possibly half-witted, I will confess that I do not understand this world at all. I do not understand people's sense of values. I cannot gather exactly what it is they want to get out of life. Take this war business as an example. Learned and industrious men, after burrowing among documents for years, give us long books on the cause of the Great War, and you pay your money and you take your choice.

But the real cause of war could be set down on a post card. It was the inevitable result of people standing about, their fingers on triggers, expecting war.

Everybody who was in the trenches will remember how, one night when all was quiet, some young ass of a sentry would fire a few quick rounds at nothing, just to warm his hands. So a German sentry would loose off a few rounds. Then more English, then more Germans. The machine guns would join. Then the light artillery and the trench mortars on both sides. Then the heavy artillery would be called in, until finally the night would be a daft inferno. That's war. And that is how the war started.

The most dangerous lunatics we have had to do with this century, have been the "Be Prepared" agitators. To be prepared, you have to amass big guns and little guns and heaps of explosives.

Once you have done that, the rest follows. Some fool gets a fright and pulls a trigger—and then you are off. You cannot have dangerous weapons without wanting, at some time, to use them. We are not in the habit of killing one another where I live, being nice, peaceable ratepayers, but suppose we were told that murder was inevitable and all began to go armed to the teeth, what do you think would happen? Why, very soon the place would be littered with corpses. All those people who go about saying that war is inevitable and giving us their views on the next war are either dangerous lunatics or criminal, They ought to be locked up and fed bread and water.

But one day some fool whose finger has been itching at the trigger too long will fire a shot. And the next time there won't be any learned men writing long books on the causes of it all. There won't be learned and industrious men and won't be any books.

There will only be a few idiots gibbering among the ruins. And sometimes even I feel like one of them.

⌀

9. French Veterans' Appeal

Citizens!

The Men of the War wish to celebrate 11 November.

The 11 November 1918 marks the end of the most terrible slaughter which has ever afflicted the modern world. For 52 months whole nations faced each other on immense battlefields. *Forty million men fought. Six million were killed. Fifteen million were wounded.* Populous and wealthy regions were ravaged; it will take a quarter century to restore them to life.

It is *Germany* who in the eyes of posterity will bear the responsibility for bloodshed and heaped-up ruins. It is *imperialist Germany, pan-Germanist and militarist, who wanted this war,* who declared war and pursued it by the most criminal methods.

VIII.9   From Antoine Prost, *In the Wake of War* (Oxford: Berg, 1992), 61. Reprinted with permission of Berg Publishers, an imprint of Bloomsbury Publishing plc.

Republican and peaceful France fought for justice, for freedom and for the law. *The Men of the War* fought against imperialism, against militarism: THEY MADE WAR ON WAR. *Seven and a half million* Frenchmen risked their lives in battle! ONE MILLION FIVE HUNDRED THOUSAND are dead! *A million* are permanently disabled! *Eight hundred thousand* children have no father! *Seven hundred thousand women* have no husband!

French citizens!
The Men of the War want THEIR VICTORY to consecrate THE ABOLITION OF WAR!
They want guilty Germany to pay for the war she unleashed!
They want victorious France to remain the Nation of Law and the Warrior of Peace.
They want anarchy among nations to be replaced by the reign of law among nations.
Men of the War, in remembrance of the great struggles which we suffered and in the name of our dead brothers, we are the peaceful servants of the LEAGUE OF NATIONS.
CITIZENS!
Join the *Men of the War*, be *Men of the Peace. On 11 November*, the day of *Victory*, the day of our *remembrance*, day of our *mourning*, day of our *hope*, join us, let us resolve together with all our hearts:
Liberty, Justice, peace among citizens!
Justice for France!
Peace in the World!

⌘

10. An African Veteran Reflects

I received many lasting things from the war. I demonstrated my dignity and courage, and [I] won the respect of the people and the [colonial] government. And whenever the people of the village had something to contest [with the French]— and they didn't dare do it [themselves] because they were afraid of them—I used to do it for them. And many times when people had problems with the government, I used to go with my decorations and arrange the situation for [them]. Because whenever the *Tubabs* [term for foreigners derived from the "two bob" or standard two-shilling fee British colonialists used to pay natives for work] saw your decorations, they knew that they [were dealing with] a very important person . . . And I gained this ability—of obtaining justice over a *Tubab*—from the war.

[For example], one day a *Tubab* came here [to the village]—he came from the *service de genie* (he was a kind of doctor)—to make an examination of the people. So he came here, and there was a small boy who was blind. And [the boy] was

VIII.10   From Joe Lunn, *Memoirs of the Maelstrom* (Portsmouth, NH: Heinemann, 1999), 232. Reprinted with permission of Boydell & Brewer Ltd.

walking, [but] he couldn't see, and he bumped into the *Tubab*. And the *Tubab* turned and pushed the boy [down]. And when I saw that, I came and said to the *Tubab*: "Why have you pushed this boy? [Can't] you see that he is blind?" And the *Tubab* said: "Oh, *pardon, pardon*. I did not know. I will never do it again, excuse me." [But] before the war, [no matter what they did], it would not have been possible to do that with a *Tubab*.

⚘

11. Africa Petitions Britain's King

May It Please Your Majesty—

1. We, the Chiefs and delegates assembled at Johannesburg, this 16th day of December, 1918, in the Special Session of the South African Native National Congress, a political body representing the various tribes of the Bantu people in South Africa, record the expression of our satisfaction and thankfulness in the triumph of righteousness in this great war by the victory of the forces of Great Britain, her noble Allies, and the United States of America.

2. We beg to convey to Your Majesty our affectionate loyalty and devotion to Your Majesty's person and Throne and the sincerity of our desire that Divine Blessing and prosperity may attend Your Majesty and all Your Majesty's Dominions in the dawn of a better age.

3. We further express the hope and wish that during Your Majesty's Reign all races and Nations will be treated fairly and with justice, and that there will be no discrimination on account of colour or creed; and will enjoy the right of citizenship, freedom and liberty under your flag. . . .

6. We are mindful of the great main fact that Great Britain and her Allies as well as the United States of America went into war (inter alia) for the protection of small and weak nations: for the enforcement of international treaties and agreements; to liberate oppressed nations; to grant every nation, great or small, the right to determine its sovereign destiny and the free choice of its own government and flag; and to allow subject races to express their voice in the final control and disposal of their territories and to choose the flag under which they desire to be protected; to make the world fit and safe for every man to live in with freedom to choose his own destiny.

7. The Bantu people of South Africa have ever been impressed with the high ideals permeating the British Constitution, and in this connection have always held the memory of the late Queen Victoria, The Good, with reverence and devotion. It was in her illustrious reign that the black people were emancipated from slavery in 1834 [actually during the reign of William IV].

In Her late Majesty's Proclamation of Natal in 1843, any discrimination in the eyes of the law on account of race, colour, or creed, as well as slavery in

VIII.11 From "Petition to King George V from the South African Native National Congress, 16 December 1918."

any shape or form, were distinctly repudiated. Even under the two Conventions in the Transvaal in 1881 and 1884, the late Queen Victoria discountenanced slavery in any shape or form. All these Proclamations and Conventions contain principles, which are still regarded by Your Majesty's subjects as their Magna Charter [*sic*].

It is with painful regret that we remind Your Majesty that these Victorian principles with which our people associate with the high ideals of the British Constitution have been departed from and in the main dishonoured and ignored by Your Majesty's representative Governments in South Africa.

We humbly submit to Your Most Gracious Majesty that the black inhabitants of this land who are Your Majesty's subjects, on account of their race, colour, language and creed, live under a veiled form of slavery. The subject's inherent right of freedom and the right to move at liberty is unwarrantably restricted, and the individual cannot bargain, under existing laws with his labour as he chooses. Equal opportunities for trading are denied and the avenues of civilized advancement are limited. . . .

9. In pursuance of Great Britain's war aims and her love for free institutions for all peoples under her flag and these aims being adapted and consonant with those of Her Allies and the United States of America, the only solution therefore is to have those principles applied to South Africa so that we may have a voice in the affairs of the country, and have full protection so as to check reactionary legislation and unpopular one-sided laws. To put these principles into effect it may please Your Majesty to cause a revision of the South African Constitution in such manner as to grant enfranchisement of natives throughout the Union; and further so as to make provision for the protection of the aboriginal national institutions being respected and developed . . .

In conclusion, we, Your Majesty's most loyal and humble subjects, lay this Memorial before Your Majesty on this supreme and unique occasion of the cessation of hostilities with thankfulness and satisfaction that Your Majesty's Memorialists have taken an active part in bringing about victory and peace, and in full confidence that the position of Your Majesty's subjects under the sun will be improved and be readjusted in terms of this Memorial.

Source References

The following are the complete bibliographic references for each extract.

Chapter I: The Mood of 1914

1. Mildred Aldrich, *Hilltop on the Marne: Being Letters Written June 3–September 8, 1914* (Boston: Houghton Mifflin, 1915), 45–47, 49–54, 57–64.
2. Felix Klein, *Diary of a French Army Chaplain* (London: Andrew Melrose, 1915), 18–19, 24–27.
3. Marc Bloch, *Memoirs of War, 1914–15*, trans. Carole Fink (Ithaca, NY: Cornell University Press, 1980), 78–79. © Carole Fink. Reprinted with kind permission.
4. W. Mansell Merry, *Two Months in Russia* (Oxford: Blackwell, 1916), 74–76, 78–79.
5. Vasilii I. Gourko, *War and Revolution in Russia, 1914–1917* (New York: Macmillan, 1919), 19–20.
6. Daniel Horn, ed. *War, Mutiny and Revolution in the German Navy: The World War I Diary of Seaman Richard Stumpf* (Brunswick, NJ: Rutgers University Press, 1967), 24–27. Copyright © 1967 by Rutgers, the State University. Reprinted by permission of Rutgers University Press.
7. Olga Hess Gankin and H.H., Fisher eds., *The Bolsheviks and the World War: The Origin of the Third International* (Stanford: Stanford University Press, 1940) 57–59. Excerpts from Olga Hess Gankin and H.H, Fisher eds., *The Bolsheviks and the World War: The Origin of the Third International* (Stanford: Stanford University Press, 1940), 57–59. Copyright © 1940 by the Board of the Trustees of the Leland Stanford Junior University, renewed 1968. All rights reserved. Used with the permission of Stanford University Press. www.sup.org.
8. Ralph Haswell Lutz, ed., *Fall of the German Empire, 1914–1918*, 2 vols. (Stanford: Stanford University Press, 1932) 2: 6–7. Copyright © 1940 by the Board of Trustees of the Leland Stanford Junior University, renewed 1960. All rights reserved. Used with the permission of Stanford University Press. www.sup.org.
9. Philipp Witkop (ed.) and A.F. Wedd (trans.), *German Students' War Letters* (London: Methuen, 1929), 17.

Empires, Soldiers, and Citizens: A World War I Sourcebook, Second Edition.
Edited by Marilyn Shevin-Coetzee and Frans Coetzee.
© 2013 John Wiley & Sons, Ltd. Published 2013 by John Wiley & Sons, Ltd.

10. Basil Thomson, *Queer People* (London: Hodder & Stoughton, 1922) 33–34, 36–38.

11. Coulson Kernahan, *The Experiences of a Recruiting Officer* (London: Hodder & Stoughton, 1915), 28–31.

12. Donald Hankey, *A Student in Arms* (London: Melrose, 1916), 25–29.

13. Frederick George Scott, *The Great War as I Saw It* (Toronto: F.D. Goodchild, 1922), 15–17, 19.

14. J.G. Mullen, "The View from the Cameroons," *Gold Coast Leader* (October 14, 16, and 28, 1916), as reprinted in *Africa* 78 (2008): 401–409.

Chapter II: War on the Western Front

1. Marc Bloch, *Memoirs of War, 1914–15*, trans. Carole Fink (Ithaca, NY: Cornell University Press, 1980), 159, 161–166. Copyright © Carole Fink. Reprinted with kind permission.

2. Guy Chapman, ed., *Vain Glory* (London: Cassell, 1967), 167–173. Reprinted with permission of PFD www.pfd.co.uk on behalf of the estate of Guy Chapman.

3. Julian Grenfell, "War is Like a Big Picnic". Excerpt from Laurence Housman, ed., *War Letters of Fallen Englishmen* (London: Victor Gollancz, 1930), 117–119.

4. Melville Hastings, "All the World over a Boy is a Boy, a Mother a Mother". Excerpt from Laurence Housman, ed., *War Letters of Fallen Englishmen* (London: Victor Gollancz, 1930) 122–125.

5. D. Sutherland, *War Diary of the Fifth Seaforth Highlanders, 51st (Highland) Division* (London: J. Lane, 1920), 43–44, 69–71.

6. Siegfried Sassoon, "A Working Party" from Siegfried Sassoon, *Collected Poems of Siegfried Sassoon*. Copyright © 1918, 1920 by E. P. Dutton. Copyright © 1936, 1946, 1947, 1948 by Siegfried Sassoon. Reprinted with kind permission of Barbara Levy Literary Agency, on behalf of the Estate of George Sassoon, and Viking Penguin, a division of Penguin Group (USA) Inc.

7. Private John Erskine Lockerby, "A Canadian in the Trenches," April 18, 1915, Canadian Great War Project, http://www.canadiangreatwarproject.com/transcripts/transcriptDisplay.asp?Type=L&Id=224.

8. "Report of the Afternoon's Actions," October 13, 1915, Canadian 26th Battalion to 5th Canadian Infantry Brigade, Library and Archives Canada, www.collectionscanada.gc.ca. Reproduced with the permission of the Minister of Public Works and Government Services Canada 2011. Source: Library and Archives, Canada/Ministry of the Overseas Military Forces of Canada fonds/RG9–III–D–3/13 October 1915, Appendix F, p 2/e000948726.

9. David Omissi, ed., *Indian Voices of the Great War: Soldiers' Letters, 1914–1918* (Houndmills, Basingstoke: Macmillan, 1999), 45–46, 50–51, 102. Reprinted with permission of Palgrave Macmillan.

10. Franz Blumenfeld, "The Readiness to Make a Sacrifice". Excerpt from Philipp Witkop (ed.) and A. F. Wedd (trans.), *German Students' War Letters* (London: Methuen, 1929) 17–21.

11. Herbert Weisser, "My Life is no Longer my Own". Excerpt from Philipp Witkop (ed.) and A.F. Wedd (trans.), *German Students' War Letters* (London: Methuen, 1929), 107–110.

12. Alfons Ankenbrand, "I Look upon Death and Call Upon Life". Excerpt from Philipp Witkop (ed.) and A.F. Wedd (trans.), *German Students' War Letters* (London: Methuen, 1929), 72–73.

13. Kurt Peterson, "Here One Becomes Another Man". Excerpt from Philipp Witkop (ed.) and A. F. Wedd (trans.), *German Students' War Letters* (London: Methuen, 1929), 149–150.

14. Ernst Jünger, *Copse 125* (London: Chatto and Windus, 1930), 55–57, 99–100.

15. *Wipers Times*, 25 December 1916.

16. *The B.E.F. Times*, 10 April 1917.

17. *The B.E.F. Times*, 10 April 1917.

Chapter III: War to the East and South

1. Vasilii I. Gourko, *War and Revolution in Russia, 1914–1917* (New York: Macmillan, 1919), 74–77.

2. John Morse, *An Englishman in the Russian Ranks* (London: Duckworth, 1915), 252–256, 262–265.

3. Bernard Pares, *Day by Day with the Russian Army, 1914–1915* (London: Constable, 1915), 245–247.

4. General Anton I. Denikin, *The Russian Turmoil* (London: Hutchinson & Co., 1922), 127–129.

5. V. Ladizhensky, *Poems Written during the Great War* (London: George Allen and Unwin, 1918), 63.

6. Francis Rolt-Wheeler and Frederick E. Drinker, eds., *The World War For Liberty* (Philadelphia: National Publishing Co., 1919) 129–133.

7. Edwin Dwinger, *The Army Behind Barbed Wire: A Siberian Diary* (London: George Allen & Unwin, 1930), 108, 120–121, 243–245.

8. Elsa Brandstrom, *Among Prisoners of War in Russia & Siberia* (London: Hutchinson, 1929), 117–123.

9. Thomas Nelson Page, *Italy and the World War* (New York: Charles Scribners Sons, 1920), 303–309, 311.

10. Major John Graham Gillam, *Gallipoli* (London: George Allen & Unwin, 1918), 72, 135–137.

11. "Daily Trench Life for Otago Mounted Rifles Regiment," *Australian Imperial Force Unit War Diaries 1914–1918. New Zealand Units.* http://www.awm.gov.au. Reprinted with permission of The Australian Army History Unit and The New Zealand Defence Force.

12. Mehmed Fasih, *Lone Pine (Bloody Ridge) Diary of Lt. Mehmed Fasih, 5th Imperial Ottoman Empire, Gallipoli, 1915* (Istanbul: Denizler Kitabevi, 2001), 56–61. Reprinted with permission.

13. Captain O. Teichman, *Diary of a Yeomanry M.O.: Egypt, Gallipoli, Palestine and Italy* (London: T. Fisher Unwin, 1921), 202–207, 237–245.

14. Sol Plaatje, *Native Life in South Africa* (London: P.S. King, n.d. 1916 ?), 279–283.

15. H.F.B. Walker, *A Doctor's Diary in Damaraland* (London: Edward Arnold, 1917), 52, 137–140.

16. "Petition to King George V from the South African Native National Congress, 16 December 1918." Reprinted in Thomas Karis and Gwendoline M. Carter, eds., *From Protest to Challenge: Documentary History of African Politics*, vol. 1 (Stanford: Hoover Institution Press, 1977), 138–139.
17. Jefferson Jones, *The Fall of Tsingtau: with a study of Japan's Ambitions in China* (Boston: Houghton Mifflin, 1915) 70–76, 78–79.
18. Jefferson Jones, *The Fall of Tsingtau: with a study of Japan's Ambitions in China* (Boston: Houghton Mifflin, 1915), 186–190.

Chapter IV: Combat in the Machine Age

1. F.V. Longstaff, *The Book of the Machine Gun* (London: Hugh Rees, 1917), 179–183.
2. George G. Nasmith, *Canada's Sons and Great Britain in the World War* (Toronto: John C. Winston, 1919), 179–181, 183–184.
3. Captain Howard Clouston, "Gas at the Front," Canadian Great War Project [originally written to his mother and then published in *Huntingdon Gleaner,* Huntingdon, Quebec, on October 10, 1918] (www.canadiangreatwarproject.com).
4. J.F.C. Fuller, *Tanks in the Great War*, (New York: E.P. Dutton & Co, 1920), 120–123. Excerpts reprinted with permission of David Higham Associates Limited.
5. Charles S. Myers, *Shell Shock in France, 1914–1918* (Cambridge: Cambridge University Press, 1940), 11–12, 25–26, 37–40. Reprinted with permission of Cambridge University Press.
6. Paul Jones, *War Letters of a Public-School Boy* (London: Cassell and Company, 1918), 138–139, 160–161.
7. Stephen King-Hall, "Battle at Sea," *A North Sea Diary, 1914–1918* (London: Hazell, Watson & Viney Ltd, n.d.), 54–56.
8. Daniel Horn, ed., *War, Mutiny and Revolution in the German Navy: The World War I Diary of Seaman Richard Stumpf* (Brunswick, NJ: Rutgers University Press, 1967), 81–83. Copyright © 1967 by Rutgers, the State University. Reprinted by permission of Rutgers University Press.
9. George von Hase, "The Two White Nations," in *The Battle of Jutland, 31 May–1 June 1916, Monograph #1* (Newport, RI: Naval War College, 1920), 19–20, 22–23, 27–29, 32.
10. Baron Spiegel of Peckelheim, *The Adventures of the U-202* (New York: Century, 1917), 50–57, 172–173.
11. *Hansard's Parliamentary Debates,* 16 February 1916, vol. 80, cols. 86–89. © Crown Copyright material reproduced with the permission of The Controller HMSO.
12. John Charles Carlile, *Folkestone During the War, 1914–1918: A Record of the Town's Life and Work* (Folkestone: F. J. Parsons, Ltd, n.d.), 96–99.
13. *Hansard's Parliamentary Debates,* 16 February 1916, vol. 80, cols.150–152. © Crown Copyright material reproduced with the permission of The Controller HMSO.
14. Oswald Boelcke, *An Aviator's Field Book* (New York: National Military Publishing Co., 1917), 91–96, 101–105.
15. John E. Tennant, *In the Clouds above Baghdad* (London: C. Palmer, 1920), 59–63.

Chapter V: Mobilizing the Home Front

1. J.A. Hobson, "Liberty as a True War Economy," *The Nation*, 29 July 1916.
2. John Crombie, "The State as the Supreme God". Excerpt from Laurence Housman, ed., *War Letters of Fallen Englishmen* (London: Victor Gollancz, 1930), 80–81.
3. Albrecht Mendelssohn-Bartholdy, "Germany's Government at War". Excerpts from Mendelssohn-Bartholdy, *The War and German Society* (New Haven: Yale University Press, 1937), 108–110. Reprinted with permission of Carnegie Endowment.
4. Ralph Haswell Lutz, ed., *Fall of the German Empire, 1914–1918*, vol. 1 (Stanford: Stanford University Press, 1932), 178–181. Copyright © 1940 by the Board of Trustees of the Leland Stanford Junior University, renewed 1960. All rights reserved. Used with the permission of Stanford University Press. www.sup.org.
5. "War, Prostitution and Venereal Disease: The Position in Germany," *The Lancet*, 23 September 1916, 567–568.
6. Frank Golder, ed., *Documents of Russian History, 1914–1917* (Gloucester, MA: Peter Smith, 1964), 146–149.
7. Paul Ignatiev, Dimitry Odinetz and Paul Novgorotsev, *Russian Schools and Universities in the World War* (New Haven: Yale University Press, 1929), 72–77, 83–84. Reprinted with permission of Carnegie Endowment.
8. David Mitrany, *The Effect of the War in Southeastern Europe* (New Haven: Yale University Press, 1936), 157–161. Reprinted with permission of Carnegie Endowment.
9. Paul Eltzbacher, *Germany's Food: Can It Last?* (London: University of London Press, 1915), 1–3, 6–10.
10. Anna Pöhland, *Die Pöhlands im Krieg* (Bonn: Pahl-Rugenstein, 1982), 105–106, 113. Translated by Marilyn Shevin–Coetzee.
11. Excerpts from Ralph Haswell Lutz, ed., *Fall of the German Empire, 1914–1918*, vol. 2 (Stanford: Stanford University Press, 1932), 106–109. Copyright © 1940 by the Board of Trustees of the Leland Stanford Junior University, renewed 1960. All rights reserved. Used with the permission of Stanford University Press. www.sup.org.
12. M. Ferguson, "The Family Budgets and Dietaries of Forty Labouring Class Families in Glasgow in Wartime," *Proceedings of the Royal Society of Edinburgh*, 37 (1916–17), 117, 126–127, 130–131.
13. Mae Byron, *Mae Byron's How-To-Save Cookery* (London: Hodder and Stoughton, 1915), 1–5.
14. Marie W. Seers, "Women in Banking," in Gilbert Stone, ed., *Women War Workers* (London: G.G. Harrap & Co., 1917), 90–92, 98–99, 107.
15. Helena Swanwick, *The War in its Effect Upon Women* (n.p., 1916), 3–11, 13, 23–25.
16. Mary Gabrielle Collins, *Branches unto the Sea* (London: Erskine Macdonald, 1916), 24.
17. Helena Lange, "Speech before the Congress of the Union of German Women Teachers," 1915. Reprinted in Susan Groag Bell and Karen M. Offen, eds., *Women, the Family, and Freedom*, vol. 2 (Stanford: Stanford University Press, 1983), 262–263. Copyright © 1983 by the Board of the Trustees of the Leland Stanford Junior University. All rights reserved. Used with the permission of Stanford University Press. www.sup.org.

18. Magda Trott, "Women's Work: A Substitute for Men's Work," 1915. Reprinted in Susan Groag Bell and Karen M. Offen, eds., *Women, the Family, and Freedom*, vol. 2 (Stanford: Stanford University Press, 1983), 277–279. Copyright © 1983 by the Board of the Trustees of the Leland Stanford Junior University. All rights reserved. Used with the permission of Stanford University Press. www.sup.org.

19. Ute Daniel, *The War from Within: German Working-Class Women in the First World War* (Oxford: Berg, 1997), 68–69. Reprinted with permission of Berg Publishers, an imprint of Bloomsbury Publishing plc.

20. Ute Daniel, *The War from Within: German Working-Class Women in the First World War* (Oxford: Berg, 1997), 101. Reprinted with permission of Berg Publishers, an imprint of Bloomsbury Publishing plc.

21. Maria Botchkareva, *Yashka: My Life as Peasant, Officer and Exile* (New York: Frederick Stokes, 1919), 72–81.

22. Robert Weldon Whalen, *Bitter Wounds: German Victims of the Great War, 1914–1939* (Ithaca, NY: Cornell University Press, 1984), 77–80. Copyright © 1984 by Cornell University. Reprinted with permission of Cornell University Press.

Chapter VI: Whose Nation?

1. Lloyd George, *The Great War: Speech Delivered at the Queen's Hall, London, on September 19, 1914* (Toronto: Hodder and Stoughton, 1914), 15–16.

2. *Hansard's Parliamentary Debates*, vol. 72 (10 June 1915), cols. 391–394; vol. 95 (3 July 1917), cols 982–985. © Crown Copyright material reproduced with the permission of The Controller HMSO.

3. R.H. Tawney, "Reflections of a Soldier," *The Nation*, 21 October 1916.

4. Michael Kettle, *Salome's Last Veil* (London: Granada, 1977), 7–9, 18–19, 98, 143–144, 146, 224, 229.

5. Maurice Barrès, *The Faith of France* (Boston: Houghton Mifflin, 1918), 2–3, 88–89, 195–196.

6. Oswin Creighton, "A British Clergyman at the Front". Excerpt from Laurence Housman, ed., *War Letters of Fallen Englishmen*, (London: Victor Gollancz, 1930), 77–79.

7. Donald Hankey, *A Student in Arms*, (London: Melrose, 1916), 104–111.

8. Hendrik de Man, *The Remaking of a Mind: A Soldier's Thoughts on War and Reconstruction* (New York: Scribners, 1919), 206–211.

9. Leo Baeck, "A German Rabbi in the field". Exerpt from Eugen Tannenbaum, *Kriegsbriefe Deutscher und Österreichischer Juden* (Berlin: Neuer Verlag, 1915), 82–88. Translated from the German by Marilyn Shevin–Coetzee.

10. *The Jews in the Eastern War Zone* (New York: American Jewish Committee, 1916), 111–117.

11. Josef Galantai, *Hungary and the First World War* (Budapest: Akademiai Kiado, 1989), 95–102. Reprinted with permission of Akademiai Kiado, Hungary.

12. February 9, 1918 report by American consul Leslie Davis (Harput, Turkey), 13–16, 19, 34–35. http://www.gomidas.org/gida/index_and_%20documents/867.4016_index_and_documents/docs/4016.392.pdf.

13. Edwyn Bevan, *Brothers All: The War and the Race Question, Papers for Wartime #4* (Oxford: Oxford University Press, 1914), 3–16. Reprinted with permission of Oxford University Press.

14. *Hansard's Parliamentary Debates,* 29 June 1916, cols. 1055–1069, 1079–1080. © Crown Copyright material reproduced with the permission of The Controller HMSO.

15. *The Times,* 18 September 1914.

16. Ralph Haswell Lutz, ed., *Fall of the German Empire, 1914–1918,* vol. 1 (Stanford: Stanford University Press, 1932), 74–75. Copyright © 1940 by the Board of Trustees of the Leland Stanford Junior University, renewed 1960. All rights reserved. Used with the permission of Stanford University Press. www.sup.org.

17. *Report of the Committee on Alleged German Outrages* (London: HMSO, 1915), 39–44. © Crown Copyright material reproduced with the permission of The Controller HMSO.

18. Fernand van Langenhove, *The Growth of a Legend: A Study Based Upon the German Accounts of Franc Tireurs and "Atrocities" in Belgium* (New York: G.P. Putnams Sons, 1916), 299–303.

19. George Bruntz, *Allied Propaganda and the Collapse of the German Empire in 1918* (Stanford: Stanford University Press, 1938), 85–89, 102–104, 106–107, 109. Copyright © 1938 by the Board of Trustees of the Leland Stanford Junior University, renewed 1966. All rights reserved. Used with the permission of Stanford University Press. www.sup.org.

Chapter VII: Dissent, Mutiny and Revolution

1. *The Nation,* 20 May 1916.

2. *Hansard's Parliamentary Debates,* 26 June 1917. © Crown Copyright material reproduced with the permission of The Controller HMSO.

3. Hélène Brion, "L'Affaire Hèlen Brion au 1. Conseil de Guerre," 1918. Reprinted in Susan Groag Bell and Susan Groag Offen, eds., *Women, the Family, and Freedom,* vol. 2 (Stanford: Stanford University Press, 1983), 273–275. Copyright © 1983 by the Board of the Trustees of the Leland Stanford Junior University. All rights reserved. Used with the permission of Stanford University Press. www.sup.org.

4. James Maxton, "War Resistance by Working-class Struggle," in Julian Bell, ed., *We Did Not Fight, 1914–1918: Experiences of War Resisters* (London: Cobden-Sanderson, 1935) 213–222.

5. Edwin Canaan, "Industrial Unrest," *The Economic Journal* (December 1917), 454–459.

6. Henri Desagneaux, *A French Soldier's War Diary* (Morley: Elmsfield Press, 1975), 38–40. Excerpts from Henri Desagneaux, *A French Soldier's War Diary* (Morley: Elmsfield Press, 1975), 38–40. First published in France as "Journal de Guerre 14–18" by Henri Desagneaux, Denoel. Reprinted with permission of Editions Denoel.

7. Olga Hess Gankin and H.H. Fisher, eds., *The Bolsheviks and the World War: The Origin of the Third International* (Stanford: Stanford University Press, 1940), 469–471. Copyright © 1940 by the Board of the Trustees of the Leland Stanford Junior University, renewed 1968. All rights reserved. Used with the permission of Stanford University Press. www.sup.org.

8. Ralph Haswell Lutz, ed., *Fall of the German Empire, 1914–1918,* vol. 2 (Stanford: Stanford University Press, 1932), 201–205. Copyright © 1940 by the Board of Trustees of the Leland Stanford Junior University, renewed 1960. All rights reserved. Used with the permission of Stanford University Press. www.sup.org.

9. Daniel Horn, ed., *War, Mutiny and Revolution in the German Navy: The World War I Diary of Seaman Richard Stumpf* (Brunswick, NJ: Rutgers University Press, 1967),

344–347, 420–427. Copyright © 1967 by Rutgers, the State University. Reprinted by permission of Rutgers University Press.

10. Annie Besant,"The Case for India": The Presidential Address Delivered by Annie Besant at the Thirty–Second Indian National Congress Held at Calcutta, 26 December 1917, http://www.gutenberg.org/ebooks/12820), 12–14.

11. *The Times,* May 1, 1916.

12. Olga Hess Gankin and H.H. Fisher, eds., *The Bolsheviks and the World War: The Origin of the Third International* (Stanford: Stanford University Press, 1940), 140–143. Copyright © 1940 by the Board of the Trustees of the Leland Stanford Junior University, renewed 1968. All rights reserved. Used with the permission of Stanford University Press. www.sup.org.

13. Paul Miliukov, "Stupidity or Treason?" Excerpt from Frank Golder, ed. *Documents of Russian History, 1914–1917* (New York: Peter Smith, 1964), 154–155, 164–165.

14. General Anton I. Denikin, *The Russian Turmoil* (London: Hutchinson & Co., 1922), 40, 61–62.

15. Maria Botchkareva, *Yashka: My Life as Peasant, Officer and Exile* (New York: Frederick Stokes, 1919), 139–145.

Chapter VIII: Legacies

1. Sir Frederic Kenyon, *War Graves: How the Cemeteries Abroad Will Be Designed* (London: HMSO, 1918), 3–14. © Crown Copyright material reproduced with the permission of The Controller HMSO.

2. Rupert Brooke, *Collected Poems of Rupert Brooke* (London: John Lane, 1918), 110.

3. Paul G. Konody, *Art and War: Canadian War Memorials* (London: Colour Ltd, 1919), 14–15.

4. C. Reginald Grundy, *Local War Museums: A Suggestion* (London: W. Claude Johnson, 1917), 5–12.

5. Charles Arthur Mercier, *Spiritualism and Sir Oliver Lodge* (London: Watts, 1917), 4–5, 10–12.

6. John Galsworthy, "The Sacred Work," in *Another Sheaf* (New York: Charles Scribner's Sons, 1919), 4–13.

7. Cecil W. Hutt, *The Future of the Disabled Soldier* (London: John Bale, 1917), 15–18, 63–67.

8. J.B. Priestley, "The Lost Generation" (Washington D.C.: Women's International League for Peace and Freedom, 1930). Reprinted by permission of United Agents on behalf of The Estate of J. B. Priestley.

9. Antoine Prost, *In the Wake of War* (Oxford: Berg, 1992), 61. Reprinted with permission of Berg Publishers, an imprint of Bloomsbury Publishing plc.

10. Joe Lunn, *Memoirs of the Maelstrom* (Portsmouth, NH: Heinemann, 1999), 232. Reprinted with permission of Boydell & Brewer Ltd.

11. "Petition to King George V from the South African Native National Congress, 16 December 1918." Reprinted in Karis and Carter, eds., *From Protest to Challenge: Documentary History of African Politics*, vol. 1 (Stanford: Hoover Institution Press, 1977) 138, 140–142.

Suggestions for Further Reading

General Surveys

Audoin-Rouzeau, Stephane, and Annette Becker. *14–18: Understanding the Great War*. New York: Hill and Wang, 2002.

Beckett, Ian F.W. *The Great War 1914–1918*. New York: Longman, 2001.

Brose, Eric Dorn. *A History of the Great War: World War One and the International Crisis of the Early Twentieth Century*. New York: Oxford University Press, 2009.

Das, Santanu, ed. *Race, Empire and First World War Writing*. Cambridge: Cambridge University Press, 2011.

Englund, Peter. *The Beauty and the Sorrow: An Intimate History of the First World War*. New York: Alfred Knopf, 2011.

Ferguson, Niall. *The Pity of War: Explaining World War I*. New York: Basic Books, 1999.

Ferro, Marc. *The Great War 1914–1918*. London: Routledge and Kegan Paul, 1973.

Fischer, Fritz. *Germany's Aims in the First World War*. New York: Norton, 1967.

Horne, John, ed. *A Companion to World War I*. Oxford: Wiley-Blackwell, 2010.

Howard, Michael. *The First World War*. Oxford: Oxford University Press, 2002.

Keegan, John. *The First World War*. New York: Knopf, 1999.

Keene, Jennifer D., and Michael S. Neiberg, eds. *Finding Common Ground: New Directions in First World War Studies*. Leiden: Brill, 2010.

Morrow, John Jr. *The Great War: An Imperial History*. London: Routledge, 2003.

Neiberg, Michael S. *Fighting the Great War: A Global History*. Cambridge, MA: Harvard University Press, 2005.

Offer, Avner. *The First World War: An Agrarian Interpretation*. Oxford: Clarendon Press, 1989.

Robbins, Keith. *The First World War*. Oxford: Clarendon Press, 1984.

Schmitt, Bernadotte, and Harold Vedeler. *The World in the Crucible*. New York: Harper and Row, 1984.

Sondhaus, Lawrence. *World War One: The Global Revolution*. Cambridge: Cambridge University Press, 2011.

Empires, Soldiers, and Citizens: A World War I Sourcebook, Second Edition.
Edited by Marilyn Shevin-Coetzee and Frans Coetzee.
© 2013 John Wiley & Sons, Ltd. Published 2013 by John Wiley & Sons, Ltd.

Stevenson, David. *The First World War and International Politics.* Oxford: Clarendon Press, 1988.

_____. *Cataclysm: The First World War as Political Tragedy.* New York: Basic Books, 2004.

Stone, Norman. *World War I: A Short History.* London: Allen Lane, 2007.

Strachan, Hew. *The First World War: To Arms.* New York: Oxford University Press, 2001.

_____, ed. *World War I: A History.* New York: Oxford University Press, 1998.

Winter, J.M. *The Experience of World War I.* New York: Oxford University Press, 1989.

_____, et al., eds. *The Great War and the Twentieth Century: Reflections on World War I.* New Haven: Yale University Press, 2000.

Winter, Jay, and Antoine Prost. *The Great War in History: Debates and Controversies, 1914 to the Present.* Cambridge: Cambridge University Press, 2005.

Origins and the Mood of 1914

Afflerbach, Holger, and David Stevenson, eds. *An Improbable War? The Outbreak of World War I and European Political Culture Before 1914.* New York: Berghahn Books, 2007.

Berghahn, Volker. *Germany and the Approach of War in 1914.* 2nd ed. New York: St. Martin's, 1993.

Bosworth, Richard. *Italy and the Approach of the First World War.* London: Macmillan, 1983.

Evans, R.J.W., and H. Pogge von Strandmann, eds. *The Coming of the First World War.* Oxford: Clarendon Press, 1988.

Hamilton, Richard F., and Holger H. Herwig. *Decisions for War, 1914–1917.* Cambridge: Cambridge University Press, 2005.

Herrmann, David. *The Arming of Europe and the Making of the First World War.* Princeton: Princeton University Press, 1996.

Hewitson, Mark. *Germany and the Causes of the First World War.* Oxford: Berg, 2004.

Joll, James, and Gordon Martel. *The Origins of the First World War.* 3rd ed. London: Longman, 2006.

Keiger, John. *France and the Origins of the First World War.* London: Macmillan, 1983.

Lieven, Dominic. *Russia and the Origins of the First World War.* London: Macmillan, 1983.

McMeekin, Sean. *The Russian Origins of the First World War.* Cambridge, MA: Harvard University Press, 2011.

Mombauer, Annika. *Helmut von Moltke and the Origins of the First World War.* Cambridge: Cambridge University Press, 2001.

_____. *The Origins of the First World War: Controversies and Consensus.* London: Longman, 2002.

Neiberg, Michael S. *Dance of the Furies: Europe and the Outbreak of World War I.* Cambridge, MA: Harvard University Press, 2011.

Rüger, Jan. *The Great Naval Game.* Cambridge: Cambridge University Press, 2007.

Stevenson, David. *Armaments and the Coming of War.* Oxford: Oxford University Press, 1996.

Stibbe, Matthew. *German Anglophobia and the Great War, 1914–1918.* Cambridge: Cambridge University Press, 2001.

Verhey, Jeffrey. *The Spirit of 1914: Militarism, Myth and Mobilization in Germany.* Cambridge: Cambridge University Press, 2000.

Williamson, Samuel. *Austria-Hungary and the Origins of the First World War.* London: Macmillan, 1991.

Zuber, Terence. *Inventing the Schlieffen Plan: German Miliary Planning, 1871–1914*. New York: Oxford University Press, 2002.

National and Area Studies

Africa

Farwell, Byron. *The Great War in Africa, 1914–1918*. New York: Norton, 1986.

Lunn, Joe. *Memoirs of the Maelstrom*. Portsmouth, NH: Heinemann, 1999.

Page, Melvin, ed. *Africa and the First World War*. New York: St. Martin's, 1987.

Paice, Edward. *World War I: The African Front: An Imperial War on the Dark Continent*. New York: Pegasus Books, 2008.

Australia and New Zealand

Andrews, Eric. *The Anzac Illusion*. Cambridge: Cambridge University Press, 1993.

Bean, C.E.W. *The Story of Anzac 2 vols*. Sydney: Angus & Robertson, 1921–1924.

Eldred-Grigg, Stevan. *The Great Wrong War: New Zealand Society in World War I*. Auckland: Random House, 2010.

Pugsley, Christopher. *The Anzac Experience: New Zealand, Australia and Empire in the First World War*. Auckland: Reed, 2004.

_____. *Te Hokowhitu a Tu: the Maori Pioneer Battalion in the First World War*. Auckland: Reed, 1995.

Thomson, Alastair. *Anzac Memories. Living with the Legend*. Melbourne: Oxford University Press, 1994.

Asia

Dickinson, Frederick. *War and National Re-Invention: Japan in the Great War, 1914–1918*. Cambridge, MA: Harvard University Press, 1999.

Guoqi, Xu. *China and the Great War*. Cambridge: Cambridge University Press, 2005.

_____. *Strangers on the Western Front: Chinese Workers in the Great War*. Cambridge, MA: Harvard University Press, 2011.

Austria-Hungary

Galantai, Jozef. *Hungary in the First World War*. Budapest: Akademiai Kiado, 1989.

Healy, Maureen. *Vienna and the Fall of the Habsburg Empire: Total War and Everyday Life in World War I*. Cambridge: Cambridge University Press, 2004.

Herwig, Holger. *The First World War: Germany and Austria-Hungary*. London: Arnold, 1997.

Rozenblit, Marsha. *Reconstructing a National Identity: The Jews of Habsburg Austria during World War I*. New York: Oxford University Press, 2001.

Britain

Bourne, J.M. *Britain and the Great War, 1914–1918*. New York: Routledge, 1989.

Gregory, Adrian. *The Last Great War: British Society and the First World War*. New York: Cambridge University Press, 2009.

Harris, J.P. *Douglas Haig and the First World War*. Cambridge: Cambridge University Press, 2008.

Marwick, Arthur. *The Deluge*. London: Macmillan, 1965.

Turner, John. *British Politics and the Great War*. New Haven: Yale University Press, 1992.

Watson, Janet. *Fighting Different Wars. Experience, Memory and the First World War in Britain*. Cambridge: Cambridge University Press, 2004.

Wilson, Trevor. *The Myriad Faces of War: Britain and the Great War, 1914–1918*. Cambridge: Polity Press, 1986.

Winter, Jay. *The Great War and the British People*. Basingstoke: Macmillan, 1985.

Canada

Cassar, George H. *Hell in Flanders Fields: Canadians at the Second Battle of Ypres*. Toronto: Dundurn Press, 2010.

Cook, Tim. *Shock Troops: Canadians Fighting the Great War, 1917–1918*. Toronto: Viking Canada, 2008.

Hayes, Geoffrey, Andrew Iarocci, and Mike Bechthold, eds. *Vimy Ridge: A Canadian Reassessment*. Waterloo, Ont: Wilfrid Laurier University Press, 2007.

Keshen, Jeffrey. *Propaganda and Censorship During Canada's Great War*. Edmonton: University of Alberta Press, 1996.

Mackenzie, David, ed. *Canada and the First World War: Essays in Honour of Robert Craig Brown*. Toronto: University of Toronto Press, 2005.

Morton, Desmond. *When Your Number's Up: The Canadian Soldier in the First World War*. Toronto: Random House, 1993.

Morton, Desmond, and J.L. Granatstein. *Marching to Armageddon: Canadians and the Great War 1914–1919*. Toronto: Lester & Orpen Dennys, 1989.

France

Becker, Jean-Jacques. *The Great War and the French People*. Leamington Spa: Berg, 1986.

Flood, P.J. *France, 1914–1918: Public Opinion and the War Effort*. Basingstoke: Macmillan, 1990.

Fogarty, Richard. *Race and War in France: Colonial Subjects in the French Army, 1914–1918*. Baltimore: Johns Hopkins University Press, 2008.

Darrow, Margaret. *French Women and the First World War*. Oxford: Berg, 2000.

Downs, Laura Lee. *Manufacturing Inequality: Gender Division in the French and British Metalworking Industries, 1914–1939*. Ithaca, NY: Cornell University Press, 1995.

McMillan, James. *Housewife or Harolot. The Place of Women in French Society, 1870–1940*. Brighton: Harvester, 1981.

Roberts, Mary Louise. *Civilisation without Sexes: Reconstructing Gender in Postwar France, 1917–1927*. Chicago: University of Chicago Press, 1994.

Smith, Leonard V., S. Audoin-Rouzeau, and A. Becker. *France and the Great War, 1914–1918*. Cambridge: Cambridge University Press, 2003.

Germany

Chickering, Roger. *Imperial Germany and the Great War, 1914–1918*. Cambridge: Cambridge University Press, 1998.

_____. *The Great War and Urban Life in Germany: Freiburg, 1914–1918*. Cambridge: Cambridge University Press, 2007.

Donson, Andrew. *Youth in the Fatherless Land: War Pedagogy, Nationalism and Authority in Germany, 1914–1918*. Cambridge, MA: Harvard University Press, 2010.

Feldman, Gerald. *Army, Industry and Labor in Germany, 1914–1918*. Princeton: Princeton University Press, 1966. Reprinted by Berg, 1992.

_____. *The Great Disorder: Politics, Economics and Society in the German Inflation, 1914–1924*. New York: Oxford University Press, 1993.

Herwig, Holger. *The First World War: Germany and Austria-Hungary*. London: Arnold, 1997.

Horne, John, and Alan Kramer. *German Atrocities 1914: A History of Denial*. New Haven: Yale University Press, 2001.

Hull, Isabel V. *Absolute Destruction: Military Culture and the Practices of War in Imperial Germany*. Ithaca, NY: Cornell University Press, 2005.

Nelson, Robert L. *German Soldier Newspapers of the First World War*. Cambridge: Cambridge University Press, 2011.

Stibbe, Matthew. *German Anglophobia and the Great War, 1914–1918*. Cambridge: Cambridge University Press, 2001.

Verhey, Jeffrey. *The Spirit of 1914: Militarism, Myth and Mobilization in Germany*. Cambridge: Cambridge University Press, 2000.

Ziemann, Benjamin. *War Experiences in Rural Germany: 1914–1923*. Oxford: Berg, 2007.

Ireland

Gregory, Adrian, and Senia Paseta, eds. *Ireland and the Great War: "A War to Unite Us All?"* Manchester: Manchester University Press, 2002.

Jeffery, Keith. *Ireland and the Great War*. Cambridge: Cambridge University Press, 2000.

Johnson, Nuala. *Ireland, the Great War and the Geography of Remembrance*. Cambridge: Cambridge University Press, 2003.

Italy

Bosworth, Richard. *Italy and the Approach of the First World War*. London: Macmillan, 1983.

Schindler, John. *Isonzo. The Forgotten Sacrifice of the Great War*. Westport, CT: Praeger, 2001.

Thompson, Mark. *The White War: Life and Death on the Italian Front, 1915–1919*. London: Faber & Faber, 2008.

Ottoman Empire and the Middle East

Aksakal, Mustafa. *The Ottoman Road to War in 1914: the Ottoman Empire and the First World War*. Cambridge: Cambridge University Press, 2008.

Balakian, Grigoris. *Armenian Golgotha: A Memoir of the Armenian Genocide, 1915–1918*. New York: Knopf, 2009.

Bloxham, Donald. *The Great Game of Genocide: Imperialism, Nationalism and the Destruction of the Ottoman Armenians*. Oxford: Oxford University Press, 2005.

Hart, Peter. *Gallipoli*. New York: Oxford University Press, 2011.

Satia, Priya. *Spies in Arabia: The Great War and the Cultural Foundations of Britain's Covert Empire in the Middle East*. New York: Oxford University Press, 2008.

Suny, Ronald G., Fatma Muge Gocek, and Norman Naimark, eds. *A Question of Genocide: Armenians and Turks at the End of the Ottoman Empire.* New York: Oxford University Press, 2011.

Woodward, David R. *Hell in the Holy Land: World War I in the Middle East.* Lexington, KY: University of Kentucky Press, 2006.

Russia

Dowling, Timothy C. *The Brusilov Offensive.* Bloomington: Indiana University Press, 2008.

Fitzpatrick, Sheila. *The Russian Revolution.* Oxford: Oxford University Press, 1982.

Gatrell, Peter. *A Whole Empire Walking: Refugees in Russia During World War I.* Bloomington: Indiana University Press, 1999.

_____. *Russia's First World War: A Social and Economic History.* Harlow: Pearson/ Longman, 2005.

Holquist, Peter. *Making War. Forging Revolution. Russia's Continuum of Crisis 1914–1921.* Cambridge, MA: Harvard University Press, 2002.

Jahn, Hubertus. *Patriotic Culture in Russia during World War I.* Ithaca: Cornell University Press, 1995.

Kaiser, Daniel. *The Workers Revolution in Russia, 1917. The View from Below.* New York: Cambridge University Press, 1987.

Koenker, Diane. *Moscow Workers and the 1917 Revolution.* Princeton: Princeton University Press, 1981.

Koenker, Diane, and William Rosenberg. *Strikes and Revolution in Russia, 1917.* Princeton: Princeton University Press, 1989.

Lieven, Dominic. *Russia and the Origins of the First World War.* London: Macmillan, 1983.

Lincoln, W. Bruce. *A Passage Through Armageddon: The Russians in War and Revolution.* New York: Oxford University Press, 1994.

Lohr, Eric. *Nationalizing the Russian Empire: The Campaign against Enemy Aliens during World War I.* Cambridge, MA: Harvard University Press, 2003.

Petrone, Karen. *The Great War in Russian Memory.* Bloomington: Indiana University Press, 2011.

Sanborn, Joshua. *Drafting the Russian Nation.* DeKalb, IL: Northern Illinois University Press, 2003.

Siegelbaum, Lewis. *The Politics of Industrial Mobilization in Russia, 1914–1917.* London: Macmillan, 1984.

Stone, Norman. *The Eastern Front 1914–1917.* London: Hodder & Stoughton, 1975.

Wildman, Allan. *The End of the Russian Imperial Army.* 2 vols. Princeton: Princeton University Press, 1980–1987.

The Western Front

Ashworth, Tony. *Trench Warfare 1914–1918.* London: Macmillan, 1980.

Beckett, Ian F.W., and Keith Simpson, eds. *A Nation in Arms: A Social Study of the British Army in the First World War.* Manchester: Manchester University Press, 1985.

Bidwell, Shelford, and Dominick Graham. *Fire Power.* London: Allen & Unwin, 1982.

Bond, Brian, ed. *The First World War and British Military History*. Oxford: Clarendon Press, 1991.

Doughty, Robert. *Pyrrhic Victory: French Strategy and Operations in the Great War*. Cambridge, MA: Harvard University Press, 2005.

Ferro, Marc, *et al.*, eds. *Meeting in No Man's Land: Christmas 1914 and Fraternisation in the Great War*. London: Constable, 2007.

French, David. *British Strategy and War Aims, 1914–1916*. London: Allen & Unwin, 1986.

Giraudoux, Jean. *Campaigns and Intervals*. Providence: Berghahn, 1994.

Greenhalgh, Elizabeth. *Foch in Command: The Forging of a First World War General*. Cambridge: Cambridge University Press, 2011.

Guoqi, Xu. *Strangers on the Western Front: Chinese Workers in the Great War*. Cambridge, MA: Harvard University Press, 2011.

Haber, Lutz. *The Poisonous Cloud*. Oxford: Clarendon Press, 1986.

Harris, J.P. *Douglas Haig and the First World War*. Cambridge: Cambridge University Press, 2008.

Horn, Alistair. *The Price of Glory: Verdun 1916*. London: Penguin, 1962.

Horne, John, and Alan Kramer. *German Atrocities 1914: A History of Denial*. New Haven: Yale University Press, 2001.

Keegan, John. *The Face of Battle*. London: Allen Lane, 1975.

Kramer, Alan. *Dynamic of Destruction: Culture and Mass Killing in the First World War*. Oxford: Oxford University Press, 2007.

Leed, Eric J. *No Man's Land. Combat and Identity in World War I*. New York: Cambridge University Press, 1979.

MacDonald, Lyn. *They Called It Passchendaele*. London: Michael Joseph, 1978.

_____. *Somme*. London: Michael Joseph, 1983.

Middlebrook, Martin. *The First Day of the Somme*. London: Allen Lane, 1971.

Prior, Robin, and Trevor Wilson. *The Somme*. New Haven: Yale University Press, 2005.

Simkins, Peter. *Kitchener's Army*. Manchester: Manchester University Press, 1988.

Smith, Leonard V. *Between Mutiny and Obedience: The Case of the French Fifth Infantry Division During World War I*. Princeton: Princeton University Press, 1994.

Travers, T.H.E. *The Killing Ground: The British Army, the Western Front and the Emergence of Modern Warfare 1900–1918*. London: Allen & Unwin, 1987.

_____. *How the War Was Won: Command and Technology in the British Army on the Western Front, 1917–1918*. London: Routledge, 1992.

Winter, Denis. *Death's Men*. London: Allen Lane, 1978.

Watson, Alexander. *Enduring the Great War. Combat, Morale and Collapse in the German and British Armies, 1914–1918*. Cambridge: Cambridge University Press, 2008.

The Eastern Front

Dowling, Timothy C. *The Brusilov Offensive*. Bloomington: Indiana University Press, 2008.

Liulevicius, Vejas. *War Land on the Eastern Front: Culture, National Identity and German Occupation in World War I*. Cambridge: Cambridge University Press, 2000.

Stoff, Laurie. *They Fought for the Motherland: Russia's Women Soldiers in World War I and the Revolution*. Lawrence, KS: University of Kansas Press, 2006.

Stone, Norman. *The Eastern Front 1914–1917*. London: Hodder & Stoughton, 1975.

Wildman, Allan K. *The End of the Russian Imperial Army*. Princeton: Princeton University Press, 1980.

Naval and Air War

Campbell, John. *Jutland: An Analysis of the Fighting*. New York: The Lyons Press, 1998.

Gordon, Andrew. *The Rules of the Game: Jutland and British Naval Command*. Annapolis: Naval Institute Press, 2000.

Halpern, Paul G. *A Naval History of World War I*. Annapolis: Naval Institute Press, 1994.

Horn, Daniel, ed. *War, Mutiny and Revolution in the German Navy: The World War I Diary of Seaman Richard Stumpf*. New Brunswick: Rutgers University Press, 1967.

Hough, Richard. *The Great War at Sea*. Oxford: Oxford University Press, 1983.

Kelly, Patrick J. *Tirpitz and the Imperial German Navy*. Bloomington: Indiana University Press, 2011.

Kennett, Lee. *The First Air War, 1914–1918*. New York: Free Press, 1991.

Morrow, John Jr. *The Great War in the Air*. Washington, DC: Smithsonian Institution Press, 1993.

Wohl, Robert. *A Passion for Wings: Aviation and the Western Imagination, 1908–1918*. Vol. 1 New Haven: Yale University Press, 1994.

The Home Front

Becker, Jean-Jacques. *The Great War and the French People*. Leamington Spa: Berg, 1986.

Braybon, Gail. *Women Workers in the First World War*. London: Croom Helm, 1981.

Coetzee, Frans, and Marilyn Shevin-Coetzee, eds. *Authority, Identity and the Social History of the Great War*. Providence: Berghahn, 1995.

Burk, Kathleen, ed. *War and the State*. London: Allen & Unwin, 1982.

_____. *Britain, America and the Sinews of War 1914–1918*. London: Allen & Unwin, 1985.

Carsten, F.L. *War against War: British and German Radical Movements in the First World War*. Berkeley: University of California Press, 1982.

Ceadel, Martin. *Pacifism in Britain, 1914–1945: The Defining of a Faith*. Oxford: Clarendon Press, 1980.

Daniel, Ute. *The War from Within: German Working-Class Women in the First World War*. Oxford: Berg, 1997.

Davis, Belinda. *Home Fires Burning: Food, Politics and Everyday Life in World War I Berlin*. Chapel Hill, NC: University of North Carolina Press, 2000.

Frevert, Ute. *Women in German History*. Leamington Spa: Berg, 1988.

Fridenson, Patrick, ed. *The French Home Front*. Providence: Berg, 1992.

Godfrey, John. *Capitalism at War: Industrial Policy and Bureaucracy in France, 1914–1918*. Leamington Spa: Berg, 1987.

Grayzel, Susan R. *Women's Identities at War: Gender, Motherhood, and Politics in Britain and France during the First World War*. Chapel Hill, NC: University of North Carolina Press, 1999.

Gregory, Adrian. *The Last Great War: British Society and the First World War.* New York: Cambridge University Press, 2009.

Haimson, Leopold, and Charles Tilly, eds. *War, Strikes, and Revolution.* New York: Cambridge University Press, 1988.

_____, and Giulio Sapelli, eds. *Strikes, Social Conflict and the First World War.* Milan: Annali della Fondazione Feltrinelli, 1993.

Hardach, Gerd. *The First World War.* Berkeley: University of California Press, 1976.

Higonnet, Margaret, *et al.*, eds. *Behind the Lines. Gender and the Two World Wars.* New Haven: Yale University Press, 1987.

Hinton, James. *The First Shop Stewards' Movement.* London: Allen & Unwin, 1973.

Horne, John. *Labour at War. France and Britain, 1914–1918.* Oxford: Clarendon Press, 1991.

Kent, Susan Kingsley. *Making Peace. The Reconstruction of Gender in Interwar Britain.* Princeton: Princeton University Press, 1993.

Kocka, Jürgen. *Facing Total War.* Cambridge, MA: Harvard University Press, 1984.

Marwick, Arthur. *The Deluge. British Society and the First World War.* 2nd ed. Basingstoke: Macmillan, 1991.

McMillan, James F. *Housewife or Harlot: The Place of Women in French Society.* Brighton: Harvester, 1981.

Panayi, Panikos. *The Enemy in Our Midst: Germans in Britain during the First World War.* Providence: Berg, 1991.

_____, ed. *Minorities in Wartime.* Providence: Berg, 1993.

Patterson, David S. *The Search for Negotiated Peace: Women's Activism and Citizen Diplomacy in World War I.* New York: Routledge, 2008.

Pedersen, Susan. *Family, Dependence and the Origins of the Welfare State: Britain and France, 1914–1945.* Cambridge: Cambridge University Press, 1993.

Proctor, Tammy. *Female Intelligence: Women and Espionage in the First World War.* New York: New York University Press, 2003.

_____. *Civilians in a World War, 1914–1918.* New York: New York University Press, 2010.

Roberts, Mary Louise. *Civilization Without Sexes: Reconstructing Gender in Postwar France, 1917–1927.* Chicago: University of Chicago Press, 1994.

Robbins, Keith. *The Abolition of War: The Peace Movement in Britain, 1914–1919.* Cardiff: University of Wales Press, 1976.

Thom, Deborah. *Nice Girls and Rude Girls: Women Workers in World War I.* London: I.B. Tauris, 2000.

Vellacott, Jo. *Pacifists, Patriots and the Vote: The Erosion of Democratic Suffragism in Britain during the First World War.* Basingstoke: Macmillan, 2007.

Vincent, C.P. *The Politics of Hunger: The Allied Blockade of Germany, 1915–1919.* Athens, OH: Ohio University Press, 1985.

Wall, Richard, and J.M. Winter, eds. *The Upheaval of War: Family, Work and Welfare in Europe, 1914–1918.* Cambridge: Cambridge University Press, 1988.

Whalen, Robert Weldon. *Bitter Wounds. German Victims of the Great War, 1914–1939.* Ithaca, NY: Cornell University Press, 1984.

Winter, J.M. *The Great War and the British People.* Basingstoke: Macmillan, 1986.

Winter, J.M., and Jean-Louis Robert, eds. *Capital Cities at War: London, Paris, Berlin, 1914–1919.* 2 vols. Cambridge: Cambridge University Press, 1997–2007.

Woollacott, Angela. *On Her Their Lives Depend: Munitions Workers in the Great War.* Berkeley: University of California Press, 1994.

Culture

Audoin-Rouzeau, Stephane. *Men at War 1914–1918. National Sentiment and Trench Journalism in France during the First World War.* Providence: Berg, 1992.

Eksteins, Modris. *Rites of Spring. The Great War and the Birth of the Modern Age.* New York: Anchor, 1990.

Field, Frank. *British and French Writers of the First World War. Comparative Studies in Cultural History.* Cambridge: Cambridge University Press, 1991.

Fuller, J.G. *Troop Morale and Popular Culture in the British and Dominion Armies 1914–1918.* Oxford: Clarendon Press, 1991.

Fussell, Paul. *The Great War and Modern Memory.* New York: Oxford University Press, 1975.

Hynes, Samuel. *A War Imagined.* New York: Atheneum, 1991.

Kavanagh, Gaynor. *Museums and the First World War: A Social History.* New York: St. Martin's, 1994.

Leese, Peter. *Shell Shock: Traumatic Neurosis and the British Soldiers of the First World War.* Basingstoke: Palgrave Macmillan, 2002.

Lerner, Paul. *Hysterical Men. War, Psychiatry and the Politics of Trauma in Germany, 1890–1930.* Ithaca, NY: Cornell University Press, 2003.

Lewis, Beth Irwin. *George Grosz. Art and Politics in the Weimar Republic.* Princeton: Princeton University Press, 1991.

Malvern, Sue. *Modern Art, Britain and the Great War.* New Haven: Yale University Press, 2004.

Mosse, George. *Fallen Soldiers.* New York: Oxford University Press, 1990.

Pick, Daniel. *War Machine: The Rationalization of Slaughter in the Machine Age.* New Haven: Yale University Press, 1993.

Roshwald, Aviel, and Richard Stites, eds. *European Culture in the Great War. The Arts, Entertainment and Propaganda, 1914–1918.* Cambridge: Cambridge University Press, 1999.

Sanders, M.L., and Philip Taylor. *British Propaganda during the First World War.* London: Macmillan, 1982.

Shephard, Ben. *A War of Nerves: Soldiers and Psychiatrists in the Twentieth Century.* Cambridge, MA: Harvard University Press, 2003.

Silver, Kenneth E. *Esprit de Corps. The Art of the Parisian Avant-Garde and the First World War, 1914–1925.* Princeton: Princeton University Press, 1989.

Stromberg, Roland. *Redemption by War. The Intellectuals and 1914.* Lawrence, KS: The Regents Press of Kansas, 1982.

Weinstein, Joan. *The End of Expressionism. Art and the November Revolution in Germany, 1918–1919.* Chicago: University of Chicago Press, 1990.

Wohl, Robert. *The Generation of 1914.* Cambridge, MA: Harvard University Press, 1979.

Memory

Fussell, Paul. *The Great War and Modern Memory.* New York: Oxford University Press, 1975.

Goebel, Stefan. *The Great War and Medieval Memory.* Cambridge: Cambridge University Press, 2006.

Johnson, Nuala C. *Ireland, the Great War and the Geography of Remembrance*. Cambridge: Cambridge University Press, 2003.

Mosse, George. *Fallen Soldiers: Reshaping the Memory of the World Wars*. New York: Oxford University Press, 1990.

Petrone, Karen. *The Great War in Russian Memory*. Bloomington: Indiana University Press, 2011.

Prost, Antoine. *In the Wake of War. "Les Anciens Combattants" and French Society 1914–1939*. Providence: Berg, 1992.

Saunders, Nicholas J., ed. *Matters of Conflict: Material Culture, Memory and the First World War*. London: Routledge, 2004.

Todman, Dan. *The First World War: Myth and Memory*. London: Hambledon Continuum, 2005.

Watson, Janet S.K. *Fighting Different Wars: Experience, Memory, and the First World War in Britain*. Cambridge: Cambridge University Press, 2004.

Winter, Jay. *Sites of Memory, Sites of Mourning: The Great War in European Cultural History*. Cambridge: Cambridge University Press, 1995.

_____. *Remembering War: The Great War between Memory and History in the 20th Century*. New Haven: Yale University Press, 2006.

Index

Empires, Soldiers, and Citizens: A World War I Sourcebook, Second Edition.
Edited by Marilyn Shevin-Coetzee and Frans Coetzee.
© 2013 John Wiley & Sons, Ltd. except sources 1 to 11. Published 2013 by John Wiley & Sons, Ltd.